Reason and Value

Reason and Value

Themes from the Moral Philosophy of Joseph Raz

EDITED BY

R. Jay Wallace

Philip Pettit

Samuel Scheffler

Michael Smith

CLARENDON PRESS · OXFORD

OXFORD
UNIVERSITY PRESS

Great Clarendon Street, Oxford ox2 6dp

Oxford University Press is a department of the University of Oxford.
It furthers the University's objective of excellence in research, scholarship,
and education by publishing worldwide in

Oxford New York

Auckland Cape Town Dar es Salaam Hong Kong Karachi
Kuala Lumpur Madrid Melbourne Mexico City Nairobi
New Delhi Shanghai Taipei Toronto

With offices in

Argentina Austria Brazil Chile Czech Republic France Greece
Guatemala Hungary Italy Japan Poland Portugal Singapore
South Korea Switzerland Thailand Turkey Ukraine Vietnam

Oxford is a registered trade mark of Oxford University Press
in the UK and in certain other countries

Published in the United States
by Oxford University Press Inc., New York

British Library Cataloguing in Publication Data

Data available

Library of Congress Cataloging in Publication Data

Data available

Typeset by SPI Publisher Services, Pondicherry, India
Printed in Great Britain
on acid-free paper by
Biddles Ltd, King's Lynn

ISBN 0-19-926188-1   978-0-19-926188-8
ISBN 0-19-929764-9 (Pbk.)   978-0-19-929764-1 (Pbk.)

1 3 5 7 9 10 8 6 4 2

PREFACE

Joseph Raz is one of the leading philosophers of the present day. His many publications have made major contributions in a wide range of areas, including jurisprudence, political philosophy, and the theory of practical reason. This volume of essays engages with prominent themes in Raz's work that are particularly significant for moral philosophy. The subtlety and power of Raz's many reflections on ethical topics—including especially his explorations of the connections between practical reason and the theory of value—make his writings a fertile source for anyone working in moral philosophy. Our hope is that this volume of original papers will both honour Raz's accomplishments in the area of ethical theorizing and contribute to an enhanced appreciation of the significance of his work for the subject.

The editors would like to express their appreciation to Jeremy Waldron and the Center for Law and Philosophy at Columbia University for hosting a conference in March 2002, at which drafts of many of the papers were discussed in the company of virtually all who have contributed to the volume.

R. Jay Wallace
Philip Pettit
Samuel Scheffler
Michael Smith

CONTENTS

CONTRIBUTORS

Michael E. Bratman is U. G. and Abbie Birch Durfee Professor in the School of Humanities and Sciences, and Professor of Philosophy at Stanford University. He is the author of *Intention, Plans, and Practical Reason* (Harvard), *Faces of Intention: Selected Essays on Intention and Agency* (Cambridge), and various articles in philosophy of action and related fields.

John Broome is White's Professor of Moral Philosophy in the University of Oxford and a Fellow of Corpus Christi College. He is the author of *Weighing Goods* (Blackwell) and *Ethics Out of Economics* (Cambridge).

Ruth Chang is Assistant Professor of Philosophy at Rutgers University. She edited the collection *Incommensurability, Incomparability, and Practical Reason* (Harvard). Her current interests lie in issues concerning the role of evaluative comparison in understanding practical reason and value.

Jonathan Dancy is Professor of Philosophy at the University of Reading. He has written extensively on the theory of reasons. Relevant books are *Moral Reasons* (Blackwell), *Practical Reality* (Oxford), and *Ethics without Principles* (forthcoming).

Harry Frankfurt is Professor of Philosophy at Princeton University. His books include *Demons, Dreamers, and Madmen* (Bobbs-Merrill), *The Importance of What We Care About* (Cambridge), and *Necessity, Volition, and Love* (Cambridge).

Ulrike Heuer is Assistant Professor of Philosophy at the University of Pennsylvania. Her work is mainly in meta-ethics, moral psychology, and theories of practical reason.

Philip Pettit teaches political theory and philosophy at Princeton University, where he holds the William Nelson Cromwell Chair in Politics. His books include *Republicanism: A Theory of Freedom and Government* (Oxford), *Three Methods of Ethics: A Debate*, with Michael Slote and Marcia Baron (Routledge),

The Common Mind: An Essay on Psychology, Society and Politics (Oxford), *A Theory of Freedom: From the Psychology to the Politics of Agency* (Polity Press and Oxford), and *Rules, Reasons and Norms: Selected Essays* (Oxford).

Peter Railton is John Stephenson Perrin Professor of Philosophy at the University of Michigan. He is the author of *Facts, Values, and Norms* (Cambridge), a collection of essays on moral philosophy.

Donald H. Regan is William W. Bishop, Jr. Collegiate Professor of Law and Professor of Philosophy in the University of Michigan. He is the author of *Utilitarianism and Co-operation* (Oxford), which shared the Matchette Prize of the American Philosophical Association for 1979–80. In addition to moral philosophy, his principal writing has been on American constitutional law. His current work centres on the law of the World Trade Organization.

T. M. Scanlon is Alford Professor of Natural Religion, Moral Philosophy, and Civil Polity at Harvard University. He is the author of *What We Owe to Each Other* (Harvard) and of numerous papers in moral and political philosophy.

Samuel Scheffler is the Class of 1941 World War II Memorial Professor of Philosophy and Law at the University of California, Berkeley. He is the author of *The Rejection of Consequentialism* (Oxford), *Human Morality* (Oxford), and *Boundaries and Allegiances* (Oxford), and editor of *Consequentialism and its Critics* (Oxford).

Seana Valentine Shiffrin is Associate Professor of Philosophy and Professor of Law at UCLA. Her research and teaching interests are in ethics, political philosophy, and theoretical issues pertaining to law.

Michael Smith is Professor of Philosophy in the Research School of Social Sciences at the Australian National University. He is the author of *The Moral Problem* (Blackwell), and editor of *Meta-Ethics* (Ashgate).

Michael Stocker is Guttag Professor of Ethics and Political Philosophy at Syracuse University. He is especially interested in ethics, moral psychology, and the connections between them. He has written *Plural and Conflicting Values* (Oxford) and (with Elizabeth Hegeman) *Valuing Emotions* (Cambridge).

Michael Thompson is Associate Professor of Philosophy at the University of Pittsburgh. He is interested in all aspects of practical philosophy and is writing a book, *Life and Action*, about some of the metaphysical problems that arise in ethics and the philosophy of action, and a monograph about the ideas of right and recognition.

R. Jay Wallace is Professor of Philosophy at the University of California, Berkeley. He is the author of *Responsibility and the Moral Sentiments* (Harvard), and editor of *Reason, Emotion and Will* (Ashgate) and *The Practice of Value* (Oxford).

1

Shared Valuing and Frameworks
for Practical Reasoning

Michael E. Bratman

1. Frameworks

Intentions, plans, and policies provide background frameworks that structure deliberation and practical reasoning. These background frameworks
have a characteristic stability over time. They shape practical reasoning,
sometimes by shaping what options are to be considered, sometimes by
shaping what is to count as a consideration of significance in favour of or
contrary to options considered. In providing such frameworks our intentions, plans, and policies help constitute and support important forms of
cross-temporal co-ordination and organization both within the life of an
individual agent and socially, across different lives. These forms of organization—both intra- and inter-personal—are central to our ability to
achieve complex, temporally extended goals. Our capacities for such intention-like attitudes, and associated structures of planning and practical
reasoning, are, for temporally persisting and social agents like us, more or
less all-purpose, universal means: they are means to an extremely wide
range of potentially divergent human goals.[1] And that is one basic reason

---

[1] So these capacities (and/or the social conditions that support them) are candidates for the
role of a Rawlsian primary good. See John Rawls, *A Theory of Justice* rev. edn. (Cambridge,
Mass.: Harvard University Press, 1999), 62, 92–3. Crystal Thorpe explores the implications of a
related idea for the idea that there are reasons that we all share (in a sense that differs from

why distinctive norms introduced by these organizing and co-ordinating structures have rational force for us.

Or so I have argued on several different occasions in developing what I have called the planning theory, a theory that I have also characterized as a modest theory of the will.[2] My aim in the present essay is to highlight these themes and then to extend them. My hope is that we can thereby arrive at a deeper understanding of a wide range of interrelated practical phenomena. We can, in particular, begin to develop a model of an important range of social phenomena that, because of their framework-providing role, are plausibly understood as forms of *shared valuing*.

2. Four Kinds of Framework

Let me begin by briefly noting four kinds of cases in which, as I see it, relevant intentions, plans, and/or policies provide various kinds of background frameworks for practical reasoning. I will then turn to a somewhat more detailed discussion of each of the cases.

that of 'shared valuing' to be discussed below.) See her 'A Puzzle about Humean Theories of Practical Reason' (unpublished MS).

[2] Early statements are in 'Intention and Means–End Reasoning', *Philosophical Review* 90 (1981), 252–65, and in 'Taking Plans Seriously', *Social Theory and Practice* 9 (1983), 271–87. I develop these ideas (and some important qualifications) further in *Intention, Plans, and Practical Reason* (Cambridge, Mass.: Harvard University Press, 1987; reissued by CSLI Publications, 1999), and *Faces of Intention: Selected Essays on Intention and Agency* (New York: Cambridge University Press, 1999). A more recent development is sketched in 'Reflection, Planning, and Temporally Extended Agency', *Philosophical Review* 109 (2000), 35–61. In my 'Introduction' to *Faces of Intention*, 5, I describe the planning theory as a modest theory of the will, one that does justice to the role of the will in our practical lives while avoiding Davidsonian concerns with 'mysterious acts of the will'. (See Donald Davidson, 'Intending', in his *Essays on Actions and Events* (New York: Oxford University Press, 1980), 83–102, at 83.)

In 'Reflection, Planning, and Temporally Extended Agency' I argue further that certain planning structures help constitute and support cross-temporal connections and continuities central to a broadly Lockean view of personal identity, and thereby to (what I call) agential authority. A full story of the norms characteristic of these planning structures would appeal as well to these considerations and their connections to issues of autonomy. But to keep the present discussion manageable, I will mostly put these matters aside here. For a related but different appeal to roles in constituting and supporting Lockean continuities and connections see Agnieszka Jaworska, 'Caring, Identification, and Internality' (unpublished MS).

In the first—and basic—case a background framework is provided by an individual's prior intentions and plans concerning her more or less specific future courses of action. Perhaps she has settled on a complex plan for her day, and this structures her ensuing practical thinking and action. Her plan poses problems about means and the like, and it filters options inconsistent with the plan. Or anyway, it does this so long as it is not reconsidered and changed; and the role of such plans in organizing our lives—in part in tandem with our limited cognitive resources—exerts rational pressure against such reconsideration and change.

Second, similar frameworks can be provided by *shared* intentions—intentions that involve more than one individual agent and concern shared, coordinated activities of those individual agents. Perhaps you and I share an intention to organize and run a conference together. This shared intention then structures our relevant, interlocking practical reasoning—including relevant bargaining and negotiation—about how to execute our shared intention.

In yet a further kind of case, plan-like frameworks concern not only courses of action, but what considerations are to be given justifying significance or weight in relevant deliberation and practical reasoning. In a central case this framework is provided by policies about how to treat certain considerations in relevant practical reasoning. Perhaps, for example, you have a policy of discounting in your deliberation concerns with revenge, despite your susceptibility to strong desires for it. In this case the cited policy about practical reasoning is a policy of an individual: namely, you. But it also seems that certain groups can have analogous policies: perhaps, for example, a philosophy department has a policy of not allowing considerations of congeniality to enter into its faculty hiring decisions.

So we have four main cases:

1. *Individual intentions and plans concerning individual action*: Individual S's prior intentions and plans concerning her own future conduct frame her practical reasoning by posing problems and filtering options.
2. *Shared intention concerning shared action*: S_1's and S_2's shared intention to J frames their interlocking deliberation and bargaining by posing problems and filtering options.
3. *Individual policies concerning what to treat as a justifying reason*: Individual S's policies, concerning the justifying significance or weight to be given

to consideration C in her own practical reasoning, frame that practical reasoning.

4. *Shared policy concerning what to treat as a justifying reason*: S_1 and S_2 have a shared policy concerning the justifying significance or weight to be given to consideration C in relevant contexts of shared deliberation.

I have discussed (1)–(3) in earlier work. Here I want to highlight certain themes from these earlier discussions. I will then turn to (4) with the hope that ideas from (1)–(3) can be extended in ways that shed light on (4). In this way I hope to shed light on forms of shared valuing.

3. Individual Intention concerning Individual Action

Begin with intentions and plans of an individual agent concerning more or less specific courses of action of that agent.[3] I intend, let us suppose, to work on this paper for several hours this morning, then finish reading a recent Ph.D. thesis draft, then, if it is sunny, to meet Susan for lunch in the park. I arrived at these intentions, and the plan in which they are embedded, for various reasons. Some of these reasons are specific to particular elements of the plan, and some of them concern the overall organization of the plan and its relation to other, larger plans of mine (e.g., to take a vacation next week).

Such intentions and plans engage distinctive norms of consistency, coherence, and stability—norms that go beyond those that apply to ordinary desires. Other things equal, an agent's intentions and plans are to be, taken together, consistent with each other and with her beliefs about the world. Further, one's intentions and plans, while typically partial, need to be filled in appropriately as time goes by. They need to be filled in with sub-plans concerning means and the like, sub-plans that are at least as extensive as one believes is (now) needed in order to do what one intends and plans; otherwise these intentions and plans will be threatened with means–end incoherence.[4]

---

[3] See *Intention, Plans, and Practical Reason*, esp. chs. 2 and 3.

[4] See ibid. 31. Note that this demand for means–end coherence can exert rational pressure in favour of a decision among several means none of which is, taken individually, a necessary means; for it may be (and frequently is) that what is necessary for one to achieve one's intended end is that one reach some decision or other concerning alternative, non-necessary but individually sufficient means.

And, finally, while such intentions and plans are not, of course, irrevocable, they are normally stable: their reconsideration and change—typically (but not always) in light of new information—is itself subject to distinctive norms of reasonable stability. Responsiveness to these demands for consistency, coherence, and stability promotes our general interests in the overall, cross-temporal organization of our lives, both individual and social. These general interests in what is for us the universal means of such cross-temporal organization help give these demands for consistency, coherence, and stability a distinctive rational force.[5]

Do such intentions themselves give the agent yet further reasons for action? Here we face conflicting pressures. On the one hand, we do not want to say simply that my intention to A gives me a new reason to A, a reason that is of the same sort as the reasons for A that will normally have led me to my intention in the first place. We do not want to say this because we do not want to sanction a simple form of bootstrapping. We do not want to say that simply by forming an intention in favour of an action that, I know, would otherwise not be one I have sufficient reason to perform, I directly give myself a new reason for so acting that can tip the scale of reasons. Irrationally forming an intention to act in a way that is contrary to the balance of one's acknowledged, prior reasons for action does not seem to be a way of making it straightforwardly rational for one to go ahead and act in the way one intends.[6]

On the other hand, even if one's initial intention is itself rationally criticizable, it nevertheless engages demands of means–end coherence: we nevertheless recognize a kind of rational pressure to settle on means and the like, and engage in associated practical reasoning.[7] Further, we

---

[5] One way to put the point is that responsiveness to these demands partly constitutes planning agency, and planning agency is, for reasons noted, a universal means for temporally persisting and social agents like us. So means–end reason enters twice: as a norm of means–end coherence on one's intentions and plans; and in an argument that one has reason to be, as one is, a planning agent, since planning agency is, for us, a universal means.

[6] For many of the points in this and the next paragraph see 'Intention and Means–End Reasoning' and *Intention, Plans, and Practical Reason*, 23–49.

[7] See the discussion of Mondale's intention to challenge Reagan's 'Star Wars' plan in the Presidential debate in *Intention, Plans, and Practical Reason*, 24–49. R. Jay Wallace emphasizes a closely related point in his 'Normativity, Commitment, and Instrumental Reason,' *Philosophers' Imprint* vol. 1 no. 3 (2001) <www.philosophersimprint.org/001003>. Wallace emphasizes that choice, decision, and intention bring with them distinctive demands of instrumental reason even in the absence of the agent's endorsement of the intended end as good. I am in agreement with Wallace on this point.

sometimes settle on a course of action—form an intention in its favour—even though, so far as we can see, this course of action is not, at least prior to our decision, superior to some conflicting competitor. Sometimes, in what I have called Buridan cases, we suppose that these courses of action are evaluatively on a par.[8] Sometimes we may suspect or know that one course is superior but not know which one.[9] Sometimes we may think that each of several conflicting options has something to be said for it, but these considerations are in a way incommensurable and there is no further fact, or judgement to be made, about which option is better.[10] In any of these cases we nevertheless recognize that once we decide on a particular course of action, we are under rational pressure to settle matters of means and the like. And this suggests that our intention or decision really does provide a new reason for action.

I have tried to do justice to both of these conflicting pressures by appealing to the idea that such prior intentions and plans provide *framework reasons*.[11] This appeal to framework reasons involves four ideas. First, in the absence of reconsideration or abandonment, prior intentions and plans structure further reasoning about means and the like, reasoning that is sensitive to rational demands for consistency and means–end coherence of one's plans. They do this by posing problems for such reasoning, problems of how to fill in one's partial plans in the pursuit of means–end coherence. And they do this by providing a filter on options by way of demands for consistency

---

[8] See my 'Davidson's Theory of Intention', reprinted in *Faces of Intention*, esp. 219–20. See also Edna Ullmann-Margalit and Sidney Morgenbesser, 'Picking and Choosing', *Social Research* 44 (1977), 757–85.

[9] See Frank R. Stockton's 1882 story, 'The Lady, or the Tiger?', in Thomas K. Parkes (ed.), *The American Short Story* (New York: Galahad Books, 1994), 202–7.

[10] See Joseph Raz, 'Incommensurability and Agency', in his *Engaging Reason: On the Theory of Value and Action* (Oxford: Oxford University Press, 1999), 65. See also Richard Holton, 'Intention and Weakness of Will', *Journal of Philosophy* 96 (1999), 245.

[11] See *Intention, Plans, and Practical Reason*, 28–35. John Broome is concerned with a similar tension between avoiding bootstrapping and providing a normative role for intentions. This leads him to distinguish reasons from what he calls 'normative requirements'. On his view, there is a normative requirement not to intend an end without intending a known, necessary means; but this does not mean that intending the end is a reason for intending those means. My account of the demand for means–end coherence parallels Broome's account of the normative requirement connecting intended ends and necessary means. I think, though, that we differ in the account we would give of what I call reasonable stability of intention. See John Broome, 'Are Intentions Reasons? And How Should We Cope with Incommensurable Values?', in Christopher W. Morris and Arthur Ripstein (eds.), *Practical Rationality and Preference: Essays for David Gauthier* (Cambridge: Cambridge University Press, 2001), esp. 114–19.

with prior intentions and plans, taken together with relevant beliefs. Second, we can nevertheless step back and criticize the entire plan-like structure that emerges—including both intended end and derived, intended means—in light of reasons for and against these larger structures. Even if this larger plan is coherent and consistent, it may nevertheless be insufficiently supported by relevant reasons. Third, there are important, general reasons—reasons grounded in central features of our temporally extended agency—that favour stability of one's framework of prior intentions and plans. But, fourth, such intentions and plans are not irrevocable. They remain open to reconsideration and change, especially in certain cases in which one newly learns that the reasons for which one originally arrived at one's intentions are no longer in force, or recognizes that one's original reasons were even then, and continue to be, insufficient to justify one's initial decision. And this leads us to recognize an important question: what are appropriate norms of intention and plan stability?[12]

This question about reasonable stability is, I think, quite difficult. It raises deep questions about the interaction between two features of our planning agency. On the one hand, we engage in long-term planning aimed at determining future conduct in ways that are sensitive to our cognitive limitations and achieve important forms of cross-temporal organization that are able to bear scrutiny over the temporally extended stretch of the planned activity. On the other hand, at the time of action it is the agent *at that time* who is in control, not some 'past self' who settled on a prior plan, or 'future self' at, so to speak, plan's end. Different views of stability respond differently to these twin features of our planning agency; and disagreements here are at the bottom of debates about versions of 'sophistication' and 'resolute choice'. These are not, however, matters we need go into in detail here.[13] All that is

---

[12] In his seminal 1976 paper, Gilbert Harman emphasized that 'the system of intentions has an inertia that keeps it going when desire fades' ('Practical Reasoning', reprinted in Gilbert Harman, *Reasoning, Meaning, and Mind* (Oxford: Oxford University Press, 1999), at 62). In appealing to the reasonable stability of intention, I am agreeing with this idea of Harman, but I am also emphasizing that this is a phenomenon that can be assessed in light of relevant norms of reasonable stability. I briefly indicate relations between this approach and broadly Deweyian ideas about deliberation and 'entanglements' in 'Taking Plans Seriously', 277–8. Richard Holton also emphasizes the significance of the normative dimension of stability in his 'Intention and Weakness of Will', 247–51.

[13] I discuss these issues in 'Toxin, Temptation, and the Stability of Intention', in *Faces of Intention*, 58–90, where I defend a view in the space between 'sophisticated' and 'resolute' choice. The *locus classicus* for the idea of resolute choice is Edward F. McClennen, *Rationality and Dynamic Choice: Foundational Explorations* (Cambridge: Cambridge University Press, 1990).

needed for present purposes is the recognition of the theoretical importance of norms of reasonable stability of prior intentions and plans.[14]

This idea of reasonable stability is a key to the relation between demands for consistency and means–end coherence, on the one hand, and framework reasons, on the other. Consistency and means–end coherence are requirements on one's overall package of intentions and plans, given one's beliefs. By themselves, however, these requirements do not fully explain the idea of framework reasons. To explain that idea, we need also to appeal to reasonable stability. For example, given an intention in favour of E, and a belief that to achieve E one must settle on an intention in favour of means M, one is faced with means–end incoherence if one intends E but does not intend M. So one needs either (a) to intend M, or (b) to give up one's intention in favour of E. So far there is no presumption in favour of either (a) or (b). Once we add reasonable stability as a feature of the prior intention in favour of E, however, there is a presumption specifically in favour of intending M. One can, of course, override this presumption by abandoning the intention in favour of E; but that will raise issues about potentially unreasonable instability (though, of course, it will sometimes be *un*reasonable *not* to abandon an ill-formed prior intention). When we in this way tie demands for consistency and coherence of our intentions and plans together with norms of reasonable stability of those intentions and plans, we arrive at a model of intentions and plans as framework reasons.[15]

The picture that emerges is that prior intentions and plans, so long as they are not reconsidered or abandoned, structure further reasoning about means and the like, and they do this in ways that are shaped by requirements for consistency and coherence of those intentions and plans. So long as one does not reconsider or abandon those plans, they are poised to play this framework-providing role in practical reasoning. But we may on occasion—especially in light of relevant, new information—reasonably reconsider and, perhaps, abandon such prior intentions and plans. Here norms of reasonable stability come to the fore. Finally, the norms of stability that ground these framework-setting roles are

---

[14] See my *Intention, Plans, and Practical Reason*, ch. 5; see also Holton, 'Intention and Weakness of Will', 247–51.

[15] I briefly consider relations between the idea of a framework reason and Joseph Raz's notion of an exclusionary reason in *Intention, Plans, and Practical Reason*, 180 n. 11. See Joseph Raz, *Practical Reason and Norms* (London: Hutchinson, 1975; reissued by Princeton University Press, 1990).

themselves grounded not solely in the particular reasons for the particular intentions and actions at issue. They are also grounded, more broadly, in our general interest in the overall, cross-temporal organization and coherence of our practical thought and action.

4. Shared Intention concerning Shared Action

Turn now to shared intention—our shared intention, for example, to organize a conference together. In a series of papers,[16] I have proposed that you and I share an intention to *J*—at least in the basic case—when we each intend that we *J*, we each intend that we *J* in accordance with and because of each of our intentions that we *J* and their meshing sub-plans, and all this is common knowledge.[17] Further, in the context of the shared intention the persistence of each of our intentions that we *J* is dependent on the known persistence of the other's intention that we *J*, and this mutual interdependence of these intentions of each is common knowledge.[18]

The idea, then, is that such a shared intention consists of a complex structure of interlocking and interdependent practical attitudes of the individual participants, in a context of common knowledge. Such shared intentions lie behind important kinds of shared activity, including what I have called *jointly intentional activity* and *shared co-operative activity*. I will not repeat here all the details of these models of shared intention and shared agency; but I do want to emphasize several points.

First, when two people share an intention to *J*, they each intend that their *J*-ing proceed by way of both of their intentions that they *J* and their meshing sub-plans. In this sense their individual intentions interlock, and

---

[16] See my 'Shared Cooperative Activity', 'Shared Intention', 'Shared Intention and Mutual Obligation', and 'I Intend that We *J*'—all in *Faces of Intention*.

[17] For a qualification see my 'I Intend that We *J*', in *Faces of Intention*, 143–4.

[18] See ibid. 153. The claim is only that there is this known mutual interdependence in this basic case of shared intention. There can be special cases in which I intend that we *J* even though my intention is, I know, not dependent on a corresponding intention of yours. Margaret Gilbert has emphasized related forms of mutual interdependence in her extensive work on shared agency. On her view, however, the relevant mutual interdependence always involves an obligation-constituting joint commitment, whereas on my view this need not always be so. See, e.g., her 'What Is It for *Us* to Intend?', in her *Sociality and Responsibility* (Lanham, M.: Rowman & Littlefield, 2000), 14–36.

they each intend that their joint *J*-ing proceed by way of the agency of each. This does not, of course, mean that when there is shared intention the participants must already have arrived at complete, meshing sub-plans. As in the case of an individual's intentions and plans concerning her own activity, shared intentions will typically be partial and will need to be filled in as time goes by. There will be rational pressure on each participant, when engaged in practical reasoning and bargaining about how to carry out the shared intention, to adjust her sub-plans in ways that will success-fully mesh with those of the other participant in the shared intention. Each person's complex intention—that they *J* by way of interlocking, meshing intentions and sub-plans of each—provides that person with a framework reason to fill in her own plans with sub-plans that support the joint activity in ways that mesh with the sub-plans of her partner.

Second, such shared intentions require neither shared reasons for the intention or the shared activity nor agreement that the shared activity is superior to its alternatives. Two people may share an intention to organize a conference even if they each have very different reasons for this: perhaps one person's reason is the advancement of scholarship, while the other person's reason has more to do with his own professional reputation. Further, even if there were agreement about which reasons are relevant, they may nevertheless disagree about which shared activity would be best. They may arrive at their shared intention by way of bargaining and com-promise. However, even given divergence in the reasons for participating in the shared intention and/or divergence in underlying value judgement, their shared intention structures and co-ordinates their reasoning and bargaining concerning relevant sub-plans and the like. It structures their planning and bargaining about, for example, when to have the conference, whom to invite, what its main topics will be, and so on. It provides a background framework for such reasoning and bargaining.

This structuring role derives from the fact that the relevant intentions of each participant favour the co-ordinated, interlocking, meshing execu-tion of each person's intentions and sub-plans in favour of the shared activity. Demands for coherence and consistency on the intentions of each of the individuals then require each to seek consistency and coherence in the overall package of sub-plans of both. So each will need to seek sub-plans that mesh with the other's sub-plans. These pressures toward mesh-ing sub-plans will help shape the reasoning and bargaining of each in the pursuit of the shared activity.

This shared framework will be subject to demands for stability. Some of these demands will derive from familiar requirements of reasonable stability on the intentions of each. In this respect there is a commonality with the case of an individual's prior plans about her own activities. But it is also true that some relevant demands for stability will normally derive also from associated inter-personal obligations, obligations that are normally (though, on my view, not universally) generated in cases of such shared intentions by way of associated assurances, promises, intentionally induced reliance, and the like.[19]

Throughout, a central source of these demands for stability, consistency, and coherence is a general concern with organization and co-ordination. Even in the case of an individual's plans about her own activities, these concerns with organization have a social dimension: a main reason for constructing plans is to help make oneself a reliable participant in forms of social co-ordination. But in the case of shared intentions and plans, concerns with inter-personal organization take centre stage.

Note that these structures can also arise in cases of shared *policies*—for example, your and my shared policy of meeting weekly to discuss the philosophy of action. This shared policy will frame our relevant reasoning and bargaining about, say, where to meet, what journal article to talk about, and so on. And our shared policy will be subject to analogous pressures—both individually and socially based—for stability.

I will return below to this idea of a shared policy; but first it will be useful to highlight certain commonalities that have emerged from the discussion so far.

5. Partiality and Frameworks

We have noted that in both the individual and the shared cases relevant intentions, plans, and policies concerning action are typically partial: they specify certain actions or ends, but typically leave certain issues about means, preliminary steps, specifications, and the like to later practical reasoning and, especially in the case of shared intention, bargaining. This partiality makes room for important forms of further practical reasoning and bargaining. Relevant intentions provide a background framework, and

---

[19] See my 'Shared Intention and Mutual Obligation'.

associated framework reasons, for that further practical reasoning and bargaining. They provide this framework in the following ways:

(1) They pose problems about further means and the like, problems driven by the need for forms of plan coherence.

(2) They constrain solutions to those problems given the needs for plan consistency.

(3) They play roles (1) and (2) in so far as they are not reconsidered or abandoned; and their reconsideration, and potential change, is itself subject to relevant norms of reasonable stability.

In the individual case the plans whose coherence, consistency, and stability are at stake are those of the individual concerning her own activity. In the shared case what is of primary interest are the interdependent plans of each concerning the joint activity of both, a joint activity that each intends to issue from interlocking intentions and meshing sub-plans of each. These distinctive complexities in what is intended by each participant in a shared intention lead, by way of demands of consistency and means–end coherence on the intentions of each, to corresponding rational pressures towards meshing, co-ordinated sub-plans among all the participants. In the shared case, further, interactions among the individuals may well, by way of norms about promissory obligations, assurances, and the like, generate further, special grounds for the stability of the shared intentions. (Of course, there is also room for assurances and the like in the case of an individual's plans about her own activity. The point here is only that the roles of assurance-based obligations and the like are particularly salient in the case of shared intention.)

In both individual and shared cases the grounds for these demands for consistency, coherence, and stability include general concerns with overall organization and co-ordination, both within a single person's temporally extended life and socially, across lives. And in both cases these demands do not in general depend on the prior superiority of the relevant course of action: both the individual and the shared cases can, for example, sometimes be Buridan cases, or involve relevant forms of incommensurability or of weakness of will; and shared intentions, and their sub-plans, can be a compromise in the face of disagreement about the best. In all these cases prior intentions—individual or shared—provide (albeit, revocable) framework reasons for relevant means, preliminary steps, specifications, and the like.

So there are deep commonalities across the cases of individual and shared intentions. As we will now see, there are also, in many cases of both sorts, important links to relevant policies about what to treat as a justifying reason for action.

6. Individual Policies concerning what to Treat as a Reason

The first step is to turn to a different kind of framework for the practical reasoning of an individual.[20] The basic idea here is that an agent may have policies—as I call them, *self-governing* policies—that say which considerations are to be given what sort of justifying significance or weight in her motivationally effective practical reasoning.[21] A person might, for example, have a policy of discounting or bracketing in her practical reasoning various forms of anger or resentment; another person might have a policy of sexual abstinence, a policy that involves refraining from giving weight in her deliberation to her desires for sexual activity; a third person might have a policy of giving great significance in his deliberation and action to style and verve; a fourth might have a policy that assigns great weight to certain religious practices in her deliberation about what to do; a fifth a policy that gives weight to honesty in her public assessments of the work of her colleagues, even if this is personally difficult.

Such self-governing policies provide a framework for practical reasoning. As I have emphasized, individual or shared intentions and plans concerning specific activities also provide frameworks for practical reasoning. Let me say a bit about how these frameworks are related to each other.

One's intentions concerning specific activities normally pose, in light of demands for coherence, problems of how to fill in one's associated partial plans of action with specifications of means and the like; and they constrain solutions to those problems by way of demands for consistency. The frame-

[20] See my 'Reflection, Planning, and Temporally Extended Agency'; 'A Desire of One's Own', *Journal of Philosophy* 100 (2003), 221–42; and 'Autonomy and Hierarchy', *Social Philosophy and Policy* 20 (2003), 156–76.

[21] For some related ideas see T. M. Scanlon, *What We Owe to Each Other* (Cambridge, Mass.: Harvard University Press, 1998), 45–53, a discussion to which I am indebted. I discuss some of these ideas from Scanlon in 'Identification, Decision, and Treating as a Reason', in my *Faces of Intention*, 196–7.

work-providing role of these intentions consists in part posing problems and constraining solutions. In filling in one's plans, however, one will typically need to weigh various pros and cons concerning alternative means or the like. And here one's self-governing policies can provide a relevant background framework of commitments to treating certain considerations as having weight or other kinds of justifying significance in such deliberations.

So, to a first approximation, intentions concerning specific activities and self-governing policies provide different kinds of frameworks that normally interact with each other in the indicated way. However, it should also be noted that self-governing policies may also pose their own, distinctive problems of means. They are, after all, policies about how to reason; and one may find that, in order for one to reason effectively in the way favoured by one's policy, one needs to take related steps. Such steps may well include forms of management of the impact of related desires or emotions—for example, of the impact on one's practical reasoning and action of anger or indignation.[22]

As I see it, such self-governing policies will themselves normally be to some extent responsive to and grounded in judgements about value, judgements that are subject to characteristic inter-subjective pressures.[23] However, such judgements of value many times leave underdetermined important details about how to live one's life.[24] Self-governing policies are sometimes in part a response to such underdetermination by value judgement and the resulting need to go beyond prior judgements concerning multiple, conflicting values in shaping one's own life (while recognizing the value of alternatives). Self-governing policies are, as I have already suggested, also sometimes in part an element in our efforts at self-management, given our need to reflect on and manage various forms of first-order motivation.[25] A person's policy of bracketing forms of anger or

---

[22] This is a version of a central theme of Harry Frankfurt. See esp. his *The Importance of What We Care About* (Cambridge: Cambridge University Press, 1988).

[23] Though in a particular case such policies may in fact not be responsive to any such judgements.

[24] See, e.g., Joseph Raz, *The Morality of Freedom* (Oxford: Oxford University Press, 1986), ch. 14, and Robert Nozick, *Philosophical Explanations* (Cambridge, Mass.: Harvard University Press, 1981), esp. 446–50. My own discussion is primarily in 'A Desire of One's Own'. And compare John Broome's discussion of the interaction between such issues and the normative role of intention in his 'Are Intentions Reasons?', esp. 114–19.

[25] I discuss interactions between these two different roles of self-governing policies, and the relevance of these interactions to hierarchical models of autonomous agency, in my 'Autonomy and Hierarchy'.

resentment can be in part a policy of reflective self-management, and in part a (in some cases and to some extent, life-defining) response to complex and conflicting evaluative pressures concerning the role of the reactive emotions in a human life. And a person's policy of bracketing forms of embarrassment and personal discomfort when it comes to certain kinds of professional assessments may also play an analogous, dual role. Given these characteristic roles in our practical lives—the response to underdetermination by value judgement, the role in self-management, the provision of associated structures to practical reasoning—it seems reasonable to say that such self-governing policies are a kind of *valuing*, a kind of valuing that is related to but different from value judgement.[26]

Our self-governing policies are under pressure to be consistent with each other, and to constitute, when taken together, a coherent framework for practical reasoning. One result of such pressures can be that such policies involve significant context relativity. I can, for example, have a policy of not giving weight to certain kinds of considerations of friendliness in job interviews or the like, even though I do give those considerations great weight in other contexts. There are limits here concerning how fine-grained such context relativity can be before it undermines important forms of personal coherence; but this is not a matter we need to resolve here.

Again, it also seems clear that norms of stability will be of great importance in this domain, and this for general reasons about cross-temporal organization and coherence within one's temporally extended life. While such self-governing policies are normally not irrevocable or, to use an idea from Harry Frankfurt, volitionally necessary,[27] their frequent, significant change would tend toward a seriously fractured life.

Self-governing policies help shape what we treat as having justificatory weight or significance in our reasoning about what to do. In this way they help to determine what I have called the 'subjective normative authority'

---

[26] See also my 'Valuing and the Will', *Philosophical Perspectives* 14 (2000), 249–65, and 'Autonomy and Hierarchy'. Concerning the distinction between valuing and value judgement see Gary Watson, 'Free Action and Free Will', *Mind* 96 (1987), 145–72, at 150; and Gilbert Harman, 'Desired Desires', as reprinted in his *Explaining Value and Other Essays in Moral Philosophy* (Oxford: Oxford University Press, 2000), 129–30. Let me note that I think some such distinction, and my treatment of it here, is available to a range of different views in meta-ethics, including both forms of expressivism and forms of cognitivism.

[27] See his 'On the Necessity of Ideals', in his *Necessity, Volition, and Love* (Cambridge: Cambridge University Press, 1999).

of certain considerations.[28] They help provide a framework of justificatory significance that responds, in a co-ordinated way, to the dual pressures both to manage one's motivational life and to respond to underdetermination by value judgement. The pressure to respond to underdetermination by value judgement is, then, rooted in a kind of partiality—a partiality in one's operative framework of reasons, given only one's inter-subjectively accountable judgements of value. So there is here a certain parallel with the partiality of ordinary plans of action. However, whereas the partiality of plans of action is a partiality in their specification of courses of action, the partiality at issue here, and to which self-governing policies are in part a response, is one engendered by underdetermination by value judgement of broad features of significance in a life of one's own.

Brief reflection on related work of Joseph Raz is useful here. Raz sees reasons for action as frequently not determining a uniquely rational course of action. Reasons, rather, frequently only pick out a set of options each of which would be compatible with the reasons there are antecedent to the choice. There remains a need for the agent to choose from these reason-eligible alternatives:

reasons for action are better characterized as making actions eligible rather than requiring their performance on pain of irrationality. In typical situations, reason does not determine what is to be done. Rather it sets a range of eligible options before agents, who choose among them as they feel inclined . . . the will plays a role in human agency separate from that of reason, a role that neither kowtows to reason by endorsing its conclusions nor irrationally rebels against it by refusing to endorse them.[29]

Judgements about reasons frequently only identify a number of 'eligible' options among which one must choose. It is the latter role that is played by 'the will'. In acknowledging this role of the will, Raz endorses what he calls the 'classical' conception of human action, in contrast with what he calls the 'rationalist' conception.[30]

---

[28] See my 'Two Problems about Human Agency', *Proceedings of the Aristotelian Society* 101 (2001), 309–26.

[29] Raz, 'Incommensurability and Agency', 65. Elsewhere Raz calls this *'the basic belief'*—the view 'that most of the time people have a variety of options such that it would accord with reason for them to choose any one of them and it would not be against reason to avoid any one of them. . . . The basic belief applies to large as well as to small decisions'. ('Explaining Normativity', in *Engaging Reason*, 100). Raz endorses this basic belief in ibid. 101.

[30] Raz, 'Incommensurability and Agency', 47.

Now, in emphasizing the roles of first-order planning structures, at times in the face of a sort of underdetermination to which Raz points, my view shares an important feature with what Raz calls the classical conception. Does my appeal to the roles of self-governing policies in shaping what has subjective normative authority, at times in the face of underdetermination by value judgement, also correspond to Razian themes? The answer is complicated.

Raz emphasizes ways in which choice of particular actions in the face of underdetermination by reasons helps make 'us into who we are'.[31] In this way choices of particular actions can have an indirect impact on an agent's reasons, by way of the values of integrity and self-respect.[32] And Raz suggests that these choices may also have an impact by way of closing off certain options as not possible for that agent.[33] So far, however, it is choices of particular options that are seen as partially shaping one's reasons.

However, Raz also emphasizes that we can choose general goals from among a myriad of potential goods, and that such goals provide reasons for action that one did not have prior to having those goals. They provide such reasons because the satisfaction of such goals is part of the agent's well-being.[34] Such chosen goals, then, seem to function to some extent like self-governing policies, as I understand them.

As I see it, though, a self-governing policy may give significance to considerations that are more like side constraints than goals—for example, a policy of honesty in public assessments of work of colleagues, or of bracketing the impact of retributive desires. Further, my account highlights not primarily a direct relation to well-being but, rather, a relation between self-governing policies and our general interest in the cross-temporal organization of our practical thought and action, a cross-temporal organization that is a kind of universal means for temporally persisting and social agents like us.[35] As Michael Friedman once put it in conversation, the normativity comes from the constraints of cross-temporal organization. And this relation to cross-temporal organization helps make the characteristic

---

[31] Raz, 'The Truth in Particularism', in *Engaging Reason*, 242.

[32] Ibid. 243.

[33] Ibid. 241.

[34] Raz, 'Incommensurability and Agency', 63–4. See also Raz, *Morality of Freedom*, ch. 12. Thanks to Nadeem Hussain for emphasizing the significance to the present discussion of this aspect of Raz's views.

[35] And that helps constitute and support important Lockean ties. See n. 2.

functioning of self-governing policies in our practical lives *ceteris paribus* a case of rational, proper functioning.

Return now to the interaction between the different kinds of framework-providing phenomena I have been discussing. Note that these different framework-providing phenomena will many times be part of a unified package of commitments. A commitment to pursue a certain kind of scientific career, for example, is likely to be in part a first-order plan of action, and in part a policy about what considerations to treat as justifying in certain professional contexts. Indeed, full participation in the planned activity may well require commitment to some such associated self-governing policy.

Finally, as this last example suggests, these phenomena may well also involve *shared* intentions and plans, and their characteristic, shared frameworks for practical reasoning and bargaining. After all, to continue with the example, a commitment to pursue a certain kind of scientific career is also likely to involve participation in relevant shared intentions, and in the shared co-operative activities associated with the pursuit of the science.[36] Participation in scientific research—like many other important human activities—is, at least normally and in part, participation in a distinctive kind of shared activity.[37] Here individual intention, shared intention, and individual self-governing policies are intertwined within a complex package of interrelated commitments. And this takes us within a step of the phenomenon of shared policies about what to treat as a reason.

7. Shared Policies concerning what to Treat as a Reason

We have seen how individuals can participate in shared intentions or policies concerning their shared activities. And we have seen how individuals can have self-governing policies concerning the justifying significance to be given to various considerations in their deliberation about what to do. We can now put these ideas together and arrive at the idea of shared policies concerning what to treat as having justifying significance in contexts of shared activity and associated shared deliberation.

---

[36] Here I was helped by conversation with Michael Friedman.

[37] This is compatible with recognizing that it is a kind of shared activity that tends to issue in knowledge. See Alvin Goldman, *Knowledge in a Social World* (Oxford: Oxford University Press, 1999).

A philosophy department, for example, may have a shared policy about how to take into account issues of sub-field in its searches and associated deliberations.[38] This is a matter on which departments may reasonably diverge. One department may have a shared policy of ignoring such issues; another may have a policy of always restricting consideration to candidates in a previously designated sub-field. In each case the policies are, we may suppose, grounded to some extent in considerations about what makes a good department, as well as in other shared policies (e.g., about who gets to vote on such matters). It is possible that the members of the department agree about which policy would be (prior to any departmental commitment to a policy) best, and that this is why the department has that policy. But such shared policies may well go beyond such judgements about value, and do not require agreement in those judgements. Such shared policies nevertheless constitute a commitment, on the part of the individuals in the group, to structuring their shared deliberation and planning in a certain way. In participating in such a shared policy, one need not suppose that it is the best such policy. One may think there is no single best policy; or one may think that a different policy would be best. Indeed, each member of the department may have a different view of what the best policy would be, but nevertheless come to be committed to a shared policy that (prior to the department's commitment to it) no one sees as best.[39]

Again, different universities may have different shared policies about the justifying weight to be given to legacy considerations in deliberations about undergraduate admissions. One may work in the admissions office and be committed to its policy about such issues without thinking it is the best such policy.

In some cases particular shared policies concerning what to treat as a reason in certain contexts of shared activity are more or less definitive of the group whose policies they are. If you are going to be a member of a certain scientific research group, you may need to participate in a shared policy of giving weight in scientific debate to certain kinds of evidence, but

---

[38] For discussions of related examples see J. David Velleman, 'How to Share an Intention', as reprinted in his *The Possibility of Practical Reason* (Oxford: Oxford University Press, 2000), 200–20, and Christopher Kutz, 'The Judicial Community', *Philosophical Issues* 11 (2001), 442–69.

[39] Though I will not argue for this here, it is not even necessary, I think, that each member thinks the actual policy is best given that the department is committed to it.

not to whether or not the person offering the evidence is your friend.[40] Central to certain groups may be a shared policy of treating conformity to particular religious texts or traditions or rituals as a justifying reason for action. Again, a club may have a shared policy of giving justifying weight to, say, religious affiliation, or race, in its deliberations about membership; and that may be why you do not want to be a member of that club. And members of a jury may be required to share a policy of refraining from giving justifying weight to their felt empathy with the defendant, or to information not presented at the trial, when deliberating together in their official capacity as jurors.

As these examples suggest, such shared policies about what to treat as justifying will normally be part of a larger package of commitments, one that includes shared intentions in favour of associated shared activities. A group might have both a shared intention to worship together each Saturday, and a shared policy to treat associated rituals and traditions as providing justifying reasons for action on those occasions of shared worship. And a scientific research group might have shared intentions to engage in a certain line of research, together with shared policies about what is to count as a justifying consideration in the group's associated deliberations about what to publish. In each case participation in the relevant shared co-operative activities of religious worship or scientific research involves as well participation in related shared policies about what to treat as a justifying reason in the context of those shared activities.

Such shared policies about what to treat as a reason can help frame shared deliberation in ways analogous to ways in which an individual's self-governing policies help frame her individual deliberation. And this may be so even though there is reasonable disagreement about which such policy would be best. The deliberations of different undergraduate admissions committees may be framed by different shared policies about the justifying role of the fact that a candidate's parents attended that university. And the deliberations of different scientific research groups may be framed by different shared policies about the justifying role of the usefulness of secrecy in the pursuit of lucrative patents.

---

[40] The policy here will probably concern both treating certain considerations as reasons for action, and treating certain considerations as evidence for something like belief formation—perhaps for forms of context-relative acceptance, in a sense I discuss in 'Practical Reasoning and Acceptance in a Context', in *Faces of Intention*.

These shared policies bring with them associated demands for consistency, coherence, and stability. The ground of these demands includes, again, general concerns with co-ordination and organization over time and inter-personally. And, as in the case of shared intentions and policies concerning courses of action, there may well be pressures in favour of stability that arise specifically from associated assurances and the like. Joining a group, for example, may sometimes involve (perhaps, implicit) promises to participate in certain shared policies about what to treat as justifying in relevant shared contexts.

8. The Core Case and Forms of Shared Valuing

Suppose our committee has a shared policy to give justifying weight to legacy considerations in admissions decisions: we intend to treat such considerations as justifying in our relevant shared deliberation. Our shared policy is, then, a special kind of shared intention, one whose targeted activity is a certain kind of shared deliberation.

This suggests that we try to understand in what such a shared policy consists by appeal to our earlier story about shared intention. According to this earlier story, we intend to *J*, in the basic case, just when, in a context of common knowledge, we each intend that we *J* in accordance with and because of each of our intentions that we *J* and their meshing sub-plans, and our individual intentions that we *J* involve an appropriate kind of mutual interdependence.

So let us apply this story to our cited shared policy about our shared deliberation. We have such a shared policy just when, in a context of common knowledge, we each intend that we give justifying weight to legacy considerations in our shared deliberation, and that this proceed in accordance with and because of each of our intentions that we give such weight and their meshing sub-plans; and there is mutual interdependence between each of our intentions that we give such weight.

And now let us generalize. In what I will call the *core case* the following holds in a context of common knowledge:

(a) We each intend
    (i) that we give weight to R in relevant shared deliberation, and
    (ii) that (i) proceed by way of each of our (a)(i) intentions and their meshing sub-plans.

(b) There is mutual interdependence between each of our (a) intentions.

Note that in the core case the shared policy concerns shared deliberation. To see the significance of this limitation, consider an example. Suppose that you and I, in a context of common knowledge, each have a policy of giving forgiveness justifying weight in our individual interactions with others. Though in a very weak sense we share a policy about what to treat as justifying, the targeted context is not one of our shared deliberation: each intends only that he or she deliberate in the cited way in contexts of individual deliberation and action. So this is not a core case.

Note also that the core case requires mutual interdependence between the intentions of each concerning what is to be treated as justifying. Indeed, in the absence of appropriate mutual interdependence each participant would not normally have an intention that *they* give weight to R in shared deliberation.[41] In some cases such interdependence will be a result of the need to fix on a group policy in the face of divergence in relevant value judgements of the individuals. But there will also be cases of such interdependence in the presence of agreement in relevant value judgement. Perhaps, for example, all the members of a committee agree, for similar reasons, that a particular policy about legacy considerations would be best. Nevertheless, it may also be true that, given their recognition of the need for co-ordination in such matters, they are each committed to the policy in part also because others are.[42]

It does seem, however, that there are possible cases in which participants in a shared activity each have mutually *in*dependent policies about what to give justifying weight in the context of that shared activity. Such cases would not be core cases even if the cited policies favoured the same considerations. Here is an example: You and I each have a policy of giving weight, in the context of our joint research project, to seeking out related published works and acknowledging them in our own publications. We recognize that our shared project might break down were we not to agree in this way. Nevertheless, we are each committed to a policy of giving weight to these considerations whether or not the other does, and in each case our reason for our policy does not refer to the other's policy.

[41] See my 'I Intend that We J'.

[42] Scott Shapiro makes a related point in a different context. See his discussion of his example of the ancient Hebrews in his 'Law, Plans, and Practical Reason', *Legal Theory* 8 (2002), 387–441. My discussion here has benefited from Shapiro's discussion.

While such a case is possible, it is important to see that there will also be significant pressure in the direction of mutual interdependence. This pressure comes from the structure of the targeted shared activity: in this case, the activity of the joint research project. After all, it is required that there be intentions that this activity proceed by way of meshing sub-plans. And part of the way the activity frequently proceeds is by way of relevant, shared deliberation. When it does proceed in this way each participant is committed to there being meshing sub-plans concerning that deliberation. So each participant is committed to there being a mesh in the relevant policies about what to give weight to in that deliberation. So each has *a* reason to adjust her policies about such weights in order to mesh with her partners' corresponding policies. So when there is such mesh—as there is in our case in which each has the same policy about the weight to be given to certain kinds of scholarship—each will have *a* reason for her contribution to that mesh, a reason that derives from each person's commitment to mesh together with facts about the other's policy. Granted, it remains possible that this reason is not a reason *for which* the person has her relevant policy. So a certain kind of independence remains possible. But it also seems that, given the intentional structure of the shared activity and associated deliberation, there will frequently be the kind of mutual interdependence that is built into the core case.

The core case, then, involves the condition, first, that the target is shared deliberation and, second, that the intentions of the individuals about what is to be given weight in that deliberation are themselves mutually interdependent. The shared policy in a core case will normally be to some extent responsive to relevant judgements of value on the part of the various participants. In this respect there is a parallel with the case of an individual's valuings. Nevertheless, the shared policy in the core case requires neither agreement nor disagreement in underlying value judgements: the core case is neutral about this matter. Return, for example, to our policy about seeking out related works by others. We might have this policy because we are in agreement that it is required by broad considerations of scholarship. But perhaps, instead, one of us participates in this policy for this reason, while another participates because he thinks it is a good way to win friends.

Further, the core case can allow for the possibility that the participants recognize the value of alternative policies. A department may be committed to a policy about the relevance of sub-field considerations in its searches even while its members recognize that a case can also be made for an alternative policy.

A shared policy in the core case provides a background framework that structures relevant shared deliberation. It helps fix on certain (in some cases, group-defining) modes of shared deliberation, modes of deliberation that can be at the heart of associated shared activities. It plays these framework-providing roles in the shared deliberation of the group in a way that is neutral concerning the presence or absence of agreement in underlying value judgement, and that can allow for recognition of the value of alternatives. Such shared policies are related to, but distinguishable from, the value judgements of the individuals, even in cases of agreement in such judgements.

These framework-providing roles of such shared policies in the core case to some extent parallel the roles of self-governing policies in the life of an individual agent. Since it was those roles that supported the proposal that those self-governing policies were a form of valuing, should we say that such shared policies in the core case are a kind of *shared valuing*?

The issues are delicate. On the one hand, a shared policy in favour of giving significance to R in the core case does not ensure either that the individual participants each judge that R is good, or that the individual participants each individually value R. The individual participants must, of course, each be committed to a policy that gives significance to R in certain shared deliberative contexts. Nevertheless, it may be that none of the participants has a self-governing policy that gives weight to R in contexts outside this special shared context. In this sense it may be that none of the participants individually values R even though they are each participants in the shared policy in favour of R. So it may seem strained to say that a shared policy in the core case in favour of R is a kind of shared valuing.

On the other hand, such a shared policy does help determine what is to be treated by the participants as a justifying consideration in relevant shared practical contexts. It plays a basic, structuring role in the normatively guided deliberation and action of the group. In this respect it seems a reasonable candidate for a form of shared valuing.

My tentative proposal is that we see such shared policies in the core case as a form of shared valuing, but also recognize that it may be important whether or not there are also other forms of agreement.[43] Shared valuings

---

[43] As Seana Shiffrin noted in conversation, such a shared policy may also articulate a shared rationale, one that may be useful when we come up against hard cases. For example,

that also involve agreement in the valuings and/or value judgements of the participants may have a special significance in certain important contexts—for example, in the context of certain kinds of friendship.[44] This generic model of shared valuing allows us to describe these stronger conditions of agreement, but also to highlight the broad and important commonality that is captured by the conditions of the core case.[45]

Granted, if I am a participant in a core case in our shared policy to, say, give weight to legacy considerations, but think this is a bad idea and do not value it, then it might be odd for me simply to say 'We value giving weight to legacy considerations.' But I am inclined to see the oddity here in terms of a conversational implicature. What I need to do is tell you 'But I myself, as an individual, do not value this.' Without that qualification my original remark may be true but misleading.

9. Inter-connected Frameworks and the Will

I have emphasized parallels and interrelations between shared valuing, in the sense of the core case, and other framework-providing phenomena noted earlier in this essay. By exploring these parallels and interrelations we may hope to clarify important features of shared valuing, provide conceptual resources for distinguishing among cases of shared valuing, distinguish shared valuing from related but different phenomena, highlight the significance of such shared valuing to our lives, and provide models of shared valuing that are sufficiently articulated to do serious theoretical work in our understanding of important social phenomena.

I want to conclude by commenting on two general themes. The first is that there is an important range of human activities that involve, in ways that are organically interconnected, all four of these kinds of framework-providing phenomena. As a member of a scientific research team, for

---

we will give weight to legacy considerations as a way of creating donor loyalty. Shiffrin suggested that such further content in the shared policy may be necessary for shared valuing; but here I find it better just to note that this is one common case of shared valuing.

David Copp discusses a related idea of a 'society's values' in his *Morality, Normativity, and Society* (New York: Oxford University Press, 1995), 190–91.

[44] Several discussants of this paper at the 2003 Moral Psychology Conference at Franklin and Marshall College emphasized this case of friendship.

[45] In these three paragraphs I benefited from discussion with the Stanford ethics discussion group and with the Bay Area Forum for Law and Ethics.

example, I have relevant, individual research plans and self-governing policies that apply to these contexts; and I am a participant in shared intentions to engage in a certain shared research project, as well as shared valuings that structure our deliberation in the pursuit of that shared project. Again, to take an example from a different domain, there will likely be analogous, interconnected planning and policy structures when actors join together in a dramatic production.

A final example comes from the law.[46] Jules Coleman argues that legal officials—including judges, legislators, and administrators—can be seen as engaged in a shared co-operative activity aimed, in part, at 'making possible the existence of a durable legal practice'.[47] Coleman argues that this point is central to a defence of legal positivism; but that is not a matter we need discuss here. What is important for present purposes is that it is plausible that such shared activities in law would normally involve the quartet of framework-providing structures we have been examining. In particular, Coleman emphasizes that these structures include 'parameters of reason[s] that are recognized as appropriate or good'.[48] And that seems likely to involve shared valuings concerning relevant legal contexts.

The second theme returns us to the very idea of the will. In each of the four kinds of cases outlined at the beginning of this essay, a framework for practical reasoning is provided by intention-like attitudes that bring with them distinctive norms of consistency, coherence, and stability. These intention-like attitudes are frequently grounded to some extent in inter-subjectively accountable value judgement. However, they may well need to go beyond those judgements in order to fix on sufficiently contoured and articulated courses of action or modes of deliberation, both individual and social. Our need to fix on such courses of action or modes of deliberation is grounded in large part in our need for organizing, cross-temporal structure in our practical thought and action, both individual and social. And we have seen reason to believe that a wide range of important human

---

[46] See Jules L. Coleman, *The Practice of Principle* (Oxford: Oxford University Press, 2001), esp. 95–100. Coleman credits Scott Shapiro with the basic idea. Shapiro develops the idea in a somewhat different way, and in fascinating detail, in his 'Law, Plans, and Practical Reason'. I discuss some of these views of Shapiro in my 'Shapiro on Legal Positivism and Jointly Intentional Activity', *Legal Theory* 8 (2002), 511–17.

[47] Coleman, *Practice of Principle*, 97.

[48] Ibid. 98.

activities involve an interrelated quartet of structures whose function it is to help constitute and support such cross-temporal organization.

I think that it is natural to say that these organizing, intention-like structures are elements of the will.[49] A characteristic, defining function of the will, so understood, is the cross-temporal organization of our individual and shared practical thought and action, in ways that respond to the underdetermination by judgements about value of the specific contours of our lives, both individual and social; in ways that can allow for recognition of, and respect for, the value of alternative modes of thought and action; and in ways that help us achieve a wide range of human ends. Shared valuing, in particular, is a kind of shared willing.[50]

[49] This is a further development of the idea that the planning theory is a modest theory of the will.

[50] Thanks to Talbot Brewer, John Broome, Edward Hinchman, Simon May, Peter Railton, Gideon Yaffe, members of the Stanford ethics discussion group and the Bay Area Forum for Law and Ethics, and participants in discussions of this essay at Georgetown University, the Analytic Legal Philosophy Conference at Yale Law School, the Australian National University, and the Moral Psychology Conference at Franklin and Marshall College. Work on this essay was supported by a fellowship from the John Simon Guggenheim Memorial Foundation.

2

Reasons

John Broome

1. Introduction and Preliminaries

Within the philosophy of normativity, the 1970s was the age of the discovery of reasons.[1] Joseph Raz was one of the first explorers. In his *Practical Reason and Norms*, Raz carefully codified the concept of a reason, and he has been a leader in its development ever since. Since those years of discovery, reasons have come to dominate thinking about normativity. Some authors now believe normativity consists of little else. Raz himself says: 'The normativity of all that is normative consists in the way it is, or provides, or is otherwise related to reasons.'[2] All is reasons.

But it is not. Reasons are undoubtedly important, but normativity has other important features, and our preoccupation with reasons distracts us from them. I think we need to look at normativity more widely. I shall begin this paper with an example of the harm that is done by our preoccupation. My description in this section is brief; it is merely a preview of arguments to come in section 5.

---

[1] I take this picturesque idea from the tentative title of Derek Parfit's forthcoming book *Rediscovering Reasons*. Michael Bratman reminded me that the concept of a reason first became prominent in the philosophy of action, and only later in the philosophy of normativity. For instance, it is in Elizabeth Anscombe's *Intention* (Oxford: Blackwell, 1957). Interestingly, Raffaele Rodogno has shown me a discussion of reasons within moral philosophy dating from 1952: Austin Duncan-Jones, *Butler's Moral Philosophy* (London: Penguin, 1952), 77–86.

[2] Joseph Raz, *Engaging Reason: On the Theory of Value and Action* (Oxford: Oxford University Press, 1999), 67.

Often 'you ought' governs a simple infinitival phrase. You ought to do something, know something, intend something, or believe something, for instance. But also often, 'you ought' governs a conditional: you ought (to Φ if X). The requirements of correct reasoning take this form, for instance. One of them is the requirement that, when a proposition q follows obviously from another p, you ought (to believe q if you believe p). You ought (to believe the world was made in less than a week, if you believe the world was made in six days).

I am forced to the ugly expedient of using brackets in order to avoid an ambiguity. I do not say that, if you believe p, you ought to believe q. That may well be false, even when q follows obviously from p. No one ought to believe the world was made in less than a week; the evidence is strongly against it. Even if you believe the world was made in six days, still it is not the case that you ought to believe it was made in less than a week. Nevertheless, you ought (to believe the world was made in less than a week, if you believe it was made in six days). You can satisfy this requirement either by not believing the world was made in six days or by believing it was made in less than a week. As it happens, you ought to satisfy it the first way. You ought not to believe the world was made in six days, even if you do.

As a useful piece of terminology, when you ought (to Φ if X), I say that X *normatively requires* you to Φ.[3] Believing the world was made in six days normatively requires you to believe it was made in less than a week.

Another example: intending an end normatively requires you to intend whatever you believe is a necessary means to the end. You ought (to intend to M if you intend to E and you believe your M-ing is a necessary means to your E-ing). I do not say that, if you intend an end, you ought to intend whatever you believe is a necessary means. That may be false. If you ought not to intend the end, it may well be false that you ought to intend whatever you believe is a necessary means to it. Still, intending the end normatively requires you to intend whatever you believe is a necessary means to it.

Relations among your beliefs and intentions are regulated by oughts that govern these relations—'wide-scope oughts' I shall call them. They imply no narrow-scope normative conditions on individual beliefs or intentions. This seems to me clear and straightforward, but many authors do

---

[3] When I introduced this term in my 'Normative Requirements' (*Ratio* 12 (1999), 398–419), I gave it a slightly narrower meaning.

not recognize it. I think this is partly because they habitually think only about reasons. They treat all normative questions as questions about what is or is not a reason for what. They ask: when q follows obviously from p, is believing p a reason to believe q? Or: is intending an end a reason to intend a means to it?

Intending an end clearly stands in some sort of normative relation to intending a means. So if the only normative relation you think of is the relation of being a reason to, you are likely to think that intending an end is a reason to intend a means. Then your view implies that, if you intend an end, you have a reason to intend a means. That is to say, if you intend an end, the narrow-scope normative property of your having a reason to applies to your intending a means.

But this is to misunderstand the logical structure of the situation. Suppose you intend to visit Rum, and the only way you can get there is to take the boat. A reason to intend to take the boat is that the boat will carry you to the wild and beautiful island of Rum. This reason exists independently of your intention to visit Rum. But if this intention was also a further reason to intend to take the boat, it would be a reason you create yourself by forming the intention to visit Rum. It is puzzling how you could create a reason in that way; Michael Bratman calls it 'bootstrapping' the reason into existence.[4] At any rate, this reason would have to be a different sort from the first. So the idea that your intention constitutes a reason raises the possibility of different sorts of reason. This is the 'dualism of reasons' that T. M. Scanlon considers and rejects in 'Reasons: A Puzzling Duality?', chapter 10 in this volume.

But actually there is a difference of scope, not merely of sort. A wide-scope ought governs the relation between intending to visit Rum and intending to take the boat: you ought (to intend to take the boat if you intend to visit Rum). On the other hand, the fact that the boat will carry you to this wild and beautiful island gives you a narrow-scope reason: it makes it the case that you have a reason (to intend to take the boat). This is a major difference in logical structure. To miss it is a serious error caused by a preoccupation with reasons.

I think we should reassess the importance of reasons. We need to codify the concept of a reason once more, and mark off its boundaries. This paper

---

[4] Michael E. Bratman, *Intention, Plans and Practical Reason* (Cambridge, Mass.: Harvard University Press, 1987; reissued by CSLI Publications, 1999), 24–7.

tries to do that. I shall boldly define a reason. Indeed, I shall distinguish two normative senses of 'a reason', and define them in sections 2 and 3 respectively. More precisely, I shall define two senses of 'a reason for you to Φ'. The second of my senses is a *pro tanto* reason, and in section 4 I shall consider how prevalent *pro tanto* reasons are. Then in sections 5 and 6, I shall identify features of normativity that are often thought to be reasons, but are not reasons as I define them. I shall argue that to call them reasons is to misunderstand them.

Ought facts

The key to understanding the concept of a reason is to look at how facts of a particular type are explained. I mean facts of the form that P ought to Φ, where 'P' stands for the name of an agent and 'to Φ' for an infinitival phrase. I shall call them 'ought facts'. An example is the fact that you ought to carry an umbrella in Glasgow. If you think there are no such facts, understand me to be speaking of ought truths instead. If you think there are no such truths, this paper will probably not make much sense to you.

To be friendly, I shall generally speak of *you* instead of a universal person *P*. What I say about you applies to anyone, of course. But unfortunately, I cannot avoid using the letter 'Φ'. I want to cover all normative cases where 'you ought' governs an infinitival phrase. There is no universal verb in English that covers all these cases, so I have to resort to the schematic letter. Moreover, I intend 'You ought to Φ' to cover some cases that, strictly grammatically, it does not cover. For example, I intend it to cover 'You ought not to dive here' and 'You ought either to forget her insult or challenge her'.

Some infinitival phrases that substitute for 'to Φ' refer to actings, intendings, believings, knowings, and so on. Others cannot be so neatly categorized. For example, when you ought either to believe p or not believe q, 'you ought' governs a phrase that refers to a relation between believings, rather than an individual believing. For another example, in his account of exclusionary reasons, Raz argues that sometimes you ought not to do a particular act for a particular reason, and he does not mean simply that you ought not to do this particular act.[5] So we have to allow 'not to G for

---

[5] Joseph Raz, *Practical Reason and Norms* (London: Hutchinson, 1975; reissued by Princeton University Press, 1990; repr. Oxford University Press, 1999), 185.

reason X' as a substitution for 'to Φ'. 'You ought' can govern all sorts of things.

Ought and explain

I shall take the concept of ought and the concept of explain as primitives. I shall use them rather than try to give an account of them. However, these concepts are afflicted by some ambiguities, and I need to specify how I shall use them.

First, 'ought'. This word can sometimes be used non-normatively. For example, suppose you ought to be exhausted by now—the 'ought' in that sentence is non-normative. But in this paper, I use 'ought' only normatively. Of facts of the form that P ought to Φ, I count as ought facts only those in which the ought is normative.

Some philosophers think 'ought' also has several normative senses. They think, for one thing, that it sometimes means the same as 'morally ought'. I would be surprised if this were so. The effect of an adverb is not usually to give a new sense to the verb it governs. There is no sense of 'finished' in which it means the same as 'partly finished' or 'hurriedly finished'. So I doubt that 'ought' can correctly be used to mean the same as 'morally ought'. However, if it can, that is not how I use it. I do not treat 'ought' as a solemn word with moral connotations. I treat it as our ordinary, work-aday, normative verb.

Next, 'explain'. First, this term is ambiguous in common usage. In one of its senses, Darwin explained evolution. In another sense, *The Origin of Species* explains evolution. In another, natural selection explains evolution. I shall stick to this third sense. As I use 'explain', an explanandum is explained by an explanans. It is not explained by a description of the explanans, nor by a describer of it.

'Explanation' is correspondingly ambiguous in common usage. It may refer to an act of explaining, to a description of an explanans, or to the explanans itself. I shall stick to the third sense. With a little regimentation, I shall take an explanation always to be a fact: a fact that explains an explanandum. I take the explanation of evolution to be the fact that natural selection occurs.

Second, although I have just specified a limit on my use of 'explain' and 'explanation', in another respect I use these terms broadly. When I say one fact X explains another Y, I mean simply that Y obtains because of X. As I understand it, the explaining relation is merely the inverse of the because relation. I have nothing to say about the nature of these relations; I take them as primitive.

Some philosophers use 'explanation' more specifically, sometimes for causal explanations only. But many explanations are not causal. For example, here is a grammatical explanation of why 'ought' takes an infinitive and not a 'that' clause: 'ought' is an auxiliary rather than a lexical verb, and an auxiliary always takes an infinitive (with or without 'to'). I shall mostly be dealing with non-causal explanations in this paper.

Third, although I shall not try to describe the nature of the explaining or because relation, I do need to say something about the individuation of explanations. Suppose Joanne broke a slate a while ago, and as a result the roof leaks. It rained last night, and today the carpet is wet. When we enquire why the carpet is wet, you might say the explanation is that it rained last night. I might say it is that Joanne broke a slate. Someone else might say it is that the roof leaks. The three of us make statements that are literally contraries: 'The explanation of why the carpet is wet is that it rained last night', 'The explanation of why the carpet is wet is that Joanne broke a slate', and 'The explanation of why the carpet is wet is that the roof leaks'. Still, our explanations are not rivals, and we would not feel we were contradicting each other. Nor would you be inclined to draw back from your assertion, and say only that the fact it rained last night is *an* explanation of why the carpet is wet. That would conversationally suggest it is only a putative explanation, which might turn out not to be the explanation at all. So our use of articles is confusing. What is going on?

My suggestion is that we think there is really one big explanation of why the carpet is wet. It is a complex fact that includes as parts all the separate facts the three of us mentioned. Each of us is picking out a part to stand in for the whole. We call it *the* explanation because it is standing in for the one big explanation. We are employing a sort of synecdoche. Which part we pick out will depend on our context: our background knowledge, our interests in the matter, and so on.

Whether or not this suggestion about individuation is right, I think we should not fuss about the confusing state of the articles 'a' and 'the' attached to 'explanation'. It is generally a mistake to look for *the* canonical explanation of some fact. We may accept several different facts as the explanation, and prefer one to another simply according to context.

Non-normative reasons

Another confusing feature of English is that the explanation of why a fact obtains is also called 'the reason' why it obtains. Here, 'the reason' is used in a non-normative sense. In this sense, it may be applied to any explanation, whether of a normative or a non-normative fact. The reason why pigs cannot fly is that they have no wings.

A useful distinguishing mark is that 'the reason' in this non-normative sense is usually followed by 'why'. Unfortunately, that is not invariably so; it is not so in 'The reason for the cow's death was BSE'. But, with or without a 'why', we must distinguish this sense of 'reason' from normative senses. This paper is about normative senses, but I cannot ignore the non-normative sense because it strongly influences the normative ones, as we shall see immediately.

2. Perfect Reasons

Preliminaries over, I come to explanations of ought facts. Suppose you ought to Φ. And suppose the explanation of this fact is some other fact X. Then X is the reason why you ought to Φ. This is only because X is the explanation of why you ought to Φ, and 'the reason why' is being used to mean the same as 'the explanation of why'. Since it means the same as the non-normative expression 'the explanation of why', 'the reason why' is here not normative.

In this case, the relation of being the reason why holds between the fact X and the fact that you ought to Φ. The latter fact is normative, but nevertheless the relation is non-normative. Normative facts can have non-normative properties. For example, if you ought to shut up and I say so, then the normative fact that you ought to shut up has the non-normative property of being stated by me.

However, in 'X is the reason why you ought to Φ', the non-normative 'reason' is so closely conjoined with the normative 'ought' that we find it impossible to resist a slide. We slide from 'X is the reason why you ought to Φ' to 'X is the reason for you to Φ', meaning exactly the same thing by it. The non-normative 'reason' (meaning explanation) slides into the normative 'ought', yielding a normative sense of 'reason' that combines the meaning of both.

In this sense, a reason for you to Φ is defined as an explanation of why you ought to Φ. So we have a reason defined in terms of the two notions of ought and explanation.

Later, I shall define a second normative sense of 'a reason'. I shall distinguish a reason in this first sense by calling it 'a perfect reason'. A perfect reason for you to Φ is defined as a fact that explains why you ought to Φ.

All the complications of the notion of explanation are inherited by the notion of a perfect reason, and it is not my business to sort them out. An explanation need not be full or complete, and what counts as an explanation may depend on the context. For instance, it may depend on our background knowledge. All this is true of a perfect reason, too. So long as a fact explains why you ought to Φ, it is a perfect reason for you to Φ.

A perfect reason therefore need not be a unique canonical reason. Suppose you ought not to drink home-made grappa because it damages your health. The fact that home-made grappa damages your health explains why you ought not to drink it, so it is a perfect reason for you not to drink it. Another explanation of why you ought not to drink home-made grappa is that it contains methyl alcohol. This is not a rival explanation; it is consistent with the first. So a perfect reason for you not to drink home-made grappa is that it contains methyl alcohol. Now we have two distinct perfect reasons for you not to drink home-made grappa. This is confusing, but only because the individuation of explanations is confusing. We need not fuss about it.

'You ought to Φ' and 'There is a perfect reason for you to Φ' are equivalent statements. That is to say, you ought to Φ if and only if you have a perfect reason to Φ. If there is a perfect reason for you to Φ, this means there is an explanation of why you ought to Φ. But that can only be so if, actually, you ought to Φ. Conversely, if you ought to Φ, no doubt there is an explanation of this fact; presumably no ought fact is inexplicable. Consequently, there is a perfect reason for you to Φ.

However, 'There is a perfect reason for you to Φ' does not *mean* the same as 'You ought to Φ'. The equivalence of the two sentences is not analytic, because it is not analytic that, if you ought to Φ, there is an explanation of this fact. 'There is a perfect reason for you to Φ' means more than 'You ought to Φ'. It means you ought to Φ and this fact has an explanation. The concept of a perfect reason is complex, incorporating the two elements of normativity and explanation. In the next section we shall see that the same is true of the concept of a *pro tanto* reason.

The element of explanation in a reason must not be forgotten. Raz says: 'We can think of [the reasons for an action] as the facts statements of which form the premises of a sound inference to the conclusion that, other things being equal, the agent ought to perform the action.'[6] This must be wrong. Section 6 identifies one fault in it. In his 'Enticing Reasons' in this volume, Jonathan Dancy identifies another. He points out that, by Raz's criterion, conclusive evidence that you ought to perform an action would be itself a reason to perform the action, and that is certainly not so. Reasons do not merely imply the agent ought to perform the action; they explain why she ought to. Evidence does not do that.

3. *Pro Tanto* Reasons

Besides perfect reasons, there must be reasons of another normative sort, because we often say some fact X is a reason for you to Φ, when it is not the case that you ought to Φ. In these cases, X evidently does not explain the fact that you ought to Φ, since there is no such fact. So X is evidently not a perfect reason. A reason of this second sort is often called a '*pro tanto* reason'. I shall now set out to describe and ultimately define a *pro tanto* reason.[2] In this section, 'reason' unqualified always refers to a *pro tanto* reason.

The idea of a *pro tanto* reason arises when the explanation of an ought fact takes a particular form. This form is governed by a mechanical analogy. *Pro tanto* reasons are said to have a 'strength' or 'weight', and these metaphorical terms signal an analogy with mechanical weighing.

The mechanical analogue is this standard explanation of why a pair of scales tips to the left, when it does: the objects in the left-hand pan of the scales have a total weight greater than the total weight of the objects in the right-hand pan. Each object in a pan is associated with a number called its weight. The numbers associated with the objects in the left-hand pan add up to more than the numbers associated with the objects in the right-hand pan. That is why the scales tip to the left.

Suppose you ought to Φ. An explanation strictly analogous to mechanical weighing would be this. There are reasons for you to Φ and reasons for you not to Φ. Each reason is associated with a number that represents

---

[6] Joseph Raz, *Practical Reason and Norms* (London: Hutchinson, 1975; reissued by Princeton University Press, 1990; repr. Oxford University Press, 1999), 187.

its weight. The numbers associated with the reasons to Φ add up to more than the numbers associated with the reasons not to Φ. That is why you ought to Φ.

Such a strictly analogous explanation rarely seems appropriate. For one thing, it often seems inappropriate to associate a reason with anything so precise as a number that represents its weight. Secondly, although we can aggregate the weights of several reasons, to aggregate them simply by adding up also often seems inappropriate. So-called organic interactions between reasons often mean that their aggregate effect differs from the total of their weights.

Still, when the fact that you ought to Φ is explained by *pro tanto* reasons, the explanation retains central elements of the mechanical analogy. It includes one or more reasons for you to Φ, and it may also include reasons for you not to Φ. These reasons are analogous to the objects in the left-hand and right-hand pans of the scales. Each reason is associated with a metaphorical weight. This weight need not be anything so precise as a number; it may be an entity of some vaguer sort. The reasons for you to Φ and those for you not to Φ are aggregated or weighed together in some way. The aggregate is some function of the weights of the individual reasons. The function may not be simply additive, as it is in the mechanical case. It may be a complicated function, and the specific nature of the reasons may influence it. Finally, the aggregate comes out in favour of your Φ-ing, and that is why you ought to Φ.

When an explanation of why you ought to Φ takes this form, I shall call it a 'weighing explanation'. The idea of a *pro tanto* reason arises in the context of a weighing explanation.

I have identified a weighing explanation by an analogy with mechanics, and the analogy is not very tight. It is not tight enough to determine a sharp boundary between weighing explanations and others. Still, I can identify some features that are essential to weighing explanations. They will be enough to allow me later to give examples of explanations that are definitely not of this sort.

Here are some essential features of a weighing explanation of why you ought to Φ. The explanation must include one or more facts that it identifies as *pro tanto* reasons, either for you to Φ or for you not to Φ. Each of these reasons must be associated with something that is identified as its 'weight'. The reasons and their weights play a characteristic role in the explanation. The role is that the weights of all the reasons are aggregated in some way, and the aggregate determines whether or not you ought to Φ.

Any weighing explanation of why you ought to Φ must include at least one *pro tanto* reason for you to Φ. This reason must have a weight. But sometimes the explanation will include no other reason—in particular, no reason for you not to Φ. In that case, you ought to Φ, whatever the weight of the reason for you to Φ. But if that is so, how does the weight of this reason play any role in the explanation? It plays a role counterfactually. If there *were* other reasons for you to Φ or not to Φ, and this reason still held and had the same weight, its weight would participate in determining whether or not you ought to Φ. This would only be so if, were the contrary reasons weighty enough, it would be the case that you ought not to Φ. So a characteristic of any *pro tanto* reason is that it is possible for it to be outweighed. Indeed, this is what the term '*pro tanto*' implies.

Definition

I am now in a position to define a *pro tanto* reason. I have described the characteristic role that *pro tanto* reasons play in an explanation of why you ought to Φ: each has a weight, and the fact that you ought to Φ is explained by the fact that the reasons for you to Φ outweigh the reasons for you not to Φ according to an aggregating function. A *pro tanto* reason is defined as a fact that plays this characteristic role in a weighing explanation.

However, I need to define more specifically a *pro tanto* reason for you to Φ, and this calls for some more detail. Suppose you ought to Φ and this fact has a weighing explanation. In the explanation, the reasons for you to Φ play one role, and the reasons for you not to Φ play another. Let us call these respectively the 'for-Φ role' and the 'against-Φ role'.

Suppose alternatively that you ought not to Φ, and this fact has a weighing explanation. In this explanation, the reasons for you to Φ play the against-not-Φ role and the reasons for you not to Φ play the for-not-Φ role, as I have just defined these roles. Let us rename these roles respectively the 'for-Φ role' and the 'against-Φ role' in this explanation.

Sometimes it is not the case that you ought to Φ, and also not the case that you ought not to Φ. Various explanations might account for this conjunctive normative fact. For example, it may be that your Φ-ing has no normative significance. But on some occasions the conjunctive fact has a weighing explanation. It would take this form: there are reasons for you to

Φ and reasons for you not to Φ, each having a weight, and the reasons on neither side outweigh those on the other. This could be because the reasons exactly balance. More often it will be because the weights of the reasons are not numbers but some vaguer entity that does not permit precise comparison of weights, and in the particular case neither side outweighs the other. In this sort of case, the reasons are often said to be 'incommensurate'.

In a weighing explanation of why it is not the case that you ought to Φ and not the case that you ought not to Φ, the reasons for you to Φ and those for you not to Φ play opposite but symmetrical roles. Let us once more call them the 'for-Φ role' and the 'against-Φ role' respectively.

Now we have enough roles. My definition is this: a *pro tanto* reason for you to Φ is a fact that plays the for-Φ role in a weighing explanation of why you ought to Φ, or in a weighing explanation of why you ought not to Φ, or in a weighing explanation of why it is not the case that you ought to Φ and not the case that you ought not to Φ.

Three objections

This definition implies that, when the reasons for you to Φ outweigh the reasons for you not to Φ, then you ought to Φ. But several people have told me this is not necessarily so. I shall review three of their objections.

The first is Jonathan Dancy's, presented in his 'Enticing Reasons'. According to Dancy, the reasons for you to Φ may fall into two classes: enticing reasons and others. The others are 'peremptory', whereas the enticing reasons merely make Φ-ing attractive. Suppose there are no non-enticing reasons either for you to Φ or for you not to Φ, but there is an enticing reason for you to Φ. Then, taking all the reasons together, the reasons for you to Φ outweigh those for you not to Φ. But Dancy thinks it is not the case that you ought to Φ, since what counts in favour of your Φ-ing is only an enticing reason. He thinks enticing reasons do not lead to oughts.

In his paper, Dancy reports my response correctly. I think you ought indeed to Φ. I think enticing reasons lead to oughts. As I said in section 1, I do not treat 'ought' as a heavyweight word. I recently advised a guest that he ought to try a mangosteen, on the grounds that mangosteens taste delicious. That they taste delicious would have to count for Dancy as an enticing reason. Nevertheless, I believe I spoke correctly.

I did not think my guest was obliged to try a mangosteen; 'obliged' is more heavyweight. I did think he ought to try one, but I simultaneously thought it would be permissible for him not to. Dancy generously points out that 'permissible' can be used in a way that makes these thoughts consistent. I am happy to adopt this usage.

The second objection was put to me separately by David McNaughton and Michael Smith. Sometimes the reasons for you to Φ outweigh those for you not to Φ, but it is not the case that you ought to Φ, because Φ-ing would be very demanding—it would be supererogatory. So they said. But I think that, if the reasons for you to Φ outweigh those for you not to Φ, then indeed you ought to Φ. If Φ-ing is supererogatory, then you are not obliged to Φ. Also, it is permissible for you not to. One more, this is to use 'permissible' in the sense licensed by Dancy.

Those two objections do not require me to adjust my definition of a *pro tanto* reason, but the third one does. This one came from Seana Shiffrin. Sometimes you ought to Φ, and you have a *pro tanto* reason either to Φ or not to Φ, but this reason plays no role in the explanation of why you ought to Φ because the explanation is not a weighing one. It might be a simple deontic principle, say. In a case like this, your *pro tanto* reason does not fit my definition.

Cases like this will occur when a simple deontic principle operates as a side constraint—when it specifies conditions that are sufficient for determining that you ought to Φ, but not necessary. Here is an example. Suppose you (a president) ought not to invade another nation, and this is because you have no authority from the UN and a simple deontic principle says you ought not to invade a nation without authority from the UN. This explanation is not a weighing one. Nevertheless, you might also have a *pro tanto* reason not to invade—for instance that doing so would kill thousands of people. This reason plays no role in explaining why you ought not to invade.

However, *pro tanto* reasons of Shiffrin's sort do play a role in a *potential* weighing explanation. They play a role in an explanation that would exist if the other, non-weighing explanation of why you ought to Φ were cancelled somehow. In the example, if, counterfactually, you had authority from the UN, then the fact that invading would kill thousands of people would play a role in a weighing explanation of why you ought not to invade, if you ought not, or of why you ought to invade, if you ought.

Accordingly, I need to adjust my definition by including potential weighing explanations as well as actual ones. I get: a *pro tanto* reason for you to Φ is a fact that plays the for-Φ role in a potential or actual weighing explanation of why you ought to Φ, or in a potential or actual weighing explanation of why you ought not to Φ, or in a potential or actual weighing explanation of why it is not the case that you ought to Φ and not the case that you ought not to Φ.

Counting in favour

'The reasons for an action are considerations which count in favour of that action.'[7] These are Raz's words, but the remark is a commonplace.[8] My definition of a *pro tanto* reason is a version of it, tightened up enough to make it a genuine definition. The definition specifies just what counting in favour of amounts to. To count in favour of Φ is to play a particular role in an explanation of why you ought to Φ. Counting in favour of is sometimes thought to be the basic normative notion.[9] But it cannot be, because it is complex. It incorporates the two elements of normativity and explanation. The notion of a reason has the same complexity.

I defined a *pro tanto* reason for you to Φ in terms of: first, the concepts of ought and explanation; second, the various concepts needed to describe a weighing explanation, such as 'aggregation'; and third, the distinction between the for-Φ role and the against-Φ role in a weighing explanation.

Do not overestimate the importance of this distinction in my definition. I defined a *pro tanto* reason without it, as any fact that plays the characteristic role of a reason in a weighing explanation. I needed the distinction only to separate a *pro tanto* reason to Φ from a *pro tanto* reason not to Φ. A weighing explanation allocates two symmetrical roles to reasons. The distinction is needed to pick out one of these roles rather than the other.[10] In the same way, the distinction between left and right is not needed to understand the idea of a weight, but it would be needed to pick out the weights in the left-hand pan of a pair of scales, rather than those in the right-hand one.

---

[7] Ibid. 186.

[8] Another example is in T. M. Scanlon, *What We Owe to Each Other* (Cambridge, Mass.: Harvard University Press, 1998), 17.

[9] For instance in Jonathan Dancy, *Ethics without Principles* (Oxford: Oxford University Press, forthcoming), ch. 2.

[10] Adrian Moore and Timothy Williamson pointed out to me that I need a way of picking out these separate roles.

Perfect and *pro tanto* reasons

Often, a *pro tanto* reason for you to Φ by itself constitutes an explanation of why you ought to Φ. If so, it is also a perfect reason for you to Φ. Suppose you ought to take an umbrella because it is raining. Then the fact it is raining explains why you ought to take an umbrella; it is a perfect reason for you to take one. However, no doubt there is also a fuller, weighing explanation of why you ought to take an umbrella. In that explanation, the fact it is raining would figure as a reason that outweighs contrary reasons. It is therefore a *pro tanto* reason too.

4. How Prevalent are *Pro Tanto* Reasons?

I think that, when philosophers speak of reasons, they are most often thinking of *pro tanto* reasons. For example, Raz says: 'Reasons have the dimension of strength.'[11] At that point he must have been thinking of *pro tanto* reasons, because this is true only of them. Only *pro tanto* reasons can participate in a weighing explanation, so only they have weight or strength. The idea of perfect reasons exists only because of the irresistible slide from 'the reason why you ought to Φ' to 'the reason for you to Φ'. It is a pity the slide is irresistible, because having two senses of 'a reason' complicates the discussion of reasons. But since it is irresistible, we have to put up with the complication and be alert to it. Still, I believe that most philosophers, when they think of reasons, generally think of *pro tanto* ones.

How prevalent are *pro tanto* reasons in the normative domain? How common are they in explanations of what we ought to do, think, want, and so on? They figure only in weighing explanations, so their prevalence depends on the prevalence of weighing explanations. There is a case for thinking that every ought fact has a weighing explanation. I call this view 'protantism'. In this section, I shall argue that protantism is questionable. I shall also argue that, even if every ought fact does have a weighing explanation, many ought facts also have more significant explanations that are not weighing ones.

Here is a putative counterexample to protantism—a putative example of an ought fact that has no weighing explanation. You ought not to believe both that it is Sunday and that it is Wednesday. A plausible explanation of

[11] Raz, *Practical Reason and Norms*, 25.

why not is that 'It is Sunday' and 'It is Wednesday' are contrary propositions, and you ought never to believe both a proposition and a contrary
proposition. This is not a weighing explanation. Neither of the facts included in it has a weight that plays any part in the explanation, and the
explanation does not involve aggregating weights.

You might doubt this is a genuine explanation of why you ought not to
believe both that it is Sunday and that it is Wednesday. You might doubt
the normative principle it calls on: that you ought never to believe both a
proposition and a contrary proposition. Suppose the only way a nuclear
war can be averted is by your believing two contrary propositions. You
might doubt that, in those circumstances, you ought not to believe both.

Some philosophers—call them 'evidentialists'—think that what you
ought to believe is determined only by considerations that are directly
connected with the truth of what you believe, so any benefit that may
arise from your beliefs is irrelevant. These philosophers will think that,
indeed, you ought never to have contrary beliefs. (They may think you
ought sometimes to bring it about that you have contrary beliefs, but they
think that is a different matter.[12]) So they will think my example of a fact
that has no weighing explanation is genuine. They will reject protantism.

But other philosophers—call them 'pragmatists'—take the opposite
view. They think you ought to have contrary beliefs if having them will
avert a nuclear war. At least, in those circumstances they think it is not
the case that you ought not to have contrary beliefs. They disagree with
the normative principle contained in my putative explanation. They accept
only a defeasible or conditional version of it. According to them, a correct
principle might be: you ought never to believe both a proposition and a
contrary proposition unless it would be extremely beneficial to do so.

Pragmatism does not immediately imply protantism, because even
according to pragmatism, my ought fact has a non-weighing explanation.
Suppose we grant pragmatists that the unconditional principle is false. I
can easily reformulate my putative explanation to use the conditional
principle instead. I am assuming circumstances are normal, so it is not
extremely beneficial for you to have contrary beliefs. In these normal
circumstances, you ought not to believe both that it is Sunday and that it

[12] See Derek Parfit, 'Rationality and Reasons', in Dan Egonsson, Jonas Josefsson, Bjørn
Petersson, and Toni Ronnow-Rasmussen (eds.), *Exploring Practical Philosophy: From Action to Values*,
(Aldershot: Ashgate, 2001), 17–39.

is Wednesday. The reformulated explanation of this ought fact is as follows. 'It is Sunday' and 'It is Wednesday' are two contrary propositions. You ought not to believe both a proposition and a contrary proposition unless it would be extremely beneficial to do so. But it would not be extremely beneficial to do so. So you ought not to believe both these propositions.

Pragmatists will think this is a correct explanation. But it is not a weighing explanation. None of the three facts included in it has a weight that plays a part in the explanation, and the explanation does not involve aggregating weights. So my ought fact still has a non-weighing explanation, even given pragmatism.

Nevertheless, for this example protantism is very likely to follow from pragmatism. Protantists think every ought fact has a weighing explanation; they need not deny that ought facts may also have non-weighing explanations. Granted pragmatism, it seems very likely that my particular ought fact has a weighing explanation, which would underlie the non-weighing explanation I have given. This weighing explanation would explain the conditional form of the normative principle, and it would go like this. When two propositions are contraries, there is a *pro tanto* reason for you not to believe both of them, stemming from the logical error in doing so. There may also be *pro tanto* reasons for you to believe both, stemming from benefits that will arise from doing so. But unless these benefits are extremely large, the *pro tanto* reason for you not to believe both outweighs the *pro tanto* reason for you to believe both, so you ought not to believe both. Therefore, in the normal circumstances you are actually in, you ought not to believe both.

I think a pragmatist should accept this weighing explanation. Take an extreme case where it is extremely beneficial for you to believe two contrary propositions. In that case, a pragmatist thinks it is not the case that you ought not to believe them both. Even so, she should surely think the fact that the propositions are contraries is a reason not to believe them both. She should think this reason exists, although it does not outweigh the great benefit of believing both. So she should think this reason is a *pro tanto* reason, and there is a weighing explanation in this extreme case. She should think this same reason exists in the normal case, too. In the normal case it outweighs other reasons, though it would not outweigh them if the case were extreme. So the explanation is a weighing one in the normal case too, and the reason in that case too is *pro tanto*.

I think, therefore, that a pragmatist should be a protantist for this example. On the other hand, the example shows that an evidentialist must deny protantism. So the issue of evidentialism versus pragmatism is crucial for the truth of protantism. But I am sorry to say that this issue is too big for this paper. For that reason, I say only that protantism is questionable. My evidence is that several authors have denied pragmatism, at least by implication. Several authors assert that, whatever benefit might come from your having particular beliefs, that benefit cannot constitute a reason for you to have those beliefs.[13]

Here is a second putative counterexample to protantism. Suppose you ought to pay £12,345 in income tax for 2003. A putative explanation of this fact is that £12,345 is what the tax laws say you owe, and you ought always to pay what the tax laws say you owe. A more detailed explanation will spell out the details of your tax calculation. It will contain a mass of complicated conditions and calculations. It will include complex conditional clauses, necessary and sufficient conditions, necessary conditions for other conditions to be sufficient, and so on. None of the facts included in this mass will have a weight that participates in any sort of aggregation. So this seems to be a normative fact that does not have a weighing explanation.

However, my putative explanation is certainly incorrect as it stands. It depends on the normative principle that you ought always to pay what the tax laws say you owe, and this is certainly incorrect. The analogue of pragmatism is certainly true for this example. If great good could be done by your disobeying the tax laws, it is not the case that you ought to obey them. A correct statement of the principle would certainly contain some condition. It might be: you ought to pay what the tax laws say you owe unless great good would result from your not paying it.

I could reformulate the explanation of why you ought to pay £12,345 in income tax, now using the conditional principle. The reformulated explanation is this: the tax laws say you owe £12,345; you ought to pay what the tax laws say you owe, unless great good would result from your not paying it; but great good would not result from your not paying it; so you ought to pay it. This is a non-weighing explanation, and it is plausibly a correct one.

---

[13] For example, ibid.; Peter Railton, 'Truth, Reason, and the Regulation of Belief', *Philosophical Issues* 5 (1994), 71–93; Jonathan Adler, *Belief's Own Ethics* (Cambridge, Mass.: MIT Press, 2002); Louis Pojman, 'Believing and Willing', *Canadian Journal of Philosophy* 15 (1985), 37–56. I thank Andrew Reisner for this list, and for urging on me the merits of pragmatism.

However, as before, a weighing explanation surely underlies it. The weighing explanation will explain the conditional normative principle that the non-weighing explanation depends on. It goes like this. The law constitutes a *pro tanto* reason for paying your taxes. There may also be *pro tanto* reasons against paying them, given by the benefits of not doing so. You ought to pay them if the *pro tanto* reason for paying outweighs the *pro tanto* reasons against paying.

It seems to me that the weighing explanation is more clearly correct in this example than in my previous example. So I think this example is unsuccessful as a counterexample to protantism. I mention it because I want to draw a different lesson from it.

We are looking for the explanation of why you ought to pay £12,345 in income tax. The weighing explanation I have given is unlikely to interest us in practice. Generally in practice, we take it for granted that you ought to pay your taxes, and we are interested in why it is £12,345 that you ought to pay. This calls for an explanation consisting of the mass of complicated conditions and calculations that I mentioned. This mass does not constitute a weighing explanation, and it includes nothing resembling a *pro tanto* reason for or against paying £12,345 in income tax. For example, somewhere in the explanation is the fact that you bought a car for £20,990 in August 2001. Your tax liability is reduced by some fraction of the car's cost, calculated in a complicated way, provided you use it in your business more than some specified amount. The fact that you bought this car is not a *pro tanto* reason either to pay £12,345 in tax or not to pay £12,354 in tax.

So even if protantism is true and every ought fact has a weighing explanation, the interesting explanation of an ought fact may include many facts that are not *pro tanto* reasons, and none that are *pro tanto* reasons. In general, we should recognize that explanations of ought facts take all sorts of forms. Explanations of other facts take all sorts of forms; weighing explanations are rare in mechanics, for instance. It would be a prejudice to expect normative explanations always to take a weighing form, and to consist of *pro tanto* reasons.

I think it is widely recognized that the explanations of ought facts are often not weighing ones. One of Raz's contributions has been to show how varied the explanations of ought facts can be. One of his examples is cancelling. He points out that a reason for you to Φ may be cancelled by some consideration that is not a reason either for you to Φ or for you not to Φ.[14]

---

[14] Raz, *Practical Reason and Norms*, 27.

He says that if you have promised to meet a friend at Carfax, that would be a reason to go to Carfax, but this reason is cancelled if your friend releases you from the promise. The fact that your friend releases you from the promise is neither a reason to go to Carfax, nor a reason not to. So this is not a case of one reason's weighing against another.

Exclusionary reasons are another of Raz's examples. Raz thinks the law is one source of exclusionary reasons. In so far as the law gives you a reason to do what it tells you to do, it also gives you an exclusionary reason, which is a reason not to act on particular contrary reasons, such as benefit to yourself.[15] The contrary reasons are genuine reasons, Raz thinks, but they do not weigh against the law's reason. So in a case where you ought to keep the law, the explanation of why you ought to keep it is not simply that the reason to keep the law outweighs opposing reasons. It is more complicated than that; it involves the exclusion of other reasons.

Scanlon also draws attention to the variety of explanation of ought facts.[16] He recognizes there are many sorts of explanation of why you ought to Φ besides weighing ones. However, Scanlon seems to assume nevertheless that the facts included in these explanations will be reasons. They will not be reasons for you to Φ or not to Φ, but reasons for something else. For example, the explanation may include a reason, X, for not taking some other fact, Y, as a reason for you to Φ.[17] I think Scanlon takes X to be a *pro tanto* reason.

Raz recognizes that explanations may include facts that are not reasons. But nevertheless, like Scanlon, he concentrates very much on reasons. When he emphasizes the complexity of normative explanations, he concentrates particularly on exclusionary reasons.[18] I believe he takes exclusionary reasons to be *pro tanto*.

But once we have noticed the great variety of explanations of ought facts, that should diminish our interest in *pro tanto* reasons. We should investigate all sorts of explanation, and not concentrate only on those that contain *pro tanto* reasons.

[15] Ibid., particularly 73–6. See also 185–6.
[16] Scanlon, *What We Owe to Each Other*, 51–3.
[17] Ibid. 51.
[18] Raz, *Practical Reason and Norms*, 35–48 and 178–99.

5. Reasons and Reasoning

I now come to two popular views that are inconsistent with my account of the normative meaning of 'a reason'. Each uses 'a reason' normatively, but apparently in a sense that differs from the two I have described. We could draw the conclusion that each correctly uses 'a reason' in a further normative sense. But, as I shall explain, I think we do better to draw the conclusion that each view is incorrect.

The first is the view, encapsulated, that reasoning is concerned with reasons: that it is a process of discovering reasons. For theoretical reasoning, it is more precisely the view that, when you reason correctly, your reasoning brings you to have a belief there is a reason for you to have. Take a simple example of correct reasoning. You say to yourself, 'The world was made in six days, so it was made in less than a week.' You start with a belief that the world was made in six days, and by reasoning end up with a new belief that it was made in less than a week. According to the view I have in mind, the fact that you believe the world was made in six days is a reason for you to believe it was made in less than a week.

Applied to practical reasoning, the view is that correct reasoning brings you to have an intention there is a reason for you to have. I think the view is mistaken for both theoretical and practical reasoning, but in this paper I shall concentrate on theoretical reasoning only. I shall examine the view that the fact you believe a proposition is a reason for you to believe the proposition's obvious consequences. Briefly, I call this the view that beliefs are reasons. I shall argue against it.

Let us first try applying my two definitions of a reason. Each gives us a version of the view that beliefs are reasons. First, there is the view that beliefs are perfect reasons. My example shows this is false. Suppose you believe the world was made in six days. Then if beliefs were perfect reasons, there would be a perfect reason for you to believe the world was made in less than a week. That is to say, there would be an explanation of why you ought to believe the world was made in less than a week. It would follow that you ought to have this belief. But this is false. The evidence is such that you ought not to have it; certainly it is not the case that you ought to have it.

The second version is the view that beliefs are *pro tanto* reasons. This is not so quickly shown to be false, but we should reject it none the less. There are two objections to it.

The first is just that this view is implausible. There are perhaps various pieces of evidence for the proposition that the world was made in less than a week, and certainly there are many pieces of evidence against it. It is plausible that these pieces of evidence constitute *pro tanto* reasons for believing it and against believing it. There may also be some other *pro tanto* reasons for or against; perhaps you find it reassuring to believe it, and perhaps this is a reason for believing it. But now suppose you believe, against the balance of evidence, that the world was made in six days. How could this belief of yours add to the reasons there are for believing the world was made in less than a week? How could your believing something create in this way a new reason for belief? It would be bootstrapping a new *pro tanto* reason into existence by means of your beliefs. It is implausible that you can do it. Let us call this the 'bootstrapping objection' to the view that beliefs are *pro tanto* reasons.

I can reinforce it by varying the example. The proposition that the world was made in six days is itself an obvious inference from the proposition that the world was made in six days. So the view that beliefs are *pro tanto* reasons implies that believing the world was made in six days is a *pro tanto* reason to believe the world was made in six days. That would be truly implausible bootstrapping.

The second objection is that this view does not explain an important normative connection between believing the world was made in six days and believing the world was made in less than a week. Suppose you believe the world was made in six days, and you do not believe it was made in less than a week. Whatever evidence you may have one way or another, your beliefs are definitely not as they ought to be. This is just because the proposition that the world was made in less than a week follows obviously from the proposition that it was made in six days.

But the view that beliefs are *pro tanto* reasons does not explain why your beliefs are definitely not as they ought to be. So far as this view is concerned, they might be entirely as they ought to be. Your belief that the world was made in six days gives you a *pro tanto* reason to believe it was made in less than a week, but this *pro tanto* reason might be outweighed by a stronger *pro tanto* reason not to believe it was made in less than a week.

On the other hand, a good explanation is available of why your beliefs are definitely not as they ought to be. It depends on the general normative principle that you ought to believe the obvious consequences of your beliefs: if *q* is an obvious consequence of *p*, you ought (to believe *q* if you believe *p*). The brackets indicate that the condition 'if you believe *p*' is within the scope of 'you ought'. To use the expression I introduced in section 1: believing *p* normatively requires you to believe *q*. I shall call this the principle that beliefs are normative requirements.

I should add a detail for clarity. The principle is that you ought (to believe *q* at a particular time if you believe *p* at that time). It does not connect a belief at one time with a belief at another. If you believe *p* at one time but not *q* at that time, then at that time you are not satisfying the principle. You can come to satisfy it either by coming to believe *q* or by stopping believing *p*.

This principle accurately explains why, if you believe the world was made in six days, but do not believe it was made in less than a week, your beliefs are definitely not as they ought to be. You ought (to believe the world was made in less than a week if you believe it was made in six days). Since you do not satisfy the condition in the brackets, your beliefs are not as they ought to be.

The principle that beliefs are normative requirements is not subject to the bootstrapping objection. Suppose you believe the world was made in six days. This belief normatively requires you to believe the world was made in less than a week. However, it does not follow that you have a reason to believe the world was made in less than a week. From 'you believe the world was made in six days' and 'you ought (to believe the world was made in less than a week if you believe it was made in six days)' we cannot derive 'you ought to believe the world was made in less than a week' or 'you have a reason to believe the world was made in less than a week'. So there is no implication that your belief the world was made in six days bootstraps into existence a reason to believe the world was made in less than a week.

In general, from 'you believe *p*' and 'you ought (to believe *q* if you believe *p*)', we cannot derive a detached normative conclusion about your believing *q*. We cannot derive that you ought to believe *q* or have a reason to believe *q*. Normative requirements do not permit this sort of detachment.

For these reasons, the principle that beliefs are normative requirements is far superior to the view that beliefs are *pro tanto* reasons. We should reject the latter.

The view that beliefs are *pro tanto* reasons implies that there is a *pro tanto* reason for you (to believe the world was made in less than a week), if you believe the world was made in six days. The principle that beliefs are normative requirements implies that you ought (to believe the world was made in less than a week, if you believe the world was made in six days). Comparing these statements shows that the view that beliefs are *pro tanto* reasons mistakes a wide-scope ought for a narrow-scope reason. It gets the logical structure wrong, and that is a serious mistake.

Protantism

The fact that q follows obviously from p explains why you ought (to believe q if you believe p). So this fact constitutes a perfect reason for you (to believe q if you believe p). Protantists think that in some circumstances it might be outweighed by contrary reasons, so they think it is a *pro tanto* reason. This appears to be Raz's view when he says: 'That a certain proposition follows from certain premises is, other things being equal, a reason for not believing the premises without believing the conclusion.'[19]

Do not mistake Raz's view for the view that beliefs are reasons. The reason has a wide scope. Applied to my example, it is the view that there is a reason for you (to believe the world was made in less than a week if you believe it was made in six days). Even if you believe the world was made in six days, we cannot derive the conclusion that you have a reason to believe it was made in less than a week. A detached normative conclusion cannot be drawn.

Another sort of reason?

I have argued we should reject the view that beliefs are reasons in either of my two normative senses of 'a reason': a perfect reason or a *pro tanto* reason. Does this mean we should recognize a third normative sense? We could define a sense of 'a reason' this way: 'X is a reason for you to Φ' means that X normatively requires you to Φ. Under this interpretation, the view that beliefs are reasons would be identical to the view that beliefs are normative requirements. Since indeed beliefs are normative requirements, the view that beliefs are reasons would be true under this interpretation.

This would be a disastrous route to follow. To say 'X is a reason for you to Φ', when X is a fact, invites us to draw the conclusion that there is a

---

[19] Raz, *Engaging Reason*, 70.

reason for you to Φ. In my example, it invites us to draw the conclusion that there is a reason for you to believe the world was made in less than a week. But this is just the conclusion we must not draw. It is a detached normative conclusion about your believing the world was made in less than a week. A normative requirement does not permit this sort of detachment. So we must not express a normative requirement using a form of words that permits it.

We should recognize it as simply false that beliefs are reasons. That would be a major step towards clarity in the philosophy of normativity. It is vital to maintain the distinction between a reason and a normative requirement, because it is a distinction of logical structure. We should not confuse wide-scope oughts with narrow-scope reasons.

6. Are Oughts Reasons?

Now the second common view that conflicts with my definitions of 'a reason'. Suppose you ought to Φ. Many authors think the fact that you ought to Φ is a reason for you to Φ. I shall call this the view that oughts are reasons. It is one implication of the remark of Raz's that I have already criticized in section 2: 'We can think of [the reasons for an action] as the facts statements of which form the premises of a sound inference to the conclusion that, other things being equal, the agent ought to perform the action.'[20] A statement of the fact that you ought to Φ forms the premiss of a sound inference to the conclusion that, other things being equal, you ought to Φ. So according to this remark, the fact that you ought to Φ is a reason for you to Φ.

The view that oughts are reasons is false if 'a reason' has the sense of a perfect reason: the fact that you ought to Φ is not an explanation of why you ought to Φ. It is also false if 'a reason' has the *pro tanto* sense: the fact that you ought to Φ cannot play any part in explaining why you ought to Φ. So if this view is correct, there must be another normative sense of 'a reason'. But actually it is not correct.

Various lines of thought can lead to the view that oughts are reasons. One of them starts from the idea that 'ought' and 'a reason' refer to different areas of normativity. Most commonly, the idea is that 'ought'

---

[20] Raz, *Practical Reason and Norms*, 187.

refers to morality, whereas 'a reason' refers to normativity all things considered. I do agree that the fact that you morally ought to Φ is a reason for you to Φ. It may be a *pro tanto* reason, and in some contexts it may be a perfect reason. So if 'ought' in some sense meant 'morally ought', the fact that you ought to Φ, in this sense, would indeed be a reason for you to Φ. In section 1, I cast doubt on the idea that there is such a sense of 'ought', and I declined to use it even if there is. So this line of thought does not suggest that oughts, in my sense, are reasons.

A second line of thought is this. If you ought to Φ, there is no doubt an explanation of this fact. That is to say, there is a reason in the non-normative sense why you ought to Φ. Consequently, there is a reason for you to Φ, in the normative sense of a perfect reason. So from the fact that you ought to Φ it follows there is a reason for you to Φ, in one sense. However, it does not follow that this fact is itself a reason for you to Φ. This line of thought is mistaken.

A third line of thought starts like this. If you ought to Φ, and you Φ, the explanation of why you Φ may be the fact that you ought to Φ. For example, since you ought to Φ, you may come to believe you ought to Φ through some epistemic process. Then you may Φ because you believe you ought to. If so, and if we use 'the reason why' in its non-normative sense equivalent to 'the explanation of why', the fact that you ought to Φ is the reason why you Φ.

This by itself does not suggest this fact is a reason for you to Φ in any normative sense. However, it is traditional in the philosophy of action to separate out a particular class of explanations from others. Explanations in this special class are sometimes called 'rationalizing explanations', and sometimes 'explanations by reasons'. They identify some fact as the reason for which you Φ, and not merely the reason why you Φ. If this fact is the reason for which you Φ, it must surely be a reason for you to Φ in some normative sense.

If the fact that you ought to Φ explains why you Φ, the explanation may well be of the rationalizing sort; if so, the fact that you ought to Φ is the reason for which you Φ, so it must be a reason for you to Φ in some normative sense. That is the line of thought.

It is mistaken. It goes through some subtle transitions in English—from the reason why you Φ to the reason for which you Φ to a reason for you to Φ—in order to move from the non-normative to the normative. It is natural to suspect an equivocation along the way, and indeed there is one.

A fact might be the reason for which you Φ without being a reason for you to Φ. That is, a fact might explain in the rationalizing way why you Φ, without being a reason for you to Φ. Suppose you believe the liquid in the glass in front of you is gin. The fact you have this belief might explain in the rationalizing way why you drink the liquid. But the liquid might actually be petrol, and there might be no reason for you to drink it. So there is an error in this line of thought.

It may nevertheless seem plausible in the particular case we are concerned with. This is the case where the reason for which you Φ is supposed to be the fact that you ought to Φ. This fact may seem unlike the fact that you believe the liquid is gin, in an important respect. It seems to justify your Φ-ing, in a way in which the fact that you believe the liquid is gin does not justify your drinking it. Perhaps this adds credibility to the idea that this fact is a reason for you to Φ.

'Justify' is an ambiguous word. To say that some fact X justifies your Φ-ing may mean that X makes it the case that you ought to Φ. But the fact that you ought to Φ does not justify your Φ-ing in this sense. It does not make it the case that you ought to Φ; it *is* the fact that you ought to Φ.

Alternatively, to say that X justifies your Φ-ing may mean X normatively requires you to Φ. If you believe the world was made in six days, we might say this fact justifies your believing the world was made in less than a week. Now it is plausible that, if you believe you ought to Φ, the fact that you believe this normatively requires you to Φ.[21] So it is plausible that believing you ought to Φ justifies your Φ-ing, in this sense of 'justifies'. Perhaps this plausible claim, added to the line of thought I described, could in some way support the view that the fact that you ought to Φ is a reason for you to Φ.

Perhaps it explains why some philosophers take this view. But it is not actually a ground for this view—far from it. The plausible claim is that the fact you believe you ought to Φ normatively requires you to Φ. It is not that the fact you ought to Φ is a reason for you to Φ. It is not even that the fact you believe you ought to Φ is a reason for you to Φ. To think it is confuses reasons and normative requirements in the way I have already objected to.

---

[21] Actually, I think this is incorrect, but believing you ought to Φ does normatively require you to intend to Φ. I argued for this claim in my 'Normative Practical Reasoning', *Proceedings of the Aristotelian Society*, suppl. vol. 75 (2001), 175–93.

Twist the argument how you like, the same conclusion emerges. It is just not the case that oughts are reasons.

7. Summary

A reason is either a perfect reason or a *pro tanto* reason. A perfect reason for you to Φ is a fact that explains why you ought to Φ. A *pro tanto* reason for you to Φ is a fact that plays a characteristic role in a potential or actual weighing explanation of why you ought to Φ, or of why you ought not to Φ, or of why it is not the case that you ought to Φ and not the case that you ought not to Φ. Consequently, the notion of a reason incorporates the two elements of normativity and explanation.

Many ought facts have explanations that are not weighing explanations, and so do not include *pro tanto* reasons.

Besides reasons, the normative world contains features of a different sort, which I call 'normative requirements'. Normative requirements have a different logical structure from reasons; they are wide-scope oughts. Nevertheless they are often mistaken for reasons. In particular, it is often thought that theoretical reasoning is concerned with reasons to believe and practical reasoning with reasons to intend. This is not so. Reasoning is concerned with satisfying various normative requirements that hold among beliefs and intentions.[22]

[22] I am particularly grateful to Jonathan Dancy, for a patient correspondence and discussion about reasons over several years. I do not pretend to have adequately addressed all the important points he has made to me. Among the many others who have generously given me useful comments are Maria Alvarez, Robert Audi, Ruth Chang, Robert Frazier, Brad Hooker, Kent Hurtig, Paul Markwick, Adrian Moore, Derek Parfit, Peter Railton, Joseph Raz, Andrew Reisner, Henry Richardson, Raffaele Rodogno, Bart Streumer, Jussi Suikkanen, John Tasioulas, Bernard Williams, and Timothy Williamson.

3

Can Desires Provide Reasons for Action?

Ruth Chang

On a widely accepted story of human agency, *all* reasons for acting, intending, and desiring are provided by the fact that the agent wants something or would want it under certain conditions. My reason for going to the store, for example, is provided by the fact that I want to buy some ice cream, and my reason for wanting to buy some ice cream is provided by the fact that I want to eat some.[1] According to these 'desire-based' accounts, all practical reasons are grounded in the present desires of the agent; justification has its source in the fact that *I do or would want it*.

Some philosophers, however, have been drawn to a starkly opposed story about practical reasons: *no* practical reasons are provided by the fact that one desires something.[2] On these 'value-based' accounts, reasons for acting,

---

[1] Perhaps in conjunction with my belief that going to the store will enable me to do so. I ignore the role of beliefs which I will take to be a constant background feature. The desires at stake are always present desires and may include counterfactual present desires, desires I would now have if certain conditions were met. Desire-based views have been defended by Bernard Williams, 'Internal and External Reasons', in *Moral Luck* (Cambridge: Cambridge University Press, 1981), 101–13, and Richard Brandt, *A Theory of the Good and the Right* (Oxford: Oxford University Press, 1979). The reasons at issue here are normative or justifying as opposed to motivating or explanatory. They are considerations that 'count in favour of' something, and may be invoked to recommend action or give advice.

[2] Proponents of value-based views include Joseph Raz, 'Incommensurability and Agency', reprinted in *Engaging Reason: On the Theory of Value and Action* (Oxford: Oxford University Press, 1999), 46–66; Thomas Scanlon, *What We Owe to Each Other* (Cambridge, Mass.: Harvard University Press,

intending, and desiring are provided by facts about the value of something, where being valuable is not simply a matter of being desired. My reason to go to the store is provided by the value of what is in question—namely, eating some ice cream—and the value of eating some ice cream is given by the fact that doing so would be valuable in some way—for example, that it would be pleasurable. It is not the fact that I want ice cream that makes having some pleasurable; having ice cream might be pleasurable even if I don't desire it in the way that, to borrow an example from Thomas Scanlon, exercising might be pleasurable even if I have to be dragged kicking and screaming to the gym. According to 'buckpassing' versions of the value-based view, it is not strictly the evaluative fact that provides the reason but the facts upon which the evaluative fact supervenes. So, for example, my reason to have the ice cream might strictly be given not by the evaluative fact that it would be pleasur*able* but rather by the natural facts upon which its being pleasurable supervenes, such as that it would be pleasant or that I would enjoy it.[3] Value-based views ground all practical reasons in evaluative facts or the facts that subvene them; justification has its source not in the fact that one wants something but in facts about what one wants.

The conflict between the two stories is striking because it is so stark; desire-based theorists think that *all* reasons are grounded in desires, while their value-based opponents tend to think that *none* are. As with many such conflicts, the truth may lie somewhere in the middle, and in this paper I argue that in the present case it does. Some practical reasons are provided by the fact that the agent wants something, while others are provided by the fact that what she wants is of value. Nor is one kind of reason rare or trivial; desires and evaluative facts each provide a large and important class of practical reasons.

1998); and Derek Parfit, 'Rationality and Reasons', in Dan Egonsson, Jonas Josefsson, Bjørn Petersson, and Toni Ronnow-Rasmussen (eds.), *Exploring Practical Philosophy: From Action to Values* (Burlington, Vt.: Ashgate 2001), 17–39, and in 'Rediscovering Reasons' (draft MS). I take both the desire- and value-based views to be 'pure'. Strictly speaking, however, Raz and Scanlon allow that there may be exceptional cases in which desires can in some sense provide reasons, but they think of these cases as aberrant in some way. I return to their qualifications later in the paper.

[3] See Scanlon, *What We Owe to Each Other*, ch. 1, and Parfit, 'Rediscovering Reasons'. According to Scanlon and Parfit, the property of being good or valuable is the higher-order property of having properties that are reason-providing. These reason-providing properties are typically subvening natural properties. Both Scanlon and Parfit are 'partial' buckpassers; they pass the buck from evaluative properties to subvening natural properties only in the case of *some* evaluative properties: namely, those that are most general or 'thin', like being good or being valuable.

My defence of the 'hybrid' view is in two stages. In the first stage, I argue that despite value-based arguments to the contrary, desires can provide reasons. This argument has a 'negative' and a 'positive' part. The negative part involves showing that what I take to be the leading arguments for the claim that desires cannot provide reasons—offered by Joseph Raz, Thomas Scanlon, and Derek Parfit—each trade on a view of desires that neglects or misinterprets what I believe is their essentially *affective* nature. I suggest that we should understand the desires in question as essentially involving an 'affective feel'. With respect to these value-based arguments, once desires are properly understood as affective states, it is an open question whether they can provide reasons.

The positive part of the argument attempts to show that 'affective desires' can provide a large and important class of practical reasons. I focus on one particular kind of affective desire, 'feeling like it', and argue that the fact that one 'feels like it' can provide a reason. More importantly, I argue, if 'feeling like it' can provide a reason, then any desire with an affective feel—for the most trivial object to the most significant—can provide a reason. Desires of the form 'I feel like it' are, I believe, the 'Achilles' heel' of all value-based views. With the right understanding of the nature of desires in place, the Achilles' heel becomes something of a Trojan horse.

If the arguments of the first stage are correct, then the pure value-based view must be rejected. This leaves us with either the pure desire-based or the hybrid view. Here we turn to the second stage of argument, which provides a coda to the first. I do not attempt to argue that the hybrid view is to be preferred to its desire-based rival; for my purposes, I can simply assume that the desire-based view is mistaken. My aim is rather to lay to rest what I take to be the main reason for rejecting the hybrid account: namely, that it is not compatible with a unified account of the 'source' of practical justification. I will suggest that, despite appearances, the claim that desires can provide reasons is compatible with the conception of the source of practical justification that underwrites the value-based view.

I

Suppose I have a reason to want or to do something. Can that reason be provided by a desire? This question must be understood in a way that does not rely on extraneous substantive assumptions. There is a sense in which all reasons could be 'provided' by desires even on a value-based view if, for example, all reasons are provided by evaluative facts about what makes one's life go best, and those evaluative facts in turn reduce to facts about what one wants.[4] But the claim that certain evaluative facts reduce to facts about what one wants is an extraneous substantive claim that holds independently of the thesis that those evaluative facts provide reasons. Put another way, when we ask whether a desire can provide reasons, we are asking whether a desire can provide reasons in virtue of being a desire, and not in some less direct way.

Philosophers who argue over whether desires can provide reasons have tended to employ one of two strategies. If they think that desires can provide reasons, they tend to emphasize the quasi-cognitive aspects of desires—desires aren't all that different from beliefs, and thus, just as beliefs can justify beliefs, the belief-like element of desires can justify action. If, on the other hand, they think that desires cannot provide reasons, they tend to emphasize the affective aspects of desires—desires just involve having certain 'feels' that assail us, and surely such feelings cannot provide reasons. If the arguments of this paper are correct, we turn these strategies on their heads. It is in virtue of the affective nature of desires that desires can provide reasons.

We begin with arguments offered by Raz, Scanlon, and Parfit for the claim that desires cannot provide reasons. All three arguments depend on views about desires that we will challenge. Raz thinks that desires must be either urges that are not 'ours' or states whose survival depends on the belief that one has reasons to have them. Scanlon rightly thinks that there are desires that occupy a middle ground, but his view of what these desires are, I suggest, fails to distinguish what is essential to desires from what is a commonly found disposition that is itself no part of a desire. Curiously, both Raz and Scanlon allow that although desires do not in general provide reasons, they may do so in exceptional cases. This nod to exceptions, I believe, indicates that their understanding of desires does not carve at the joints. Parfit does not countenance any exception, but I will suggest that he should.

II

Raz's argument can be seen to involve two steps: first, any desire that can in principle rationalize must itself be backed by value-based reasons for

---

[4] See Thomas Hurka, 'Parfit on Well-Being and Personal Reasons' (draft MS). Thanks to Chris Meacham and Holly Smith for discussion on this point.

having it or its objects; and second, given that this is so, the fact that one also wants what one has value-based reasons to have cannot, on pain of double-counting, provide an additional reason to have it.[5] Therefore, Raz concludes, desires cannot provide reasons.[6]

The argument for the first step turns on a view about the nature of desires.[7] Desires are either 'urges' or what he sometimes calls 'philosophical' desires (he gives them this label to indicate that these are the desires he thinks are of interest to philosophers). Urges, Raz says, are not 'ours'; they 'attack us', are 'inflicted on us', and are 'not under our control'. As Warren Quinn has argued, urges understood as simple functional states that happen to be present in us, cannot 'rationalize'—that is, provide a reason for—action.[8] The simple functional state of a coke machine according to which the input of a dollar results in the output of a can of

[5] The locution 'to have what one wants' and its cognates should be understood as 'to take the appropriate action with respect to what one wants'. Since the appropriate action might take many forms—e.g., promoting, bringing about, respecting, and so on—I will sometimes use the neutral formulation of 'having' as shorthand for one or more of these actions. It should not be understood as implying that there might be a reason for there being a state of affairs in which one has the object one wants.

[6] What follows is my attempt to codify Raz's very rich and complex discussion of this topic. Raz's most recent statement of his view about the relation between reasons and desires is in 'Incommensurability and Agency'. All page numbers are to this article. He also discusses various aspects of this view in *The Morality of Freedom* (Oxford: Oxford University Press, 1986) and in 'On the Moral Point of View', in *Engaging Reason*, 247–72.

[7] Raz actually gives two arguments for the claim that desires presuppose value-based reasons. The second is an improved version of the common value-based complaint that desire-based theorists cannot make sense of reasoning about 'final' desires—that is, desires that a desire-based theorist thinks are at the end of a chain of justification. Raz argues that even if desire-based theorists are right in thinking that one cannot reason about which final ends one should have, they still face the problem of accounting for reasoning about what to do when final ends conflict. And, Raz thinks, the desire-based theorist must appeal to values to account for such reasoning; without such an appeal, 'reasoning' would amount to no more than sitting back and seeing which of two conflicting final desires moves one to action (pp. 51–2). One might have two responses to this argument. First, it is not clear whether desire-based theorists must admit that 'reasoning' about final ends can consist only in sitting back and seeing what one actually does. When final ends conflict, one might sit back and see which one wants more, but it is not clear that this need consist in what one actually does. Second, and more importantly, many views of practical reason allow that practical reasons at some point run out; in cases of conflict that hit rock bottom, it is inappropriate to deliberate about what to do. If this view of practical reasons is right, it will not be surprising if there are cases of conflicts between final ends in which the appropriate thing to do *is* just to sit back and see what one most wants to do.

[8] Warren Quinn, 'Putting Rationality in its Place', as reprinted in his *Morality and Action* (Cambridge: Cambridge University Press, 1993), 228–55.

coke cannot rationalize the dispensing of a can any more than a functional state (urge) of an agent according to which the input of some stimulus (the sight of a radio) results in the output of some action (turning on the radio) can rationalize the performance of that action. Someone who acts on the urge to turn on radios, paint potatoes green, or count blades of grass does not act on a reason; her action is the mental equivalent of a physical reflex.

Philosophical desires, by contrast, can in principle rationalize action because they are 'ours'; we 'endorse' them by believing that their objects are valuable in some particular way. Without believing that what we want is valuable, Raz thinks, we could not have a desire for it; our desire depends for its survival on believing that its object is good in some way. And unlike urges, Raz notes, philosophical desires 'do not have a felt quality' (p. 54). I might desire to hear a lecture on Kant or to finish my holiday shopping, but these desires do not involve my having any particular feeling towards their objects. Rather, Raz suggests, wanting those things involves believing that they are valuable in some way.

Now Raz thinks that the value of something provides a reason for having it, and thus the belief that what one wants is good is the belief that there is reason to have what one wants. Raz seems to think that the belief is not 'opaque' in this context. He writes, 'We cannot want what we see no reason to want any more than we can believe what we think is untrue or contrary to the evidence.' (p. 57). Thus philosophical desires, properly understood, are mental states that depend for their survival on the belief that there is a particular value-based reason to have their objects.[9]

If desires necessarily involve believing that one has independent value-based reasons to have their objects, there *must be* independent value-based reasons to have (or not to have) their objects. To think otherwise would be to hold the odd view that even though no rational person could ever come to see that he has a desire not backed by independent value-based reasons, he in fact may have such desires. The practical agent, no matter how rational he might be, would be incapable of coming to the correct

---

[9] There is a question as to whether Raz understands philosophical desires as involving *only* the belief that what one wants is good in some way or also the belief—whose content is entailed on Raz's view by the content of the former belief—that one has reasons to want what one wants. I interpret him as making the latter claim because I can see no other way of making sense of his argument from the nature of philosophical desires to the conclusion that all desires are backed by value-based reasons.

view about such a desire; and rather than accept this untoward consequence, it seems we should accept that every desire is in fact backed by
value-based reasons.[10]

Having concluded that our desires already presuppose value-based
reasons to have their objects, Raz then suggests, in the second step of
his argument, that desires cannot themselves provide reasons for having
their objects above and beyond the reasons that they already presuppose
(pp. 56–62). If desires depend in one way or another on value-based reasons
for having their objects, what additional normative force could be provided
by the desire itself? To think that the desire could provide a further,
independent reason would seem to involve double-counting. As he writes,
'It requires too much by way of mental gymnastics' (p. 61).

While there are many intriguing questions raised by Raz's argument, its
key point, that the only desires that could in principle rationalize action
must be 'philosophical' desires, is far from clear. Surely we can have desires
that do not depend for their survival on our believing that we have a
reason to have their objects. And such desires need not thereby be urges
beyond our control. A diabetic might want a piece of chocolate cake in a
way that does not depend on his believing that he has any reason to have
it; indeed, he might believe the opposite—he might believe that he has no
reason since he knows that he doesn't like chocolate cake and that, were
he to have even a single bite, he would fall into a diabetic coma and die. A
teenager might want to play truant *because* she believes that she has no
reason to do so and many reasons not to.[11] Sometimes, while walking
down the sidewalk, I have a desire to turn a cartwheel—doing so just
appeals to me. This appeal does not depend on my believing that I have
any reason to turn a cartwheel. Such desires are not compulsions beyond

---

[10] This paragraph fills a gap in Raz's argument in a way that I believe is supported by his
writings elsewhere. One of the deep themes running throughout Raz's work, I believe, is a
rejection at some level of the distinction between the subjective and the objective as regards
the normative. Most of his claims about what 'objectively' holds in the normative realm are
claims about what beliefs we would need to attribute to a rational agent engaged in normative discourse and deliberation. In general, Raz seems to think that we must understand the
normative by taking as our starting-point what a rational agent would believe, intend, or do.
See Raz, 'When We Are Ourselves' and 'Explaining Normativity: On Rationality and the
Justification of Reason' in *Engaging Reason*, 5–21 and 67–89.

[11] See Michael Stocker's paper in this volume for a discussion of the related idea of
someone wanting something *because* it is bad. See also his 'Desiring the Bad: An Essay in Moral
Psychology', *Journal of Philosophy* 76 (1979), 738–53.

the agent's control; they are all too familiar states we often find ourselves in—or so I will argue in due course. While we have many of our desires only because we believe that we have reason to have their objects, not all of our desires are like this.

We now turn to Scanlon's argument.[12] Scanlon offers an account of 'the commonsense notion of desire' (p. 40) that occupies a middle ground between Raz's two extremes. He suggests that ordinary desires are what he calls 'desires in the directed-attention sense' (p. 39); they are not simple functional states that are not 'ours' but nor do they necessarily involve the belief that there is a reason to have the desire. Instead, desires in the directed-attention sense necessarily involve one's attention being directed 'insistently toward considerations that present themselves as counting in favor of [having the object of one's desire]' (p. 39). To take one of Scanlon's examples, someone might have an attention-directed desire for a new computer; that is, he might find his attention being insistently drawn to the features of the computer that present themselves as reasons to buy it. At the same time, however, he might believe that the appearance of reasons is deceptive; he might believe that he has *no* reason to buy the computer—he doesn't need any of the new features, and his old computer functions perfectly well.

If ordinary desires are desires in the directed-attention sense, can they provide reasons? Scanlon argues no. Suppose I have an attention-directed desire for a new computer. If I believe I have no reason to buy the computer, then the fact that I have a tendency to judge that I have a reason to buy it provides no reason for me to go out and get one; after all, I believe that I have no reason to do so. How could the fact that I have a tendency to judge that I have a reason provide me with a reason to act in a way in which I believe I have no reason to act? (pp. 43–4). As Scanlon persuasively suggests, if I have a reason to buy the new computer, it will be provided by the fact that I will enjoy having it, that it will help me to write papers faster, that it will look nice on my new desk, or the like (p. 44).

This is not to say that desires in the directed-attention sense have no role to play in the reasons one has to do what one wants to do; some reasons have what Scanlon calls 'subjective conditions'. For example, there are many valuable ways I could spend my life, but I have good reason to

---

[12] His argument is to be found in *What We Owe to Each Other*, ch. 1. All page references are to this chapter.

choose only those pursuits that I am drawn to. My having an attention-directed desire to be a philosopher might be a subjective condition on my having good reasons to be one. But we should not think that my reason to be a philosopher is provided by the desire; I have a good reason to be a philosopher not because I want to be one but because being one is a worthwhile way to spend one's life that appeals to me (pp. 48–9).[13] Moreover, the fact that I have an attention-directed desire to be a philosopher may provide evidence that I have a reason to be one without itself providing a reason to be one (p. 45).

Scanlon's argument that desires in the directed-attention sense do not provide reasons is persuasive. But is it so clear that desires in the ordinary sense need to be understood as desires in this sense? In defence of his account, Scanlon writes, 'This idea [of directed attention] seems to me to capture an essential element in the intuitive notion of (occurrent) desire. Desires for food, for example, and sexual desires are marked by just this character of directed attention. And this character is generally missing in cases in which we say that a person who does something for a reason nonetheless "has no desire to do it," as when, for example, one must tell a friend some unwelcome news' (p. 39). I think Scanlon is right to point out that the ordinary desires of interest have a quality of drawing our attention in certain ways. We can agree that when we want things in this sense, they

---

[13] See also Derek Parfit, *Reasons and Persons* (Oxford: Oxford University Press, 1984), 121, and 'Rationality and Reasons', 19; Raz, 'Incommensurability and Agency', 64. After writing this paper, I came across several articles relevant to Scanlon's discussion of subjective conditions in the burgeoning literature on his views about reasons, including a reply by Scanlon himself. In their 'Desires, Motives, and Reasons: Scanlon's Rationalistic Moral Psychology', *Social Theory and Practice* 28 (2002), 243–76, at 269–72, for example, David Copp and David Sobel argue, among other things, that the putatively value-based reason provided by the fact that one would enjoy something is in fact a desire-based reason because *enjoyment* necessarily involves a concurrent liking of the experience or desire that the experience continue. This argument is further elaborated by David Sobel in his 'Pain for Objectivists' (draft MS). That there is this necessary connection does not, however, it seems to me, show either that the concurrent liking or desire connected to future enjoyment must itself be an 'original source' of reasons or that such future mental states are of the sort that desire-based theorists think can provide reasons. This is the line of response that Scanlon himself seems to take in his 'Replies', *Social Theory and Practice* 28 (2002), 337–40, at 339–40. I believe that Raz, Scanlon, and Parfit are correct in thinking that the dependence of some value-based reasons on subjective states of the agent—even where this dependence is conceptual in nature—does not itself undermine the value-based view of reasons. One's having a desire, for instance, conceptually depends on one's actually existing, but no one would think that the 'original source' of one's reasons is one's existence rather than one's desire.

appeal to us, we are *attracted* to them. But Scanlon seems to think that this attraction necessarily involves having the quasi-cognitive tendency to judge that one has reasons to have what attracts. I believe that the element of attraction essential to the desires of interest is best understood in terms of an 'affective feel', and that this affective feel does not necessarily involve any particular cognitive or quasi-cognitive state. This, of course, allows that there may be a causal or psychological story behind such affective feels, and that they may depend on various beliefs about their objects—for example, that they are edible, and so on. But such attractions do not require, *contra* Raz, a belief that there are reasons for what one wants or, *contra* Scanlon, a tendency to have such a belief.

In the next section, I shall provide some reasons for thinking that the desires of interest are neither the 'attention-directed' nor 'philosophical' desires favoured respectively by Scanlon and Raz. If we can show that such desires do not necessarily involve a *tendency* to believe that one has reasons, we will thereby presumably have grounds for thinking that they do not necessarily involve the *belief* that one has reasons. Thus, I focus on the question of whether desires involve this tendency. Arguing that they are not, however, is not straightforward. I suggest an analogy, present some examples, and offer a diagnosis of the temptation to think that they are.

III

Desires in the directed-attention sense are analogous to the perception of illusions, but the ordinary desires of interest need not be like such perceptions. When confronted with a stick partially submerged in water, our attention is drawn to features of the stick that present themselves as reasons to judge that the stick is bent. Our perception of the illusion necessarily involves a tendency to judge that the stick is bent, where this tendency persists even in the face of knowledge that the stick is straight.[14] Desires in the directed-attention sense are like illusory perceptions in both regards. They necessarily involve a tendency to judge that one has a reason, and this tendency persists even in the face of the knowledge or belief that one has

[14] Another example is the Müller–Lyer illusion which involves two lines of equal length, one with 'fins' pointing outward and the other with fins pointing inward. Our perception of the two lines necessarily involves a tendency to judge that the line with fins pointing outward is longer.

no reason. But ordinary desires are not like this. Suppose we want some ice cream. Our response toward the ice cream is not like our response toward the stick in the water. Our attention is drawn to what about the ice cream appeals to us; we find ourselves with an attitude of attraction towards those features. But we do not necessarily have any tendency to judge that those features provide reasons to have the ice cream in the way that we have a tendency to judge, when confronted with the perceptual illusion, that its features provide reasons to think that the stick is bent. Instead, our desire simply involves our being attracted to what we want. Unlike perceptions of illusions and desires in the directed-attention sense, ordinary desires do not seem necessarily to involve a tendency to judge that we have reasons.

Now consider examples of ordinary desires that, on the face of it, do not seem to involve any tendency to judge that one has reasons. In these cases, it might nevertheless be true that the agent has such a tendency, but it would be otiose to appeal to this tendency in understanding her desire. As I've confessed, sometimes while walking down the sidewalk, I find myself with a desire to turn a cartwheel. It doesn't seem to me that I have any tendency to judge that I have a reason to do so; rather, doing so simply appeals to me. If someone were to insist that I can't be attracted to doing so without having this tendency, I would find their insistence idle. Or, when ordering in a restaurant, I sometimes find myself with a desire to order dishes of a certain colour. I am attracted to green, say. The question is whether this involves my having a tendency to think that its being green is a reason to order the spinach fricassee. It seems to me that I can be attracted to the greenness of spinach fricassee without thereby having a tendency to judge that its being green provides me with a reason to have it. Or, sometimes students in my classes end up dating one another. Everyone in the class can witness their mutual attraction. Appeal to a tendency on their parts to judge that they have reasons to be together seems superfluous to understanding their attraction. These cases can be easily multiplied. The point is that these desires are neither pathological urges beyond the agent's control nor quasi-cognitive states. They can be fully understood as ordinary desires without appeal to a tendency on the part of the agent to judge that she has reasons to have what she wants.

A different set of examples involves cases in which having the tendency to judge that one has reasons is in some sense 'impossible'. If one can have an ordinary desire in such cases, then it would follow that such desires need not be understood in terms of this tendency.

Start with a case in which there is overwhelming reason not to have any tendency to judge that one has reasons. This might loosely be called a case of 'rational impossibility'. Consider our diabetic who is squaring off against a piece of chocolate cake. Having the taste of chocolate appeals to him. He knows from experience, however, that he dislikes the taste of chocolate; moreover, he has just tested his blood sugar level and knows that if he has a single bite, he will go into a diabetic coma and die. Can he nevertheless be attracted to the chocolate cake without having a tendency to judge that he has reason to have some? The question is not whether a story can be told according to which his tendency is quashed by his belief that he has no reason to have the cake; it is rather whether it *makes sense* to suppose that he has an ordinary desire to have the cake without thereby having a tendency to judge that he has a reason to have it. I believe it does.

Now consider a case of psychological impossibility. A teenager raised by a strict disciplinarian has the deeply ingrained belief that cutting class is taboo. Suppose she is psychologically incapable of having the tendency to judge that she has reason to play truant in just the way that a religious fundamentalist might be incapable of having a tendency to judge that there is no God. Isn't it nevertheless possible that she wants to cut class? Why can't she be attracted to breaking the rules in spite of the fact that she is psychologically incapable of having a tendency to judge that there is a reason to break those rules? This psychological incapacity might reach her conscious and unconscious states. Or consider the case of Huckleberry Finn, who is psychologically incapable of having a tendency to judge that he has a reason to help Jim escape from slavery. Nevertheless, it seems that he wants to, and that he can have this desire even though he may have only the tendency to judge that he has *no* reasons.

There is also the case of conceptual impossibility. Take a young child who lacks the concept of a reason (of 'counting in favour of'). Can she have desires in the ordinary sense? Does it make sense to suppose that a young child might have a desire for mashed carrots even though she lacks the conceptual apparatus required to have a tendency to judge that she has a reason to want the mashed carrots? Why can't the child be attracted to mashed carrots in an ordinary way without her desire having to be understood as involving a tendency to judge that she has reasons?

Finally, there is the case of logical incoherence. Suppose an eccentric philosopher has a desire for what there is no reason to have. That is, he wants things under the description 'there is no reason to have this'.

Although the content of what he wants is peculiar, he can want it in a perfectly ordinary way—he is attracted to what he has no reasons to have; this feature appeals to him. According to Scanlon, such a person would necessarily have a tendency to judge that he has reasons to have what he has no reasons to have. But can we not understand such a person as having a desire in the ordinary sense, admittedly for a strange content, without thereby thinking that he has a tendency to logical incoherence? Perhaps Dostoevsky's author in *Notes from Underground* would be such a person. In so far as it makes sense to think that someone can have an ordinary desire for this content in the same way that he can have an ordinary desire for more mundane content *without* thereby thinking that he has a tendency towards logical incoherence, such desires do not necessarily involve a tendency to see reasons.

If any of these examples succeeds, then ordinary desires need not be understood as attention-directed. Although, I believe, ordinary desires are not attention-directed in Scanlon's sense, it is easy to see why there might be a temptation to think that they are. Many ordinary desires do, indeed, involve a tendency to judge that we have reasons to have their objects. But we should not think that this tendency is part of what it is to have an ordinary desire. Instead, the tendency to judge that one has reasons to have what one wants is better regarded as an independent disposition common among people we might call 'rationalizers'; if a rationalizer is attracted to something, she will tend to believe that she has independent reasons to have what she is attracted to. But this disposition of 'rationalizing' is not itself a component of ordinary desires. For one thing, not everyone has the disposition. For another, even if everyone did, the disposition is most plausibly explained *in terms* of the distinct state of being attracted to something; one has a tendency to judge that one has reasons for something *because* one finds it attractive.

If ordinary desires need not involve having a tendency to believe that one has reasons, then presumably they need not involve believing that one has reasons; ordinary desires are neither Razian 'philosophical' desires nor Scanlonian 'attention-directed' desires. They are rather 'affective' desires—non-cognitive states essentially involving attraction to their objects without reference to any particular cognitive or quasi-cognitive element.

Now it might be thought that if affective desires are neither 'philosophical' nor 'attention-directed', they must be the urges that Raz and Scanlon rightly deride as incapable of rationalizing action. But is there not conceptual space for desires between the cognitive and quasi-cognitive states that Raz and Scanlon propose, on the one hand, and urges, on the other? Both urges and affective desires essentially involve some phenomenological feel, but only affective desires are intentional states: that is, they involve having an *attitude about some content*, while an urge—e.g., feeling hungry, thirsty, or sleepy—is a phenomenological feel but not an attitude *about* anything. When I have an affective desire to turn a cartwheel, I have an attitude *about* the act of doing so; if I have instead an urge to turn one, I have a certain phenomenological feel that is merely a motivational impulse and involves no attitude *about* the act of turning one. Since affective desires are attitudes *we* have towards contents, they are 'ours' in a way that motivational impulses that 'attack us' are not. Of course, there is a sense in which affective desires may 'attack us', but this is the same sense in which beliefs, which can rationalize thought, can sometimes 'attack us'. Our relation to urges and the like is in this sense 'passive', while our relation to affective desires is one of 'active' engagement; *we* have those attitudes.[15] This difference between affective desires and urges underwrites another. Affective desires are what we might call 'reasons-appropriate', while urges are not. While it is appropriate to ask what reasons I have to want to turn a cartwheel (even if in fact I do not have any), it is not appropriate to ask what (normative) reasons I have to be hungry; hunger is not the sort of mental state for which there could be reasons.[16]

If affective desires are neither cognitive nor quasi-cognitive conative states, on the one hand, nor urges, on the other, then, so far as Raz's and Scanlon's arguments go, it remains to be seen whether they can provide reasons.[17] The common idea underlying both their arguments is that

[15] This distinction between active and passive mental states can be found in Raz, 'When We Are Ourselves'.

[16] Though of course we might have reasons to eat. Scanlon calls the attitudes for which we can ask for reasons 'judgement-sensitive', and glosses the idea as follows: an attitude is judgement-sensitive if a rational person would come to have it upon judging that she had sufficient reason to have it, and would cease to have it upon judging that she had sufficient reason not to have it. See Scanlon, *What We Owe to Each Other*, 20. I believe this gloss leaves out likings and dislikings of states we have no independent reason to like or dislike. It *makes sense* to ask whether, for example, I have any reason to like cold showers even though my liking may be judgement-insensitive.

[17] Copp and Sobel, among others, have articulated similar misgivings about Scanlon's 'over-intellectualized' account of desires. See Copp and Sobel, 'Desires, Motives, and Reasons', 254–64. In his reply to their article, Scanlon admits that his claim that all ordinary desires are attention-directed might have been 'overly broad', but suggests that even if some ordinary

desires already presuppose reasons to have what one wants independently of the want itself. For Raz, a desire necessarily involves a belief that one has independent reasons for what one wants; for Scanlon, it necessarily involves a tendency to judge that one has such reasons. On these understandings of desires, it is not altogether surprising that desires do not plausibly provide reasons apart from the independent reasons they already presuppose. If, however, we understand desires as essentially affective states that do not necessarily involve reference to independent reasons, it becomes an open question whether such desires can provide reasons.[18]

IV

Curiously, both Raz and Scanlon can be seen as admitting that there are affective desires in the sense we have suggested, and, moreover, that such desires can provide reasons. This is because both allow that there may be exceptions to their conclusion that desires cannot provide reasons, and these exceptions are best understood as involving affective desires.

After arguing vigorously that no desire can provide a reason, Raz ends his argument with the following unexpected concession:

There remains the simple point that if of two acceptable options one wants one thing and does the other, one is acting irrationally. If when offered a pear or a banana, I have reason to take one and it does not matter which one, then if I

desires do not fit his model, ordinary desires are *in general* attention-directed. See Scanlon, 'Replies', 338. My arguments attempt to show that ordinary desires are not in general attention-directed and that the temptation to think that they are can be explained by mistakenly assimilating to such desires a common but distinct disposition to see independent reasons for what one wants.

[18] There is, of course, much more that needs to be said about affective desires. To my knowledge no one has yet provided a satisfactory account of them. I suspect that phenomenological accounts are inadequate because they end up treating affective desires as mere compulsions, and that dispositional accounts, according to which an affective desire involves a disposition to have an affective feel in certain circumstances, get the explanation front to back; there are 'one-off' attractions that cannot plausibly be explained in terms of a disposition. For a phenomenological view, see W. D. Falk, 'Ought and Motivation', *Proceedings of the Aristotelian Society* 48 (1948), 111–38, at 116–17; and for a dispositional account of phenomenological feel (and of desires generally) see Michael Smith, *The Moral Problem* (Oxford: Blackwell, 1994), pp. 114 ff. For a defence of the desire-based view that draws on the affective nature of desires, see Stephanie Beardman, 'Affective Deliberation: Toward a Humean Account of Practical Reason' (Rutgers University Ph.D. dissertation; Ann Arbor: UMI Dissertation Services, 2000).

want the banana but take the pear, I have acted irrationally. Moreover, in situations of the kind just described, one can explain and justify taking the banana by pointing out that one wanted the banana, and not the pear. In such contexts we refer to what we want as we do to reasons. Here they function as reasons. In these circumstances, wants are reasons, though in being limited to this case they are very peculiar reasons. (p. 62)

As we have already noted, since Raz thinks that the only desires that are 'ours' are 'philosophical' desires—that is, desires necessarily involving the belief that one has a reason for what one wants—the want in this passage must be a philosophical want. But then it is hard to see how wanting the banana in this sense could rationalize taking it. For the case Raz imagines involves my believing that I have no more reason to take the one piece of fruit over the other; this is what Raz means when he says that both the pear and the banana are 'acceptable'. I believe that I have a reason to take the pear, but I do not want the pear. I believe that I have a reason to take the banana, and I want the banana. I also believe that neither reason is stronger than the other. If I take the banana, my belief that I have reason to take it cannot rationalize my action, for I also believe that I have a no less strong reason to take the pear. If my wanting to take the banana is to rationalize my taking it, it must involve some element beyond my belief that I have a reason to take it. This further element is very plausibly my *attraction* to the banana.

Raz's case, I believe, is better understood as showing that there is a kind of desire beyond urges and philosophical desires that can sometimes rationalize action. Suppose the desires at issue in his case are affective desires. I find myself attracted to the banana but not the pear. If I believe that the value-based reasons for having one over the other are 'evenly matched', then it would be irrational for me to go for the pear when I am attracted to the banana.[19] My being attracted to the banana rationalizes my action of going for it. Note that this case can also be understood in a more objectivist vein. Instead of talking about what it would be *rational* for me to choose, we might ask what I would have *most reason* to choose. In this case, we have to ask whether my normative belief about the way the reasons shake out is true. If in fact there is no more value-based reason to have the banana

[19] There are perhaps three ways in which the reasons might be 'evenly matched': they are equally good, 'on a par', or incomparable. 'On a par' is a term of art that holds of two comparable items that are not equal, yet neither is one greater, better, or stronger than the other. See my 'The Possibility of Parity', *Ethics* 112 (2002), 659–88.

rather than the pear, the fact that I want it seems to provide reason for me to go for it. Since most value-based theorists seem to recognize this distinction between what might be rational for me to do, understood as relative to my beliefs, and what I might have most reason to do, understood as relative to the facts, I will understand this exception in an objectivist vein. The exception so understood, then, is that affective desires can provide reasons when the value-based reasons for and against having what one wants are evenly matched.

Scanlon is somewhat more circumspect about the possibility of an exception to his claim that desires cannot provide reasons. He recognizes, however, that there are cases in which what one is justified in doing seems to be a matter of doing what one 'feels like'. He writes:

There is, however, a class of cases in which the fact that I 'feel like' doing a certain thing (have a desire to do it in the directed-attention sense) may seem to provide me with a reason. For example, when I am walking from my home to my office, I often choose one route rather than another 'just because I feel like it'; *that is to say, I choose it just because it is the alternative that presents itself as attractive at the time.* This may be because I take this direction of my attention as a sign that I will enjoy that route more or that it has any other specific benefits. But it is possible that, considerations of enjoyment aside, I simply let the matter be decided by what happens to appeal to me at the time. One might say that in such a case I act for no reason. But even if in some such cases the fact that I 'felt like' doing something is a reason in the standard normative sense, these are special, rather trivial cases, not central examples that provide the pattern on which all other cases of doing something for a reason should be modeled. (p. 48, emphasis added)

The important point for present purposes is that in this passage Scanlon seems to recognize that sometimes one's attention can be directed towards something in a way that essentially involves only one's being attracted to it, without there being any additional 'sign'—for example, given by a tendency to judge that one has reasons for it—that it will be enjoyable. He seems to allow, in other words, that 'feeling like it' is a mental state that involves attraction but not necessarily any quasi-cognitive tendency to judge that one has reasons. This is plausibly what we have identified as an affective desire. Moreover, he seems willing to allow that such a desire might provide reasons when 'I simply let the matter be decided by what happens to appeal to me at the time'. It seems, then, that when I make such a decision, my 'feeling like it' can provide a reason for doing what I feel like.

Now both Raz and Scanlon allow their exceptions somewhat grudgingly; the reasons these desires provide, if they do, will be 'very peculiar' or 'special [and] rather trivial'. But the fact that the desires they take as possible exceptions are of a unified sort—namely, affective—suggests that the views of desires on which their arguments rely neglect the possibility that desires understood as essentially affective states can rationalize action. If desires rationalize in virtue of their affective nature, then it remains to be seen whether such desires can in general provide practical reasons.

V

There is another exception to value-based views that can be extracted from an argument offered by Derek Parfit. In recent and forthcoming work, Parfit argues that *no* desires can provide reasons.[20] Parfit focuses on 'final' desires, desires that desire-based theorists think are at the end of a chain of justification. For reasons we need not go into here, Parfit thinks that all final desires are 'intrinsic' desires—that is, desires for something not as a means to something else but for its intrinsic features.[21] He argues that for all final desires, the reasons to have what one wants are provided not by the fact that one wants it but either by intrinsic features of what one wants or by 'indirect' facts about what one wants. And if there are neither intrinsic nor 'indirect' reasons to have what one wants, there are *no* reasons to have what one wants.

The reasons to have what one wants in most cases of final desires, Parfit thinks, will be provided by intrinsic facts about what one wants. To illustrate that this is so, he invokes his case of the man with 'Future Tuesday Indifference'. At all times he cares in the normal way about pains and

[20] See Parfit, 'Rediscovering Reasons', especially the draft chapters 'Reasons and Motives' and 'Rationality and Reasons', and *idem*, 'Rationality and Reasons', esp. 20–7. Since some of what I want to take issue with in his argument is in unpublished work, the reader will have to rely on my summary of it. I am grateful to Parfit for illuminating conversations about his draft, much of the fruit of which is not included in my discussion here.

[21] Parfit, 'Rationality and Reasons', 20–1. Final desires need not be intrinsic, however. They might be 'extrinsic', or they might be what I later call 'feature-free'. I might want an object for its extrinsic features, such as for the fact that it used to belong to my mother or constitutes some other thing that I want; or I might want it *as such* and not for any of its particular features. See Christine Korsgaard, 'Two Distinctions in Goodness', reprinted in *Creating the Kingdom of Ends* (Cambridge: Cambridge University Press, 1996), 249–74.

pleasures he is or will be experiencing, '[b]ut he never cares about possible pains or pleasures on a *future* Tuesday'.[22] This man has true beliefs about all matters relevant to his desire; he understands that pain hurts, that Tuesday is merely a conventional calendar division, that it will be him suffering on future Tuesdays, and so on. Still, he is indifferent to his pain on future Tuesdays and consequently would always prefer to undergo excruciating pain on a future Tuesday than to suffer a minor pain on any other day— he would choose torture on a future Tuesday to a hangnail on Wednesday. Surely, Parfit argues, the fact that the torture is intrinsically painful gives him a reason to prefer the mild pain and to have it instead of the excruci- ating torture, and the fact that the torture occurs on a Tuesday gives him no reason to prefer it or to have it instead of the hangnail. And, Parfit goes on to claim, while the intrinsic fact that the torture is excruciatingly painful provides reasons for him to have the hangnail instead, the fact that he prefers the torture because it is on a Tuesday provides no reason for him to have it instead of the hangnail. Parfit extrapolates from cases of this kind to urge that, as a general rule, the reasons one has to have what one wants are not provided by the fact that one wants it but by intrinsic facts about what one wants.

Now Parfit allows that there may be some final desires for things whose intrinsic features provide no reasons to have them or not to have them. We might call such desires and their objects 'intrinsically neutral'. For instance, I might want to wear pink or to get a haircut or to turn a cartwheel. There is no intrinsic reason to do or not to do any of these things. But, Parfit thinks, in such cases there will be an 'indirect' value- based reason to have or not to have what one wants; or if there isn't, there will be no reason at all. 'Indirect' reasons are value-based reasons that depend in some way on the fact that one wants something; they are reasons with subjective conditions. Parfit gives two examples of such reasons. First, I might have a reason to have what I want because the thought of being in a state in which my desire is satisfied fills me with pleasure. If the thought of my wearing a pink jumpsuit fills me with glee, then I have a reason to take the steps required to get myself in that state. It is the fact that this thought is pleasant that provides a reason for me to wear pink, not the fact that I want to wear pink. Second, I might have a reason to have what I want because my not having it will distract me from

---

[22] Parfit, *Reasons and Persons*, 124.

doing other things.[23] For example, although I have no intrinsic reason to get a haircut, my not getting one will distract me from getting on with my work. It is the fact that I will be distracted that provides me with a reason to get a haircut, not the fact that I want to do so. If there is no indirect value-based reason to have what one wants, then, Parfit thinks, there are *no* reasons to have what one wants. Desires in these cases, according to Parfit, are merely urges or compulsions and do not themselves provide reasons to have their objects. In any case, the fact that one wants something does not provide a reason to have it; either one's reason is given by an indirect value-based fact or one has no reason.

There is one kind of intrinsically neutral desire, however, that I believe Parfit—and all value-based theorists—should admit as an exception to this claim. These are what Parfit calls 'hedonic desires', the likings or dislikings of *present conscious states* that 'make' those states painful, pleasant, or unpleasant.[24] Parfit gives as examples liking a cold shower, disliking the sound of squeaking chalk, and disliking the touch of velvet. Some people like the touch of velvet while others, such as Parfit, dislike it. Since there are no intrinsic features of the sensation that provide a reason to like or dislike it, those who like and those who dislike it are not making any mistake. Hedonic desires are neither rational nor irrational.

Can hedonic desires provide reasons? It seems clear that they can. Since desire-based theorists take only *present* desires to provide reasons, we focus on the question whether *present* hedonic desires can provide reasons.[25] If I now like the present sensation of touching velvet, my now liking it seems to provide me with a reason to continue to touch it; and if I now dislike the present sound of squeaking chalk, my now disliking it seems to provide a reason for me to remove myself from its vicinity. In general, it seems that my present likings and dislikings of (intrinsically neutral) present sensations can provide reasons to continue or cease having those sensations.

---

[23] Compare Stephen Schiffer, 'A Paradox of Desire', *American Philosophical Quarterly* 13 (1976), 195–203, who seems to think that the way a desire provides reasons is by being like a nagging itch waiting to be scratched. As value-based theorists might say, the reason to scratch the itch is not provided by the desire but by the fact that not scratching has unpleasant consequences. See also George Schueler, *Desire: Its Role in Practical Reason and the Explanation of Action* (Cambridge, Mass.: MIT Press, 1995), 80–97.

[24] Parfit 'Rationality and Reasons', 26, and 'Reasons and Motives', draft p. 5.

[25] It is worth pointing out that the argument that present hedonic desires can provide reasons also shows that future hedonic desires can provide reasons; if I will tomorrow dislike the sound of squeaking chalk I will then hear, I have reasons now to take steps to avoid hearing it.

Now it might be thought that it is not the fact that I now dislike the sensation that provides a reason to stop having it but rather the fact that having it is painful. As Parfit says, however, the disliking 'makes' the sensation painful, and here the 'making' relation is most plausibly one of constitution: the fact that now hearing the squeaking chalk is painful just consists in the fact that I now dislike it. Indeed, since the sensation is not intrinsically painful, it is hard to see in what else its being painful could consist other than the fact that I dislike it. Thus, my reason to flee from the present sound of squeaking chalk is provided by the fact that I now dislike it. And so, if this is right, we have an exception to Parfit's claim that no desires can provide reasons.

To avoid this result, Parfit must think either that there are always 'indirect' reasons to continue or to cease having the objects of one's present hedonic desires or that such desires are like urges, which provide no reason to do what one has the urge to do. It is implausible to think, however, that there is always some indirect reason to continue or cease having a sensation one likes or dislikes. I need not always find the thought of continuing to have a sensation I like pleasurable. I like the sensation of rain against my face, for example, but while I am having that sensation I need not contemplate how continuing to have it would be pleasant; indeed, if I were to contemplate the matter, I might not take any pleasure in the thought. And when I put up my umbrella, the fact that I am no longer having a sensation I like does not distract me or impede me from carrying on with my day. Sometimes there are such indirect facts that provide reasons for me to continue or cease having a sensation I like, but there need not be. Moreover, it would be a mistake to think that because there are no value-based reasons to continue having the sensation one likes, one has *no* reason to continue to have it. It would be odd to think that even though I now intensely dislike the present sound of squeaking chalk, I have no reason to remove myself from it. Hedonic desires are not like urges to turn on radios or count blades of grass which provide no reason to have their objects.

If this is right, then Parfit must allow present hedonic desires as an exception to his claim that no desires can provide reasons. When I put this to Parfit, he agreed that he might have to qualify his claim that *no* desires can provide reasons, but he insisted, à la Raz and Scanlon, that even if he did have to allow an exception for hedonic desires, such desires are peculiar and cannot form the basis of a general argument that desires can provide reasons. This is because, he thinks, hedonic desires are crucially different from desires proper, in that the former *must* be directed at present states while the latter need not be and are typically directed at future states— and desire-based theorists take as their paradigm present desires directed at future states. I cannot now like a sensation I will have tomorrow; my present likes must be directed at present states. And the disposition of liking a kind of sensation whenever it occurs is a different kind of mental state from an occurrent liking. Thus even if present likings and dislikings of present sensations can provide reasons, there is no reason to think that paradigmatic desires can.[26]

Whether Parfit can effectively quarantine the exception provided by hedonic desires is a delicate matter, and an adequate examination of the possible ways in which he might attempt to do so would lead us too far afield. There are grounds, however, for thinking that his cited reason— that hedonic desires must be directed at present states, and ordinary desires need not be—will not do the trick.

If the exception provided by hedonic desires is to be harmless, Parfit must maintain that there is a relevant distinction between one's present liking or disliking of a present sensation and one's present desire that that sensation continue or cease. For if my liking the present sensation of touching velvet can provide a reason for me to continue to touch it, and if this liking is not relevantly different from the present desire that this sensation continue, then the present desire that it continue provides a reason for me to continue to touch it. In this case, we would have an example of a paradigmatic desire that provides reasons, and the value-based view would begin to unravel.[27]

---

[26] There is an alternative, seemingly less concessive response available to the value-based theorist. Instead of conceding that present hedonic desires can provide reasons to have their sensations continue, he might argue that only *future*, and not present, hedonic desires can provide reasons. Since present likings of present sensations do not guarantee that one will continue to like that sensation, how can a present liking provide a reason to continue to have a sensation that one might detest in the next instant? Only *future* likings of concurrent sensations can provide reasons: if, for example, tomorrow I will like having the then-present sensation of touching velvet, that gives me a reason now to touch velvet at that time tomorrow. But allowing that *future* hedonic desires can provide reasons does not threaten to unravel the value-based view because, in so far as desire-based theorists want to keep the connection between reasons and motivation, *future* mental states are not the sort of state that they think can provide reasons. Compare Scanlon, 'Replies', 339–40. This line of response is, I believe, problematic in ways similar to Parfit's concessive response; detailed arguments might be developed to show that it is difficult to draw a line between the two kinds of states.

[27] Parfit calls desires about one's present and future pleasures and pains 'metahedonic desires'. (Although in 'Rationality and Reasons', 26, he defines them as desires about one's

The question, then, is whether there is some relevant difference between my present liking of the present sensation of touching velvet and my present desire that this sensation continue. Parfit cites the fact that the former must be directed at present states, while the latter can also be directed at future states. But the thought that this difference could account for why likings can provide reasons but paradigmatic desires cannot is bizarre. For suppose I have two conative states that differ only in that one must be directed at present states while the other can be directed at present or future states. Suppose too that only one of these conative states can provide reasons. It would be strange to think that the fact that the conative attitude might be directed at future states prevents that attitude from providing a reason. Indeed, given a choice between either being necessarily directed at present states and being possibly directed at future states as a condition that prevents a mental attitude from providing a reason, it would be natural to choose the former, not the latter. It is hard to see how the fact of being possibly directed at future states can *block* a conative state from providing a reason. Parfit may have identified a difference between present likings and present desires for future states, but this difference could not plausibly ground the claim that only likings can provide reasons and paradigmatic reasons cannot.

Moreover, there is a relevant *similarity* between the two states that suggests that if present likings can provide reasons, then so too can paradigmatic desires. If my now liking the present sensation of touching velvet can provide a reason for me to continue to touch it, it does so in virtue of the *liking* or attraction I have to the sensation. A present desire that the sensation of touching velvet continue, if affective, will also involve attraction to the sensation of touching velvet. In this case both my liking and my present desire that the sensation continue involve attraction to their objects. If the attraction rationalizes in the one case, why not in the other?[28]

_____

future pleasures and pains, he means to include desires about one's *present* pleasures and pains as well, such as the desire that one's present pleasure continue.) While he might allow that the present liking of a present sensation can provide a reason to continue to have that sensation, he must deny that the metahedonic desire that one's present pleasant sensation continue can provide a reason to continue having the sensation.

[28] This is not to say that *all* present desires that a present sensation continue need involve having an affective feel. Some such desires might be 'motivated'; I might now want to stop taking a cold shower because I believe that I will catch a cold or that I have reasons to get back to work. My point is only that if I now like a present sensation, then I might plausibly have (perhaps I must have) an affective desire that this pleasant sensation continue; and if the attraction in the one case can provide a reason, why not in the other?

Although Parfit does not offer any explicit account of desires, his implicit account seems to assume, like Raz's and Scanlon's, that the affective feel of a desire cannot rationalize action. Indeed, the general form of his argument against desire-based views seems to assume that if there are value-based reasons to have what one wants, the fact that one wants it does not provide a further independent reason to have it. This assumption might have some plausibility if, like Raz and Scanlon, Parfit assumes that desires already depend on value-based reasons to have their objects; for in this case, there would seem to be double-counting. If, however, affective desires are independent of such reasons, then Parfit's arguments, like Raz's and Scanlon's, leave open the possibility that affective desires can in general provide reasons.

VI

Thus three leading value-based theorists each recognize that there may be an exception to their claim that desires cannot provide reasons. From Raz, we have the case in which an attraction to one option seems to provide a reason to go for it when the independent value-based reasons for the options are evenly matched (one has reason to go for the banana over the pear because one is attracted to the banana). From Scanlon, we have the case in which it seems that 'feeling like it' can provide a reason when one decides to let what one feels like determine what one will do (one has reason to take the route home one feels like taking). And finally, from Parfit, we have the case of being attracted to a rationally neutral present sensation; that attraction can provide a reason to continue to have the sensation (one has a reason to continue to touch velvet if one likes the sensation). Each of the desires, we suggested, is an affective desire.[29]

I now want to outline a positive argument for thinking that affective desires can, indeed, provide reasons, and thus that the three exceptions are

---

[29] The three exceptions might be understood as successive restrictions on one another. Raz's is arguably the broadest: an affective desire for something can provide a reason to have it on the condition that the other reasons for having it and not having it are evenly matched. Scanlon's can be understood as a restriction on Raz's: affective desires can provide a reason only when one 'decides' to let what one does be so determined, and the cases in which it is appropriate to decide this are 'trivial'. Parfit's exception can be seen as restricting further the trivial cases to ones in which the choice is between otherwise rationally neutral present sensations.

instances of a broad class of cases in which desires can provide reasons. The argument begins by examining what I take to be the 'Achilles' heel' of any value-based views, the case of 'feeling like it' when all other relevant reasons are evenly matched. Once it is allowed that 'feeling like it' can rationalize action in these cases, there is good reason to think that affective desires generally can rationalize action.

We start by distinguishing two kinds of affective feel or attraction that one can have towards an object. Most attractions are to particular features of an object; one is attracted to the creaminess of the banana, the scenic beauty of a certain route home, the plushness of the touch of velvet. We might call these attractions 'feature-bound'. Some attractions, however, are not directed toward any particular feature of an object; one is simply attracted to the object *as such*. Affective desires with 'feature-free' attractions are desires for the object itself but not under any particular description. To distinguish feature-bound from feature-free affective desires, I will call the latter 'feelings like it'. (In common usage, 'feeling like it' covers both feature-free and feature-bound attractions.) If one 'feels like' wearing pink, there need be no particular feature of wearing pink that attracts one; one *just feels like* wearing pink. Or one might simply feel like tying one's shoe-laces with the double-loop method or turning a cartwheel down the sidewalk or writing with a pencil instead of a pen, without being attracted to any particular feature of doing so.

'Feeling like it' can rationalize action when the other relevant reasons for or against having what one feels like are evenly matched. Consider Buridan's famous ass, poised between two equidistant and qualitatively identical bales of hay. There are, by hypothesis, no independent reasons for him to eat the one bale rather than the other. Now suppose that he 'feels like' the hay on the left, not because it is to the left or for any other feature of it—he just wants *that* bale. If he is attracted to the bale on the left but goes for the one of the right, surely he would not be doing what he has most reason to do. He has most reason to eat the bale on the left since all other reasons are evenly matched and he is attracted to that bale.

Now it might be conceded that the ass does have more reason to eat the bale on the left but that it is a mistake to suppose that his 'feeling like it' can provide a reason for him to do so. Rather, the value-based theorist might say, his feeling like it provides evidence for the fact that he would enjoy it more but does not itself provide a reason for him to eat that bale;

his reason for going for the left bale would then be that he would enjoy it more. Or perhaps what provides his reason to eat on the left is not that he 'feels like it' but that he has 'decided' to do so.

Given that the bales are identical, if he enjoys eating one bale more, his greater enjoyment must *consist in* the fact that he feels like eating that one; his attraction to the one bale is what makes eating it all the more pleasurable. Thus what provides the reason is his 'feeling like it', not some independent fact that he would enjoy it more.

More importantly, even if his 'feeling like it' does not constitute the fact that he would enjoy having it more—and thus he would enjoy having either bale equally—the fact that he 'feels like' the bale on the left can nevertheless provide a reason for him to go left. If he goes left, his action can be rationalized by pointing out that he felt like having the bale on the left. If he goes right, we would need some explanation for this puzzling act; what reason does he have to go right given that he would enjoy each of the two identical bales equally and feels like having the one on the left? What we would be looking for is a reason to go right that counteracts his reason to go left provided by the fact that he feels like it. The point here is that 'feeling like it' need not be cashed out in terms of facts about greater enjoyment; the fact that one is attracted to something can *per se* provide a reason to go for it when all other reasons are evenly matched. Finally, if the bales are identical and he 'decides' to go left, his decision can provide a reason only in so far as it is based upon some reason-providing consideration—for instance, that he feels like the bale on the left. In this case, it is not the decision, but the fact that he 'feels like it', that provides the reason.[30]

In order to avoid the conclusion that his 'feeling like it' provides a reason to go left, the value-based theorist might deny that in going left the ass acts for a reason. Perhaps 'feeling like it' is just an urge; if, in going left, the ass is just satisfying an urge, he acts for *no* reason. 'Feeling like it', however, is not an urge. First, as an affective desire, it involves having an attitude towards something and is not a 'passive' motivational impulse like thirst. Second, it is a reasons-appropriate attitude, while an urge is not. Even though the ass may have no reason to feel one way or another, it is appropriate to ask whether he has reason to feel the way he does. Feeling thirsty, by contrast, is not the kind of state for which one can sensibly ask for reasons.

---

[30] See Michael E. Bratman, *Intention, Plans, and Practical Reason* (Cambridge, Mass.: Harvard University Press, 1987; reissued by CSLI Publications, 1999).

Although 'feeling like it' is not an urge, perhaps going to the left bale because he 'feels like it' is, nevertheless, going to the left for no reason. (Recall that Scanlon suggests that his exception could be a case of this sort.) But doing something because one feels like it does not seem like cases in which one does things for no reason. I sometimes drum my fingers against my computer keyboard for no reason. Many people, while sitting in their car waiting for a red light to change, will start to hum for no reason. Doing things for no reason usually involves absent-mindedly not attending to what one is doing. Sometimes when one acts arbitrarily, one is acting for no reason. When one feels like something, in contrast, one has a definite phenomenological attraction to something that draws one's attention. The ass has his attention fixed on the two bales of hay; he finds himself attracted to the one on the left. When he moves to eat the one on the left, he does so in full awareness of his attraction. He does not act for no reason; on the contrary, he acts for the reason that he feels like having it.

Nor need there be any 'indirect' reasons that rationalize the ass's going for the left bale rather than the right. He needn't find the thought of eating the left bale pleasing, nor need it be true that he feels distracted or bothered if he doesn't get to eat the left bale but is stuck with the right bale instead. Not all affective desires need be 'nagging' desires; I might be attracted to the touch of velvet but not feel bothered or distracted if I don't touch it. Our ass feels like eating the left bale, but if he ends up eating the right one, he will just shrug his shoulders and happily munch away.

Therefore, if one is faced with a choice between two relevantly identical alternatives, 'feeling like it' can rationalize one's act of going for it. And this type of case is more common than one might think. Suppose you are at a supermarket and are confronted with row upon row of identical cans of soup. You might simply arbitrarily pick one for no reason. However, you might instead 'feel like' having a certain can—the one that catches your eye, for example. If you feel drawn to one can but take another, you fail to act on a reason you have.[31] Or suppose that at dinner you are served a plate of three identical slices of beef. Where should you start? If you feel like starting with a particular slice, that provides a reason to do so. Or

---

[31] Note that whether you deserve to be called 'irrational' depends on how irrationality is understood. If one thinks that in these cases the agent would not be irrational in not doing what she felt like doing, that would not by itself show that 'feeling like it' did not provide a reason.

suppose a magician friend asks you to choose a card, any card. The cards, fanned out, are identical in all relevant respects. But one might be drawn to a particular card, and that attraction provides a reason to choose it. In all of these cases, it would be puzzling if you did not do what you felt like doing. If, on the other hand, you did what you felt like doing, the fact that you felt like it would rationalize your action, and no further explanation would be required.

This conclusion can be extended to cases in which one is faced with a choice, not between identical alternatives, but between non-identical alternatives for which the independent reasons for and against are evenly matched. We then have a modified version of the Buridan's ass case, since the way in which the independent reasons are evenly matched does not simply follow from the fact that the alternatives are relevantly identical. But the way in which the independent reasons are evenly matched cannot make a difference to whether 'feeling like it' can provide a reason. Scanlon's two-routes-home case might be an example. The two routes home are different—one is scenic and long, the other is short and lined with strip malls—but the reasons for taking one rather than the other are evenly matched. Suppose that one has a feature-free affective desire for the longer route. If one takes the shorter route instead, one would fail to act in the way one has most reason to act. Being attracted to the longer route provides a reason to take it when all other independent reasons are evenly matched. Thus, 'feeling like it' can provide a reason to have what one feels like whenever the other independent reasons relevant to what one should do are evenly matched regardless of whether the alternatives are identical or very different.

Now this extended conclusion might be understood in a limited way; for perhaps 'feeling like it' can 'provide' reasons not in the deep sense of providing an independent reason in its own right but only in a *conditional* sense: when the A-team of reasons—that is, value-based reasons—have 'run out', the B-team of reasons, such as 'feeling like it', can take over. This would imply that 'feeling like it' is something like a coin toss, a consideration that operates as a decision procedure when all relevant reasons have run out. Perhaps 'feeling like it', like the outcome of the coin toss, 'provides a reason' only in this conditional sense.[32]

---

[32] Compare Raz, who thinks that although desires do not provide reasons, they 'become relevant when reasons have run their course'. After value-based reasons have run out, one

Although it may sometimes operate in this way, 'feeling like it' can also provide a relevant reason for choice in its own right. Whether it does depends on whether the consideration of what one feels like is relevant to what one should do in a given choice situation. In an ordinary choice between saving one drowning stranger or two, what one 'feels like' doing is not relevant to the choice. But it is hard to believe that what one feels like is not relevant in a choice between things to eat, places to go, and people to see. If I must choose between an Italian and a Chinese meal for dinner tonight, surely the consideration of what I feel like is relevant to the choice, even if my feeling like Chinese is an attraction to having the Chinese meal not under any particular description but simply to *that* cuisine. Given that what I feel like is relevant, the fact that I feel like Chinese provides a reason to have it. Thus if I feel like Chinese but have Italian, I act against my reasons. This is not necessarily because, having seen that the reasons for either sort of meal were evenly matched, I adopt a decision procedure according to which I will go for what I feel like. Rather, my attraction to *that* cuisine provides an independent reason for me to have it. Thus the cases in which 'feeling like it' can rationalize action are not restricted to ones in which the other reasons are evenly matched. Even if with respect to all the other reasons having Italian is better than having Chinese, the fact that I feel like Chinese provides a reason to have Chinese. In general, even if one option is significantly better than another, the fact that I 'feel like' the worse option can itself provide a reason to have it.

There is, however, another way in which it might be thought that 'feeling like it' rationalizes only conditionally. Perhaps 'feeling like it' can provide a reason only on the condition that nothing much of value turns on what one does in the choice situation. This may be what Scanlon has in mind when he suggests that 'feeling like it' can rationalize action if one 'decides' to let what one will do turn on what one is attracted to doing. Presumably, one's 'deciding' in this way can have its intended normative

---

might act on one's desire, which, according to Raz, is acting for *no* reason. None the less, Raz holds, one's desire can 'rationalize' one's action in the sense that, in such cases, not doing what one wants 'usually manifests an unconscious desire for punishment, self-hate, patho-logical self-doubt, or something else' which is 'irrational'. See Raz, 'Incommensurability and Agency', 63. I find this view unstable because it maintains that desires cannot provide reasons while at the same time maintaining that not doing what one wants when reasons have run out is irrational. How can one be irrational if one does something one has no reason not to do?

effect only if the relevant reasons sanction such a decision,[33] and, arguably, such a decision is sanctioned by the relevant reasons only in 'special, rather trivial cases'. Even if, for example, the reasons for taking one route outweigh the reasons for taking another, there is a higher-order reason (perhaps deriving from the values of spontaneity and variety in the way one chooses what to do) to let some of one's choices turn on what one feels like when nothing much turns on what one does. 'Feeling like it', then, might be a reason in virtue of a higher-order reason to take it as a reason in cases of trivial importance. The normative force of such a reason would then depend on the fact that 'first-order' reasons are of trivial importance.

It is not clear, however, that 'feeling like it' rationalizes only in cases of trivial importance. In choosing between two very different careers, for instance, the fact that one has an attraction to one *as such* seems to be of relevance at the first-order level. What one feels like seems relevant in choices between careers, loves, places to live, and so on. But even if 'feeling like it' can provide a reason only when it does not much matter which alternative one chooses, we should not be misled into thinking that it thereby has only conditional rationalizing force. In so far as doing what one feels like is relevant to what one should do, 'feeling like it' can rationalize as an independent reason in its own right, not as a reason that is conditional on the other reasons being of trivial importance.

'Feelings like it', I believe, are the Achilles' heel of value-based views of reasons. I do not know of any value-based view that can avoid admitting these cases as exceptions. Importantly, once we allow that 'feeling like it' can provide reasons, we must also allow that affective desires involving *feature-bound* attractions can provide reasons. Feature-bound attractions rely on certain features of what one wants that ground one's affective feel towards the object. Because they depend on features of an object, it is easy to recast such attractions as value-based facts about the object, such as that one will enjoy having it. But if feature-free attractions can provide reasons, then so can feature-bound ones. This is because such attractions differ only in their objects; being attracted to a feature of an object is being attracted to an object *as such*, where the object *as such* in this case is the feature. In being attracted to a feature, one need not be attracted to a feature of that feature. If being attracted to an object *as such* provides a reason to have that

---

[33] See Bratman, *Intention, Plans, and Practical Reason,* and Scanlon, *What We Owe to Each Other,* 46–7.

object, then attraction to a feature (as an object *as such*) provides a reason to have that feature, and thereby provides a reason to have the object with that feature. The distinction between feature-free and feature-bound attractions, then, is not one that makes a difference to whether attractions can provide reasons.

If affective desires in general can provide reasons, then they provide a large and important class of reasons. For being attracted to features of objects is relevant to choices involving a great many important matters, such as choosing a career, a life-partner, or a place to live. Indeed, having an attraction towards something is in principle unlimited in scope; whether this attraction provides a reason depends on whether the choice situation is one in which one's attractions are relevant to the question of what one should do. Where they are and one has such an attraction, the attraction need not have great normative weight; the most weighty reason I have to spend my time thinking about philosophical issues is plausibly provided by the fact that doing so is worthwhile, but the fact that I am attracted to philosophy provides an independent reason to pursue it. Sometimes, however, one's affective desires provide the most important reasons to do something, for example, in choosing what to wear or how to spend one's leisure time. Regardless of their relative weight, such reasons can 'tip the scales' against one's value-based reasons. I might, for example, have most value-based reason to be a doctor, but the fact that I have an affective desire to be a philosopher may give me, all things considered, reason to be one. Having an affective desire for something, then, can make a significant difference to what we have, all things considered, reason to do.

VII

The conclusion that affective desires can provide reasons is consistent with the view that *all* reasons are provided by desires. But as I said, I am going to assume that this view is false.[34] Instead, I want to try to undermine what I take to be the most serious obstacle to thinking that the hybrid view is true.

[34] It may be worth noting that this assumption is not *obviously* unwarranted. Although desire-based views are the received orthodoxy, the reasons for preferring such views to value-based views are somewhat obscure. There are three general grounds commonly cited for such a preference, but they are in fact neutral between the two views. These are (1) that reasons

The conflict between desire- and value-based views can be understood at a deeper level as deriving from two competing conceptions of the source of practical justification. According to the *internalist* conception, all practical justification has its source in facts that are in some sense 'internal' to the agent, and according to desire-based theorists these facts are that the agent wants something. According to the *externalist* conception, by contrast, all practical justification derives from facts that are in some sense 'external' to the agent; and the only facts these could plausibly be, according to

must be naturalistically respectable and thus, it seems, must be provided by facts that the agent wants something, not by queer facts about the value of what she wants; (2) that reasons must be able to figure in motivational or causal explanations of rational action and therefore, it seems, must be provided by an agent's motivations; and (3) that reasons must be 'inescapable' in the sense that if one recognizes one has a reason, one must be motivated to do what one has reason to do, and thus it seems that the only kind of consideration that could guarantee this motivation would itself be a motivation.

On the first ground, whatever sort of facts provide reasons, there is a normative fact in virtue of which they do, and it is an open question on both desire- and value-based views as to whether this normative fact is natural. Of course it might be pointed out that value-based views are saddled with an additional queer fact: namely, the evaluative fact that provides the reason. But, as we have already noted, some value-based views 'pass the buck' from evaluative facts to their natural subvening facts; when describing one's reasons, then, one may eschew all mention of evaluative facts. In this way, a commitment to naturalism does not itself favour the desire-based as opposed to the value-based view.

On the second, as Thomas Nagel pointed out long ago, a rational agent might be motivated to do something, such as empty his sick relative's bedpan, not because he has an independent desire to do so but because he believes that it is his duty or that he has a reason to do it. His belief produces his motivation, which then leads him to act, or the belief itself motivates him to action via a disposition to do what he believes he has reason to do—the disposition of rationality. In either case, the reason can be provided not by his desire but by an external fact, belief in which provides the motivational link to rational action. Thus the thought that practical reasons must be able to figure in the explanation of rational action cuts across desire- and value-based views.

Finally, on the third, the 'inescapability' of reasons must be understood in the right way. Even desire-based theorists will allow that an agent with reasons might not be motivated to do what he has reasons to do. The inescapability at issue is *rational* inescapability; if I am rational, I must be motivated by the reasons I believe I have. And *any* theorist can secure inescapability in this sense simply by understanding what it is to be rational in terms of being motivated by what one believes are one's reasons. One's inescapable reason might be provided by the fact that something is good.

Many of the points of this note can be found in Williams, 'Internal and External Reasons', 102, 106–7; Thomas Nagel, *The Possibility of Altruism* (Oxford: Clarendon Press, 1970); Christine Korsgaard, *The Sources of Normativity* (Cambridge: Cambridge University Press, 1996), and *idem*, 'Skepticism about Practical Reason', as reprinted in Stephen Darwall, Allan Gibbard, and Peter Railton (eds.), *Moral Discourse and Practice*, (New York: Oxford University Press, 1997), 376–7; and Parfit, *Rediscovering Reasons*.

value-based theorists, are facts about the value of the action or its object. In the one case practical justification derives from the fact that the agent wants something, and in the other from facts about *what* she wants.

The debate about which considerations can provide reasons, then, involves a deeper debate about the source of justification—is it internal or external to the agent? Now one obvious way to defend the hybrid view is simply to insist that practical justification has dual sources; sometimes the justification of action derives from facts internal to the agent, and sometimes from facts external to the agent. But why should we think that practical justification, presumably understood in unitary fashion, is sometimes internal and sometimes external? The hybrid view faces a challenge not faced by its 'purist' rivals: it needs to demonstrate that its ecumenical spirit with respect to reasons is compatible with a non-arbitrary, coherent conception of the source of practical justification.

I want to end by explaining how the hybrid view is compatible with the *externalist* conception of practical justification. The core thought behind this conception is given by the question, How can what reasons I have be, in the end, *up to me*? The source of practical justification must lie outside the agent, in facts about the action or its object. I suggest that affective desires can provide reasons even on the assumption that all practical justification must derive from facts external to the agent. This may seem puzzling, for how can the fact that an agent wants something be a fact external to that agent? Seeing how this is possible depends on getting a better understanding of the appropriate sense in which a fact might be 'external' and of the different ways in which actions might be conceived.

As many philosophers of action have pointed out, an action is an action under many different descriptions. There is the flexing of the muscles, the pulling of the trigger, and the murdering of one's enemy. Now actions involving an object for which one has an affective desire can be conceived under two descriptions, either as a response to the world or as a response to the agent's mental state. If I have an affective desire for ice cream, my eating ice cream can be understood either as my having some ice cream or as my satisfying my affective desire for ice cream. If I feel like taking the long, scenic route home, my taking the long, scenic route home can be seen either as my taking that route home or as my doing what I feel like. And if I am attracted to the present sensation of a hot bath, then my continuing to soak can be conceived either as my continuing to take a hot bath or as my gratifying my attraction.

Actions described in these ways allow for two kinds of reasons—those provided by features of the action understood as a response to the world and those provided by features of the action understood as a response to an affective desire. Suppose, for example, that I am intensely afraid of cockroaches; the thought of touching one sends shivers down my spine. Now when I run away from a cockroach, my action is both a running away from a cockroach and an allaying of a state of fear. What reasons do I have for my action? Given that cockroaches are harmless creatures—they do not carry disease or bite, and are God's nimblest creatures, capable of changing direction twenty-five times in a single second—there are no intrinsic value-based reasons to run away from them. Perhaps there are indirect value-based reasons, but we can rig the case so that these are eliminated; if I do not run away, I will still be fearful of the cockroach but will not, for instance, be distracted from doing other things. Although there are no intrinsic or indirect value-based reasons for me to flee from the cockroach, the fact that I fear it provides a desire-based reason to run away. My desire-based reason derives from features of the action under its desire-responsive description as the allaying of a state of fear; and my lack of value-based reasons derives from features of the action under its world-responsive description as the flight from a cockroach. Nor does the example depend upon there being no value-based reasons. Suppose you are afraid of scorpions and I am not. We both have value-based reasons to avoid a creature whose bite is painful. But you have an additional reason based upon your fear that I lack, for even though both our actions can be described as a fleeing from a dangerous creature, only yours can be de-scribed and hence rationalized as a response to a conative attitude.[35]

The fact that I want something (or fear it, respect it, etc.) is 'external' in the sense that it can be seen to rationalize *as* a fact about an action or its object. The act of fleeing from a cockroach is an act of allaying a fear and, as such, provides me with a reason to respond in the appropriate way to the object of my action: namely, my fear. Of course, there is in some sense

---

[35] It is perhaps worth noting that the question of when a consideration is 'relevant' to a choice situation—that is, when it is potentially a reason for choosing—cuts across the question of whether desires or value-based facts provide reasons. Just as the fact that I want something is not always relevant to a choice, so is the fact that something is beautiful not always relevant to a choice (e.g., between two candidates for a philosophy job). On the view under consideration, external facts would determine what is relevant to a choice, and it is plausible to think that these facts would determine relevance for types of action.

no real difference between my act of fleeing from the cockroach and my act of allaying my fear (and perhaps no difference at all). But, all the same, these two different ways of conceiving the action make a significant difference to whether the fear can be taken to rationalize the action under an externalist conception of the source of justification.

If this way of understanding reasons provided by desires is correct, there is a lesson for both value- and desire-based theorists. Value-based theorists are mistaken in assuming that the fact that one wants something cannot be a fact external to the agent that can justify action. Indeed, I suspect that resistance from most value-based theorists to the idea that desires can provide reasons derives from the mistaken assumption that the externalist conception precludes such reasons. And desire-based theorists are mistaken in supposing that if desires are to provide reasons, the internalist conception of practical justification must be correct—desires can provide reasons even under the externalist conception.

By accepting the hybrid view, we do not thereby sacrifice the unitary character of practical justification. Although there are two distinctive kinds of consideration that provide reasons, there is unity at a deeper level: all practical reasons are provided by facts with a single source—they are provided by facts about the action or its object that are appropriately external to the agent.[36]

---

[36] My warmest thanks to Kit Fine, Derek Parfit, and Jacob Ross for very useful and incisive comments on earlier versions of this paper, and to John Broome and Sigrun Svavarsdottir for very helpful discussion of parts of an early draft. Although this paper is in some ways critical of the views of Joseph Raz, Thomas Scanlon, and Derek Parfit, anyone who knows their work will recognize their salutary influence throughout. The ideas in the paper were developed in response to a conversation I had with Joseph Raz many years ago while I was a graduate student at Balliol College. I am grateful to him for his continued philosophical friendship and guidance, and for his challenging and illuminating work which informs so much of my own.

4

Enticing Reasons

Jonathan Dancy

In this paper I consider the possibility of a general distinction between two sorts of reason: those that entice and those that are, as I will later say, more 'peremptory' in style. The main idea here is that some reasons are obviously in the business of more or less telling us what to do—though this way of putting the point will turn out not to be quite right, and I use it here only to help you see what I am getting at; moral reasons are an obvious case in point, but many reasons of prudence do the same (the reasons for having your brakes checked are peremptory, in my sense). Other reasons, however, are more to do with making an option attractive rather than demanded, required, or right. At its most basic, the distinction I am after is between those reasons that say 'Come on, I'd be nice', and those that say something of a more forceful sort such as 'You'd better do this'.

I will be trying to pin-point the real basis of this distinction later, but an initial suggestion is that there is no underlying requirement that one choose the most attractive option. There may not even be *a further* reason of any sort (enticing or peremptory) to choose the most attractive option, any more than there is a *further* reason to do the action that overall one ought to do. It may be wrong to do an action when there is more moral or prudential reason to do something else: you *should* get your brakes checked, you *should* help the afflicted. But, I will suggest, it is not wrong (morally or otherwise) to do a less enticing action when there is a more enticing one available.

1. Reasons against Enticers

The most direct attack one could mount on the notion of an enticing reason would go something like this. John Broome writes: 'if you have a reason to q and no reason not to q, then you ought to q.'[1] I take it that on this view the term 'reason' *means* (among other things, perhaps) a consideration which one would be wrong not to act on in the absence of any opposition; that you ought to q is a trivial and analytic consequence of your having a reason to q and no reason not to q. This being so, the idea of a reason that it is not wrong to fail to respond to, in the absence of opposing considerations, is effectively self-contradictory. But supposed enticing reasons are of just this sort. For if there is no rational requirement that one choose the most attractive option, there will be enticing reasons that it is not wrong to fail to respond to—not to act on, that is.

This stance seems really to beg the question against enticing reasons. To announce at the outset that good reasons are considerations it is wrong not to act on unless they are outweighed or otherwise defeated by other reasons is simply to contradict those who suggest that some good reasons are not like this. Once the notion of an enticing reason is presented as a possibility, more than this will need to be said if that notion is to be rejected as incoherent.

There is in this an interesting question just what is meant by saying that it is wrong not to act on a winning consideration (or set of considerations, I presume). On some accounts, 'wrong' here means 'irrational'. But I agree with Tim Scanlon[2] that someone who fails to act on an undefeated good reason need not be subject to so severe a charge as that of being irrational. The charge of irrationality should be reserved for grosser failures with respect to reasons. There are less dramatic complaints that we can make; among these is that it is wrong, though not irrational. But it need not be necessary to go even that far. I would not say that it is irrational, or that it is wrong, not to act on an enticing reason when the alternative is to do something for which there is no reason whatsoever (enticing or non-enticing): it is not irrational just to do nothing at all. This would not mean

---

[1] John Broome, 'Normative Requirements', in J. Dancy (ed.), *Normativity* (Oxford: Blackwell, 2000), 78–99, at 80. Broome does not believe this any more, I think; I am quoting old Broome, not new Broome.

[2] T. M. Scanlon, *What We Owe to Each Other* (Cambridge, Mass.: Harvard University Press, 1998), 26–8.

that there was no style of criticism whatever that is applicable in such a case. One might say about a person who does something for which there is nothing to be said at all, when there was a nice-ish alternative, that he was plain silly. There is certainly some criticism to be made, then, that lies within the broad domain of the rational, but it would be of the soft kind that we would also use of someone who chose a not very nice option when he had a stunningly nice one available. It is not irrational to do this, and it is not that one ought not to do it, but it is just silly to pass up such a nice way of spending the day, or whatever.

My conclusion so far is that this direct attack on the notion of an enticing reason is a failure. But there are more subtle attacks to be considered. One such is offered by Joseph Raz. His paper 'Reason and the Will' has a section that discusses, and defends, what he calls 'the basic belief':

most of the time people have a variety of options such that it would accord with reason for them to choose any one of them and it would not be against reason to avoid any of them.[3]

Raz introduces a potential distinction between 'enticing' and 'requiring' reasons as one possible way of defending the basic belief. (Another way, the one Raz actually adopts, is to appeal to incommensurability.) In my discussion of Raz, I will initially follow his terminology; but I will eventually suggest that the term 'requiring reasons' is a mistake. According to Raz, then,

Enticing reasons make an option attractive, and render following them intelligible. But they do not bear at all on the reasonableness of not conforming with them. Failure to conform with enticing reasons is never wrong, unreasonable, or irrational.[4]

There follows a two-page discussion of enticing reasons[5] in which Raz tries to show that the notion is incoherent. He starts by understanding the enticing/requiring distinction as a distinction between two types of reason; 'reasons are divided into two types', he suggests. He then suggests two difficulties for this division. The first is that 'the very same considerations which in some circumstances seem to be enticing reasons are under other

---

[3] Joseph Raz, *Engaging Reason: On the Theory of Value and Action* (Oxford: Oxford University Press, 1999), 90–117, at 100.

[4] Ibid. 101.

[5] Ibid. 101–2.

conditions requiring reasons'. Now this itself would be no difficulty. The idea should not be that there are two sorts of reason, so that each consideration is either of one sort or of the other, but not both. Rather, it is that there are two normative relations, the requiring relation and the enticing relation. These are, we might say, 'styles' of favouring (more on this later). One and the same consideration can stand in either or both of these relations—though probably it cannot both require and entice us to do one and the same action at the same time. Which relation it is standing in on a given occasion will no doubt depend on the context.

Raz's second difficulty here is that if we start with an enticing reason, and add further reasons to it, we may end up with a conclusive reason of which the allegedly enticing reason is a part. He asks, 'Should we say that enticing reasons are enticing one by one, but not in combination?' If we do say this, we undermine the official purpose of introducing enticing reasons in the first place, which was to explain the basic belief.

What is the supposed problem here? We are understanding the suggestion to be that there are two normative relations at issue: enticing and requiring. On that account, there is no reason to deny that if you change the context by adding further reasons, the original enticer may be converted into a requirer, without the possibility of such conversions doing anything to undermine the distinction between enticing and requiring. I think that Raz may have two possibilities in mind here, both of which need to be addressed. The first is that the addition of an enticer to a requirer may result in a combination that is a stronger requirer, maybe even a conclusive reason. The second is that enough enticers will amount to a conclusive reason, even though they themselves retain their individual status as enticers, and do not become requirers. If we allow the latter possibility, he says, we undermine the supposed purpose of introducing enticing reasons in the first place, which was to explain 'the basic belief'.

To make sense of all this, we need to get clearer on the relation between the contributory and the overall (which Raz sometimes calls 'conclusive'). In particular, we need to distinguish between the conclusive, the overall, and the requiring. (A decisive reason is probably the same as a conclusive reason.)

A conclusive reason (as I understand and use the term) is a consideration which, though there may be others on both sides, really is the one that decides the issue in the present case. The sum total of the reasons in favour is not itself properly called conclusive; there may be overall more reason to do the action than not, without any of the contributing reasons being conclusive, and without the combination of them being conclusive either. In such a case, the matter should be expressed as I have just done, using the notion of what there is overall most reason to do, rather than the notion of a conclusive reason.

Sometimes the notion of overall reason is combined with that of a sufficient reason. It is common to say that where the reasons come down on one side rather than the other, those reasons are sufficient and the reasons on the other side are insufficient. But this is to abuse the notion of the sufficient. That notion goes best with enticing reasons (though I don't at all mean to suggest that it does not apply in the domain of Raz's requirers). Sufficient enticing reason is something that can be shared by more than one option. An enticing reason (or a set of enticing reasons) is sufficient if it makes its option worth doing. There may be more than one thing that is worth doing, as things stand. An action that is worth doing, in this sense, is one that is above a certain absolute threshold; it is not a comparative matter, though there are always comparative questions about whether one action is more worthwhile than another. There can be something to be said for an action without the action being interesting enough (say) to be worth doing.

One of the most striking differences between theoretical and practical rationality is that if I have sufficient practical reason for more than one option—that is to say, if more than one option lies above the threshold—I am rationally permitted to choose any of them, so long as they are roughly equally well supported. By contrast, if I have sufficient and equally good reason for each of a set of alternative beliefs, I am not rationally permitted to choose any of them in preference to the others. This is all part of what Raz is getting at with what he calls the basic belief.[6]

Our question, however, does not really concern sufficient reasons. There is no mystery about how several enticing reasons can combine to make a

[6] Note that the basic belief is not concerned only with the sorts of reason that I am thinking of as enticers. Like enticers, requirers come in stronger and weaker forms; situations call for certain responses, and different features of the situation may call for different responses. (This notion of 'calling for' is one way to introduce a weak form of requirement.) It is possible for there to be a situation in which several different responses are called for with approximately equal strength, in such a way that the agent is not rationally at fault in choosing any of them. This shows, it seems to me, that Raz's complex account of potential enticers may introduce a feature that is not restricted to enticers, but which they share with other sorts of practical reasons.

sufficient case for doing the action they promote; together they make the action worth doing, though severally none of them would have been able to do so. Our question (Raz's question, that is) was rather how it can be that a *conclusive* reason can consist of features that stand individually only in the enticing relation to the action. Part of the answer to this is that an enticing reason can be conclusive (for this to be the case, there must be no requirers present, of course) or, if only requirers are capable of being conclusive, a sufficient combination of individually insufficient enticers should not be thought of as a conclusive reason at all, so that Raz's problem does not arise. Though elsewhere he appears to accept the distinction between being conclusive and requiring,[7] Raz seems to conflate these notions in his second possibility. For he supposes that one can add enticing reasons to enticing reasons until one gets to a conclusive reason; the non-conclusive reasons together, he says, 'constitute a conclusive reason'. And he then supposes that if there is a conclusive reason, it is one that it would be wrong to act in breach of. But, first, it seems to me wrong to identify what there is overall, or even merely sufficient, reason to do with what there is conclusive reason to do; there may be overall reason but no conclusive reason. And, second, what there is overall enticing reason to do will not amount to a reason that it is wrong to act in breach of. We get this result only with overall requiring reasons. To suppose otherwise is to beg the question against the notion of an enticing reason.

It may help at this point for me to present a little map of distinctions and concepts here. First we have enticing reasons versus the others (which Raz calls requiring reasons). Here we are dealing with two styles of rational support linked to a distinction in subject matter. Second there is the distinction between contributory reasons and overall reason. There are no overall reasons; the proper phrase, as I see it, is not 'I have an overall reason to do this rather than that' but 'I have overall reason to do this rather than that'. If one has overall reason to do this, one certainly has sufficient reason to do it, even if none of the reasons one has is itself sufficient. One can, however, have sufficient reason to do it without having overall reason to do it (as when two actions are both pretty good and roughly equally good). If one has overall reason to do it, one probably does not have a conclusive reason to do it. A conclusive reason is one whose presence is enough in the

---

[7] See Raz, *Engaging Reason*, 229, where Raz says that reasons 'are conclusive when they prevail over all conflicting reasons'.

context to determine the issue; there may be more to be said for the action than this, but saying that more is really redundant in the circumstances. If there is such a conclusive reason present in the case, it is a bit odd (though not exactly wrong) to say that there is overall reason to do the action, because talking about the 'overall' seems to introduce conceptions of several reasons acting together. Since there are no overall reasons, no overall reasons are conclusive reasons. Conclusive reasons and decisive reasons are the same thing.

This leaves us with Raz's notion of a requiring reason, and the rather similar notion of a demanding reason. But I will not attempt to map those notions with respect to those mapped in the previous paragraph, since I will eventually suggest that we should abandon them altogether. No contributory reason either requires or demands, I will be claiming. If, then, the notion of a requiring reason is not the same as that of a conclusive reason, we will have to drop it completely. But I will continue to use Raz's contrast between enticers and requirers at least until the end of the present section of this paper.

With all this in hand, we can deal with Raz's other supposed possibility, that by adding requirers to an enticer we may get 'a conclusive reason'. Understanding the notion of a conclusive reason as suggested above, this possibility can hardly arise, unless the several combined reasons somehow become one. If the idea is merely that the combination of enticer and requirers may give us overall or sufficient reason, that seems innocuous.

Of course Raz did not only suggest that his two possibilities were somehow internally incoherent. He also said that if one allows them, one prevents the notion of an enticing reason from being used in support of the basic belief. Should we accept this? No. There is nothing in the situation, as we are now understanding it, that prevents a person from having enticing reasons for more than one action, some stronger than others, in such a way that it would accord with reason for them to choose any one of [those actions] and it would not be against reason to avoid any of them'.

There is an issue here about whether Raz is right to speak of a combination of reasons as a reason. Sometimes he talks about a complete reason; at one point he speaks of 'his reason in its entirety'.[8] In a long footnote in his paper on particularism[9] he defines a stipulative notion of a complete reason as consisting of all the facts stated by the non-redundant premisses of a sound,

---

[8] Ibid. 228.   [9] Ibid. 228–9 n. 22.

deductive argument entailing as its conclusion a proposition of the form 'There is a reason for A to V'. He claims, in support of this definition, that 'An examination of the use of expressions such as "this is a different reason", "this is the same reason", and similar expressions, will show that this notion of complete reason captures an important aspect of our understanding of reasons', though he does allow that those expressions are ordinarily used in ways that invoke differing, context-dependent, standards of completeness.

It is in fact easy to show that this definition of a complete reason is inadequate. I presume that the complete reason we are dealing with is a complete reason for A to V. Here is a sound deductive argument whose conclusion is in accordance with Raz's definition above:

> Someone in the room has a reason to V.
> There are only three people in the room, A, B, and C.
> Neither B nor C has a reason to V.
> So A has a reason to V.

It seems to me that none of the premises of this argument is a reason for A to V, and the combination of them is not a reason either, complete or otherwise. All we have here is a guarantee that there is a reason, which is not at all the same thing as a specification of the reason that is guaranteed to exist. Further, on Raz's account the reason mentioned in the conclusion is not the same reason as the one specified in the first premise, which is surely peculiar.

Leaving these criticisms aside, my own view about Raz's stipulative definition of a 'complete reason' is that it distorts the relation between contributing and overall reason. (This is one reason why it is no defence of the definition that it is stipulative.[10]) This criticism, if it is correct, will apply equally to versions of the view that escape the objections in the previous paragraph. One worry here is that if the only complete reasons are sets of considerations that together operate as a guarantee for something or other, the status of the contributory begins to appear odd. For contributory

---

[10] There is a further way in which Raz's definition of a complete reason is prejudicial, which is significant if the notion of a complete reason is to play any part in a sound response to particularist remarks about contributory reasons. If, for instance, I just defined as a 'complete reason' for an action's being wrong the supervenience base for that wrongness, and then announced that, whatever particularism had to say about anything less extensive than that, still, once we reached complete reasons rather than parts of reasons, generalism was blatantly sound, surely one would not be tempted to take this very seriously. Particularists would probably say that this sort of a reason is no reason at all.

reasons will have to be understood as incomplete, or partial, or something like that. But there is nothing incomplete about an ordinary contributory reason. Whatever it is that such reasons do, they do it perfectly well, and completely. They are not hopelessly trying to do something else, something that can be done only by several considerations acting together (as Raz would have it, acting as the several premises of an argument to the conclusion that there is a reason for A to V). Furthermore, in defining 'complete reason' as he does, he is in danger of making it impossible to understand the relation between what is contributed by an ordinary, incomplete reason and what is achieved by a complete one. Finally, whatever it is that a contributory moral reason does, it must, just in virtue of that contribution, be capable of standing as the ground for overall duty. If it were the only relevant feature, the only one actually making a difference here, our duty overall would be to do the action which it favours. But it is not at all clear, on Raz's picture, that an incomplete reason is capable of playing this sort of role; only complete reasons can do that, for him.

We started by suggesting that we have two normative relations: requiring and enticing. A set of enticing reasons can be sufficient to make the action they recommend worth doing, fun, exciting, attractive, and so on. (These are the sort of thick concepts we are dealing with in the domain of enticers.) One may have several such sets present at once. If one has only one, the action it recommends is the one that there is overall most enticing reason to do. But one is, as it were, in charge of one's enticing reasons. It is never irrational or wrong to choose an enticing action other than the one that is most enticing—even though it can be pretty silly to do so, and, in this weak sense, contrary to reason.

This seems to mean that though there can be both enticing and requiring reasons, the requiring ones, no matter how weak, will always win in a head-to-head fight. If it is contrary to reason to fail to respond to a requiring reason, but there is no rational requirement that one respond to an enticer, then reason, we might say, requires that the requirer wins.[11] This

---

[11] I don't think we should be muddled by the apparently parallel thought that enticers 'entice' that the enticer wins. This is just one expression of the idea that all reasons win *in their own terms*. Horticultural reasons, for example, defeat moral ones in gardening terms. The point in the main text is merely that one lays oneself open to the complaint that one has failed to respond to the nature of a certain reason if one complies with the enticer rather than with the requirer, and one does not lay oneself open to an analogous complaint if one complies with the requirer.

issue is raised by Raz's second argument against enticing reasons, to which I now turn. Assume that enticing reasons cannot defeat requiring reasons, though they can defeat weaker enticers (not, however, in a way that makes it contrary to reason to yield to the weaker enticement). Now suppose that Mary has enticing reason to go to the last night of the play this evening, and requiring reason to visit her aged mother. The reason requiring her to visit her mother does not require her to do so this evening. Mary could go any day this week. So as a requiring reason it is not very strong—or perhaps we should say that though strong it is unfocused. The question that Raz asks is this: 'if the enticing reason to go to the play could have justified her deferring the visit to the next day, does it not show that enticing reasons can defeat requiring ones?'[12] If so, he suggests, there is no relevant difference between enticers and requirers; it is just a question of strong versus weak. For wherever an enticer defeats a requirer, it will be wrong (contrary to reason) to do what the requirer requires. And this will convert the enticer into a requirer.

There is something odd about this example, because Mary's requiring reason is not a reason to visit her mother this evening, while the enticing reason only applies to this one evening. So the conflict between them is not a direct conflict. If it were a direct conflict, the requirer would certainly win, so long as it is stronger than negligible. (This is not the same as saying that moral requirers always defeat other requirers.) But as things stand, Mary will not have acted in breach of the requiring reason if by the end of the week she has made the required visit. So I don't really see the difficulty at this stage. Deferring her visit until the next day is not something that Mary needs to have a reason to do, if she is to escape censure for doing so.

One might think that the difficulty could be revived in the following way. Suppose that Mary has an enticing reason for each day of the week, and a requiring reason to visit her mother on at least one day, unspecified. What is to happen? The situation seems to me to be like this. On each day, Mary has a choice, and faces no censure whatever she chooses, until she gets to the last day. On the last day, assuming that the visit has not yet been made, it must be made, and the enticer is powerless.

I conclude that Raz's attempt to show the notion of an enticing reason to be incoherent is a failure. But it has raised significant issues about

---

[12] Raz, *Engaging Reason*, 102.

exactly how we are to conceive of an enticer, to which I now turn. If we want to know what is the real difference between enticers and others, what resources have we to call on? The following possibilities have all been thrown up, implicitly or explicitly, in what has gone before:

1. *Lexical domination*: any requiring reason can defeat any enticer.
2. *Styles of criticism*: mishandling of enticing reasons invites special sorts of criticism, and the use of members of a distinctive family of thick concepts (e.g., the silly rather than the irrational).
3. *No oughts*: no matter how strong our enticing reasons, they never generate an 'ought' (or a 'right', or a 'wrong').
4. *Discounting*: an agent may discount his own enticing reasons.
5. *Permissibility*: it is always permissible to choose not to do the action one has most enticing reason to do.

Which, if any, of these is really the central point? It cannot be *lexical domination*, one would say, since even if we allow that any requiring reason can defeat any enticer, we want to know why, and the answer to this question seems to be given by something like *no oughts* or *permissibility*. Nor, I would think, can the central point be *styles of criticism*. For, again, we would want to know what makes this family of thick concepts distinctive—that is, what is distinctive about the sort of praise or criticism that they bring along with them? And, again, it seems as if the answer to this question might be given by *no oughts*, or by *permissibility*. So it seems as if the first two possibilities cannot stand independently, which reduces us to the last three. But *no oughts* can be challenged. John Broome suggested to me that we can have pretty weak (though still overall) oughts. If so, why bother denying that enticers can generate such a thing? At least where there is a considerable difference between the strength of one enticer and another, there is rational criticism (that is, criticism of the rational sort) of someone who fails to choose to act in accordance with the stronger reason. This is just what I was after when I said, of such a person, that he would be plain silly. Broome's view is that one ought not to be plain silly.

Suppose that we accept this view. This would deprive us of *no oughts*. It would not itself unsettle *discounting*, or *permissibility*, but it would show that the latter notions are going to have to be rather special in this connection. On the *discounting* front, normally (and I have supererogation in mind here) that which is discounted is not an ought—or the ground for an 'ought'; by discounting it one exactly prevents the formation of the 'ought'—that is the whole purpose of discounting. Surely, we might say, to discount a reason is to prevent it from contributing to the overall level at which 'oughts' are to be found. But the sort of discounting we are engaged in with enticers would, if Broome were right, be the discounting of 'oughts'. One ought to choose the strongest enticer, though it is somehow rationally permissible not to. This throws the pressure on to *permissibility*. Normally we would say that if one ought to do something, it is *not* permissible not to. But we are now supposing that though (in the weak sense) one ought to choose the strongest enticer, it is permissible to choose a weaker one. One ought to do this, but it is not wrong not to do it; one ought to do this, but one has a right not to. These remarks seem to make sense in the present context, whereas in ordinary discussion of moral reasons they would be thought to be straightforwardly contradictory. So permissibility for enticers is not the same thing as permissibility for requirers. This is not impossible. The familiar notion of permissibility—the one that is defined in terms of 'oughts'—was created by people who had not considered the possibility of enticing reasons. If we understand a permissible action as one that it is not wrong to do, and a wrong action as one that it is not permissible to do, we get a nice interconnection which reminds us strongly of the relation between necessity and possibility. But if we once allow that there can be an action that we ought to do but which it is not wrong not to do, or which it is permissible not to do, that nice interconnection between the various deontic concepts (ought, right, wrong, permissible) fails.

Note that Broome's point only concerned 'ought'. Perhaps one ought to do the action which entices most strongly (in the weak sense of ought), but it is not wrong not to do so. It is not only permissibility, then, whose tight link with 'ought' has been broken; the link between 'ought' and 'wrong' has been broken too. Perhaps *no oughts* should be renamed *no wrongs*.

I said that the notion of permissibility at issue here is not the one we are used to. A further respect in which that will be true is that ordinarily, where something is permissible, no criticism is attracted by those who choose it. But here, we are supposing, even though it is, in a sense, permissible to choose a noticeably less enticing option, criticism is still appropriate. As we might say, you can do this but it would be pretty silly of you to do so. We might even say that though it is silly, you have a perfect right to make that choice. This is not itself unfamiliar. We say, perhaps, that you have a right to gamble all your money away, even though this is something that you should not (ought not to) do. You have a right to do it, but this does not mean that you are immune from criticism if you decide to do so.

But what might it mean to say that you have a right to do this, or that it is permissible to do it, even though you ought not to do it and can be criticized quite severely if you do? Can these notions really survive if their normal connections with 'oughts' are severed? Let us not forget that most of the difficulties that have emerged stem from admitting Broome's claim that there is a sort of weak 'ought' operating here; if we had chosen to tough it out, we could have insisted that there are no 'oughts', not even weak ones, but that there is discountability (of the normal type) and permissibility (again of a normal type). And it does seem to me that toughing it out is the best way forward here for someone interested in making sense of enticers. Doing so restores the standard connections between discountability, permissibility, 'wrong', and 'ought', whose rupture caused us all the complications we have just been struggling through.

But even if we do choose to tough it out, there is still the idea that one has a right to discount, a right to choose the less enticing option. What sort of right is that? There is one clear difference between the sort of right that we would be dealing with here and anything worth thinking of as a moral right. This is that moral rights are rights *against* other agents, as it is usually, though rather unbeautifully, put. What this means is that if I have a right to do it, it is wrong of you to do anything to prevent me. We get something of this with enticers. If I have a perfect right to do an enticing action (of any sort, now, whether it be the strongest enticer or not), this can only be because I have no moral reason not to do it, and so I already have a moral right to do it; it would, therefore, be wrong of you to interfere. In this sense, my right is a right against others, just like any other. But that is not the point. The point is that I have a right to choose the less enticing action even if I ought (in the weak sense) to choose the most enticing. Though I suppose one could say that you ought not to interfere in order to make me choose the most enticing action, this hardly seems to be the right point to focus on. The real point seems to be that certain sorts of criticism are not appropriate. But this throws us back to our starting-point.

Can we now do better? What sort of criticism is inappropriate? I have already suggested that selecting the less enticing option should not be thought of as irrational. We would be more likely to think of a person who does this as silly. Does this amount to anything more than saying that severe criticism of the rational sort is not appropriate in this type of case? Mild criticism, on the other hand, is fine. If that were all there is to it, the idea that enticing reasons are distinctive would be under some threat. Mild criticism of the rational sort is appropriate in many cases where we are dealing only with requiring reasons. We might keep going by pointing out that the severity of the criticism should be somehow related to the disparity between the reasons. If criticism of someone who selects an enormously less enticing option is still only mild, this would itself be significant. But I think there is more to be said. The idea is that there is a sort of blip in the judgement of someone who decides to take one option when he knows full well that another is more required. Such a person asks himself the question what is the thing to do, and then fails to attend to his own answer. There is no such blip in the judgement of someone who prefers the less enticing option. That person may have decided that the more normative question 'What is the thing to do?' has no answer in the present case. But this does not mean that nothing is left to determine his choice. He starts by asking 'What shall I do?' If he decides that there is one course of action that is the one to do, that is the way he has to go, on pain of the blip. But if he decides that nothing is here required of him, he can continue to ask 'What shall I do' by asking what it would be nice to do, and he can then act according to his answer to that question. But he is not at odds with his answer to it if he decides to do something nice enough, but less nice than something else.

I return to these issues in my final section.

2. The Contributory and the Overall

If there are such things as enticers, why have they escaped notice? A possible answer to this question is that we have all been working with a general conception of what I call a contributory reason, which obscures the possibility of enticers, but which is in fact mistaken. The *locus classicus* of this mistaken conception is Jean Hampton's posthumously published *The Authority of Reason*.[13] When Hampton talks about reasons, she constantly uses terms that are, one would have thought, quite inappropriate for the merely contributory. She says that reasons are 'directive' (pp. 51, 85), have

---

[13] J. E. Hampton, *The Authority of Reason* (Cambridge: Cambridge University Press, 1998). Parenthetical page references in this section are to this book.

'obligatory force' (p. 99), have 'compelling rightness' (pp. 93, 99), are 'prescriptive' (p. 87), are or express commands (p. 88), concern the 'ought to be' (p. 92), 'feel like orders' (p. 106), and have a 'compelling quality' (pp. 91–2). But all these remarks seem to be more appropriate at the overall level. An overall 'ought', we might say, is a directive; in a perfectly clear sense (at least for present purposes), it tells us what to do—what we should do. It expresses a command, maybe; it has a compelling quality; it has 'obligatory force' in some sense or other; it feels like an order and directs us to do this rather than that. The question, then, is whether contributory reasons do the same as the overall does. And the answer is surely that they don't. If an overall 'ought' commands, it cannot be that contributory reasons command as well; there is no such thing as a *pro tanto* command. We have reasons on both sides of the question, often enough. Is it that each reason on either side commands, and then that somehow the sum total of them commands as well? I don't think this is a coherent scenario; there are too many commands floating about.

Raz's notion of a requiring reason, and of a 'demanding' reason, are vulnerable to similar criticism. For contributory reasons neither require nor demand, whether they are on the winning or the losing side. Of course they do do something that is a *bit like* requiring; though it would be inadequate to say that they do something like requiring but weaker. Requiring and demanding are things that, though they come in degrees, happen only at the overall level. So from now on we will have to abandon Raz's contrast between the enticing and the requiring. What is more, the way in which I started this paper, where I talked of reasons that are in the business of more or less telling us what to do, or of saying 'You'd better do this', will have to go as well.

My main point here is that if one does think of the contributory as requiring, compelling, or demanding, the idea of an enticing reason is probably not going to occur to one at all. And if it does occur, it will probably be only in a distorted form. Hampton does sometimes speak in ways that look as if they are intended to capture the enticing. She talks of reasons as having 'a pull, an attractiveness' (pp. 91–2), and at one point discusses the nature of a reason to have a haircut on Sunday afternoon. This looks like an enticer, I think; the idea is not that she ought to have her hair cut on Sunday afternoon, but that going to the hairdresser might be an agreeable relaxation. But Hampton distorts this reason in two ways. First, she has already cast all such reasons as 'directives', which is surely part of what lies behind her thinking of them as commands. A directive sounds pretty like a requirer to me. Second, she attempts to use Raz's distinction between mandatory and permissive reasons to capture the difference between her reason to have a haircut and her reason to care for her baby. She writes, 'some reasons command us, and thereby give us mandates, and others direct us in ways that indicate permissions, rather than commands' (p. 90). But this is surely wrong. It is not that I am permitted to have a haircut on Sunday (though let us suppose that I am, and that without this permission the enticing reason to do so would be silenced). It is that there is a reason in favour of doing so, which cannot be simply that it is permitted nor what makes it permissible.[14] Where there is permission but no favouring consideration, there is normally no reason, and all that we have is the absence of reasons against.

One might reply here that Hampton has just chosen the wrong terminology. Permissions are indeed not what is at issue in the debate about enticers; but Hampton's substantial remarks show that she does not really mean to appeal to the notion of permission. After all, she says that these reasons 'merely guide us' (p. 90)—as opposed, I suppose, to requiring us. This talk of guiding, however, is no improvement on what we have seen already. It is common to use the notion of guiding for overall oughts. My course of action is surely guided by thoughts about what I ought overall to do. (I don't necessarily go on to do those things, sadly.) Is it the case that I am guided also by thoughts about contributory reasons? Well, yes it is, but it cannot be the same sort of guiding as before, on pain of incoherence. Hampton's talk of guiding only shows, I think, that though she means to distinguish guiding from requiring, or something like that, both of these notions find their place within a general concept of a directing reason—a directive.

It is within the domain of the directive that the distinction between the mandatory and the permissive is to be found. The notion of a directive, like that of the mandatory, is deontic. It is tightly related to oughts. The notion of an enticer is not deontic, since no oughts are involved (as we eventually decided); this is what makes it significant as a possibility within the theory of reasons, since it is normal to see people casting the general notion of a reason within the deontic *rather than* the evaluative domain. (Both of these domains lie, supposedly, within the more general domain of

---

[14] I don't mean that the fact that something is permitted can never be a reason to do it, only that it is not in this case, let us suppose.

the normative.) What about the notion of a permission? Well, a permission is normally understood as the absence of an 'ought-not', and so functions in the deontic domain—the domain of directives, one might say. And Hampton says that permissives are like mandatory reasons in having a sort of 'compelling rightness' (p. 91). This shows, I think, that the real mistake is to start with the notion of a directive and then try to put everything under that label; Hampton is, hopelessly, trying to do everything in terms of force, compulsion, and necessity. Attractiveness, grounded in enticing reasons, is nothing at all like compelling force, grounded in mandating reasons—even though there are attractions that one cannot resist. The absence of a mandating reason is not itself an enticing reason.

If all this is right, Hampton's attempt to capture what she calls 'the authority of reasons' in terms of anything like an obligatory force (p. 99) is a mistake. If there is such a thing as a single style of authority belonging to all reasons, we need a quite different account of it.

One possibility that has not yet been mentioned is that we should try to understand the authority of reasons by saying that reasons apply to us irrespective of what we like, what we want, or what appeals to us. But though moral reasons may be like this, it is extremely contentious to say the same about practical reasons in general; and to do so would leave no room for enticing reasons in particular. What is enticing for one person is not for another, and properly so. (This is another interesting aspect of the enticing.) Perhaps we are going to find ourselves driven to saying that only some reasons have the sort of authority that Hampton is talking about. But if we say this, have we abandoned the attempt to isolate the normative nature of reasons? Is it that enticing reasons are not 'normative' at all? They are, after all, capable of rendering an action intelligible, sensible, worth doing, and so on. I now turn, therefore, to consider what could be meant by saying that the very notion of a reason is a normative notion.

3. The Normativity of Reasons

Raz claims that '[t]he normativity of all that is normative consists in the way it is, or provides, or is otherwise related to reasons'.[15] Let us distinguish between two questions:

---

[15] Raz, *Engaging Reason*, 67.

1. Is there one normative concept in terms of which all others can be defined, or at least understood?
2. Is there one normative concept in terms of whose normativity the normativity of all other terms can be understood?

Raz's remark, quoted above, hovers between these questions. He doesn't exactly say that the normativity of other concepts is related to the normativity of the concept of a reason. But he doesn't quite commit himself to the view that other normative concepts can be defined in terms of a reason either.

It is possible that even if the answer to the first question is no, the answer to the second is yes. It is possible, for instance, that there are various normative concepts, forming a local holism, so that each member of the normative family can be understood in terms of its relations to the others, and none is more basic than any other. Even so, it might be that the notion of normativity is centrally to be understood in terms of one member of the family, that of reason.

It is however possible that there is one central normative concept in terms of which all other normative concepts can be defined and which cannot itself be defined in terms of others. If so, it would be very tempting to try to understand the normativity of the other concepts in terms of that of the central concept. And many people think this is the way things actually are. For many, there is one central normative concept, that of 'ought', and all other normative concepts can be defined in terms of some relation to 'ought', and in this way get their normativity from that of 'ought'.

This picture is not Raz's picture, and there is a weakness in it, which is that it simply takes for granted (at least as we have expressed it so far) the normativity of 'ought'. If asked to say what makes 'ought' normative, it is hard to find an answer because there is nothing left to say. Raz's picture, however, has the same weakness, because he doesn't really tell us what makes the concept of a reason normative. I don't see how one could make progress without saying something about how to conceive of normativity itself.

The fact that one ought to do this rather than that, and the fact that one has reason to do this rather than that, bear their practical relevance on their face; they are explicit answers to the question what to do. Let us suppose that the central concepts in such facts, those of 'ought' and of 'reason', are therefore pivotal members of a special family of concepts, the family of normative concepts. We need not be sure yet which other concepts are members of this family. (Perhaps the concept of relevance is one such.) Any fact expressed in ways in which those concepts play no role may have practical relevance; some such facts are perhaps necessarily practically relevant. But that such facts are practically relevant is a further fact about them. As Derek Parfit puts it,[16] a fact that has normative significance need not for that reason be a normative fact. The difference here is between facts that might be mentioned in answers to the question what to do, and the facts that those facts are relevant to the question what to do. To give a *very* contentious example of this difference: the fact that this action would make many more comfortable and none less comfortable could well be mentioned in an answer to the question whether it is the thing to do, but is not the same fact as the fact that it is relevant to what to do. On this account, therefore, it is not a normative fact, though it is a fact of normative significance, one that makes a difference to what to do.

Some normative facts, then, are more complex than the simple fact that one ought to do this; they contain that fact, but they also contain what makes that simple fact the case. Such facts are of this form: that p makes it the case that one ought (or has reason) to act in way w. These meta-facts are facts about some matter-of-fact and about its making a difference to how to act. They constitute direct answers not only to the practical question what to do, but to the question why. It is these meta-facts that I think of as the central normative facts, by reference to which the normativity of all others is to be understood. Each such fact is the fact that some other fact stands in a certain normative relation to an action (or a belief or a feeling or a desire . . .); we have mentioned two such normative relations, that of 'being a reason for' and that of 'making it the case that one ought'. Let us hope that these will prove to be enough.

If this is to be our starting-point, the question whether we are to conceive of enticing reasons as normative is not decided by the fact that they do not generate 'oughts', for our account of the normative does not require anything of the sort. It would be enough if enticers can be thought of as relevantly similar to other reasons. Let us now fix on a term for the 'other reasons'. We have already decided that ordinary contributory reasons neither

---

[16] Derek Parfit, 'Reasons and Motivation', *Proceedings of the Aristotelian Society*, suppl. vol. 71 (1997), 99–130.

require, nor command, nor direct. But they are, I would say, still *peremptory* in style. So from now on I will work with a distinction between enticing reasons and peremptory reasons. The peremptory ones were the ones I had primarily in mind in laying out my conception of normativity. The question now is whether that conception is sufficiently flexible to allow us to think of enticing reasons as normative. I am going to suggest that it is.

One way to capture what it is that peremptory contributory reasons do is to say that they stand in a certain normative relation to action, the favouring relation. A reason for doing an action is a consideration which counts in favour of that action; it makes an independent contribution to the case for doing it. As far as this goes, there is no problem in thinking of enticing reasons as standing in just such a relation to the actions which they are reasons to do. We will want, of course, to distinguish the style of favouring done by peremptors from the style of that done by enticers. But this is just the old question of the difference between the peremptory and the enticing—a question which needs further consideration but which should not alarm us.

In particular, no special problem derives from the suspect thought that the concept of a reason is a deontic concept rather than an evaluative one. (Here I am just underlining a point that I made in section 2.) We have already seen that attempts to capture what contributory peremptors do in deontic-sounding terms like 'command', 'require', and 'direct' are all failures. The only way we can retain our sense that these peremptors are deontic is to try to characterize what they do in terms of some relation to 'oughts'. This is a big topic, but my own view is that every attempt to do this is a failure[17]—except possibly for one. The one survivor is the claim that if there is a reason in favour of doing something and no reason against, one ought to do it. I don't see a big difference between this claim and the claim that if there is more reason to do something than to do anything else, one ought to do it. These things may (both?) be true; and it is true that, on our present showing, enticing reasons do not generate 'oughts' in this sort of way. But if this relation to 'oughts' is all that being deontic amounts to, it is not a *further* difference between enticers and peremptors. It is just the same difference again. Introducing the notion of the deontic is not a step forward.

---

[17] I argue this point in detail in ch. 2 of my forthcoming *Ethics without Principles* (Oxford: Oxford University Press).

So far, so good. The difficulty, if there is one, in understanding enticing reasons as normative derives from the way I tried to explicate the notion of normativity. Normative concepts are those which play pivotal roles in direct answers to the question what to do. Now: is the question what to do the question to which specification of enticing reasons as reasons is an answer? If it is not, enticing reasons are not normative in the way that peremptory ones are. And there are two views one could take on this issue. One could say that the question what to do is one to which one could respond by saying that there is no action here that is the thing to do, and that this leaves us free to concentrate on which action would be most fun. Or one could say that in the absence of peremptory reasons, the most enticing course is the thing to do.

The question 'What is the thing to do?' is perhaps not quite the same as the question 'What shall I do?' There is a similar difference, it seems, between the question 'What should I decide to do?' and the question 'What shall I decide to do?' To the latter question, there is no doubt that specification of enticing considerations as reasons is directly relevant; to the former one, not. But which of these questions was the one we were thinking of as 'the practical question'? If it was the former, there was a covert appeal to an 'ought' in setting up the notion of normativity, and that was something that I was trying to avoid. It must therefore have been the latter. But to that question, the answer 'You have enticing reason to do this rather than that' is directly relevant, and in this sense the notion of an enticing reason is as normative as the notion of any other sort of reason.[18]

In thinking of things in this way, we are weakening the notion of the normative. The question 'What shall I do?' is less deontic in style than the question 'What should I do?', but we are understanding the normative in terms of the former rather than the latter.

Nobody denies that enticers speak in favour of the action they commend. They may speak in a discountable way (that is, one can discount what they say), and they may commend rather than recommend. But this favouring, or speaking in favour of, seems none the less to be recognizably similar as such to other more peremptory sorts of favouring. If that is right, my overall suggestion is that we should weaken our conception of the

---

[18] Of course, the answer 'This would be more pleasant than that' is not the same answer as any answer that explicitly uses the concept of a reason. (This is just an echo of Parfit's distinction between what is of normative significance and what is normative.)

normative so as to include all forms of the favouring relation, the non-peremptory as well as the peremptory.[19] Being normative, in this weaker sense, will turn out to have nothing especially to do with norms—at least, not in the way that we usually think of norms.

One consideration that supports this weakening of the concept of the normative is that the debate between naturalists and non-naturalists about the irreducibility or otherwise of the normative in general seems to apply just as much to the weaker, non-peremptory sort of favouring as to the stronger, peremptory sort. The reducibility or otherwise of the weaker relation that stands between that which entices and the action that it favours (or commends) is going to be as interesting and contentious—from the naturalist's point of view—as that of the strong relation of requiring. If it is normativity *as such* that engages the reductivist aspirations of naturalism, this is further evidence that we would be wrong to think of enticing reasons as non-normative.

Another commonality between peremptors and enticers is a functional one: they are both notions that have a place within the context of practical deliberation, being considerations relevant to the substantive questions from which deliberation begins, and which it aims to resolve (either 'What shall I do?' or 'What is the thing to do?'). And we see the same structure both sides, the structure given us by the distinction between the contributory and the overall; we see the same relation between considerations favouring one alternative and those favouring another, and the same relation between considerations favouring one alternative and those disfavouring it. (There is a difference between speaking against an option and speaking in favour of something else.)

These common features, which I invoke in order to increase our confidence that enticers can be thought of as normative, will of course make it

---

[19] One might wonder whether Broome's normative requirements would be left out of account, on this approach, so that there would remain something normative whose normativity we have failed to capture. The matter will turn on whether we are to think of a normative requirement in this sense as anything more than a non-detachable requirement on a complex. In his 'Normative Requirements' Broome did think there was more to a requirement than that, but, as I understand it, he now thinks, as I always did, that the whole story of these requirements can be told in terms of non-detachability. If so, the normativity of these requirements will be able to be told in the terms I suggest. For any such non-detachable requirement will be a reason, or an ought. For instance, the requirement that if one believes that p and that $(p \rightarrow q)$ one should also believe that q amounts to no more than that one non-detachably ought not to believe that p and that $(p \rightarrow q)$ and fail to believe that q.

harder to show that enticers are really as different from peremptors as I have earlier tried to suggest. The more we stress the similarities between the two, the harder it will be to draw the sort of distinction I appealed to; in particular, the harder it will be to say that peremptors generate 'oughts' while enticers do not. I now return, therefore, to that issue.

4. The Difference between Enticing and Peremptory Reasons

If there are both enticing and peremptory reasons, there must be a difference between them. Reasons of both sorts favour, perhaps; but they must favour in different ways, if one sort of favouring can somehow generate an 'ought' and the other cannot. Up to now, I have been talking about a difference in style. Can we say any more about this difference?

One might think it would be enough here to say that peremptory reasons are reasons that one has no right simply to discount; the relevant agent is not in charge here. One is not ordinarily rationally permitted to discount a peremptory reason. By contrast, one can discount enticing reasons of one's own (though not those of others), without thereby causing them to cease to be reasons.

We have seen something like this phenomenon of discountability elsewhere, in the theory of supererogation, and indeed more generally in the theory of agent-relative reasons. In the case of supererogation, I will assume the picture for which I argued in my *Moral Reasons* (chs. 8 and 12). This has it that the reason for me to sacrifice myself is (let us suppose) that three others will die if I hold back. This reason is non-discountable. If it is not to make it wrong for me not to sacrifice my life for the sake of the others, some other reasons must be found on the other side. Naturally we should not ignore such considerations as the loss to me, but this is obviously less of a reason as it stands than the combined losses to the other three. The question is how to work it so that, despite this imbalance, reason does not require me to sacrifice myself; we hope somehow to leave it that I act outstandingly well if I make the sacrifice, but that I do not act against the reasons if I fail to do so. If one is to achieve this while working solely within the realm of reasons, one must, it seems, resort to factoring in some supposedly agent-relative reasons, all the neutral reasons having been counted in already. Suppose now that we find some agent-relative reasons capable of justifying my failing to sacrifice myself. We do not want to say that the balance of reasons now makes the sacrifice wrong, if I choose to make it. The way in which we avoid saying this is by announcing that the agent-relative reasons are discountable by the agent.[20] The other reasons, assuming that none of them are enticers, are non-discountable.

Nothing in this picture requires, however, that any of the relevant reasons are enticers. It may be that the agent-relative reasons, though discountable, are not to do with the fun, the amusing, the attractive, and so on. The cost to me may lie not in the loss of amusement or anything like that, but rather in things to do with the education, health, or safety of my (soon to be orphaned) children. The whole story of supererogation given above makes no essential appeal to non-peremptory reasons. This is what makes the phenomenon of supererogation noticeably more puzzling than that of discountable enticers, for in the former the reasons that are supposedly discountable are also, as we are now saying, peremptory. A discountable enticer seems much less problematic, from a theoretical point of view, than a discountable peremptor. Still, the important point is that if there are discountable peremptors, it cannot be right to understand the difference between enticing and peremptory reasons in terms of what is and what is not discountable.[21]

One thing gained by this brief discussion of supererogation is that it seems to show that normativity and discountability are not themselves at odds, which is of some help in the defence of enticing reasons. There needs, of course, to be an explanation of discountability wherever it occurs. But this is no difficulty in the present case, since our explanation of the discountability of enticers will simply appeal to the larger idea that agents are entitled to put themselves second. (This is not much of an explanation, perhaps, though I try to defend it in *Moral Reasons*, sect. 12.2.) There is, then, no general argument that enticers cannot be normative because they are discountable. But we still lack an account of the difference in style between the enticing and the peremptory.

---

[20] In the terms that Thomas Nagel uses in his *The View from Nowhere* (New York: Oxford University Press, 1986), the agent-relative reason is non-insistent; all the neutral reasons are insistent.

[21] In terms of the non-insistent, some peremptory reasons are non-insistent (if the above account of supererogation is on the right lines.

We might resuscitate here a suggestion that we previously rejected as an account of the authority of reasons. On those lines, we would say that a peremptory reason applies to us irrespective of our current likes and dislikes, enthusiasms and affections. Enticing reasons are not like this. Now if this is the difference, it is (and is only) a difference in ground. The idea would have to be that the difference in ground comes with a difference in the kind of favouring relation that lies between that ground and the relevant action. But can we extract a difference in favouring relation from a (supposed) difference in what comes on the left-hand side of it—in what is doing the favouring? Not directly, I would think.

The point is not that there are some peremptory reasons which are equally dependent on subjective conditions of likes, affections, and so on. To make that point, we might try to appeal to the duties of friendship, for example, or at least to the sorts of reasons given us by the troubles our friends get into. Relations of friendship are conditional (in some sense) on affection and liking. So, one might say, the reasons of friendship are as dependent on subjective conditions as are any enticing reasons we may have. But I would not accept this picture. We are dealing with different sorts of dependence. It is true that friendship generates peremptory reasons, and that those reasons would not exist in the absence of the subjective conditions that make friendship possible. But I would say that they are not *grounded* in those conditions in the way that enticing reasons are grounded in what one enjoys or finds amusing. It is because we find each other pleasant company that we have become friends, and by becoming friends we acquire reasons that we did not have before. There is nothing like this sort of thing with straightforward enticers, where the subjective conditions act more or less as ground.

The point is rather that one needs to do more work if a supposed difference in ground is to give one a difference in relation. And it is not obvious where to go. Suppose that, *per impossibile*, I could change my likes and dislikes at will. Would this be any help? No; we would still be facing the fact that the reasons given me by my likes and dislikes are there for me until I change what I like. So we might say that I have some reason, so long as woodwork is what I most enjoy doing of a weekend, to spend my weekends at the work-bench; it is irrelevant that this reason becomes ineffectual as soon as I come to prefer music to woodwork.[22]

---

[22] In different terms, the reason here is a non-detachable one on a combination: having the preference for woodwork and spending my weekends at the bench.

What, then, can we appeal to? Let us take a step back for a moment and ask what we would take as showing a difference between two favouring relations. We have already decided that a difference in ground is not enough. Ground is input. What about a difference at the output level? This looks more promising. Whether the input is the same or different, if the output is different, it looks as if we must be dealing with a different relation. Now we already have a supposed difference in output, since we have often claimed that peremptory reasons take us to 'oughts', while enticing reasons don't. This, then, seems to be the right sort of claim. But it itself seemed to be in need of explanation. It seemed that this could not be all there was to be said, for a difference of this sort cannot be a 'brute' difference. This is the present state of play.

But it might improve matters if instead of saying what enticing reasons don't do, we say what they do do. Here is a suggestion of that sort. Peremptory reasons take us to 'oughts', and enticing reasons take us to 'bests'. If this suggestion could be substantiated, we would have given a sense to the initially attractive idea that peremptors have a deontic focus, while enticers have an evaluative focus. We would also have sustained the normativity of enticers as similar to, but not the same as, that of peremptors.

It would be a mistake to object to this that the reasons in favour of supererogatory acts take us only to bests, not to oughts. It is true that they don't succeed in taking us to an ought (always supposing that the notion of supererogation is coherent). But the idea of taking us to an 'ought' that I am appealing to here is not that of *succeeding* in generating an 'ought'; for otherwise there would be no defeated peremptory reasons. To take us to an 'ought' is, in the sense I am after, to *try* to generate an 'ought', but not yet to succeed. Similarly, enticers try to generate a 'best', though they may not succeed either, and won't if something else generates a 'better'.

But don't some peremptory reasons take us to 'bests'? Yes, they do; but they also take us to 'oughts'. In saying what it is that enticers do, we have not avoided the idea that the main difference between them and peremptors lies in something with a deontic focus that enticers are not involved in. The point is rather that we can understand the idea that enticers are *reasons* by showing that they have a focus which is like, but different from, the sort of focus that peremptors have. (Here we can appeal to the commonalities mentioned at the end of the previous section.) They go to make a choice the best one, but not yet the one which one ought to take.

At the end of the first section I suggested, on behalf of the possibility of enticers, that there is a blip in the judgement of someone who, recognizing an 'ought', failed to respect that 'ought' in deciding what to do; such a person is one whose judgement is at odds with itself, I said. But I maintained that there is no such blip when one decides to do one thing when one recognizes that another would be more pleasant, and so better. The things I said about normativity in the previous section only serve to make this picture harder to defend. In broad terms, I was trying to build the notion of normativity on that of practical relevance. Isn't there a blip in the judgement of someone who recognizes that one car would be better than another but buys the worse one? Certainly, if there are peremptory reasons around—better brakes, for instance. But what if there aren't? The way I put it at the end of the first section was that no blip occurs if one chooses an option that is nice enough, even if one allows that another would be nicer. This is an appeal to satisficing. The idea was that there is a level above which no blip occurs whatever one chooses. So long as an option is enticing enough, one may choose it bliplessly. But the difficulty for this idea is that the agent seems to be ignoring something which by his own lights is practically relevant: namely, that some other option would be better. Why isn't this just another blip—and one not very different in style from the first one? The difference between 'best' and 'right' or 'ought' doesn't seem to get a grip here.

It is hard to be quite sure what is supposed to be explaining what at this point. I think the real pressure is only to make sure that the two aspects of the position are consistent. The two aspects are the idea of the absence of blips and the distinction between 'bests' and 'oughts'. The latter was introduced not so as to explain the former, but so as to help us accept that enticing is a favouring relation of a different style from that of the more familiar peremptory reasons. The idea of the absence of a blip was introduced in order to give some form to the idea that certain styles of criticism are not appropriate when we are dealing with enticers. The crucial question is, therefore, whether the person who says that one option would be best but that he is going to prefer another is vulnerable to criticism of the very same style as that appropriate when we fail to select the option we know we ought to select.

The person who asks what is the thing to do, answers his own question, and then fails to select that option is failing to attend to the results of his own deliberation. But when I ask 'What shall I do?', I am in a rather different case. The decision that one option is more pleasant, and from that point of view better, is not itself the decision that this is 'what I shall do'. So in failing to select that option my judgement is not at odds with itself. There is, that is, a gap between the product of evaluative deliberation and choice that we do not find between the product of deontic deliberation and choice. When I rank options for pleasurability, I do so on the way to a decision, but the ranking I emerge with lies at a distance from the decision that I will make in the light of it. What I want to know is how much fun each option will be, and in what way, and I can express my discoveries in terms of what is more or less enticing, and in those terms better or worse. With that information I will choose, but there is not the same sense that my choice has effectively already been made as there is when I have already answered the question what to do. In this way, it seems possible to suggest that the deontic blip is not present on the evaluative side.[23]

Of course, for anything like this suggestion to work, there will have to be the sort of difference between 'ought' and 'best' that some positions are officially opposed to. But we knew already that the possibility of enticers would be easier to make out on some views than on others.[24]

---

[23] One might say, in reply, that on the evaluative side the blip is that of failing to prefer (choose) what one has already preferred (judged better); in doing so, one is at odds with oneself. But to say this would be to appeal to the notorious ambiguity of 'prefer'.

[24] I am most grateful to Michael Ridge for extensive comments on earlier drafts, and also to John Broome, Roger Crisp, Brad Hooker, Christopher Hookway, Derek Parfit, and Philip Stratton-Lake for lively discussion of these issues. Comments from Jay Wallace made an enormous difference to a penultimate draft that had got out of control. I am also grateful to the British Academy for the award of a Research Readership, during my tenure of which this paper was written.

5

Disengaging Reason

Harry Frankfurt

1. The philosophical thought of Joseph Raz is characterized by provoca-
tively creative insight, remarkable analytical penetration, refreshingly
humane judgement, and a steady and far-reaching logical grasp. These
have enabled him to develop comprehensive and compelling structures of
theory and argument. Moreover, Raz is especially notable among those
who are deeply concerned with the issues to which he has devoted his
efforts, in that he is so far from being an ideologue. In articulating and
elaborating his moral and social vision, he is never moralistic or sentimen-
tal. On the contrary, he is guided invariably by a severe and selfless commitment to the most austere ideals of objectivity and of reason.

It seems to me, however, that Raz—like many philosophers—assigns to
reason a greater significance in our lives than it actually possesses. I do not
mean by this, of course, that there is something wrong in his conscientious
dedication to exploring the demands of rationality and seeking to comply
with them. Attempts like his to understand what reason requires, and to
satisfy those requirements, are valuable not merely because they are prudent or because they may be productive. They are foundational conditions
of human dignity—admirable in themselves, and indispensable to a civil-
ized culture. Nor, in suggesting that Raz exaggerates the significance of
reason in human life, do I mean that he overestimates either the extent to
which our thoughts and actions are genuinely reasonable or the extent
to which it is plausible to expect them to become so. To his astringent
intelligence, it is only too clear how often we behave foolishly, how rarely

our thinking meets even quite modest standards of rigour and coherence, and how improbable it is that this will change.

The difficulty I find in Raz's thought, then, is neither that he relies too heavily upon reason in developing and in recommending his views, nor that he is excessively optimistic concerning how far people do or might possibly manage to live up to the ideals of rationality. Rather, the difficulty as I see it is that he misjudges how indispensably the faculty of reason is engaged in constituting various structures and capacities that are distinctive of human life. In my opinion, the role of reason in making certain characteristic features of our experience possible is less decisive, and indeed less pertinent, than he supposes.

2. We are accustomed to accepting, as an authentic representation of the essential nature of our species, the ancient definition that man is a rational animal. According to this familiar conception of ourselves, it is by our rationality that we human beings are basically differentiated from other animals. What is not only unique about us, but what makes us distinctively human, is that we possess the precious faculty of reason. From this it follows that the most characteristically human aspects of our lives must necessarily be grounded in, or fundamentally dependent upon, the fact that we are rational creatures.

It is only to be expected, accordingly, that those who understand being human as a matter of being a rational animal will tend to assume that reason plays an essential role in the constitution of those capacities and possibilities that are central to our humanity.[1] The truth is, however, that rationality is not the only characteristic that it is plausible to regard as differentiating human beings in significant ways from the members of all other animal species. In fact, I believe, certain basic features of human life—which Raz mistakenly considers to be functions of rationality—do not actually depend upon the faculty of reason at all. They derive from other faculties, distinct from reason, that also do not appear to be possessed by any non-human animal and that contribute very substantially to what we are inclined to think of as especially human aspects of our lives.

In particular, there are the faculties of reflexive self-consciousness and of volition. It is by the exercise of these that we are capable both of introducing a division within ourselves, which in a certain way separates us from

---

[1] I have no particular reason to suppose, and do not mean to suggest, that Raz's thinking has actually been shaped in this way.

our own conscious states and activities, and then of coming to acquire a variety of attitudes, desires, and intentions regarding those activities and states. Our capacity to do such things is not rational or cognitive in nature. It is not basically an ability to perceive formal or other evidentiary relationships, or to fashion and grasp concepts; nor does it aim at understanding or believing or recognizing, or at anything else that might more or less plausibly be regarded as a special prerogative of reason. It is a volitional capacity, which makes it possible for us to step back from and objectify what goes on in our minds and, most critically, to accomplish a selective identification of ourselves with, or an alienation of ourselves from, elements of our own psychic life.[2]

3. I propose to consider what Raz says about the role played by reason in the constitution of two human capacities—our capacity to make choices and decisions, and our capacity to be in states of mind that are active rather than passive.[3] Each of these is of very considerable importance in shaping the character of human experience. If we were unable ever to make any choices or decisions, or if we were entirely passive with respect to all the processes and conditions of our minds, our lives would be fundamentally different than they are.

Raz maintains that reason is necessarily implicated both in making choices or decisions and in being in active states of mind. On his account, a person's state of mind is active only in so far as the person judges that state of mind to be reasonable; and an essential constituent of choosing or of making a decision is that the person has a reason for the choice or decision that he makes. In my opinion, Raz is mistaken on both counts. So far as I can see, neither choosing nor being in an active state of mind requires having a reason.[4] Choices can be made without any reason for choosing the

---

[2] Volition and reason tend to be confusingly intermingled. However, the former strikes me as more primitive than the latter, and thus as unlikely to presuppose it. My hunch is that the relationship goes the other way: reason depends upon will. I suspect that our abilities to divide ourselves by stepping back from the immediacy of our own consciousness, and then to reorganize our inner lives, are essential for even the most elementary exercise of reason.

[3] My discussion will be focused on the account that Raz develops in 'When We Are Ourselves: The Active and the Passive', one of the essays in his *Engaging Reason: On the Theory and Value of Action* (Oxford: Oxford University Press, 1999), 5–21. All page references in my text are to that volume.

[4] For the sake of convenience, I will sometimes omit an explicit reference to making decisions. It is to be understood throughout that anything said about choice extends to decisions as well.

option that is chosen, and, indeed, without any reason for making a choice to begin with; and a person's state of mind may be active rather than passive even though it is not true that the person judges his state of mind to be reasonable. A person can make choices and decisions, and he can be in active states of mind, even without engaging his reason at all.

4. According to Raz, 'choice and decision are subject to rules of rational constraint, the most important of which is that one can only choose or decide for a reason, i.e., for what one takes to be a good reason for the option chosen' (p. 8). This strikes me as quite implausible. I do not see why it should be impossible for a person to make a choice or a decision even when he does not think that he has a good reason, or even when it is clear to him that he has no reason whatever for choosing or deciding as he does.[5] That may not be a very sensible way to go about things. Nevertheless, it can be done.

So far as I am aware, Raz offers no pertinent argument to show that his account of the relationship between choosing and having reasons is correct. He offers instead an observation, supported by an illustrative example, concerning a rather different matter: namely, the relationship that must be thought to obtain between a certain choice and some consideration that is advanced as a reason for it, in order for that consideration to be taken as a good reason for the option chosen. 'I cannot choose to have coffee because I love Sophocles', Raz observes, unless it happens to be the case that 'I believe something which intelligibly can be taken to be a reason for that choice' (p. 8). That is, nothing can be construed as a reason for making a certain choice unless it is understandable in what way it tends to show that the choice is justified.

Now Raz may very well be right about this. Perhaps it is true that loving Sophocles cannot be a person's reason for choosing to have coffee unless the person has some belief that explains why his love of Sophocles should lead him to consider it reasonable to make that choice. However, this is quite irrelevant to the point at issue; it has no bearing upon Raz's thesis about choices and reasons. It provides no support for his claim that choices and decisions can be made only for what those who make them take to be good reasons.

What Raz says about loving Sophocles and choosing to have coffee has to do only with whether the former can actually serve as a reason for the latter.

---

[5] I believe that it is possible for a person to make a choice for a reason that he actually considers to be a bad reason. However, I shall not defend this view here.

It can do so, Raz maintains, only for someone whose beliefs account for the fact that his loving Sophocles seems to him to be a good reason for his choosing to have coffee. But this point concerning what can be construed as a reason has nothing to do with whether people must have reasons. It is one thing to explain what it means for a person to take something to be a good reason for making a certain choice. It is quite another to show that a person cannot make a choice unless he has what he takes to be a good reason for making it. Explaining what counts as having a reason for choosing does nothing to establish that having a reason is necessary in order to choose.

5. Raz's view that choosing or deciding is impossible without having a reason[6] might perhaps be thought to acquire some support from the fact that we are reluctant to describe subhuman animals as making decisions or choices. We are inclined to suppose that no animal of that sort can properly be described as literally having done such a thing. This reluctance tends rather stubbornly to persist, even when we take into account that the animal hesitated and looked around with evident concern before it proceeded finally to set out on one available course of action rather than on another of which it appeared to have also been aware.

It seems to us that, in the courses of action that they follow, subhuman animals are altogether passive. We do not regard them as following those courses of action because they have actively chosen to follow them, but merely because they are being moved by certain impulses or inclinations. Moreover, we more or less understandably suppose that this passivity is due to a lack of reason. After all, we are used to considering the fact that subhuman animals lack reason as the most important thing that distinguishes them from ourselves; so it is natural enough for us to suppose that it is their lack of reason that accounts for their lack of a capacity to choose. The fact that they are unlike us in not making choices, we presume, derives from the fact that they are unlike us in not being rational, and hence in having no reasons for doing what they do.

[6] In his essay entitled 'Incommensurability and Agency', in *Engaging Reason*, 46–66, Raz explains that choosing a certain option does not require that there be a reason for preferring that option to all others. Evidently what he considers indispensable for choice is just a reason for regarding the chosen option as among those that are 'eligible for choice' (p. 65) When a person has reasons for considering several options as equally eligible for choice, and no reason for choosing one in preference to the others, Raz says, 'the will plays a role in human agency apart from that of reason'. Reason is none the less essential to choice, he maintains, because it must establish the eligibility of the chosen option. My own view is that options can be chosen without any reason for regarding them as eligible for choice.

In my view, however, it is not our assumption that subhuman animals lack reason that makes attributions of choice to them seem as dissonant to us as it does. Rather, I believe, the dissonance is accounted for by a different assumption that we make about those animals: namely, that they are incapable of the reflexivity, the self-evaluation, and the selective identification with elements of their own psychic experience that are such central features of human life. It is their presumptive lack of these volitional capacities, rather than of rationality, that stands in the way of supposing that they have the capacity to make choices.

The difference between the active movement that is involved in making a choice and passive movements that are occasioned just by impulse or inclination is not that the former depends upon having a reason. The difference is that the former is constituted as active by the circumstance that the chooser supports and thereby takes direct responsibility for his own activity. He is not merely put into motion or impelled by forces that are effective in generating activity but that he himself does not mobilize. He is himself behind what he is doing. He is identified with the forces by which he is moved, and thus they are fully his own.[7]

To make a choice or a decision is to make up one's mind. Now making up one's mind is a reflexive act; it is an act that the mind performs upon itself. If it is impossible for subhuman animals to make up their minds, this is because an animal of that sort cannot divide its consciousness, or step back from itself in the way that reflexive self-awareness entails. Since it cannot take itself apart, by objectifying and focusing separately on the various elements of its own mental life, it cannot organize itself or put itself together. Thus, it cannot make itself up. What keeps animals from making choices and decisions, then, is not a lack of reason. It is a lack of the reflexive and volitional capacities that deciding and choosing require.

In making up our minds, we do various things: we form intentions, we identify ourselves with one or another inclination, we commit ourselves to a certain thought or desire. These are activities of the will, which do not appear as such to entail any exercise of reason. It is quite possible, then, for a person to choose and to decide without having any reason that legitimates his choice or his decision.

---

[7] While this is obviously nothing like an adequate analysis of the active–passive distinction, I believe that it is sufficient for the purpose at hand.

6. Is there any basis for thinking otherwise? Raz evidently considers it pertinent to argue that beliefs cannot be chosen at will. In his view, beliefs are inescapably subject to rational constraint; and he appears to think that this supports his claim that choices are similarly constrained (pp. 12 ff.). His point seems to be that since it is reasonable to suppose that no one can adopt a belief unless he considers it to be true, we may also suppose that no one can make a choice unless he regards it as a reasonable choice—that is, unless he considers himself to have a reason for making it.

Whether or not Raz's account of belief is correct, it provides no support for his account of choice. Even if deciding what to believe is subject to certain constraints, as he urges, why should this lead one to think that making decisions about other matters is also constrained in the same way? Deciding what to believe is not a paradigm for decisions and choices of all kinds. It is a special case. Let us accept Raz's view that it is in the very nature of believing that beliefs are taken by the believer to be true; and let us suppose that an act of deciding to believe something is identical with an act of deciding to believe it to be true.[8] This does not entail that it is part of the essential nature of the act of making up one's mind that the person who performs the act takes himself to be acting reasonably. When a person chooses or decides, what he does is not identical with any judgement or assumption concerning whether his doing it is justified. Making a decision or a choice is one thing, and having an opinion concerning whether the choice or decision is a reasonable one is something else.

Choosing an option is separable from, and does not depend upon, evaluating it. There is no compelling logical or conceptual basis for insisting that it is impossible to make up one's mind unless one not only possesses the reflexive and volitional capacities that performing any act of decision or choice requires but also has what one takes to be a good reason for using

---

[8] Raz appears to acknowledge that beliefs may none the less persist even after the believer finds that they are false. He avoids admitting that this provides counterexamples to his claim by characterizing such beliefs as 'pathological', and by maintaining that they are not really beliefs at all but only 'thoughts that one cannot help thinking'. The agent does not have a genuine belief, Raz insists, but is merely 'haunted by thought' (p. 15). Being haunted by thought, however, consists in being obsessed—unable to get the thought out of your mind. When people persist in beliefs they know to be false, on the other hand, they are not simply unable to get certain thoughts out of their minds; they act on those thoughts, their deliberations and decisions are guided by them, etc. It is difficult to understand why the beliefs should not be counted as genuine beliefs, except for the somewhat questionable stipulation that belief is to be understood as constrained by an assumption of truth.

those capacities in making the particular decision or choice that is being made. In fact, the act of making up one's mind can be performed for no reason at all. Performing it entails simply that the agent commits himself to a certain alternative, or enlists himself in support of it. He can do this without having any explicit or implicit belief or thought concerning whether it is a good idea for him to make that commitment.[9]

7. According to Raz, 'it makes sense to suppose' that the will is active only in so far as it is, in a somewhat weak sense, rational—that is, 'only when it responds to reasons as we see them' (p. 10). Another way of understanding when the will is active, however, strikes me as making better sense. In my view, the will is active in so far as (and only in so far as) it is whole-hearted. Roughly speaking, a person's will is 'whole-hearted' (i.e., the person wills whole-heartedly) to the extent that he wants or is willing for his will to be as it is, and that he therefore identifies with it or joins himself to it. In that case, the person is neither an indifferent bystander to his own volitional activity, nor is he a helplessly imposed-upon victim of it. He is satisfied with his will, and is in no way passive with respect to it.

Now this whole-heartedness may not be grounded in reasons. People do not require reasons in order to be satisfied with themselves (nor, even less, to be dissatisfied with themselves). Their attitudes towards themselves may be based upon considerations that are quite irrational, and that they themselves recognize as irrational; or their attitudes may be entirely baseless, and unconditioned by reasons of any kind. Whole-heartedness consists just in a certain harmonious volitional structure, which can come about independently of a response to reasons. The will may be whole-hearted, and hence active, even when it is not responding to reasons at all.

Although an active will need not be rational in the weak sense that is germane to Raz's discussion, the fact that a will is rational in that sense does

---

[9] We must distinguish (a) reason constrains the will, and (b) the will cannot function except for reasons. Raz is wrong to endorse (b), but maybe (a) is correct. Descartes thought it impossible to refrain from assenting to a proposition while perceiving clearly and distinctly that it is true. It might perhaps seem that, similarly, no one can decline to make a certain choice while he is presently and fully aware that he has a decisive reason for making it. But I wonder whether it may not be possible for someone to recognize that a certain choice is rationally required and yet be deterred from making it on account of a concomitant experience of fear, or of disgust, or of some other aversive response that does not obscure what reason requires but inhibits the person from being effectively moved by that requirement. This leaves open whether it is also possible to choose while recognizing that reason *forbids* doing so.

entail that it is active. This is not because whole-heartedness is inessential, but because weak rationality ensures whole-heartedness. To see something as a reason for (or against) a certain belief or a certain action is to see it as supporting (or as opposing) that action or that belief. Thus, responding to reasons as we see them is a matter of taking those favourable or unfavourable considerations into account in determining what to believe or what to do. Now in so far as an agent tends to regard himself as proceeding rationally in deciding what to think or how to act—in other words, in so far as he is weakly rational—he will tend to be whole-hearted in those decisions. The agent's conviction that he is behaving rationally, and that his behaviour is therefore justified, serves to eliminate the inner conflicts of self-doubt and ambivalence. It immunizes him from any hesitation or inhibition concerning whether what he is doing is what he really wants to do. To the extent that someone is weakly rational, accordingly, he is necessarily whole-hearted.

Whole-heartedness based in this way upon rationality is, however, only a special case. A person may become whole-hearted without supposing that what he is doing is justified by reasons.[10] In any event, it is essentially in virtue of his whole-heartedness, and only indirectly in virtue of his rationality, that a rational agent is active rather than passive in what he does. It is the character of his willing, not of his thinking, that counts.

8. In illustration of his view concerning the relationship between being active and being weakly rational, Raz considers a person who is irritated with a friend but who does not consider his irritation to be justified. Such a person is passive with respect to the irritation, Raz maintains, and might indicate this by saying that the irritation 'seized me in spite of myself', or the like (p. 12). Raz's characterization of this person as passive is unjustified. From the fact that a person does not think that his feeling of irritation is justified, it cannot be inferred either that the person is, or that he considers himself to be, in a passive state with respect to that feeling.

Suppose that the person does not care whether the feeling is justified. Suppose that he feels irritated, that he is entirely satisfied with feeling that way, and that he identifies himself whole-heartedly with the feeling without it even occurring to him to ask whether he has any reason for doing so.[11] In that case, he is unequivocally active with respect to feeling irritated,

---

[10] This is implicitly established above, in my discussion of choosing.

[11] In saying that the person is satisfied with the feeling, I do not mean that he makes some judgement to the effect that the feeling is acceptable to him. I mean just that he accepts the feeling, with no inclination to resist it or to dispel it.

despite the fact that he does not imagine himself to have any reason whatever for being in that state.

It is also to be noted that thinking oneself rational does not entail considering oneself to be active. That is, a person may regard himself as having been passively seized and overcome by a feeling of irritation even though he believes that the feeling is entirely reasonable and fully justified. Suppose the person has what he thinks is a foolproof method that enables him to avoid feelings of irritation even when feelings of that sort would be justified by good reasons; suppose he has foolishly made a bet or promised someone (perhaps himself) that he will never feel irritated again; suppose he is now using his method in an effort to avoid feeling irritated despite the fact that he thinks that, in his present circumstances, a feeling of irritation would be quite reasonable; and suppose he is chagrined to find that his method has failed and that he is feeling irritated in spite of himself. In that case, he will naturally consider himself to be defeated by the feeling of irritation, and will recognize his own passivity with respect to it. He will have a sense that the feeling has possessed him against his will. This sense of passivity appears to be fully compatible with a belief on his part that his being irritated is, in the circumstances, entirely justified by altogether sound and compelling reasons.

Perhaps it may be true that people tend to feel passive and out of control in so far as they believe that they are behaving irrationally, and that they tend to think of themselves as active in so far as they believe that their behaviour is rational. But people are not always concerned with whether or not they are being rational. Sometimes they busy themselves with one thing or another, and may even be whole-heartedly involved in what they are doing, with no interest at all in whether they have good reasons for doing it. They neither believe that they are acting rationally, nor believe that their behaviour is unsupported by reasons.

This lack of self-evaluation or of self-understanding does not make it impossible for them to make choices or decisions. Nor does being indifferent to one's own rationality entail, as Raz appears to believe, having a sense of being invaded, or feeling that one's will has been passively overcome. What counts in determining whether a person is active or passive is the whole-heartedness of his will in what he is doing, and not whether he has good reasons or even any reasons for doing it.

6

Raz on Values and Reasons

Ulrike Heuer

The relation of values and reasons is a major focus of Joseph Raz's recent work. He claims that reasons are based on values, that reasons depend on values, and even, surprisingly, that reasons *are* values.

In this paper I examine Raz's account of the *relation* between values and reasons, focusing in particular on *practical reasons*—reasons for acting in certain ways with respect to what is valued.[1]

As a preliminary way of delineating two basic alternatives for mapping the relation between reasons and values, let me pose a Euthyphro-style question: (1) Is something valuable because we have reason to behave in some way with respect to it? Or: (2) Do we have reason to behave in some way with respect to it because it is valuable?[2] Though helpful for contrasting different approaches, this question is still multiply ambiguous. It may be interpreted as a question concerning the metaphysical primacy of values or reasons respectively—that is, whether there have to be things of value for there to be reasons, or vice versa. There is also a question of conceptual primacy: Can 'value' be defined in terms of reasons, or can 'reason' be defined in terms of value? A related, but different question is epistemological: Does a person have to be able to master the concept of value in order to understand the concept of a reason (or, again, vice versa)? I will use these three questions as guide-lines for investigating Raz's view of the

---

[1] That there are other reasons seems trivial to me. Of course, if something is the case, there should usually be reasons to believe that this is so.

[2] In neither case is the question about the subjectivity of values. It is not a Euthyphro contrast in *that* sense.

relation of values and reasons. Are values (1) metaphysically, (2) conceptually, and/or (3) epistemologically prior to reasons? Or are reasons in all or any of these respects prior to values?

My strategy in the paper is as follows. In section 1, I locate Raz's position with respect to these three questions by contrasting his views with those of Thomas Scanlon. In section 2, I work out Raz's account of reasons and values in some greater detail. And then, in section 3, I discuss what I take to be the remaining major problem with Raz's approach.

1. The Relation of Values and Reasons

In order to elucidate Raz's position on reasons and values, let me begin by giving a few examples of practical deliberation.

It's Saturday night, and Sally is trying to decide whether or not to go to a party at the Smiths'. The party promises to be enjoyable and would allow Sally to meet some friends whom she hasn't seen for a long time. Evidently, she has reasons to attend the party, and her reasons can be phrased in terms of the perceived evaluative aspects of going: it would be fun; it would be good to see those friends again. Hence, as Raz puts it, 'We cannot understand what is of value in a party without understanding what it is a reason for, that is, when one has reason to go to one, and how one behaves at a party.'[3] More generally, 'understanding the value depends on and leads to understanding the reason'.[4]

Take another example. It's Sunday afternoon, and Paul is trying to decide whether or not to go to a concert in the park. Surprisingly, a group of musicians is going to perform some of Beethoven's late string quartets. While Paul likes this music immensely, he is somewhat doubtful that the park is the right surroundings for listening to it. He decides to go, but with considerable hesitation. While the idea of playing the music in the park is not as clearly misguided as 'having recordings of Beethoven's late quartets played in the elevators, hallways, and restrooms of an office building', it might indicate 'a failure to understand the value of music of this kind [...] a lack of understanding ... in what way it is worth attending to'.[5] Scanlon,

[3] Joseph Raz, 'Respecting People', in his *Value, Respect, and Attachment* (Cambridge: Cambridge University Press, 2001), 164 f.

[4] Ibid. 165.

[5] T. M. Scanlon, *What We Owe to Each Other* (Cambridge, Mass.: Harvard University Press, 1998), 100.

whose example I have adapted here, concludes—in terms that are strikingly similar to Raz's—that 'understanding the value of something often involves not merely knowing that it is valuable or how valuable it is, but also how it is to be valued'[6]—that is, what reasons it gives us to act.

Both Raz and Scanlon are committed to the view that one cannot understand the value of something without understanding the reasons one has for behaving in a certain way with respect to it. Further, the claim is meant to entail its contrapositive: Not knowing what one has reason to do shows that the value of the things one deals with has not been properly understood. However, neither Scanlon nor Raz is committed to claiming that understanding reasons entails understanding values, but only the converse: understanding values *entails* understanding reasons.

Putting this claim in terms of entailment may make the thesis sound improbably strong. After all, it is surely possible that a person has but a partial understanding of the value of something—for instance, Beethoven's string quartets—without any clear idea of why it is better, *ceteris paribus*, to listen to them in acoustically favourable as opposed to unfavourable conditions. But both Raz and Scanlon can accept this. What they must hold is that a *complete understanding* of the value of something does entail an understanding of one's reasons for behaving in certain ways with respect to it. This interpretation leaves room for having only an incomplete understanding of both reasons and values, and perhaps a somewhat better grip on the one than on the other; and in particular it does not deny that even complete understanding of one's reasons need not entail complete understanding of the values the reasons relate to. This latter point, I take it, establishes some epistemological priority of reasons. Hence, with respect to the epistemological question, both Raz and Scanlon agree that our understanding of reasons is prior to our understanding of values.

But how is this epistemological priority of reasons to be explained? In Scanlon's case, the claim that understanding the value of something entails understanding one's reasons for acting in a certain way simply follows from the buck-passing account of values that he advances in his book. In a nutshell it is the following:

[6] Ibid.

being valuable is not a property that provides us with reasons. Rather, to call something valuable is to say that it has other properties that provide reasons for behaving in certain ways with regard to it.[7]

Thus, the buck passing amounts to defining value in terms of reasons. 'X is of value' is equivalent to saying that X has certain (natural) properties,[8] which provide reasons for actions. So in Scanlon's case the epistemological primacy of reasons follows from their conceptual primacy. The buck-passing account of values leads to a conceptual or semantic reduction of the concept of value. Scanlon's idea is that a claim like 'This is a valuable research project' is tantamount to saying: this research project 'casts light on the causes of cancer'[9] (say) and should therefore be pursued. 'Casting light on the causes of cancer' is a 'natural' property that gives us reasons (in this case, reasons to pursue, promote, or respect the project), and saying 'that it is valuable' is just another way of reporting that the project has reason-giving properties. Thus far, Scanlon comes down quite clearly on one side of the Euthyphro contrast with respect to both the conceptual and the epistemological primacy of reasons over values. X has value because it gives us reasons, and not vice versa.

How about the metaphysical question? In his book, Scanlon advances a 'realist' view of reasons: he claims that 'being a reason for x' is an irreducible normative relation.[10] Put together with the claim we encountered above, that the concept of value can be defined in terms of reasons, it seems that he is committed to a metaphysical primacy claim as well: there have to be reasons, in order for there to be anything of value. If so, Scanlon's view would illustrate a position which, with respect to all three questions, claims that reasons are prior to values.[11] Hence, Scanlon con-

---

[7] T. M. Scanlon, *What We Owe to Each Other* (Cambridge, Mass.: Harvard University Press, 1998), 96.

[8] In the book, Scanlon refers to 'natural properties' (P. 97), or alternatively to 'propositions about the natural world' (P. 57). However, he seems to be revising his view in a more recent response to Jay Wallace's criticism of buck passing: 'My thesis was that goodness is not itself a property that provides reasons, not that the underlying properties are always natural properties, and I should not have written in a way that suggested this' T. M. Scanlon, 'Reasons, Responsibility, and Reliance: Replies to Wallace, Dworkin, and Deigh', *Ethics* 112 (2002), 513. I am not sure whether Scanlon's remarks in this article amount to rejecting buck passing after all. If so, I believe that his view of reasons stands in need of quite substantial revisions.

[9] Scanlon, *What We Owe to Each Other*, 97   [10] Ibid. 57 f.

[11] I am not going to investigate Scanlon's arguments for buck passing in this paper, but I hope to do so on another occasion.

cludes: 'My account contains [...] the claim that being valuable is not a property that provides us with reasons.'[12]

As we have seen, Raz and Scanlon agree with respect to the epistemological question. Does Raz share Scanlon's position with respect to the other two questions as well? After all, the metaphysical primacy of reasons can explain their conceptual primacy, which in turn can explain the epistemological primacy. A Scanlonian explanation could proceed thus: There is no need for a person to understand the concept of value at all—she can make do with an understanding of natural facts and reasons alone, without really missing out on anything. But if we are to use the concept of value, we have to understand that it is just another way of reporting that the thing, which is valuable, has reason-providing properties. The conceptual primacy of reasons can then be explained by their metaphysical primacy: only if and because there are reasons are there values.

But even though Raz shares Scanlon's view about 'understanding'—his view on the epistemological question—he does not agree with the other two claims of Scanlon's. According to him, there is a relation between values and reasons (they are 'intrinsically connected'), and value is prior to reason (the 'value is a reason for [action]'; 'the value...determines the reason').[13] These remarks are quite clearly not about the conceptual, but about the metaphysical priority of values. They do not explain the concept of a reason for action but, rather, address the question of what reasons are—they are (or are determined by) values. Hence with respect to the metaphysical question, Raz occupies the opposite pole of the Euthyphro contrast: we have reasons to act in certain ways because so acting is an appropriate response to value. Put differently, it is an aspect of things of value, one might say, that they are practical reasons. Or perhaps: it is an aspect of certain facts—evaluative facts—that they are reasons. While there might be different ways to understand the slogan 'Reasons are values', the one I just suggested seems the most promising to me. One alternative would be that the relation between these two might be the tightest one possible: namely, identity. If so, the Euthyphro question as a question about primacy wouldn't find a foothold. However, I believe that

---

[12] Scanlon, *What We Owe to Each Other*, 96.

[13] 'In general the value of what has value, and the action its value *is* a reason for, are intrinsically connected' (Raz, 'Respecting People', 164 (my emphasis) and *passim*, e.g. 165 f.). And also: 'the value of what is of value determines what action...it is the reason to perform' (ibid. 166).

the presumption of identity is too strong to ascribe to Raz. After all, as we have already seen, he shares with Scanlon the view that reasons are (in the sense explained above) epistemologically prior to values. If they were identical, this priority would be hard to make sense of.

That this is what Raz should be thinking, at any rate, becomes apparent if one thinks of examples of discussing the value of something. Is it a good play? Was it a good film? In discussions of this kind, many reasons for the value of a play can be advanced; there can be long and heated exchanges of reasons, which never even touch on reasons for action. Or take a different example. There are lectures, essays, and books arguing that, for instance, a certain painting cannot be by the alleged artist, because it is inferior in value to all her other well-established work. Reasons: yes; reasons for action: no. Thus it seems that there is a lot to be understood regarding values that is independent of practical reasons altogether. The original thesis that understanding values and understanding reasons are somehow wedded shouldn't be tightened to a degree that excludes the attribution of this view to Raz. 'Value' in the broad sense in which I use this concept is a notion that seems to be much richer than 'practical reason', and at least partly independent. Thus, the slogan 'Values are reasons' needs modification. Therefore, I suggest reading it as short for: It is an aspect of things of value that they are practical reasons—but it is not the whole story. I will rely on this interpretation for the remainder of this essay.

We can conclude that, like Scanlon, Raz defends an 'asymmetrical' dependence relation holding between values and reasons[14]—only that it looks in the other direction. While Scanlon takes reasons to be conceptually and metaphysically prior to values, Raz claims that values are metaphysically prior to reasons, while being rather silent on the conceptual variant of the Euthyphro question. Reasons depend for their existence on values. This claim is quite compatible with the epistemological priority of reasons that we encountered earlier. The person who fully understands the reasons she has to act may still have only an incomplete understanding of the value of the items involved. She knows only of a certain aspect of it: namely, of its reason-giving properties, but misses out on other aspects that account for the reasons. She is like the person who knows that she shouldn't be munching popcorn during a performance of Beethoven's string quartets, but without really understanding why not. The person

---

[14] 'Reason and value are inherently though asymmetrically connected' (ibid.).

who understands her reasons—and might even have complete understanding of her reasons—yet has only a rudimentary understanding of the
value misses out on exactly those aspects of value which are not reason-
giving. A full understanding of values entails a full understanding of
reasons. But that is consistent with the claim that even a full understanding of reasons need not entail a full understanding of values.

In the next section, I am going to work out some details of Raz's
account of reasons as based on values which will lead to an answer to the
as yet unanswered question about conceptual primacy on Raz's view.

2. What Reasons?

Now what does claiming that values are reasons for actions—or perhaps
more precisely that reasons are aspects of evaluative properties—really
come to? If reasons are aspects of everything that is of value, one simple
consequence is that there cannot be anything of value without there being
reasons to act. But aren't there simply too many things of value? How can it
be that there is a reason to act (for me, I presume) with respect to all the
good theatre productions, all the delicious dishes on the planet, all the
conceivable good actions, etc.? What is it that I have reason to do just
because something is, say, aesthetically pleasing? Nothing perhaps? On the
broadest construction of practical reasons, our reasons for action might
include, say, reasons for admiration. Even so, it just does not seem right
that there is always such a reason for every person. I do not have to admire,
or indeed do anything with respect to all the good things that there are.
Does an account such as Raz's have a chance to get off the ground if it is
committed to claiming that it is an aspect of everything of value to be a
reason for action? The problem is that very often there is no apparent link
between values and reasons at all—or is there? How is the reason-giving
aspect of values to be established in those cases where it does not appear as
though the acknowledged value of something gives us *any* reason to act?

A. The Razian Schema

Raz offers a general description of the kinds of reasons that values (or,
more precisely, aspects of evaluative facts) 'are'. He mentions the following
four possibilities. A person A has a reason to φ, if φ-ing is (1) the preserving

of, (2) the non-destruction of[15], or (3) the engagement with something of value[16]. And (4) *A* has reason to acknowledge the value of a thing correctly, in case she is to form any belief about its value[17].

This gives us what I would like to call 'the Razian Schema': There are reasons to

1. preserve
2. not destroy
3. engage with
4. and acknowledge

whatever is of value.

Let me take these up, starting with the last: the reason to form an adequate attitude. Raz is careful to make clear that there is no general requirement to have any views about the value of things. It is only *if* I am to form an attitude that it should be correct. Raz thinks that this extends to 'fantasies, imaginings, wishes, emotions, as well as to our plain beliefs'.[18] While the first three seem to be arbitrary thought policing to me, and the fourth needs further explanation, the last ('beliefs') is least controversial. It is but an instance of the general theoretical requirement that beliefs ought to be true—and thus, it is not really of interest in so far as our concern is with the question how reasons for actions and values are related. This leaves us with the first three kinds of reasons.

That there is a general reason not to destroy things of value (2) is not exactly a reason for action, but rather a constraint on reasons for action. That an action would not destroy something of value is hardly a reason for acting accordingly. Rather, if an action would lead to destroying something of value, but there is also an independent reason for performing the action, the prospect of destruction counts against it. A stronger interpretation of (2) as a constraint would be that only actions that do not lead to destroying anything of value are permitted. But this seems implausibly

---

[15] '[I]n general we have reason not to destroy, and furthermore to preserve what is of value' (ibid. 162).

[16] '[W]e can engage with value in appropriate ways' (ibid.). 'Ultimately, value is realized when it is engaged with' (ibid. 163). '[O]ur lives are about engaging with value, the rest being mere preliminaries' (ibid. 164).

[17] '[I]f we think of an object which is of value, we should think of it in ways consistent with its value' (ibid. 161).

[18] Ibid.

strong, especially if we follow Raz in understanding 'value' in the broadest sense as comprising, for instance, 'instrumental value'.[19]

This leaves us with (1) and (3). Both of these kinds of reasons answer directly to the central question of practical reasoning: what should one do? Yet (1) might not quite give an answer. It depends on its scope and limits. Perhaps it could be pushed towards a utilitarian interpretation (reading 'preserve' as tending towards 'promote'), and thus cover all there is to practical reason. A more modest interpretation is that I have a reason to preserve only what is threatened. If so, (1) would give me reasons to act only in very specific circumstances.

Finally, there is (3): 'engaging with' reasons. They are the most important kind of reasons with respect to everyday decisions. As they are neither just constraining nor confined to specific situations, they are the most influential in guiding people's choices.

But why accept the Razian Schema? Is there any reason to believe that the relation between values and practical reasons can be specified in precisely the way it suggests? With respect to (4) the answer is easy, since it can be seen as an instance of a general requirement of theoretical rationality. But the answer is not as obvious with respect to the other three categories. According to Raz, (1) and (2) are justified through (3). We should preserve and not destroy things of value, *because* their value is there to be engaged with, to be realized.[20] As he sees it, the same holds for (4) as well: both recognition and preservation are conditions of engaging with. Hence, 'engaging with' reasons are not only the most important kind in guiding practical reasoning; they are also the ones that ultimately explain the other kinds of reasons. (1), (2), and (4) are established on the strength of (3). Raz groups (1), (2), and (4) together, labelling them 'reasons for respect'.[21] We ought to respect what is of value, because it is there to be engaged with. But what then establishes (3)? (3) pertains to what our life is ultimately about. 'Engaging with' reasons are the reasons for 'all activities, relationships, attitudes' 'which give content to our lives'.[22] Consequently,

---

[19] After all, the use of many tools leads to their destruction. Food is instrumentally valuable for nourishment, but by eating it, I destroy it. That, however, hardly counts against eating. This consideration might show that even the weak claim that destruction is always a reason against doing something is already too strong.

[20] Ibid. 167.

[21] Ibid. 167 and *passim*.

[22] Ibid. 168.

the underlying argument has to be that the concept of a reason is to be explained as part of understanding what a meaningful life consists in. I will not try to take this argument any further here. Instead I will look more closely at the crucial third kind of reasons.

B. Engaging with Value in the Appropriate Way

What are 'engaging with' reasons? Why does the person who has Beethoven's music played in an elevator fail to engage with its value? Not because it is not a form of engaging with it, I presume, but because this is not engaging with it 'in the appropriate way'. The key to understanding the necessary connection between reasons and values is this notion of 'appropriateness'. Engaging with value *simpliciter* won't do, provided that everything one does touches on things of value in one way or another. How, then, is 'engaging with' different from 'engaging with in the appropriate way'? Raz writes: 'We do so [engage with value in appropriate ways] when we listen to music with attention and discrimination, read a novel with understanding, climb rocks using our skill to cope, spend time with friends in ways appropriate to our relationships with them.'[23] Hence, he explains 'appropriateness' by way of giving examples. There may be a temptation (that I at least feel) to ask for a more general characterization, which might in turn lead us to suspect that all of this is plainly circular. Is there an explanation of appropriateness which is more general than the examples, and does not come down to saying that one engages appropriately with something just in case one engages with it in a way that heeds the reasons it gives us? But even if there isn't, this might not be an objection. It would only show that the formulation 'engaging with in the appropriate way' does not help in figuring out what our reasons are. Note that in denying that there is a general criterion for appropriateness, Raz's conception of value-based reasons is clearly different from teleological conceptions based on the idea that value ought to be promoted. 'Promote value', one might say, would be a general answer to the question 'What does "engaging with in the appropriate way" consists of?'

Can we do without any such general answer? Looking at the examples, what makes us believe that the reasons that they exemplify are truly *reasons* and not mere expressions of conventional judgements about 'how to behave

---

[23] Ibid. 162 f.

appropriately'? I take it that Raz's answer to this is the following: the value of something is partly constituted by the reasons that we have. This follows from the metaphysical primacy claim as I interpreted it above. Hence, if a novel were not what has to be 'read...with understanding', the value of novels would be different.[24] (I don't mean how valuable it is, but which value it is.)

This interpretation of 'engaging with in the appropriate way' takes us back to the original claim that understanding values and understanding reasons are necessarily linked. They are so related, because an object of value would not be an instantiation of that very value unless it is appropriate to engage with it in certain ways, but not in others. Were it appropriate to engage with it in different ways, it would instantiate a different value.

This whole second part so far can be read as an affirmative answer to the question of whether values are conceptually prior to reasons: yes, reason can be defined in terms of value, as done in the Razian Schema.

While both Scanlon and Raz agree on the epistemological priority of reasons over values, they disagree about the answers to both of the other two Euthyphro questions. According to Scanlon, reasons are prior to values in all three respects, whereas Raz maintains the conceptual as well as metaphysical primacy of values.

C. Normative versus Evaluative: An Aside

Reasons are usually thought to be *normative*, whereas values are not normative, at least not in the same sense. The typical form of a value statement is 'x is V (where V is an evaluative property)', whereas the typical form of a practical reason might be 'A should (or must or ought to) ϕ in these circumstances'. If values provide reasons, there has to be a way of accounting for the deontic language, which is commonly associated with talk about reasons. What is the relation between values, reason statements, and deontic statements? One possible way of conceiving of the relation is the following. Values provide reasons. Reason statements entail deontic statements. That is, saying that p is a reason to ϕ is tantamount to saying that p entails the truth of a statement of the form: x ought to ϕ.

Now, there is an immediate objection to this way of thinking of reasons. After all, it can hardly be the case that I ought to do just anything that I

---

[24] An answer along these lines is also suggested in Joseph Raz, *The Practice of Value*, ed. R. Jay Wallace (Oxford: Oxford University Press 2003).

have a reason to do. Perhaps there is a reason why I would like to spend a day indulging myself by going to the cinema while at the same time I have to finish a paper in order to keep a deadline—and let's assume that there is a reason for keeping the deadline as well. Is it, then, that I ought to go to the cinema, and I ought to finish my paper, hence I am facing a dilemma? While it might be nice to think so, it is hardly true. It seems quite clear that I ought not to go to the cinema—not on the very day when my deadline is up, that is. Not every reason statement entails an ought, it seems. But of course there is a common way of dealing with this problem. Following David Ross, one could say every reason statement entails a prima-facie ought that can easily be outweighed; a reason statement entails a *sans phrase* ought statement only together with a closure statement.[25] The closure statement establishes that there is no defeating reason. Hence, while I have a reason to go to the cinema, this reason is defeated by the reasons for finishing my paper in good time. Assuming that my commitment to finishing the paper is undefeated, only it entails a *sans phrase* ought statement.

This is a common way of conceiving of the relation between reasons and ought statements. I would like to call it 'the entailment claim'. Raz endorses a version of the entailment claim. In an earlier paper he writes:

A non-relativized ought-statement [. . .] is entailed by a statement of a reason, i.e. a relativized ought-statement and a closure statement to the effect that there are no defeating facts of the relevant kind.[26]

In this quote, 'relativized' refers to a use of ought statements, such as 'You ought to do it, morally speaking'. The claim here is that a reason such as 'John promised to do *A*', together with the fact that there is no defeating reason, entails a non-relativized ought. Without the 'closure statement' the reason entails a relativized ought.[27]

---

[25] I am adopting David Ross's terminology here from his book *The Right and the Good*, ed. Philip Stratton-Lake (Oxford: Oxford University Press, 1930), ch. 2. In current discussions it has become common to replace his expressions *prima facie* and *sans phrase* by *pro tanto* and 'all things considered'. However, none of these seem entirely happy uses of terminology to me. While the replacement of *prima facie* by *pro tanto* is probably a good idea, since *prima facie* suggests that we deal with an apparent—as opposed to a real—'ought', the replacement of *sans phrase* with 'all things considered' is less successful because it suggests that in order to establish a *sans phrase* ought, we have to consider 'all things', which is both unclear and questionable.

[26] J. Raz, 'Introduction', 14.

[27] In Raz's terms the entailment claim is the view that reason statements entail either relativized or non-relativized ought statements. However, he also says: 'a non-relativized ought-statement concerning what is to be done on a single occasion entails that there is a

Put together with the account as I developed it in the last two subsections, the Razian claim amounts to the following. First, if something is of value, it also has reason-giving properties. And, second, its having reason-giving properties entails the truth of statements of the kind 'x should φ' (but 'x should φ' is not a reason).

3. The Problem

A. The 'Basic Belief', Optional Reasons, and Incommensurability

There is, however, a problem with the kind of value-based account of reasons that I have sketched so far. It turns up with Raz's specific answer to the question: What reasons do I have?

The discussion so far has established the following answer: I have reason to engage with things of value in the appropriate way and reasons of respect, which serve to preserve the conditions of 'engaging with' (remember: recognition, preservation, non-destruction). And there is the entailment claim: every reason statement entails either a relativized or a non-relativized ought statement, where a non-relativized 'ought' statement is true, just in case there is no defeating reason to do something else. Now, everything that is of value provides various reasons to engage with it, I take it. All these reasons are, presumably, my reasons (just as well as yours). Hence, I ought to read every worthwhile novel 'with understanding', provided there is no defeating reason to do something else.

And what would be a 'defeating reason'? Consider the following candidates: a stronger reason, a more stringent reason, and a reason that directly invalidates another. What makes reasons stronger or weightier is notoriously obscure. Stringency, however, might be easier to get a grip on. Say, I have a reason to read the novel, unless I have a duty to do something else. 'Duty', it seems, is more stringent than a mere *pro tanto* reason. And, finally, a reason might be defeated if it is directly invalidated as, say, when I give you a promise, but you release me from keeping it. But, here is the

conclusive reason for that action on that occasion' (ibid.). Thus, the claim seems to be even stronger than entailment, and might be thought of as logical equivalence: an 'ought' statement entails that there is a reason, and a statement that there is a reason entails an 'ought' statement.

problem: it just cannot be that I (conclusively) ought to read novels unless I have either a stronger reason or a duty to do something else. (Invalidation does not seem to be a pertinent option in this case.)

Let me introduce a further doctrine of Raz's that is meant to deal with this problem. He believes that reasons are 'optional' under certain conditions. The *optional reasons claim*[28] is meant to account for what Raz calls 'the basic belief',

that most of the time people have a variety of options such that it would accord with reason for them to choose any one of them and it would not be against reason to avoid any of them.[29]

Thus, the relieving message of this 'basic belief' is that I do not have to read novels after all. I am fine if I do, but not to blame if I don't. Yet, earlier it seemed as though the understanding of reasons as aspects of things of value, together with the entailment claim, commits Raz to a different view. How, then, does he arrive at the optional reasons claim? How does it fit in with the rest?

Here is how we can establish that a reason is optional without contradicting the entailment claim:[30]

Whenever two competing reasons fail to defeat each other [the perfect conformer with reason] will be able to conform with only one of them. Two reasons fail to defeat each other [1] either if they are equal in strength or stringency, [2] or if they have incommensurate strength or degrees of stringency.[31]

Thus, it is not only in cases when my reason to read novels is defeated that I may do something else, but also in certain cases where it is not: in those cases where I have an equally strong or stringent reason to do something else, and in other cases where I have a reason to do something else which is 'incommensurate' in strength or stringency. I take it that I have equally strong or stringent reasons in those cases where the reasons are *similar in kind*: my reason to read one novel by a particular author may be equal to my reason to read another novel by that author. Hence, if I try to decide which novel to read, I am fine (not neglecting a reason) if I read either.

---

[28] Joseph Raz, *Engaging Reason: On the Theory and Value of Action* (Oxford: Oxford University Press, 1999), ch. 5, especially 98 ff.

[29] Ibid. 100.

[30] In his discussion of 'enticing reasons' Raz considers the possibility of rejecting the entailment claim, but then rejects it (ibid. 101 f.).

[31] Ibid. 98.

What is hidden behind 'incommensurability', though? According to Raz, reasons

are incommensurate if and only if it is not true that one defeats the other, nor that they are of equal strength or stringency. They are incommensurate in strength, that is, reason does not determine which of them should be followed, not even that there is equal reason to follow either. When reasons are incommensurate, they are rendered optional, [...] because it is reasonable to choose either option [...] and it is not unreasonable or wrong to refrain from pursuing either option.[32]

I suppose that two options are likely to be incommensurate if they are *not similar in kind*. Hence, if I wonder whether I should read a novel, go for a walk, or do my taxes, all of them might be incommensurate. And again, I'll be all right if I choose any one of these alternatives.

However, none of this really makes good on what Raz called the 'basic belief'. After all, the 'basic belief' was that I am fine if I read a novel, but not in the wrong if I don't. It was not based on any comparison of novel reading with the other options available to me. Raz's attempt to account for 'optional reasons' by introducing incommensurability leads to the question how we are to understand *reasoning*. After all, there is an abundance of reasons based on values. If the rationality of my choice were to be established by comparison with other options, I would have to evaluate all these other options available to me. And 'available' can hardly just mean 'those I happen to consider'.

One may reply that so far we have been concerned only with the metaphysics of reasons, not with practical deliberation and reasoning. Metaphysically speaking, there *is* an abundance of reasons. But we only take them into account in deliberating what to do (1) if there is reason to deliberate, and (2) if they represent feasible options.[33] Hence, there are pragmatic constraints, which allow us not to take all our reasons into account for the purpose of practical deliberation. Consequently, rationality does not consist in being guided by one's reasons—not by all of them, at least. However, before I look more closely at this solution to the problem, I want to develop the problem itself a bit more.

The problem is that Raz's account of values as reasons recognizes too many reasons to engage in a comparative evaluation of their strength or

---

[32] Ibid. 103.

[33] I am grateful to Ruth Chang and Milton Meyer for pressing me on this point.

stringency in making rational decisions. Even though he allows for 'incommensurability', hence the *impossibility* of comparison, incommensurability itself is to be established by failure of comparison: by figuring out that neither of two options is equal in value to, or better than, the other.

The reasons are too many, because they are based only on certain aspects of things of value. The need for comparative evaluation of one's reasons follows from the entailment claim. We start out with a relativized 'ought', and then establish closure: that there is no defeating reason. In addition to this, the *optional reasons claim* introduces equality and incommensurability as modes of comparison. But all of this requires that a non-relativized 'ought' can be established only through extensive comparison of the reasons that there are—and there are too many of them to review anything but a random selection.[34] Raz seems to assume that incommensurability—the main road to closure—can be established quickly in many cases, simply by noting that different options are often different in kind. Consequently, Raz compares types of actions when he diagnoses incommensurability. However, the decision of the deliberating agent is about particular options, not just about types. It is less than clear whether incommensurability of types suffices to establish the incommensurability of token actions as well. For example, even if the type action 'going to the concert' is incommensurable with the type 'staying home reading a novel', it need not follow that going to *this* concert isn't clearly preferable to reading *this* novel.[35] Hence the assumption that closure can be established easily—the assumption on which Raz apparently relies—seems unwarranted.

B. The 'Basic Belief' and Subjective Conditions

But isn't there an easy way to hang on more tightly to the 'basic belief'— the belief that even though my reading a novel can be made intelligible by pointing to evaluative aspects of the novel, it is not the case that I *ought to* read the novel for those reasons, and thus I commit no rational failure if I don't? Why not add that only a person who likes novels has reason to read them? And even the person who generally likes novels might have a reason to read a particular one only if she is in the mood for it. Hence, it is not values alone that determine reasons, but rather there are other, sub-

---

[34] I am concerned only with 'engaging with' reasons at this point.

[35] I owe this point to Ruth Chang.

jective conditions that need to be met if a reason is to be ascribed to me correctly.

There are at least two different ways of understanding this reply. One is this, hinted at earlier: even though, metaphysically speaking, a person has an abundance of reasons, there are rationally permissible ways of narrowing down the range of options that she takes into account when deliberating. If the only options I am considering are whether to go to the cinema or to stay at home to read a novel, and I can also readily judge that these two options are incommensurate, I know immediately that I may (rationally) choose either one, depending on my current inclinations.[36] Even though there are lots of other reasons that I have at the very same time, they never come into play because of how I framed my choice. Hence, the metaphysical account of reasons does not immediately settle questions of practical deliberation. But this reply rests on the dubious assumption that I cannot go wrong in ignoring other courses of action that are open to me. Yet, how I happened to frame my choices might itself be objectionable.

The second way of understanding the reply is that 'engaging with' reasons are conditional reasons. I *have* those reasons only if certain subjective conditions obtain: that is, I have a reason to engage with things of value only if I desire to do so (say).

On the first interpretation, the metaphysical picture remains untouched: everyone has an abundance of reasons that they would never consider acting on. The narrowing down which is needed to successfully conduct practical deliberation is contextual. On the second interpretation, the metaphysical picture is insufficient to determine *my* reasons. Even though reasons generally depend on values, I have a reason only if I fulfil certain subjective conditions. Since the first interpretation seems to rest on a doubtful assumption that I cannot go wrong in framing choices, I will proceed by focusing only on the second one.

Are 'engaging with' reasons conditional reasons? There are various ways of understanding the theoretical assumptions that underlie the claim that they are.

1. *Desire*: A person has reason to engage with value only if she has a desire to do so.

---

[36] Raz even suggests that I would be irrational in not following my inclination in such a situation. See his *Engaging Reason*, ch. 3.

2. *Success*: A person has reason to engage with value only if she is likely to succeed in doing so.

3. *Pleasure*: A person has reason to engage with value only if she would enjoy doing so.

(1)–(3) are ways of getting rid of the too many reasons by making 'engaging with' reasons dependent on subjective features, which can be specified as desire, success, or pleasure.

Accepting the first suggestion would lead towards a different account of reasons altogether, to what is sometimes called an internalist or desire-based view. Since I want to explore the possibility of developing a value-based account, I will neglect this option here. Also, Raz clearly rejects (1): desires by themselves, he thinks, are never reasons, nor do they lead to a modification of one's reasons.[37] However, he does write:

> obviously no one has reason to engage with all valuable objects. We need not read all the novels, listen to all the music, climb all the mountains, go to all the parties, dance in all the dances, which are worthwhile.... [W]hile in one way ultimately our lives are about engaging with value...in another way the reasons of respect [recognition, preservation, non-destruction] are more basic. They are also more categorical, in not depending to the same degree on people's tastes and inclinations.[38]

Isn't this like saying that I have a reason to engage with value only if I have a desire to do so?[39] But the passage allows for a different interpretation: 'taste and inclination' may be important because without them one is unlikely to do well in engaging-with-value pursuits.[40] Thus, it is not *inclination* as such which gives me a reason, and therefore this move is compatible with the rejection of desires as reasons, as well as conditions of having reasons. It is, rather, the claim that 'inclination and taste' are a condition for engaging successfully with things of value. Understood in this way, the rationale behind the quote might be (2) rather than (1).

Now, this answer seems quite problematic to me. Do I have a reason only if I am likely to act on it successfully? That must be false. After all, I am likely to act unsuccessfully not only for lack of inclination, but also

---

[37] Raz even suggests that I would be irrational in not following my inclination in such a situation. See his *Engaging Reason*, ch. 3.

[38] Raz, 'Respecting People', 163 f.

[39] The quoted passage comes with no further explanation. It might as well hint at the optional reasons claim—but, as we have seen already, that would not help to solve the problem.

[40] Compare Raz, *Engaging Reason*, 59 f. and *passim*.

(e.g.) for lack of sufficient information about the relevant circumstances. Take the following example: I may have an incomplete understanding of what my reasons are. In this case, I would be unlikely to act successfully on them. That would, however, hardly prove that I don't have the reasons (which I don't fully understand) to begin with. Apparently, the question of whether or not I am likely to act successfully should better be dealt with separately from the question of whether or not I have a reason. Or else, is the case where I am unlikely to act successfully because I lack 'taste and inclination' different enough from the one of incomplete understanding to warrant the conclusion that if I lack 'taste and inclination' I do not have a reason to begin with? Again, that seems to be plainly wrong since often enough one discovers one's reason in pursuits one initially undertook with little or no inclination to do so. Say, a friend drags me to a film that I am not inclined to see—and it turns out to be a very good idea. In this case, 'success' (if that's what it is) does not depend on 'inclination'. Does it depend on taste, though? That seems a more promising line to take. Yet, the problem with it might be similar to the one with 'framing choices' above. Taste, I take it, is not altogether beyond rational criticism. If so, someone's given taste can hardly be a condition of her having a reason. If I happen to have very bad taste in wine, does it follow that I have more reason to have a bad wine than a good one?

There can be examples for the converse point too: people might have an inclination to do something, but lack the ability to do it successfully. Whenever one starts to learn something new—say, playing the violin— this seems inevitably to be the situation one is in. If the ability to act successfully were a condition for having a reason, there could never be a reason to learn anything. Hence, having an inclination is neither necessary nor sufficient for having the ability to act successfully. Having this ability is probably not itself a condition for having a reason either. (And in any case, we can know about it most of the time only after trying. And then trying might change the situation because it can lead to acquiring the ability.) Therefore, (2) must be false.

That leaves us with (3) as another attempt to make sense of the claim that 'engaging with' reasons are conditional reasons. The claim would again be that 'taste and inclination' are conditions of enjoyment. But, it may be obvious by now that the counterexamples to (2) could *mutatis mutandis* be recast as counterexamples to (3) as well. 'Taste and inclination' are neither necessary (as the film example shows) nor sufficient (as the violin example shows—assuming that playing badly is not enjoyable) for enjoyment.[41] And again, the ability to enjoy something is probably not itself a condition of having a reason, and can most of the time not be known about prior to trying, and might be acquired in trying.[42]

But you might feel that I dismissed (1)–(3) as subjective conditions too quickly. A suggestion, made to me by Jay Wallace, goes like this: (a) at least for a wide range of activities their value is contingent on their being either successfully engaged in or pleasant for the agent; (b) taste and inclination are conditions, in turn, of success and pleasure in many cases; (c) in cases where success or pleasure are possible without either taste or inclination, the presence of these factors might still be epistemic markers of success or pleasure. Hence, according to this suggestion, we should distinguish between the value of 'things' and the value of activities. The value of activities may well depend on subjective conditions, as will, in consequence, 'engaging with' reasons, even though not all reasons have subjective conditions. Desire would come in either as a condition of success and pleasure or as epistemically relevant in directing us towards those activities that we can perform successfully or with pleasure.

This way of putting in the subjective conditions seems plausible. Yet, as I will try to explain presently, I doubt that it can be made to work—but for reasons that will force us to go beyond the points I made above.

Let us think of someone who is not trying to learn to play the violin but already plays it reasonably well. Call her Olga. According to the current suggestion, Olga's activity of playing the violin is valuable—and consequently, she has reason to play—in most situations only if she might do

---

[41] Alon Harel suggested to me that 'taste and inclination', while not conditions of success or enjoyment, are our best and, indeed, only guide towards them. While true, it seems to me that this observation is compatible with rejecting them as conditions of having reasons, first because success and enjoyment may themselves not be conditions of having reasons, and secondly because—even if they were—our best guide is certainly fallible.

[42] There is a further reason why the idea of 'conditioned reasons' does not fit well into Raz's argument. As mentioned earlier, Raz claims that if we had different reasons with respect to a thing of value, its value would be different too. If I didn't have reason to read novels with attention, the value of novels would be different. This goes well with the original idea that reasons *are* aspects of values. But it doesn't sit well with the idea of subjectively conditioned reasons. If you have different reasons than I have (because you lack 'taste and inclination'), it apparently follows that the value of the thing you deal with must be different. That is, if having 'engaging with' reasons partly constitutes the identity of a value, the reasons cannot be different for different persons. I am grateful to Ruth Chang for directing my attention to this point.

so successfully or with pleasure, and her desire is a condition or an indicator of pleasure and success. Now, imagine that Olga decides to play for her grandmother at her birthday party. Does she have reason to do so? If she is likely to play successfully or with pleasure, she does—or so the suggestion goes. But what do success and pleasure on such an occasion consist in? Would she have to play like, say, Jascha Heifetz in order to perform successfully, or, at any rate, in a way that resembles professional playing closely enough? Hardly. But what, then, is the standard of success that we ought to appeal to in deciding whether she has reason to perform for her grandmother? Perhaps it is this: Olga would be successful in playing the violin on this occasion if her doing so gives pleasure to her grandmother (and, possibly, to the other guests at the party). But if so, it seems to me that the standard of success is not independent of the value of the activity, and can therefore not figure as a constraint on it. What success consists in depends on the value of the activity. Olga's playing the violin would be valuable if she succeeds in giving pleasure to her grandmother. Yet, the suggestion we are investigating is that Olga's activity will be valuable only if she is likely to perform successfully. But if we have to admit that her performance will be successful just in case it is valuable, and that there is no independent standard for what should count as success in this situation, success cannot be a condition of the value of the activity. Is this a peculiarity of the example, perhaps generated by the fact that Olga's playing serves a further purpose: namely, giving pleasure to her grandmother? Would the situation be different if we focused instead on a concert performance? When is she likely to succeed on such an occasion? Again, it seems to me that the standard of success is entirely dependent on the value of the activity itself. After all, there can be different kinds of concerts, and they may be valuable in different ways. In each case, success would consist in performing in such a way that the activity is valuable.

How about pleasure, the proposed second condition of the value of an activity? In order to discuss this issue properly, we need an account of pleasure—which I cannot even begin to expound here. Let me therefore be very sketchy. What is pleasure, after all? Following Aristotle, a pleasurable activity just is (1) an unimpeded[43] or (2) a completed one.[44] If we

---

[43] Aristotle, *Nicomachean Ethics* VII, 1153b10.

[44] 'Pleasure completes the activity not as the corresponding permanent state does, by its immanence, but as an end which supervenes as the bloom of youth does on those in the flower of their age' (ibid. X, 1174b30; trans W. D. Ross).

assume this understanding of pleasure, pleasure could not constitute a second condition, independent of success. If performing an activity in such a way that it realizes its value should count as success, and its completion as pleasure, the two conditions are neither independent of each other, nor of the value of the activity itself. There is, of course, a different kind of pleasure, too, which is not captured by the two Aristotelian suggestions: namely, physical pleasure. But for most activities, this will hardly be a condition of the value of the activity. It may be relevant in some cases (like lying on a beach, enjoying the sun), but when it is, it would probably have to be explained, again, by the value of the activity involved—and not as an independent condition of its value.

The discussion of subjective conditions above leads to the conclusion that our reasons to engage with things of value do not depend on subjective conditions, because we can have those reasons even in their absence. As to the suggestion that the value of activities—for the most part—depends on success and pleasure: in cases where this is true, success and pleasure are not independent of the value of an activity. What counts as success in a particular case depends, as we have seen, on the value of the activity; and an activity is pleasant if it is successful, i.e. realizes the good it aimed at—and not the converse.

How, then, can it be that 'taste and inclination' are conditions of having a reason to engage with value? Even though claiming that reasons have 'subjective conditions' seems to be the reply to my problem that many people are inclined to give, I don't see a way of explaining how this could be so, short of changing directions completely and turning to a desire-based account of reasons. Hence, if the solution to the problem is to be that reasons have subjective conditions, it would better be interpreted as (1) than as (2) or (3).

To summarize: in order to establish a non-relativized 'ought', we have to establish closure among the reasons we are considering, and also identify which of our undefeated reasons is the strongest. Raz wrongly believes that incommensurability of reasons allows us to achieve both aims quickly in most cases of practical deliberation. Discarding this option, there are two different ones that I considered, neither of which seemed satisfying: (1) Closure is established by framing our choices. We simply consider only a few of the available options. This move seems arbitrary. (2) 'Engaging with' reasons are only conditional reasons. They are reasons for a person only if she fulfils certain subjective conditions. Assuming that those subjective conditions can function as a filter, their introduction would again allow us to establish closure quickly. However, all the candidate subjective conditions (desire, success, pleasure) that I tested above seemed unsuited for the job. Therefore, it remains unclear how the metaphysical account of reasons as aspects of values can be mapped on to a satisfactory understanding of practical reasoning.

C. Rejecting the Entailment Claim

However, there is a fourth explanation of how my acting on my reasons might depend on taste and inclination—or, more generally, on subjective conditions.

4. A person has reason to engage with value, period. But whether she is rationally at fault for not doing so depends on the circumstances.

This does not reduce the number of the too many reasons, but blocks certain normative consequences. It might come closest to what Raz calls 'the basic belief'. I may have reason to engage with all the things of value that there are, but I am not in the wrong if I don't. But, for this claim, 'taste and inclination' are immaterial. It is tantamount to rejecting the entailment claim—the claim that every reason statement entails an ought statement—and is therefore not available to Raz. Yet, this is the only response to the too-many-reasons problem, so far as I can see, which captures the commonsensical understanding of the role of subjective conditions. It is neither that I only have a reason if I have an inclination to act accordingly, nor that I ought to act on certain reasons only if I have an inclination to do so. Rather, the point is that since there is an abundance of reasons to do things that will count as engaging with value, I might as well go by my 'taste and inclination'; I might as well let them determine what reasons I am going to follow. For 'taste and inclination' to play the role of a truly optional factor, which is itself void of normative implications, it seems to be necessary that *reasons* are 'optional' in a much stronger sense than the one that Raz allows for; it requires that they be optional not only because other things are as good or incommensurate. For 'taste and inclination' to play the role that they seem to play in everyday deliberation, reasons have to be optional in the stronger sense that having a reason does *not* entail an 'ought' statement. 'Taste and inclination' may well come in, if I am to decide what to do, but without being reasons or conditions of having reasons.

Therefore, I am inclined to conclude that Raz's view of reasons as aspects of things of value can only be sustained if we reject the entailment claim—at least for 'engaging with' reasons (possibly not for reasons of respect). This would, of course, call for a reinterpretation of the normativity of reasons,[45] which I cannot even attempt to begin in this essay.[46]

---

[45] Jimmy Lenman urged me to consider the possibility that a reason statement might not entail an ought statement, but rather a permission to act accordingly. This suggestion is, of course, tempting, because it preserves the link to other deontic notions, such as 'ought'. 'Ought' could then be defined as not being permitted not to do something. Yet, this suggestion seems wrong to me for the following reasons: (1) The reasons we deal with are *pro tanto* reasons only. However, there seems to be no *pro tanto* permission. Permissions are always 'all out': saying that you are permitted to φ is tantamount to saying that there is nothing that counts against φ-ing. (2) Reasons, it is often said, *count in favour* of actions. Permissions, on the other hand, are only negative: an action is permitted, if nothing counts against it. Hence, there is no contradiction in saying that while you are permitted to φ, there is no reason to φ; i.e. while nothing counts against it, nothing counts in its favour either.

[46] An earlier version of this paper was presented at a conference on 'The Ethics of Joseph Raz' in March 2002 in New York. I am grateful to the participants of the conference for comments and critical discussion. I am also much indebted to Alon Harel, Victoria McGeer, Jimmy Lenman, Joseph Raz, Randall Rose, Jay Wallace, and, especially, Philip Pettit for extremely helpful written comments. At different stages Thérèse Björkholm, Elisabeth Herschbach, and Sherry Orbach helped me with editing the manuscript. I owe a great deal to their suggestions, and I am very thankful for their generous help. Finally, I would like to thank the participants of the Philamore group for a very instructive and insightful discussion.

7

The Truth in Deontology

Philip Pettit and Michael Smith

Let a deontological constraint be a pattern of action that people ought to adopt, even when doing so will not be for the best; more precisely, even when it will not be for the best in promoting conformity to that very course of action on the part of agents overall, or perhaps on the part of that agent over life as a whole. Deontologists argue that such constraints have a widespread and fundamental presence in moral thought. They govern how we should behave across a wide front, whether in our dealings with ourselves, with one another, or with the rest of nature. And the authority they have over us is not derived from the impersonal value of satisfying them, as teleologists or consequentialists would argue; it is in that sense fundamental.

With characteristic sensitivity to the ways in which we reason about what to do in various circumstances, Joseph Raz gives a sympathetic hearing to the claims of deontological constraints.[1] He thinks that deontological patterns of thought are a mark of agents we tend to admire. And, going still further, he sets himself against the idea that consequentialism might be able to explain their authority by pointing us towards neutral goods whose promotion would explain their hold over us. Consequentialists might prescribe the satisfaction of the constraints in normal cases, where satisfying them is for the best, but would take the opposite line in perverse circumstances where it is not for the best. Raz sides with deontology in maintaining that at least some constraints have a fundamental, teleologically underivable status.

---

[1] Joseph Raz, *The Morality of Freedom* (Oxford: Oxford University Press, 1986), chs. 11–13.

Our aim in this paper is to argue that deontological constraints do indeed have a widespread presence in moral thought, being relevant in an endless range of cases. We try to show that the practice of deliberation is at the core of social life, and that it intrudes deontological constraints to which we must all claim to defer. In doing this, we take a different approach from Raz, but one that he may find complementary; we associate constraints, not with the received conception of admirable agents, but with the framework within which we conduct many of our interactions with others. But towards the end of the paper we break more decisively with his position, arguing that the case made for the widespread presence of deontological constraints does not argue for giving them a fundamental status; it does not rule out consequentialism. There is truth in deontology, but that is not to say that deontology or non-consequentialism is true.

The paper is in five sections. In the first, we show how the simple activity of playing a game can impose deontological restrictions on players; in the second we describe the practice of deliberative exchange, emphasizing the parallel with game-playing activity; in the third we show how deontological restrictions are associated with deliberative exchange; in the fourth we argue that these restrictions—unlike those involved in game-playing—are hard for people generally not to countenance; and then in a brief, concluding section we show why the truth in deontology that is thereby established does not necessarily mean that deontology is true.

1. Deontological Games

One context in which deontological attitudes are at home is that of the game. Think of the game in which different individuals or groups compete for what is deemed to be victory. Think of chess or cricket or football or whatever. In any such game there are rules that people countenance as governing the things that they may and may not do in pursuit of victory. In particular, there are rules such that not to follow them is, by received criteria, to fail to play the game. These are sometimes described as rules that are constitutive of the game, as distinct from rules that regulate how the game is best played, or fairly played, and so on.[2] They are design

---

[2] J. R. Searle, *Speech Acts: An Essay in the Philosophy of Language* (Cambridge: Cambridge University Press, 1969).

specifications on what has to be done among the parties involved in order for them to count as playing the game. Let those specifications be implemented, and a game of the relevant sort will take place; let them fail to be implemented, and it will fail to take place.

Since these truths about the constitutive rules of a game are going to be available to all, and since game playing is an intentional activity, the success of players in conforming to the rules will manifestly be within their intentional control. They will each conform intentionally to the rules. That being a fact accessible to everyone, they will each expect everyone to conform intentionally. And that in turn being a fact accessible to everyone, they will each expect everyone to expect this, and so on. That they each conform intentionally, in other words, will be a matter of common or mutual or shared awareness between them.[3]

Other patterns of common awareness will emerge to supplement this common awareness of intentional conformity. In particular, it is almost inevitable that people will come to share in a common awareness that violating a rule is a fault within the context of a game; that each naturally relies on others not to violate rules in that way; that violators will attract a negative reaction from those who relied on them; that this is something that any violator will have been in a position to predict; and so that no one who violates a rule can protest against the negative reaction of others. Violators must be taken, as the vernacular has it, to have licensed or permitted complaint about their violation of the rules; after all, they advertised themselves as game-players who were aware of the rules and aware of the reliance of others.[4]

These claims are all fairly plausible, given familiar facts about human psychology, and given that those facts are generally accessible, that their accessibility is itself generally accessible, and so on. Without trying to document them in detail, we are going to take them as granted in this paper. They entail that the constitutive rules of a game will get established among players as rules that they recognize as binding and rules that can be invoked in licensed or permitted complaint about any breach. The rules will serve within the context of the game as norms that all endorse as guiding ideals and as ideals in the name of which they allow themselves to be judged.

---

[3] David Lewis, *Convention* (Cambridge, Mass.: Harvard University Press, 1969).

[4] Margaret Gilbert, *On Social Facts* (Princeton: Princeton University Press, 1989); T. M. Scanlon, *What We Owe to Each Other* (Cambridge, Mass.: Harvard University Press, 1998).

The thing to notice now about the constitutive rules that serve in such a normative role is that they identify faults after a deontological pattern. Let us think of a violation of the rules as consequentially productive when it promises to reduce breaches generally, or even to reduce later breaches on the part of the agent. The deontological character of the constitutive rules of a game appears in the fact that a failure to abide by those rules counts as a fault, even if it is consequentially productive in reducing the overall number of breaches. Games would be impossible if players were allowed to duck in and out of compliance with the constitutive rules, depending on whether such violations were consequentially productive in that sense. So the rules which govern game-play serve as deontological norms for the players.

Putting this in other terms, the rules represent binding constraints on how the players are to interact with one another, not attractive constraints whose fulfilment they should try to promote in aggregate.[5] They determine that certain patterns of behaviour constitute wrongdoing, and they indict wrongdoing even in the case where the wrongdoing allows less wrong to be done overall. Thus they mark a distinction between wrongdoing and allowing the doing of wrong. It is against the rules of the game to violate them; it is not against the rules of the game not to reduce or eliminate violations by others or by oneself at a later time. Players are required to conform to the rules, but beyond the requirements of those rules, everything is permitted within the game.

Given that the context of a game may give rise in the manner sketched to essentially deontological norms, a natural question is whether something of the kind could be the source of those deontological requirements that many see as having an intuitive and intelligible hold on us in day-to-day life. Can we think of any game-like context which is relevant in human interactions generally—not just when we take up chess or cricket or whatever—and which might explain the fact that certain normative prohibitions, such as those on violence and lying, are often assumed to have a deontological character? Can we think of any game-like venture that is not discretionary in the way in which chess and cricket are discretionary and that deontologically shapes the expectations to which we hold one another in ordinary moral talk?

---

[5] Robert Nozick, *Anarchy, State, and Utopia* (Oxford: Blackwell, 1974).

We think that there is such a practice that we human beings undertake in common, without paying much attention to the fact, and that it can serve to explain the hold of certain intuitive prohibitions. It underwrites deontological restrictions in the manner of the constitutive rules of a game, but the restrictions underwritten have a much deeper hold on us than game-playing rules. Where we can choose or not choose to play a game like chess or cricket, we can hardly conceive of exiting from this practice. The restrictions associated with it may not be categorical, in the sense of being conditional on nothing; after all, they are conditional on participation in the practice. But they approximate categorical restrictions so far as that on which they are conditional is a mode of interaction that humans cannot easily avoid.

2. Deliberative Exchange

The practice we have in mind is that whereby human beings relate to one another as deliberative or discursive partners, seeking and offering counsel about what one or more of their number should hold or do, consulting about patterns of reciprocation that may appeal to each, or taking counsel together about what they should jointly do or hold. It may involve the assembly that has to make a collective judgement or decision. Or it may involve two or more people working out a pattern of mutually beneficial exchange. Or it may just involve two or three people comparing notes about what one of them should think or do in this or that circumstance.

In any such exchange people claim to direct one another's attention to reasons that are relevant to what they should think or do. Reasons in this sense are either considerations that explain why a decision or judgement is right or considerations that explain why they are right for someone with certain pre-existing commitments.[6] Deliberative practice purports to facilitate the access that participants have to such reasons, including reasons that may support reciprocal or joint action. It directs people to presumptive, hitherto unregistered facts and values, in particular facts and values that bear on what they ought to believe or do, individually or collectively.[7]

[6] John Broome, 'Reasons', ch. 2 in this volume.
[7] Philip Pettit, *A Theory of Freedom: From the Psychology to the Politics of Agency* (Cambridge and New York: Polity and Oxford University Press, 2001); Philip Pettit and Michael Smith, 'Freedom in Belief and Desire', *Journal of Philosophy* 93 (1996), 429–49.

What are the marks of deliberative practice? Deliberative exchange always involves people seeking to influence one another, or at least accepting that what they do may have such an influence. But the influence they seek in deliberation is not that achieved by putting obstacles or penalties or rewards in one another's path. They look for influence in deliberation by trying to affect one another's beliefs, including beliefs about the presence of such factors. But again, they don't look for influence by inducing beliefs in any old manner. They look for influence in the characteristically open fashion of communication, where it is evident that speakers intend to elicit certain beliefs, in particular beliefs that they themselves purportedly endorse; evident that they intend the audience to be aware of this; evident that they intend them to form the beliefs in virtue of that awareness; and so on in the usual Gricean explication of these things. More specifically still, they look for the sort of influence provided by sincere communication, trying to get the audience to believe things that they do actually endorse; to deceive others, after all, is hardly to deliberate with them.

Is sincere communication enough to ensure deliberation? Whether I seek to communicate sincerely how the world is in some respect or how I am in some respect—say, in respect of belief or desire or intention—I must begin with the sincere communication of what I believe: that the world is thus and so, or that I am thus and so. I must sincerely communicate what I believe—say, that p—both in the sense of communicating the content of what I believe and the fact that I believe it; I must put before you both the assumed fact that p, and the fact that I believe that p, though of course you may not be persuaded of either: communication is not necessarily successful communication. The question which arises now is whether the sincere communication of what we each believe, understood in this way, is always going to count as an instance of deliberating with one another.

The sincere communication of belief is going to count as deliberating with one another, intuitively, only so far as it involves exploring the reasons that we each have for believing, desiring, and doing things. It will involve trying to spell out the available options for belief or intention or action before us, individually or jointly, and then searching out the range and the relevance to choice of those considerations that we countenance as reasons—or, going deeper still, that we can give one another reason for countenancing as reasons. Exploring reasons with one another in this sense is an inherently epistemic project, though it may promise a practical pay-off in reciprocal or joint action, and may be pursued because of that promise. It contrasts intuitively with the attempt to engineer one another's reasons and manipulate one another's responses.

The engineering of reasons and the manipulation of responses may occur via insincere communication: deception, after all, is a standard means of manipulation. But it turns out that it may also materialize via sincere communication. Thus it is necessary to distinguish between the sincere, epistemic form of communication involved in deliberating with one another and the sincere, manipulative communication that contrasts with it.

The paradigm of sincere, manipulative communication is the threat. We are not thinking of the deceptive threat—not the bluff threat, as it might be called—since it does not count as sincere. And we are not thinking of the predictive threat in which I warn you that if you do B, I will do A, since your doing B would provide me with an independent reason for that response: a reason that would have obtained, even if I hadn't spoken to you about it. Nor, as will appear later, are we thinking of the mesmerizing threat that saps the nerve and the rationality of the audience. We have in mind the threat I might make to penalize your doing B by doing A in punitive response, where I have no independent reason to respond in that way: no reason independent of the reason I have to declare my intention and push you away from B.

This threat is a manipulative attempt to engineer or rig the reasons that are relevant to what you should do, though it may also involve exploring those reasons as they exist after the rigging. Such coercion does not count, intuitively, as an exercise of deliberation. When I threaten you in an attempt to coerce a certain response, I tamper with factors that deliberation would limit me to exploring: the options before you and the considerations available to adjudicate between those alternatives. What I do involves changing the options before you—replacing the B option with the option of doing-B-and-then-being-penalized—or, equivalently, triggering a new reason in the attempt to influence the choice: creating a penalty that constitutes a reason not to choose B. It involves engineering your reasons, as we put it, not exploring them—or at least not just exploring them— with you.

Not only does deliberation require the sincere communication of belief, then; it also has to have an epistemic character, being an attempt to explore your reasons with you. Does this stipulation rule out offers as well as threats? The deceptive offer—another sort of bluff—will be ruled out as an insincere form of communication. The predictive offer will be ruled in, on the grounds that allowed us to rule in the predictive threat. And the mesmerizing offer will be ruled out on the same grounds as the mesmerizing threat; more on this in a moment. But what about the more regular offer: the offer to reward your doing something, say D, by doing C in response, where the reason for making the C reward available, as well as the reason to let you know about it, is to motivate you to do D? Do we have to rule out such regular offers, on the grounds that they are just as manipulative as ordinary threats? Do we have to rule out those offers in which mutually beneficial co-operation may originate, for example, as when you and I make agreements and contracts?

Happily, it turns out that we do not have to take any such drastic line. The offer of a reward that you have no means of refusing—for example, the offer to broadcast your success, should you achieve some result or other—will clearly be a way just of engineering your reasons and will have to fall to the stipulation that rules out strategic threats; it represents a form of manipulation, nothing more. But most offers are not like that, since they are offers of rewards that can be refused by those to whom they are made. And this possibility of refusal makes all the difference.

What I do in making an offer of a reward for your D-ing—strictly, a reward that does not mesmerize you, say by connecting with an urgent need—is not, or at least not directly, to engineer the reasons you have in respect of the options before you. I do not interfere with any of the existing factors which deliberation would limit me to exploring: your options or the considerations relevant to the choice of those options. Rather what I do is to expand the realm of available options to include, not just D-ing and E-ing, but also D-ing-and-then-collecting-a-reward. Making such a refusable offer is friendly to deliberation so far as it does not change any of the factors that deliberation would limit me to exploring: your existing options and the considerations relevant to choosing between them.[8]

Making such a refusable offer may be cast, indeed, as itself an instance of deliberating with you. It is designed to provide information, after all, on a new option that you may be very glad to consider: that of D-ing-and-then-collecting-a-reward. I might have invited you in clear epistemic vein to

---

[8] Pettit, *Theory of Freedom*, ch. 4.

consider, and perhaps enquire into, whether a third party would be willing to reward you for *D*-ing. In the refusable offer I invite you to consider whether I would be willing to do this, and, anticipating your enquiry, I say that yes I would.[9]

This line fits with our intuitive conception of deliberation. If you seek my deliberative advice, inviting me to explore the reasons you have to do this or that, then you may reasonably complain if I directly engineer those reasons by manipulatively putting penalties in place. But you can hardly complain if I respond by expanding the range of options, arranging things so that not only can you do this or that, you can also take one of the existing options and enjoy a reward at the same time; certainly you can hardly complain if the offer is of the non-mesmerizing sort. This is an exercise in which I may seek to influence you, and perhaps enjoy success in the enterprise, but it does not involve engineering your reasons in the manipulative manner of a threat.[10]

To sum up the line of thought so far, deliberative exchange involves the sincere, epistemic communication of belief in which people attempt to explore with one other the reasons they have to form various attitudes or perform various actions, whether individually, reciprocally, or jointly. Is this enough, then, by way of a definition? Not quite, though it comes close. For the sincere, epistemic communication of belief may sometimes have the contingent effect of exposing the audience to pressures that rig the reasons available—in the manner, roughly, of coercion—or that reduce the audience's capacity to

---

[9] Many writers, following Habermas, mark a difference between the activity of bargaining with others and debating with them. See Jürgen Habermas, *A Theory of Communicative Action*, vol. 1 (Cambridge: Polity, 1984) and *A Theory of Communicative Action*, vol. 2 (Cambridge: Polity, 1989). And see Jon Elster, 'Arguing and Bargaining in Two Constituent Assemblies', *University of Pennsylvania Journal of Constitutional Law* 2 (2000), 345–421. We believe that there are various ways this distinction could be made in our terms. For example, and perhaps most plausibly, bargaining may be identified with the practice of deliberating with others and making offers in an effort at mutual accommodation, whereas debating is identified with deliberating with others in an attempt to determine what should be jointly done on the basis of jointly accepted premises.

[10] As a matter of definition, of course, I will have raised the opportunity cost of your existing options: *D*-ing or *E*-ing (and in neither case collecting a reward). Does that involve engineering your reasons, then? We hold not. What explains the fact that you ought, say, to perform *D* and accept the reward, if indeed that is what it turns out you ought to do? What in that sense—the sense signalled in the text—is your reason for taking the option? Not, except more or less tautologically, the fact that it has the lowest opportunity cost. Rather, the fact which explains why that is so: viz., that the considerations that function as reasons for you make it more attractive than the alternatives.

process reasons properly. We now propose to strengthen the characterization of deliberative exchange in a way that restricts it to cases where the interaction is not warped by such extraneous pressures.

It may seem difficult to incorporate the proposed restriction in a tighter definition, since doing so would appear to require, impossibly, a full list of the pressures that might vitiate deliberation. We would define deliberative exchange as the sincere, epistemic communication of belief that is designed to explore the audience's reasons with them, where the communication does not apply extraneous pressures *a* or *b* or *c*...It turns out, however, that no such inventory of extraneous pressures is required. The practice of deliberative exchange involves a heuristic for identifying factors that apply such pressures—we may call them 'vitiators'—and we can invoke those factors, therefore, without having a detailed list to offer. We can define deliberative exchange as involving the sincere, epistemic communication of belief, where the communication is not affected by vitiators of the kind recognized in deliberative practice.

The reason why deliberative exchange involves a heuristic for identifying vitiators goes back to a central aspect of such interaction. The parties to deliberative exchange will not just report judgements and intentions to one another, as if they were matters of incidental, theoretical interest. For reasons parallel to those rehearsed in the discussion of games, such reporting will be transformed by the emergence of certain common beliefs among them. Thus they will report their judgements and intentions in a recognition that others may rely on their holding by the views and the goals in question: that others may make their plans around the assumption that such attitudes are in place, as in commitments to reciprocal or joint action. The parties will elicit this reliance, where it is relevant, as a matter commonly accessible to all, thus depriving themselves—again, in a way that is accessible in common to all—of any basis for protesting against complaints should they not prove reliable; in this sense, they will license or permit such complaints. In order to mark this special way in which the parties to deliberative exchange may report their judgements and intentions, we can say that they avow those attitudes or commit themselves to them. They report the attitudes in a context where reliance is elicited, and exposure to complaint accepted, as a matter of common assumption.[11]

[11] Victoria McGeer, 'Is "Self-knowledge" an Empirical Problem? Renegotiating the Space of Philosophical Explanation', *Journal of Philosophy* 93 (1996), 483–515; Victoria McGeer and Philip Pettit, 'The Self-regulating Mind', *Language and Communication* 22 (2002), 281–99.

But if the practice of deliberative exchange involves avowal and exposure to complaint, it has to involve an adjudicative procedure under which complaints may be validated or invalidated. Deliberators implement such a procedure when they identify cases where a person may not have lived up to an avowal but decide that something about the original occasion of avowal excuses such a failure. Perhaps the person avowed such-and-such a belief, declared such-and-such an intention, made such-and-such a promise. No matter. It is not appropriate to hold the person to that sort of avowal because it was made under this or that extraneous pressure, and, by the criteria implicit in the validating procedure, the pressure provides an excuse—partial or full—for non-performance.

The presence of this validating procedure in deliberative practice means that we can define vitiators as factors that would be taken, under the practice, to excuse someone who made an avowal from acting on it; specifically, they would excuse such non-performance on grounds related to the character of the original exchange. Typical excusers in this category, and so typical vitiators, are the sorts of factors present when we can speak of one person oppressing or exploiting or intimidating another. Suppose I hold out a reward or a penalty—say, a predictive, otherwise acceptable penalty—of a kind that mesmerizes you with an intoxicating or terrifying prospect. Suppose I take advantage of your urgent needs by proposing to sell you a medicine you require but only at an outlandish price. Or suppose I exploit your more general dependence on me, using it—perhaps without either of us being aware of the fact—to get you on side with whatever I say or propose. Under existing deliberative practice, you have a reasonable excuse—perhaps partial, perhaps full—for later refusing to comply with certain commitments you may have made in conditions of those kinds; I cannot expect my complaints about non-compliance to be given significant weight. Those conditions, so the invalidation of the complaints suggests, vitiated the exchange of reasons involved, depriving it of a deliberative, or at least fully deliberative character.[12]

---

[12] The line taken here for downgrading certain cases where people exchange reasons—in our terms, downgrading them from fully deliberative status—should be distinguished from that adopted, for example, by Jürgen Habermas, *Moral Consciousness and Communicative Action* (Cambridge: Polity, 1990). He argues that in such cases there are always reasons put forward which flout the principle that no consideration should be allowed to carry weight with anyone unless everyone can accept it as a guide for everyone to follow. See too Christopher McMahon, 'Why There is No Issue between Habermas and Rawls', *Journal of Philosophy* 99 (2002),

This leaves us, finally, with a working definition of deliberative exchange or practice. Deliberative exchange involves sincere, epistemic and unvitiated communication on the part of the persons involved, the aim being to explore one another's reasons in the realm of thought or action, including reciprocal and joint action. Or, in full-dress definition, deliberative exchange occurs just so far as

- the parties sincerely communicate their beliefs, openly seeking to get one another to recognize and share them;
- the communication is intended as an epistemic exploration of one another's reasons for believing or doing various things, individually, reciprocally, or collectively;
- there are no vitiators present, so that any avowals of attitude—any commitments—are inescapable under the rules of the practice: only a later change of circumstances can excuse non-compliance.

This definition of deliberative exchange answers, as we have been arguing, to a range of intuitions about when it is appropriate to think that people are deliberating with one another. But it also has another merit that may make it appealing. It represents a dialogical version—a version involving two or more people—of a process that we each conduct in our own case as we try to reason anything through, whether with a view to making a judgement of fact or forming an intention about what to do.

Imagine that I am conducting a bit of theoretical or practical reasoning of this kind. I endorse a consideration, let us say, that I take to be relevant to the conclusion I am to form. Since I will only form that conclusion later, I have to think of myself down that track—perhaps seconds, minutes, or hours down that track—as someone to whom I offer the consideration in the way I offer a consideration in sincere, epistemically oriented communication. And at that later time I have to receive the consideration as my past self's testimony, treating that self in the interlocutor role in which it self-presents. It makes no sense in this epistemically driven enterprise for me at one time to think of forcing my later hand, or deceiving my later self, or putting a coercive intertemporal threat in place. I may

111–29; and Scanlon, *What We Owe to Each Other*. The line taken here promises to downgrade every case that this test would indict. And, more positively, it downgrades certain cases that that test would miss and would be wrong to miss. I may exploit your dependence on me in deliberation despite the fact that every consideration I put forward is reasonable according to Habermas's principle. And yet, intuitively, a case of that kind ought to be downgraded from full normative status.

sometimes try to do that, of course, as when I place little confidence in my later self, and think manipulation is required. But in the process of reasoning, theoretical and practical, I have to relate to myself across time in the manner described.

The definition we have offered of deliberative exchange is supposed to catch an interpersonal analogue of the intra-personal process of reasoning in this way. Just as reasoning with myself requires me to communicate sincerely and epistemically across time, with each self relying on past and future counterparts to live up to certain expectations, so deliberation with others requires analogous moves. It may be some support for the definition offered that what it requires to be in place among partners to deliberation is precisely the sort of thing that must be in place across time whenever people reason with themselves.

3. Deliberative, Deontological Restrictions

The practice of deliberative exchange makes a central place in human life for the recognition of certain deontological restrictions. Such exchange, like the sorts of games described earlier, is governed by constitutive rules. And the existence of these rules means that people who present themselves as aspiring to deliberative exchange, in an understanding of what it involves, must accept that they are going to be expected, as a matter of common knowledge, to endorse those rules and to license others to complain in a deontological way about any failures to live up to them.

Some of the rules that are constitutive of deliberation are rules of conduct—rules for the conduct of deliberation—whereas others are rules of compliance with commitments made within deliberative exchange. By the first clause in the definition of deliberative exchange, to take up the first category, every party must communicate certain attitudes, not seek to impose or inculcate them by other means; and every party must communicate those attitudes sincerely. By the second clause, every party to deliberative exchange must look for an influence on addressees of an epistemic kind. The aim of each must be to draw the attention of others to the options before them in any choice of theory or action and to search out the relevance to their choice of all those reasons that they countenance or can be given reason to countenance. And by the third clause, a number of further prescriptions and prohibitions follow. I will not be participating in deliberative exchange as such—I will be playing by different rules, playing a different game—if I look for any influence that is supported by deliberatively vitiating pressures such as those that derive from the dependency or the vulnerability or the impressionability of the addressee.

The constitutive rules of deliberative exchange also include rules of compliance. These govern, not how parties should conduct themselves in the course of deliberation, but how they should behave in its wake. They require them to comply with any commitment incurred within the exchange, as in commitments to holding by a certain belief or intention, and acting on it. This sort of commitment may emerge in any deliberative interaction, but it will be typical, in particular, of the sort that leads to co-operative or collective projects. These rules of compliance are constitutive of deliberative exchange in the sense that the practice would cease to exist if participants refused to admit that they could reasonably be challenged with failures to abide by those rules.

The existence and the accessibility of these constitutive rules mean that people who enter into deliberative exchange must disclaim, as a matter of common knowledge, any attitude or action that runs counter to them. Thus no one can aspire to deliberate with someone without being taken to rule out deception, coercion, intimidation, or infidelity to commitments undertaken. And, of course, no one can have such an aspiration without being taken to rule out equally the exercise of force and the like. To set out to deliberate with someone is to announce or present oneself in a certain guise: as a person who can be expected to honour the constraints associated with deliberative exchange.

The constraints that one explicitly or implicitly claims to endorse in assuming the profile of a deliberative partner, like the constraints associated with the games we discussed earlier, are deontological in character. Suppose that I breach a rule of deliberative exchange and try to justify myself on the grounds that this is consequentially productive. The violation involved promises to reduce the number of violations committed in general, I say, whether by me or by others. This justification won't work, if it is meant to show that the violation is to count as a deliberative overture. Deliberative overtures are defined as overtures that are consistent with the rules of deliberative exchange, and any violation of the rules is a departure from that practice. So far as I violate those rules, therefore, I have to recognize that I have broken with the practice, and that there is no hope of justifying what I do as an instance of what the practice requires.[13]

The rules of deliberative practice, to put this matter another way, dictate that any violation of those rules is deliberatively wrong; they entail that, so far as I violate those rules, I fail to act deliberatively, and can be rebuked by those I let down. But while the rules proscribe such violations, they do not proscribe the act of allowing violations to occur, say on the part of others or on one's own later part. Doing wrong is unjustifiable within the rules of the practice, but allowing wrong to be done is justifiable. And so doing wrong can never be justified as an instance of what deliberative practice requires—it can never be presented as something less than wrongdoing of that kind—on the ground that it reduces such wrongdoing in general. The constraints imposed by deliberative practice are inescapably deontological in character.

4. The Significance of these Restrictions

How important is this result? Not very, it may seem, so far as it parallels the sort of thing that is true also in chess and cricket. True, the rules of deliberative exchange may rule out more significantly objectionable activities—force, intimidation, coercion, deception, infidelity—than the rules of any such game. But just as the rules of a game have a hold on us conditionally on our wanting to take part in the exercise, and not otherwise, so the same is true here. Granted I have to disclaim resort to deception and coercion, force and intimidation, so far as I want deliberative exchange. So what? That still leaves me free to embrace those activities, and make it clear that I am doing so. All it means is that I have a choice between playing the deliberative game, thereby licensing complaint about any resort to such behaviour, and parading the fact that I do not mean to conduct myself deliberatively.

This response, however, misses out on an important feature that makes deliberative practice special. Short of explicitly cancelling such a construal, most of the ordinary overtures I make to other people will signal a willingness to deliberate, as a matter of mutual assumption. And making those

---

[13] As becomes apparent in the concluding section, there may be hope of justifying an action, period, when there is no hope of justifying it as an instance of what the practice requires.

overtures, therefore, will mean exposing myself to deliberative expectations and, if I fail to perform appropriately, to deliberative complaints. Deliberative practice haunts human interaction, intruding as a default the assumptions on the basis of which people hold one another to deliberative standards. The jurisdiction of deliberative exchange has a resilient hold on human beings, and entrenches routines of assessment and criticism in the name of associated norms.

Consider what happens when I address others with a serious observation or query or proposal; when I speak to them in a way that is not just a bid for phatic stroking or tickling. How are they to take me? Clearly, they will think, I am putting myself forward as having a communicative intention, not just as meaning to pound their ears. And clearly I am putting myself forward as a sincere speaker; to present oneself as deceptive would be self-defeating. I may be threatening and seeking to coerce them, of course. But if I am, my words will make that plain; and short of that being made plain, the default assumption among my addressees must be that this is an overture in deliberative exchange: an invitation to reason about something of concern to one or all of us. Again, I may be doing this in the hope that an extraneous pressure I activate—say, the pressure on a dependant to keep me sweet—will secure the result I want. But in the normal course of addressing others, I will keep that sort of hope in the background, as something unsaid and unsalient, not as something my addressees are invited to see.

Granted that I am going to be taken in normal exchange to have deliberative intent, the question is whether I am likely to acquiesce in being taken that way. Acquiescing would mean acquiescing in its being for me a matter of assumption shared with my interlocutors that we are each disposed to conform to the rules of deliberative exchange; that we are each disposed to rely on commitments made within the exchange; and that we are each making ourselves vulnerable, therefore, to complaints about not proving reliable.

We think that I will have little choice in the normal situation but to acquiesce in this construal of my attitudes. The only alternative will be to renounce deliberation altogether, embracing the coercive or intimidating profile of someone who announces something tantamount to: 'this is an open competition for individual advantage', 'this is a fight for victory'. I face a stark set of options: either to go along with the image of intending a deliberative exchange, whether sincerely or insincerely, with or without the hope of pressuring others into taking my preferred line; or to renounce that image in favour of a declaration of war. Faced with such alternatives, the option of endorsing the deliberative image will normally prove irresistible. So we surmise; and so everyday evidence suggests.

Acquiescing in something's being a matter of mutual assumption involves not denying that it is a matter of mutual assumption in a context where this, as anyone can see, will otherwise go through by default. And not denying that it is a matter of mutual assumption in such a context amounts, in effect, to putting it forward positively as a matter of mutual assumption. In the case envisaged, then, I manifest a positive claim that the exercise sought or in process is one in which each of us communicates his or her attitudes in a sincere, epistemic, and unvitiated fashion; one in which the norms of deliberation are taken by all to be relevant and are firmly put in adjudicative place.[14]

The thesis defended does not mean that deliberative practice itself will have a ubiquitous presence in human life. What will have that sort of presence, rather, is the pretension to deliberative practice, where that pretension may be sincere or insincere, motivated or not motivated by a desire to exert extraneous pressure. To pretend to deliberation is to present oneself as accepting and endorsing the pattern of mutual assumptions on the basis of which deliberative exchange proceeds. It is to put oneself forward as sharing in a mutual belief that everyone involved intends to conform to deliberative norms; that everyone is relying on others to abide by those norms; and that everyone licenses complaints against them, should they fail to conform. Thus it is to cast oneself as operating within the jurisdiction of deliberative practice, inviting others to hold one to the expectation that one will conduct deliberation properly, and that one will comply with any commitments made within deliberative exchange.

---

[14] The sort of claim envisaged is close to what Jürgen Habermas would describe as an implied claim to validity. See his *Theory of Communicative Action*, vols. 1 and 2. He sometimes represents validity claims as claims about the subjective sincerity of the speaker in making a remark, asking a question, giving an order; about the objective suitability of the world in making that remark true, that question relevant, that order feasible; and about the inter-subjective authority of the speaker in virtue of which the overture cannot rightly be ignored by the addressees. See Habermas, *Moral Consciousness and Communicative Action*. This taxonomy is meant to cover all sorts of speech acts in a single formula, whereas our formula is designed with assertoric overtures primarily in mind. We note, however, that it would seem to ignore the claim implicit in such overtures to be communicating one's attitudes in an epistemic manner and not to be relying on any extraneous pressures for the efficacy of the communication.

The pretension to deliberative exchange, understood in this way, may be present without such exchange actually materializing. Recognizing that I will inevitably trigger the mutual assumption that we are involved in deliberation—and that I will inevitably expose myself, therefore, to adjudication in terms of deliberative norms—I may decide to make the best of this in self-serving terms. I may be prepared, where doing so is advantageous, to tell lies or break promises or rely on unspoken pressures that I can intrude in my dealings with others. And what I may do, of course, may be done by many others. Deliberative pretension does not ensure the realization of deliberative practice, then. All it means is that the norms associated with deliberative practice will be assured of relevance; what I and others do may not live up to those deliberative norms, but it will be subject to their jurisdiction.

At the beginning of this discussion we asked whether the restrictions associated with deliberation had any deeper bite than those associated with games. The suspicion raised was that they don't. One may apparently choose not to play the deliberative game in the way in which one may choose not to play chess or cricket. But we now see that this thought misses out on the fact that deliberative pretension has a resilient presence in social life. In routine overtures with others, one will naturally seem to be playing the deliberative game, whether that is something welcome or not. And in such overtures it will be difficult not to acquiesce in the assumption. Once one acquiesces in that assumption, of course, one exposes oneself to the jurisdiction of deliberative practice and to adjudication in the name of deliberative rules. Those rules will attain relevance in the assessment of how one behaves.

For all that this says, as we mentioned, it remains possible that people will pay little or no attention to the norms of deliberative exchange, flouting them with abandon. But the line of thought we have been running also gives us reason to think that people will tend to take the norms quite seriously. Suppose that someone routinely breaches deliberative norms and, as is likely to happen, that this becomes widely known. That will mean that the person will not be able to pretend effectively to deliberation with acquaintances, since they will take his or her past behaviour to show that in all likelihood the pretension is not sincere. But if the person is unable to pretend effectively to such deliberation, then that will ensure a sort of ostracism from their community. It will mean that the person cannot hope to enjoy the fruits of deliberative exchange with acquaintances—or of the simulation of deliberative exchange—in any area where such exchange makes others vulnerable.

The sort of ostracism envisaged will have quite enormous costs. First of all, it will severely reduce the ways in which those ostracized may hope to exercise even unwelcome influence over others. They may set out to force others to do things. Or they may shamelessly threaten and try to coerce them. Or they may seek to rig things so that others are unwittingly led to act as they want. But that is about all. The reserves of influence associated with deception and fraud, insinuation and innuendo, will remain closed. They are only there to be mined, after all, by the person who can effectively pretend to deliberation.

Not only is the ability to pretend to deliberation indispensable as a tool for the abuse of others in these ways, it is also the only instrumentality available whereby people can achieve certain mutually beneficial kinds of influence. We can depend on each other to be able to expand our own reserves of evidence and understanding, and so to improve the quality of our individual judgements and decisions, only so far as we can establish deliberative relations with one another, proving ourselves to be mutually reliable over the long haul of trial and test. And we can unite with others to achieve initiatives of joint action only so far as we can establish among ourselves that we are of a common, deliberatively shaped mind. Those who rely on force or coercion to get others to act with them will only be able to have faith in those others when they are under effective scrutiny. And those who seek to expand their own evidence and understanding by interrogation of those who fear them will be exposed to the paradox of the counsellor: the paradox that only the king who abjures his kingly power can hope to have honest counsellors.

Where the resilience of deliberative pretension facilitates entry to the jurisdiction of deliberative norms—it makes it almost impossible not to enter—the feature we have just been reviewing explains why that jurisdiction may be expected to have a substantive role in determining how people in the general run behave. Let people conduct themselves with relative indifference to the norms of deliberation, and they will find themselves deprived of the ability to pretend to deliberate, and so deprived of access to those overtures that involve deliberative pretension. They will find themselves cast out from the society of their immediate fellows. The only life possible for them will be a life on the hoof, in which they move on at every point where their deliberative recalcitrance begins to register with associates.

The considerations canvassed should be sufficient to establish that the practice of deliberative exchange has a compelling character that marks it off from the games discussed earlier. The fact that that practice imposes deontological constraints on us, therefore, means that such constraints have a central place in our dealings with one another; they assume an inescapable and imposing authority in our lives. People can parade an indifference to deliberative constraints only in those cases where they are dealing with others whom they cast unthinkingly beyond the pale of ordinary conversation and commerce. And such cases are likely to be infrequent. They may arise in the relations between despots and their underlings, or between two groups which are sworn to mutual enmity, but they are hardly robust phenomena on the settled, social scene.

The centrality of deliberative norms in social life shows up in the fact that we can usefully treat them as explicating the demands of respect, at least on one interpretation.[15] On this interpretation, to respect other people—to treat each as a person—is to deal with them in a deliberative fashion or, at the least, to deal with them in a way that leaves open the possibility of deliberation. Negatively, this requires not ostracizing them from one's world and not treating them with aggression or coercion or the like. Positively, it requires, first, addressing them as minds with which one can communicate in a sincere, epistemic, and unvitiated manner; and second, giving them a hearing as voices that can reach one's own mind in reciprocal fashion. When one addresses others in this way, the epistemic character of the deliberation projected means that one never treats them as means only, but always also as ends.

This interpretation of respect is a distinctively social one. It explains why one cannot fully sustain respect in relation to people who do not reciprocate in kind. And it explains why there are different ways in which social arrangements may jeopardize the possibility of respect without anyone's being at fault. Respect will be put at risk by the sort of asymmetry which means that one party has to condescend to others, as if in gratuitous benevolence, in addressing them or giving them a hearing. That is why Kant, following a long republican tradition, insists that it is in the nature of respect that it is not given as a gift.[16] One cannot receive respect as a gift

[15] Stephen Darwall, 'Two Kinds of Respect', *Ethics* 88 (1977), 36–49.

[16] On this theme in republicanism see Philip Pettit, *Republicanism: A Theory of Freedom and Government* (Oxford: Oxford University Press, 1997), chs. 1–2. On Kant see J. B. Schneewind, 'Autonomy, Obligation, and Virtue: An Overview of Kant's Moral Philosophy', in P. Guyer (ed.), *The Cambridge Companion to Kant* (Cambridge: Cambridge University Press, 1992), 309–41.

conferred by others; one can only have the respect of others when one is sufficiently on a par to be able to command it.

5. Deontology versus Teleology: A Comment

Where, finally, does this leave the more familiar debate between deontology and teleology, non-consequentialism and consequentialism, in moral theory? We have argued that certain deontological constraints have a widespread presence in human life, coming into play with deliberative pretension and deliberative practice. The question, however, is whether this means that they have a fundamental status as norms. Can they be derived as norms we generally ought to countenance, given the neutral good that doing so promotes, as consequentialists say? Or do they resist any such derivation, as deontologists would claim?[17]

There are two reasons why the truth that we have found in deontology—the truth that deontological constraints are so widespread—may seem to establish the truth of deontology. The first is that the deontological practice of deliberative exchange is absolutely central to human interaction, giving content to the very notion of respect. The second is that deliberative practice offers the only site at which the question between deontology and teleology can be debated and, being itself subject to deontological rules, makes a judgement in favour of teleology difficult or even incoherent. Neither consideration, however, is decisive.

The second consideration, to take them in reverse order, starts from the observation that the question between deontologists and teleologists arises within deliberative exchange, so it has to be debated under the deontological rules of that exchange. I give my reasons for why I think that whether something is the right way to behave is determined by the neutral consequences associated with it. You counter with your reasons for denying

---

[17] For the record, though one of us is committed to the truth of consequentialism, the other isn't. See Philip Pettit, 'A Consequentialist Perspective on Ethics', in M. Baron, M. Slote, and P. Pettit (eds.), *Three Methods of Ethics: A Debate* (Oxford: Blackwell, 1997), 92–174; Philip Pettit and T. M. Scanlon, 'Consequentialism and Contractualism', *Theoria* 66 (2000), 228–45; and Michael Smith, 'Immodest Consequentialism and Character', *Utilitas* 13 (2001), 173–94. For an overview of issues that arise for a consequentialism that evaluates practices and other items, as well as acts, see Philip Pettit and Michael Smith, 'Global Consequentialism', in Brad Hooker, Elinor Mason and Dale E. Miller (eds.), *Morality, Rules and Consequences* (Edinburgh: Edinburgh University Press, 2000), 121–33.

this. And both of us have to conduct that debate—where else?—in the context of deliberative, deontological rules.

But the fact that the issue has to be decided under deontological rules does not guarantee a victory for deontology. Victory would be guaranteed only if it was impossible within deliberative exchange to talk about why the practice of such exchange is valuable, and to ask after whether it may not occasionally be better—however regrettable—to eschew deliberation in favour of initiatives like coercion or outright force. But of course this is not impossible.

No impossibility blocks me from trying to convince you in deliberative exchange that what makes such exchange valuable, and in general better than alternatives, is the fact that it produces various attractive results. And no impossibility blocks me from arguing that whenever circumstances are perverse enough to make the prospective results of exiting the practice and resorting to force or coercion better than those of sticking with it, then that is what I should do. If I can argue this line successfully, I will be able to vindicate consequentialism; if not, not. And for all we have seen, both possibilities remain open.

The second reason why the truth in deontology may seem to ensure the truth of deontology derives from the centrality in human life of deliberative practice. The considerations rehearsed in the paper direct us to a canonical mode of interaction between human beings. And they show that this mode of interaction is conducted, in the nature of the case, under deontological restrictions that are admitted by all. One cannot deliberate with others and not disavow consequentialist calculations about what one should say or do, just as one cannot assume the profile of a friend in dealing with others and not eschew such thoughts. But deliberating with others is the very paradigm of interpersonal relations, and its non-consequentialist character may make deontology seem like an ineluctable doctrine.

Consistently with showing that deliberative practice has such a character, however, the considerations rehearsed leave it an open question whether rightness is determined in the last analysis by the neutral value of associated consequences. Deontologists are certainly on the right track in holding that the code implicit in the practice of deliberative exchange— the practice, as we take it, of interpersonal respect—is inherently deontological; and some may think that this is all they ever really wanted to maintain. But they are not on the right track if they go beyond this and hold that this in itself establishes the truth of deontology.

No matter how central deliberative practice is in human life, it is still possible that fidelity to this practice is required, as consequentialists maintain, only so far as it makes for the best overall. Who is to say that if fidelity to the practice is going to have disastrous results, for example— say, because it will hinder the prospect of saving innocent lives—I should still remain faithful to it, abjuring the force or coercion or whatever that would save those lives?[18]

It is common for consequentialists to argue that while a practice like friendship involves eschewing consequentialist thoughts in dealing with friends, still the practice should be espoused so far, and only so far, as it promises to be for the best overall. Its centrality notwithstanding, there is nothing to block consequentialists from taking a similar line on deliberative practice. The deontological character of that practice shows that there is truth in deontology, and perhaps more truth than consequentialists have traditionally allowed. But it does not show that deontology is true; it leaves the consequentialist problematic intact.[19]

---

[18] Commitment to even the interpersonal analogue of deliberative practice described above looks like it too will be vulnerable to the value of that commitment. See Michael Smith, 'Search for the Source', *Philosophical Quarterly* 49 (1999), 384–94.

[19] An earlier version of this paper was presented at a colloquium at the Australian National University. We were greatly aided by comments from participants at that colloquium. We are also especially grateful for comments received from Jay Wallace.

8

How to Engage Reason: The Problem of Regress

Peter Railton

Learning and Doing

Like me, I suspect, you learn to use the latest version of your word-processing program simply by launching into it. This time, everything has been proceeding as usual, until you first attempt to save a file.

Saving this file will replace an existing version. Are you sure you want to replace it?

You are sure, so you click on 'Yes'. But instead of the familiar whir of machinery as the file is saved, you receive another query:

You have confirmed your previous command. Are you sure you want to confirm?

'Humpf. This new version is a bit more conscientious than the one before. Oh, well. No doubt I'll get used to it. And it's true that just yesterday I clicked "Yes" so automatically that I overwrote a file I had wanted to save. So maybe another chance to confirm is a good thing.' Once again, you click on 'Yes'. A new message appears:

You have confirmed your previous command. Are you sure you want to confirm?

By now you're getting impatient. 'This is ridiculous. Does this machine want me to confirm everything? I'll check the Confirmation Options Menu.' When you discover you can't modify the feature, you disable it. 'Risky, but I've got to be able to do my work.'

Risky indeed. And didn't you just say confirmation of confirmation might be a good idea? 'Yes. But enough is enough.' You'd like to be able to reason with the computer, so that you could exercise some *judgement* about when enough is enough rather than simply turn the confirmation function off. But isn't your problem precisely too many occasions for judgement? You preferred the older version of the program, which obeyed your first replacement-confirmation command without further question, even though this sometimes led to it taking the next step too hastily. You see at once that requiring a judgement at each step is self-defeating, so prefer to 'automatize' the process of confirming—confirmations themselves are to be 'followed blindly'. As Wittgenstein infamously said, we, too, can obey a rule—a rule of inference, say—only if we can obey a rule 'blindly', without further question, choice, judgement, or interpretation.[1]

The word 'blindly', especially in conjunction with 'obey', has an ominous ring. But the notion here is perfectly ordinary and matter-of-fact—and that is indeed the point. Consider a teacher explaining aspects of English grammar to students in a French village school. His explanations show how a rule of English grammar is being applied in a given case. The students struggle to recall and apply these rules themselves when responding to the teacher's requests for further applications. Neither he nor they are 'blindly following' these grammatical rules of English, but in their own commentaries, they are blindly following the rules of their native French. So blindly, that some students might be surprised to learn which French rules are in play, and how they might be similar to the English rules they are finding it so hard to learn. A visitor to the class, who speaks English well but French hardly at all, would find the English examples transparent—'going without saying'—and the French explanations opaque. There is a difference, then, in which rules they follow blindly in speaking and hearing. Spontaneous speaking and hearing would be virtually impossible if speaking and hearing required eyes-open rule following.

At the Altar

Nigel has thought the matter through thoroughly, going over all the reasons he has for or against marrying Megan. He has concluded, all things

---

[1] Ludwig Wittgenstein, *Philosophical Investigations*, trans. G. E. M. Anscombe (London: Macmillan, 1953), 85, 88.

considered, that he unquestionably ought to do so. He knows only too well that his own aversion to binding decisions has cost him dearly in the past, and he is confident that in this case the chief source of any uneasiness he now feels about marrying Megan just *is* uneasiness about making so weighty a decision. Were he advising someone else in his shoes, there is no question about what he'd say: 'Marrying Megan is the thing to do. Above all, don't lose your chance.'

His mind and hers made up, they schedule the ceremony. And Nigel now finds himself at the altar, facing a smiling Megan as they stand before an expectant gathering of friends and relatives. 'Do you, Nigel, accept Megan as your lawful wedded wife, for better or for worse, in sickness and in health, 'til death do you part?' Nigel replies, without hesitation, 'I've thought the whole thing through and made up my mind. There is every reason in the world for me to marry Megan, and I definitely ought to say "yes" without delay.'

Why does the ceremony grind to a halt at this point? Has not Nigel's practical reasoning faculty done its job? Via a completed inference, it has reached an all-things-considered *ought* judgement as a conclusion. Joseph Raz has written:

Statements of facts which are reasons for the performance of a certain action by a certain agent are the premises of an argument the conclusion of which is that there is a reason for the agent to perform the action or that he ought to do it. Statements of the form '*p* is a reason for *x* to ϕ' correspond to an inference of which '*p*' is the premise 'there is a reason for *x* to ϕ' the conclusion. An inference the conclusion of which is a 'There is reason to . . .' statement or an 'ought' statement is a practical inference.[2]

But if practical reason has done all its work in Nigel, and performed perfectly, why is he once again at risk of irrationally losing a chance in a way he'll bitterly regret? What *incompetence* of practical reason is being shown? None, someone might say—all the fault lies with Nigel's will, not his practical reason.

Aristotle and Kant appear to disagree. For Aristotle, the conclusion of a practical inference—not some further effect or condition—is the 'beginning of action' itself (*De Anima* 433a16):

---

[2] Joseph Raz, *Practical Reason and Norms* (London: Hutchinson, 1975; reissued by Princeton University Press, 1990), 28.

That the action is the conclusion is quite clear; but the premises which lead to the doing of something are of two kinds, through the good and through the possible. (*Movement of Animals* 701a20–5)

Nigel has reached an all-things-considered *judgement* about the good and the possible, and shown admirable reason in doing so, but his reason is not yet *practical*. On the Aristoelian account, he remains practically irrational because his reasoning has not concluded in activity *attuned* to the reasons he so well discerns.

Kant similarly places the will *within* the faculty of practical reason, which functions as it should when it *attunes* (*Stimmung*) active willing to the reasons it has discovered. Thus he distinguishes two elements in practical reasoning or action in accord with 'self-legislation'. One is a judgement of reason that applies a law or rational requirement:

In all lawgiving . . . there are two elements: **first**, a law, which represents an action that is to be done as *objectively* necessary, that is, which makes the action a duty . . . . (*MM* 6: 218)[3]

This first, objective element is *not* practical, but theoretical:

By the first the action is represented as a duty [e.g., by showing how it fits the application of a categorical imperative test], and this is a merely theoretical cognition of a possible determination of choice, that is, of practical rules. (ibid.)

In principle, this cognition could be applied equally well to a third party, to humans in general, to a fictional figure in a story or philosophical example.[4] It is not self-*legislation*, and does not give the law action-governing force. This 'merely theoretical cognition' can, however, become practical and 'enacted' if it is engaged first-personally—when I apply the objective rule or test directly to a subjective maxim of action on my part (even if the act concerns my support for or encouragement of the conduct of others)—*and* this gives rise in me to an actual 'incentive':

. . . **second**, an incentive, which connects a ground for determining choice to this action *subjectively* with the representation of the law. (*MM* 6: 218)

---

[3] References to Immanuel Kant in the text are herein abbreviated as follows: *MM* = *The Metaphysics of Morals*; *CPrR* = *The Critique of Practical Reason*. Translations are those of M. J. Gregor in *Immanuel Kant: Practical Philosophy* (Cambridge: Cambridge University Press, 1996).

[4] Indeed, Raz points out that it may be an advantage of giving an *ought* statement as the conclusion of a practical inference that this permits first- and third-person symmetry. See *Practical Reason and Norms*, 28.

The connection with a 'ground for determining choice' (*Bestimmungsgrund*) is to be found in the 'faculty of desire', where, according to Kant, the will resides.

Some philosophers have objected to the idea that the conclusion of practical reason could be an action, in part on the ground that it seems incompatible with the phenomenon of *failure* to act upon what one acknowledges as the balance of reasons, e.g., in *akrasia*.[5] But a different way of thinking about *akrasia* suggests itself, for its distinctive character is not that of an inconsistency obtaining between a judgement concerning what is best or dutiful and one's own action, but that of a conflict *within* action, a tug-of-war or battle of will. The *akratic* knows only too well this feeling of being torn in two directions, and why *strength* or *weakness* are apt descriptions, rather than mere *consistency* and *inconsistency*. This battle of will involves—and is experienced as—being torn between conflicting action-tendencies: e.g., temptation versus self-respect or commitment. Attraction arising from appetite and perception can compete with standing desire to lose weight, producing real difficulty and frustration for the agent, whichever act he chooses. To master the situation, the agent's 'rational will', itself a desire, must be strong—his attention to the reasons he most respects and identifies with must be able to mobilize sufficient motivational force behind the distant goal of losing weight to overpower the impressive motivational force of a proximate and delectable chocolate mousse. Kant has a similar picture of the 'moral feeling' of respect for the moral law that figures in action done from duty:

...sensible impressions lose their influence on moral feeling only because respect for the law is more powerful than all such feelings together. (*MM* 6: 408)

The faculty of practical reason thus must include a strong and healthy 'faculty of desire'; an akratic agent displays not the utter displacement of his faculty of practical reason, but too little musculature within it. He should feel both pulls: hunger and the presence of delicious, available food constitute a *pro tanto* reason to eat, and if his idea of losing weight were that of an anorexic, we might well hope that this reason would predominate. Moreover, he will act intentionally even when he yields to temptation: he does not eat the mousse 'by mistake'. It is within intentionality that this battle is fought, and the battle is lost when the side of feelings of self-

---

[5] Ibid.

respect and commitment—how he would like to be—cannot mobilize as much force as the side of *gourmandisme*.

There might be no more than a preference for choice of words at stake in saying whether the conclusion of a practical inference is an *ought* judgement or an efficacious balance of action-tendencies. Recall, though, that the word *rational* comes from *ratio*, or proportion. Practical reason has as its specific domain governing practice—generating actual and effective intentional action-tendencies in *proportion* to the strength of reasons. This helps us, I think, to see Aristotle's point, and why he prefers a language of 'striking the right balance'. And it helps us to see Nigel as displaying *practical irrationality*, for his vivid sense of the dangers of commitment mobilizes a reluctance that his awareness of long-term reasons cannot seem to overpower.[6]

For Aristotle and Kant, too, the inclusion of action within practical deliberation is part of what gives the deliberative process its distinctive and serious character. We all know the vast phenomenological difference between serving on an advisory commission to a legislative or executive body versus serving in the executive or legislative body itself, which must make, live with, and take responsibility for decisions or enactments. Certainly Nigel knows this difference.

Apt Responsiveness to Reasons

We have been speaking of good and bad reasons. What if we wish to focus especially on the good ones?

---

[6] A similar point applies to intentions regarding actions that will largely take place in the future. If Aristotelian practical reasoning reaches a conclusion about such an action, then we have to say that the action begins to be set in motion at that time. This, however, helps explain why a person who is *irresolute*—who decides on Tuesday to accept a position by a future deadline, after weeks of careful deliberation, but who then constantly revisits the question as if from scratch almost daily up to the deadline—has not really concluded his practical deliberation on Tuesday after all, even though he might at that time have reached an all-things-considered judgement that he ought to accept the position. Once a decision is made, an entire suite of organismic responses is set in motion—not just planning based on this decision, but expectation, selective attention, emotions of various kinds, resistance to rethinking, and so on. If I have decided to buy a Volvo next model year based on *Consumer Reports*, I will find that I perk up my ears and begin nervously eavesdropping on the conversation when I hear two strangers discussing Volvos. On the present account, irresolution or lack of attentiveness to changed circumstances or available evidence that might disconfirm one's practical premises are failures of practical reason.

Thought and action are, after all, subject to normative assessment. There are, for example, rational and irrational beliefs, rational and irrational acts. There are, as well, true or false beliefs, and good or bad acts. It is an attractive idea to bring these two species of normative assessment together, to use the notion of truth to explain the notion of rational belief, and to use the notion of value to explain the notion of rational action. The explanation is mediated by the idea of *reasons for*—facts constitute reasons for belief, goods constitute reasons for action, and rationality consists in apt appreciation of, or responsiveness to, these reasons. For example:

Aspects of the world are valuable. That constitutes reasons for action. Because we are rational animals, ones with the power of reason, we are able to conduct ourselves in light of those reasons.[7]

The normativity of all that is normative consists in the way it is, or provides, or is otherwise related to reasons. . . . So ultimately the explanation of normativity is the explanation of what it is to be a reason, and of related puzzles about reasons. (p. 67)

But is there anything to say about the normativity of reason itself?

Reason is inherently normative. That is its central characteristic (p. 68).

Our curiosity may remain: What is 'inherent normativity', and if reason can have it, why can't other things, so that we could be 'aptly responsive to reasons' more directly, by responding to *them* rather than bringing reasons into it? Raz writes:

[A]ccounts of normativity and of reason and rationality, though not identical, are interrelated. An account of rationality is an account of the capacity to perceive reasons and to conform to them, and of different forms of conforming to reasons, and their appropriateness in different contexts. (p. 68)

Animals and humans both see things and act accordingly. Could the question whether they are perceived as reasons be a matter of whether this seeing process involves *reasoning*?[8] That seems too restrictive. Many human faculties shared with 'unreasoning' animals—perception, memory, attention, motivation, etc.—are at work together in what we call rational

---

[7] Joseph Raz, *Engaging Reason: On the Theory of Value and Action* (Oxford: Oxford University Press, 1999), 1; Parenthetical references in the text are to this volume.

[8] Raz writes: 'While at least minimal reasoning ability is among the constituents of capacity-rationality, it does not exhaust it'. (p. 70).

human thought and action, without the constant intermediation of reasoning. Animals equipped with perception, memory, motivation, etc. can respond appropriately in their cognition and behaviour to objects and circumstances in the world about them—thereby aptly avoiding danger, finding food when hungry, co-operating in building, hunting, and defence. Why is this not acting 'for a reason'?

Being rational is being capable of acting intentionally, that is, for reasons as one takes them to be, and that means in light of one's appreciation of one's situation in the world. (p. 3)

What is 'appreciation of one's situation' that intelligent social animals lack, such that no 'recognition as reasons' mediates their response to these factors, and so no 'appreciation of *reasons for* what they do' could explain what they do—even when they successfully match appetite and cognition to yield effective behaviour? Christine Korsgaard writes, in 'The Normativity of Instrumental Reason':

[A]s Nagel points out in *The Possibility of Altruism*, the specifically rational character of going to the dentist to avert an unwanted toothache depends upon *how* the belief [that dentists cure toothaches] and the desire [to be rid of one's toothache] are 'combined'. It is certainly not enough to say that they jointly *cause* the action, or that their bare co-presence effects a motive, for a person might be conditioned so that he responds in totally crazy ways to the co-presence of certain beliefs and desires....If the belief and desire...operate on the person merely by having a certain causal efficacy when co-present, the rational action is only accidentally or externally different from the mad one....For the person to act rationally, she must be motivated by her own *recognition* of the appropriate conceptual connection between the belief and the desire.[9]

This certainly seems plausible, and the least we can ask of rational agents. But regress threatens even this modest proposal.

Suppose we begin with:

1. She desires: Get rid of toothache.
2. She believes: Going to the dentist gets rid of toothaches.
<*jointly cause*>
3. She initiates: Going to the dentist.

---

[9] Christine Korsgaard, 'The Normativity of Instrumental Reason', in Garrett Cullity and Berys Gaut (eds.), *Ethics and Practical Reason* (Oxford: Oxford University Press, 1997), 221–2.

Korsgaard worries that if an individual had been conditioned such that the occurrence of (1) + (2) simply triggered (3), so this sequence just 'happens to her', we would not say that she acts rationally, or for a reason. To be sure, (1) + (2) may well constitute a reason for initiating a trip to the dentist, but a bare causal sequence does not appear to make this initiation a rational activity of her own doing. Korsgaard suggests we add:

1. She desires: Get rid of toothache.
2. She believes: Going to the dentist gets rid of toothaches.
3. She recognizes: (1) + (2) have a conceptual connection such that they constitute a reason to go to the dentist.

   <*jointly cause*>

4. She desires: Going to the dentist.

   <*causes*>

5. She initiates: Going to the dentist.[10]

But couldn't sequence (1) + (2) + (3) simply 'happen to her', due to some sort of conditioning or causal coincidence? So, if this sequence is to yield (4) and (5) 'in the right way' to make this a rational action, perhaps we should add that the agent recognizes that (1)–(3) have the status of rationalizing (4):

1. She desires: Get rid of toothache.
2. She believes: Going to the dentist gets rid of toothaches.
3. She recognizes: (1) + (2) have a conceptual connection such that they constitute a reason to go to the dentist.
4. She recognizes: (1) + (2) + (3) have a conceptual structure such that they constitute a reason to want to go to the dentist.

   <*jointly cause*>

5. She desires: Going to the dentist.

   <*jointly cause*>

6. She initiates: Going to the dentist.

And yet, the sequence (1) + (2) + (3) + (4), too, could just 'happen to her', thanks to conditioning or coincidence. How would that show her to be acting for a reason?

These regresses, like the famous Lewis Carroll paradox for theoretical reasoning that they vaguely recall, seem to suggest that we had better not

---

[10] Don't we also need some recognition on her part that there are no competing, weightier reasons? Not if all we ask (for present purposes) is that she be going to the dentist 'for a reason'. Perhaps she had better reason to do other things.

be tempted by conceptions of what it is to act on a reason, or to reason following rules, that require some new, contentful operation of the mind, such as a recognition or a judgement that a rule applies, in order to link the premisses to one another or to the conclusion 'in the right way'. The premisses of a practical or theoretical inference had better suffice for the conclusion as they stand. Hume made the Lewis Carroll point *avant la lettre* when he wrote that if we could not 'exert our reason without employing more than two ideas, and without having recourse to a third to serve as a medium betwixt them' (*T* 97n), we could never follow an argument or make a judgement at all.[11] Somehow, the two ideas must suffice—for 'the mind cannot run up with its inferences *in infinitum*' (*T* 97). We must, then, be capable of 'immediate' or unmediated inference, 'without any new reasoning or conclusion' (*T* 102), yet this must be a 'true species of reasoning' (*T* 97n).

Raz is among recent authors who have recognized this problem, and he concludes that a substantial amount of our rational, intentional activity must be 'automatic', unmediated by reasoning or recognition. He considers the plight of an obsessively anxious person, Sylvia, who cannot leave home without checking once more to see if the garden gate really is locked. Each time she starts to walk away, she wonders whether she made quite sure before leaving the gate, or whether her previous test might in fact have loosened it up. At some point she must, as we saw in the word-processor example, decide that enough is enough when it comes to confirmation, and walk away, resolutely ignoring residual doubt that she realizes she cannot refute and will not test:

> to act rationally we need to preserve a proper balance between resoluteness and openness to doubt. It is not a balance we can decide upon. While Sylvia can grit her teeth and decide not to turn back again for the fifth time, such conscious decisions only minimize her irrationality. To be rational she must act 'automatically' in a way that allows for proper openness to doubt without relapsing into indecisiveness and anxiety. To be rational she, and we, must function properly, and that functioning must be automatic, rather than a product of deliberation and decision. (p. 72)

Such 'automaticity' of intentional action pervades our lives, just as 'automaticity' of rule following pervades our language use and reasoning.

---

[11] References to David Hume, *Treatise of Human Nature*, ed. L. A. Selby-Bigge (Oxford: Oxford University Press, 1988); references in the text are hereinafter abbreviated '*T*'.

Even Sylvia is showing remarkable automaticity in the very way she yields to her obsessions. After all, her anxiety and doubt have a very narrow focus: Is the gate locked? To perform a 'check' on this is possible only because it never occurs to her to question an enormous amount of apparent fact which she simply takes on trust from her perceptual experience and memory. Is her perception of size and shape, or her sensation of grasping the latch knob, veridical? Is her memory of where her house is located, or what it looks like, or even who she is, accurate? Such things she assumes 'blindly', without second-guessing, as she shuttles back and forth between gate and walkway. This vast body of unquestioning confidence— *default trust*, as I will call it—enables her to act intentionally, and for a reason ('Checking my gate lock'), whether this is a good reason or not. Moreover, we all think she has good reason for this 'automaticity' in perception, and congratulate her on being rational at least *this* far. If only she weren't stuck on questions of locks and unplugged toasters, she could be more rational by being more prone to default trust, less prone to overly conscientious enquiry.

Can we say that her default trust *is* conscientious, and based on reasoning from past experience? We can and should say that her default trust is no breach of epistemic virtue, but even 'past experience' could be no evidence of any such thing as verdical perception if one did not already accord some default trust to one's own sense of what one is experiencing, one's memories, one's sense of coherence, and so on. *That* trust could not, without regress, be 'based on reasoning'. So reasoning cannot be the ground of normative authority 'all the way down', and some authority must be default-assumed.

Hume observed that even that most self-consciously and systematically critical interlocutor, the disputatious sceptic, who extends Sylvia's powers to doubt the obvious even to ordinary experience, none the less displays a touchingly unsceptical attitude toward the power of argumentation and his own powers of thought and memory. We might add: toward his own command of language and the content of his thoughts. Remove this default confidence, and he can no more declare his words to be 'giving an argument for scepticism'—an intentional action—than 'giving a recipe for haggis' or 'scat-singing without a tune'. He has no more alternative in this than we do:

I may, nay I must, yield to the current of nature, in submitting to my senses and understanding; and in this blind submission I shew most perfectly my sceptical disposition and principles. (*T* 269)

Default, Defeasible Trust

Default trust, however 'blind', is not inherently *blinding*. On the contrary. If the sceptic trusts his ability to speak English and draw the conclusions demanded of his premisses, and I trust my own appreciation of his argument, we both will *see* (no longer be blind to) a problem that I have in defending my beliefs: Where I previously had hoped to be able always to have a reason for whatever I believe, taking nothing 'blindly' or 'without reason', I now realize that this hope is impossible—some things cannot, without regress or circularity, be argued for. Even if I say, 'Some things are simply *self-evident* in the light of reason,' I now see this is whistling in the dark: 'self-evidence in the light of reason' is just default trust in what seems evident to me, garnished with parsley. If I cannot even imagine an alternative to p, then to say that p is 'impossible' is just to trust my powers of imagination and command of p's content. If I say, 'I do not need foundations, self-evident or otherwise. Coherence is enough for me, since circles of reasons that yield no internal conflict are virtuous,' then I simply display my default trust in coherence and in my sense of it.

The sceptic takes advantage of a default trust in our command of language and reasoning that he and I share to get me to see a surprising incongruity in my own thought, from which I can learn something I certainly did not expect. On a smaller scale, an individual's default trust in her senses and memory allows her to be surprised by incongruities in her daily experience—particular bits of perceptual data can give rise to conflicting expectations, surprise, and questioning. This is possible because each of these bits has some default authority—it generates a real expectation of how things are or will be. Were she incapable of according any such default trust to thoughts or experiences, and formed no expectations from experience, such learning by surprise and incongruity would be impossible. Blind trust is part of seeing—seeing an argument's point, seeing the familiar garden gate, or seeing that there is a conflict between two bits of sensory evidence. Since it can generate loss of confidence, as well as sustaining or strengthening confidence when conflict is absent, let us therefore speak of it as default, defeasible trust.

Philosophers are familiar with default, defeasible trust in a different sphere: prisoner's dilemma situations. Rapaport's well-known tit-for-tat strategy commits the agent to an initial, unsecured, no-questions-asked co-operation in the first encounter with any new player. This default trust is, however, defeasible—it will be withdrawn for the next round of play with that individual if he or she defects. Game theorists, prone to more guarded and less 'naive' strategies than tit-for-tat, were at first startled when Rapaport proposed blind co-operativeness on the first play. Yet this default trust proves as essential for the strategy's success in self-stabilizing in a population as its default 'punishment' for defectors.[12]

The tit-for-tat strategy in prisoner's dilemma games does not require that the agent's default trust be an internal attitude of confidence. It is sufficient if the player *acts as if* he trusted the other, whatever he happens to feel about the matter himself. Is default trust absent in such cases of pretence? Hardly. Consider a player who takes himself to be 'playing the tit-for-tat strategy' or 'co-operating' or 'punishing' on a particular round of play. This player is manifesting a great deal of sincere default trust in his perceptual and reasoning faculties. Acting *as if* it were the case that *p* is itself a form of intentional action, and thus requires not simply behaving in a way that externally resembles *p*, but also trusting oneself to be *doing q*.

The word 'trust' might seem freighted already with normative notions and conceptual content, and we must be careful when talking about 'default trust' for present purposes to use a much simpler idea than that. As I am understanding 'trust' herein, it can be felt without even possessing the concept of 'trust', much less the concept of 'meriting trust'. I assume, for example, that well-tended very young infants come to trust their care-givers in much the same sense that we characteristically trust our sensations. Certainly no 'judgement of trustworthiness' is involved on the infant's part. Indeed, this attitude does not necessarily take a propositional object. A 2-year-old trusts her pet dog not to bite, a schoolchild trusts his chair and the schoolhouse not to collapse, a tourist in a new city trusts a subway map on the wall to be accurate, and a bicyclist trusts his eyes and his steering and balance when negotiating between two parked cars. Trust,

---

[12] For discussion, see Robert Axelrod, *The Evolution of Cooperation* (New York: Basic Books, 1984).

as we have said, has as its signature that it gives rise to *expectation*, which can be more or less strong according as the trust is more or less firm. I trust a neighbourhood dog not to bite, and so am surprised when he suddenly nips me; I much more firmly trust my fellow passengers on the bus not to bite, and so am absolutely astonished when one does.[13]

Trust gives a companion, an animal, or an object a distinctive role in shaping what one does or does not do, and what one does or does not find surprising. We can also think of it as always containing a kernel of *de se* self-trust as well. If one could not in some measure and in some ways spontaneously rely upon one's feelings, sensations, thoughts, faculties, and continuity over time, one could hardly rely upon anyone or anything else, spontaneously or otherwise. Such *de se* self-trust could hardly be mediated by a quasi-linguistic proposition or 'self-concept', since a pre-linguistic infant could not learn language in the first place without it. Even if children were equipped from birth with Mentalese, they would still need default trust in regularities in their experience to learn which English or Urdu words go with which concepts. And for adults, regularities of experience can only *be* regularities of experience if individuals have some default trust in sensation, memory, and personal continuity, spontaneously taking seeings, touchings, and memories as *intimating* how things are. So we never outgrow our need for spontaneous trust. As Allan Gibbard writes:

we could not avoid taking things on our own authority, even if we resolved to ... [even though such] fundamental authority ... [c]learly ... is non-rational in one sense in which philosophers commonly use the term.[14]

Normative Attitudes

If reason is to enable us to respond aptly to good reasons, it must first be engaged; it must at least be able to get going. But it cannot be engaged thanks to reason 'all the way down', whether one is speaking of causation or justification. Such a claim may seem paradoxical. If sustained, it might

---

[13] On the developmental aspects of trust, see M. D. S. Ainsworth and S. M. Bell, 'Attachment, Exploration, and Separation: Illustrated by the Behavior of One-Year-Olds in a Strange Situation', *Child Development* 41 (1970), 49–67, and John Bowlby, *A Secure Base: Parent–Child Attachment and Healthy Human Development* (New York: Basic Books, 1988).

[14] Allan Gibbard, *Wise Choices, Apt Feelings* (Cambridge, Mass.: Harvard University Press, 1990), 177–8.

seem to undermine reason's legitimacy. How could anything worthy of the name of reason have its genesis and acquire its authority in thought and action from something deserving the name of unreason? The paradox is no deeper than this—a certain blindness enables us to see; default trust allows us to take the first step in learning and reasoning; default trust then allows us to take a second step, and notice its conflict or accord with the first; default trust further allows us to take the third step, as conflict is 'allowed to' weaken subsequent trust while accord 'is allowed' to strengthen it; and so default, defeasible trust enables us to learn and unlearn.

Philosophers have tended to assume that Hume is abandoning the idea of a normative epistemology when he writes of 'blind submission' to the 'current of nature'. His theory of belief has been rejected as 'associationalist' and 'passive'—leaving no place for an epistemic agency responsive to reasons or reasoning. Christine Korsgaard, for example, writes:

I don't think that Hume believes in rational belief any more than he does in rational action. His view is that beliefs are sentiments which are caused in us by perceptions and habits. Reason doesn't really enter into it.[15]

And Raz writes:

For Hume, and for some of those who followed him, the assertion that belief is not voluntary was an expression of the empiricist view that belief is passive. Hume's empiricist account of belief and belief formation has long been discarded. (p. 7)

Hume's defence is straightforward. If we are to display agency, follow arguments, or deploy reasoning, we must indeed have certain sentiments—such as default, defeasible trust—not themselves found in logic proper or based upon reasons or choice. For example, he takes the 'association of ideas'—a spontaneous thought-transition from one idea to another, without the intermediation of a third—to be necessary if even a simple argument is to be followed without Tortoise-like regress. He writes:

After the most accurate and exact of my reasonings, I can give no reason why I shou'd assent to it; and feel nothing but a *strong* propensity to consider objects *strongly* in that view, under which they appear to me. ... Without [that] quality, by which the mind enlivens some ideas beyond others (which seemingly is so trivial, and so little founded on reason) we cou'd never assent to any argument. (*T* 265)

---

[15] Korsgaard, 'Normativity of Instrumental Reason', 223 n.

But how could so passive and non-judgemental an attitude as default trust be the foundation for a form of reason-disciplined agency? Can Hume reply to the criticism that this appears to be a 'merely causal' process—association rather than logical inference—indistinguishable so far as we have said from such phenomena as animal conditioning?

We have seen that regress awaits schemes that would reintroduce rational agency in a causal process by inserting a 'recognition' or other rational operation between steps in a thought process, or between belief-desire premises and practical conclusions. If we cannot *add* normativity to the premises of a theoretical or practical inference, perhaps we can find it there already—by showing that belief and desire themselves are *normative attitudes*, not mere causal tendencies or tugs.

Notice that our question is not about the *concepts* of belief and desire, but about the actual mental states or attitudes to which these concepts apply. These states or attitudes need not in themselves be 'normative entities' of some unfamiliar sort. Thus, the copy of this paper you are now holding in your hands might be an entity to which the complex normative concept 'a hopeless tangle of confusions made worse by length' applies, but in itself the entity is just pressed wood pulp and patterns of dried ink. To show that a state is normative, one must do more than show that it qualifies for normative labelling. The state must have the structure or character to play a normative role in its own right—thought- or action-guidingness in rational agents.

The idea that normativity in this sense might be present *inside* belief and desire, or belief-desire pairs, seems promising. Then belief and desire could suffice as premises for action, but not at the expense of normativity. But how are we to characterize an attitude as 'inherently normative'? One possibility is to see the matter in terms of *how the attitude presents itself or its object to us*. A belief that *p* might present *p* as 'meriting belief' or *credible*, or present itself as 'aiming at the truth concerning *p*'. A desire to *q* might present *q* as 'meriting pursuit' or *desirable*, or present itself as 'aiming at what it is worthwhile to do' . Thus, concerning belief, David Velleman writes:

belief must be characterized, not just as the attitude having the motivational role, but rather as a truth-directed species of that attitude: to believe a proposition is to regard it as true with the aim of thereby accepting a truth.[16]

---

[16] David Velleman, *The Possibility of Practical Reason* (Oxford: Oxford University Press, 2000), 247. See note 19 (below), however, for further discussion.

And Dennis Stampe proposed in his effort to explain the 'authority' of desire:

Desires constitute reasons for us to act because their contents are represented as states of affairs the realization of which would be good.[17]

Raz would appear to agree:

since we desire only what we think of as worth desiring, our desires are among our responses to perceived reasons. This is true of a desire to drink when thirsty as much as of the desire to become a good teacher. (p. 74)

However, we had better not try to explain this notion of a desire or belief 'presenting' its object as desirable or credible in terms of a *judgement*, even implicit. Consider the proposal that belief is distinguished from mere hypothesis by the fact that believing that *p* is or requires 'judging that *p* is credible'. To make the necessary judgement of *p*, I will have to have or arrive at a belief with the conceptual content '*p* is credible'. And for that I need to judge whether '*p* is credible' is credible. For that, in turn, I will need yet more beliefs, more credences. Nor can the problem be evaded by making the judgements required 'implicit' or 'tacit': an infinite number of implicit or tacit operations can no more be performed in finite time than an infinite number of explicit ones.

An approach that might avoid regress is *functional*. What matters is not that one judge or deem a proposition credible or a state desirable—it suffices that there is a suite of cognition and motivation that constitutes one *expecting* or *finding* it so, perhaps without ever judging this. A normative state is thus one whose nature is to realize a certain regulative role in an individual's functional mental architecture or, more vividly, an individual's 'whir of organism'.[18] This sort of approach has been associated with behaviourism, but behaviourism is only a *species* of it—one that takes difference in explicit behaviour as the touchstone for distinguishing functions. But psychology has long since moved beyond the behavioural frontier, to

---

[17] Dennis Stampe, 'The Authority of Desire', *Philosophical Review* 96 (1987): 335–81, at 355.

[18] In this sense, even the hard-core causal-functionalist cannot shrug off the idea of 'normative states' as inherently unclear. After all, he himself almost certainly accepts the notion that functional properties are not equivalent to material properties, even though material properties embody them. For the functionalist, a belief is a mental state that *realizes a certain functional role* in an individual's mental architecture. In actual humans, this role might be played by certain neurophysiological states, but in some other creature or machine it might be played by quite different material states.

include all manner of internal and non-behavioural evidence concerning cognitive, affective, and motivational processes.

Consider *perception*, which has been called a normative state in the functional sense, since a bit of experience constitutes a perception in so far as it is part of the working of a belief system that aims at—or has as a 'proper function' to track—the truth about one's surroundings.[19] As a result, a misperception is none the less a perceiving. Contrast *hallucination*, which can also yield experiences that more or less accurately paint the world that happens to be around me, but for which we don't have the notion of *mishallucination*. Perception, then, is a state whose character is partly fixed by its role in the 'epistemic space' of reasons for belief, a non-judgemental, causal process which none the less has conditions of correctness.

We had a hint of this idea above, when it was suggested that a Humean notion like default, defeasible trust might be a state with a nature such that it can enable us to realize the normative role of *learning*. 'Learning' is a concept of truth-tracking or error-correction, and so default, defeasible trust is in that sense apt for playing a part in the normative role of belief. If Hume—and perhaps Wittgenstein as well—are right that this sort of attitude is also essential to following rules of language and logic, then here is another aspect of the normative role of belief that default, defeasible trust is 'by its nature capable of'.

What about the case of desire? Let us turn from Hume to Kant, who gave us a compelling model of desire in part to show how action from duty, action in accord with objective requirements of practical reason, is

---

[19] Well, which is it—aiming or functioning? Here philosophers differ, and the choice could be consequential, since accounts formulated in terms of 'aiming' run the risk of reinserting a judging or deciding agent between one's attitudes and their objects, thereby launching a regress. David Velleman proposes to give a causal-functional understanding of belief's inherent 'aiming at truth':

Belief aims at truth in the normative sense only because it aims at the truth descriptively, in the sense that it is constitutively regulated by mechanisms designed to ensure that it is true.... - What distinguishes belief from other states that take their prepositional objects as true is that, unlike assumption or fanatasy, belief tends to track what *is* true, when its regulatory mechanisms are functioning as designed.... Belief thus aims at truth in the same sense that the circulation aims to supply body tissues with nutrients and oxygen. (*Possibility of Practical Reason*, 17)

The challenge now is to understand how this functional understanding might be structured, how it could constitute 'truth-aiming', and how it might work together with other functional elements of psychology to yield structured thought and behaviour worthy of such names as 'inference' or 'intentional action'.

psychologically possible. Since desire—if it is to play a normative role—is supposed to 'track value' much as belief is supposed to track truth, we might expect a somewhat similar *learning*-permitting architecture for desire. This, indeed, is just the sort of account Kant gives in the *Critique of Practical Reason* and the *Metaphysics of Morals*: desire is a direct *liking* for an idea that gives rise to activity in the agent aimed at producing the state the idea represents, which renders the agent subject to potential satisfaction, or frustration and surprise.

An example might help us introduce this account. I read or hear a description of a kind of food, and find the description very appealing. I *like* the idea of trying it, even though I have never tasted this cuisine. As a result, I now also *want* to try it—that is, I am prepared to spend some effort pursuing it, with some expectation that I will find it enjoyable. 'Why are you suddenly so keen to go to this Catalan restaurant tonight?—You've never had Catalan food.' The appeal need not be simple pleasure or novelty, however. I might like the idea of reading a book that promises deep enlightenment, or of trying a career that promises self-development. Even an object of obligation can be liked, as Kant observed. If I have strong team spirit and a sense of obligation to my team-mates, and my coach tells me that the team badly needs me to develop the skills of blocking, then even though I hate and dread the thought of throwing myself into the path of large, fast-moving, cleat-shod defensive players, I will none the less *want* badly to work on the arduous and painful blocking drills, even to the point of exhaustion. That I genuinely want this is shown by my painful frustration and self-dissatisfaction if I give up too soon, relaxing and welcome as I find that in other respects. Here is Kant's eloquent way of putting it:

Life is the faculty of a being to act in accordance with laws of the faculty of desire. The **faculty of desire** is a being's faculty to be *by means of its representations the cause of the reality of the objects of these representations*. Pleasure [*Lust*] is the *representation of the agreement of an object or of an action with the* subjective *conditions of life* .... For the purposes of this *Critique*, I have no further need of concepts borrowed from psychology. (*CPrR* 5: 8n)

Consider *moral feeling*, that motivation which Kant posits to serve as the basis for distinctively moral action:

Moral feeling. This is the susceptibility to feel *Lust* or *Unlust* merely from being aware that our actions are consistent with or contrary to the law of duty. Every determination of choice proceeds *from the representation of a possible action to* the deed through the feeling of *Lust* or *Unlust*, taking an interest in the action or its effect. (*MM* 6: 399)[20]

It is this 'susceptibility' or 'feeling' that constitutes the respect that motivates action from duty:

Respect (*reverentia*) ['for the law, which in its subjective aspect is called moral feeling', 6: 465] is, again, something merely subjective, a feeling of a special kind, not a judgment about an object that it would be a duty to bring about or produce. (*MM* 6: 402)

The moral feeling of respect does not involve a *moral judgement* that this respectful attitude is required or a duty, that its object 'deserves respect'. For this would launch an immediate regress of just the kind we have discussed:

such a duty, regarded as a duty, could be represented to us only through the *respect* we have for it. A duty to have respect would thus amount to being put under obligation to duties. (*MM* 6: 402)

Moral action does indeed depend upon *moral belief*, but moral belief is not a practical attitude, it presupposes and yields no distinctive motive to action. This secures, for Kant, its independence from inclination or 'wishful thinking'. Moral action also depends upon *moral feeling*, which is not a belief but a practical attitude—specifically, a desire. What brings these two elements together in the process of action from duty is the *idea* or representation that they share: that a certain act is consistent (or inconsistent) with the moral law. Indeed, we may think of the action as *organized around* this idea—belief embodied in a trusting expectation that the subjective maxim of the act accords with the test of universality, and desire embodied in a direct liking for this idea. The *dutiful intention*, as we may call it, thus is this sort of belief-desire pair. This intention can explain an agent's action

---

[20] *Lust* and *Unlust* are not so much sensory pleasantness, but 'spirited interest'. *Lust* has the same root as the archaic English *list*, so that *Unlust*, for example, is translated 'listless'. This is what psychologists call 'incentive salience'. Anticipated sensory pleasantness is just one way of feeling an incentive or liking for an idea or image—it is a form of inclination (*Neigung*) or the '*lower faculty of desire*', which Kant distinguishes from the full domain of desire proper (*Begierde*), since the object of desire can be wholly free of any promise of personal pleasure. It owes its 'incentive salience' to the *idea* that it takes as its object, as in love of a country, love of a person, love of duty. Such an incentive can incite motivated pursuit of actions that promise no personal pleasure, and even fly in the face of it.

because the moral feeling in him or her can be motivationally preponderant. Kant writes, 'sensible impressions lose their influence on moral feeling only because respect for the law is more powerful than all such feelings together' (*MM* 6: 408). When the moral feeling is 'so strengthened' as to become a standing 'predisposition (*praedispositio*)' that is no momentary 'enthusiasm', but none the less remains 'on the side of feeling' and does not presume to *judge*—thus allowing theoretical reason to make the objective discernment of what is or is not consistent with the moral law—then we have 'the true strength of virtue', the 'state of *health* in the moral life' (*MM* 6: 409).

Should we be surprised that, for Kant, a non-voluntary feeling of direct liking can combine with belief around an objective idea to yield voluntary, intentional action 'under that idea'—moral duty itself? On the contrary. If instead Kant required an intelligent volition or intention *in order to form a dutiful intention*, he would be in just the sort of regress that would arise if a judgement or belief were required in order to form a belief, a rule required in order to follow a rule.

Rational Action without Regress

Interestingly enough, the very categories of volition that Kant deploys in his analysis of the faculty and functioning of desire are perfectly at home in contemporary motivational psychology: a desire is an attitude of *immediate affect* directed toward a *mental representation*, which elicits motivation to bring about the object of that representation; it thus brings with it *frustration* with failures in this pursuit, *incentive* to continue, and *intrinsic reward* in successes at realizing this representation.[21] Kant was not far off, therefore,

---

[21] On the distinction between direct liking and motivated pursuit, see, e.g., Kent C. Berridge, 'Reward Learning: Reinforcement, Incentives, and Expectations', in D. L. Medin (ed.), *The Psychology of Learning and Motivation* 40 (New York: Academic Press, 2000), 223–78; on the neurophysiological embodiment of learning and reward, and especially the role of surprise and disappointment in shaping evaluation, motivation, and expectation, see W. Schultz, P. Dayan, and P. R. Montague, 'The Neural Basis of Prediction and Reward', *Science* 275 (1997), 1593–9. Note that the 'intrinsic reward' of success *in* an action or activity is independent of the further question whether the *outcome* of the activity in the end is what one had hoped for. Thus, one is pleased when one succeeds in locating a hard-to-find restaurant a friend had warmly recommended, even if this pleasure fades after tasting the food and finding it is not to one's liking. To be sure, failing to enjoy the meal will affect subsequent motivation to find the restaurant again.

in saying that all he needed from empirical psychology for his theory of practical agency was this much of a possibility: the existence of a faculty of desire that could take as its immediate object not only personal welfare-related goals, but also non-personal goals.[22]

Similarly, the categories of Hume's theory of belief are also at home in modern empirical psychology: belief is an attitude of more or less confident *default trust* directed towards a *mental representation* situated in an *associative network*, which permits *unmediated inference* and elicits *expectancies* for states as represented by these attitudes. This attitude is *modulated* by experience—strengthened by positive outcomes and weakened by surprise at failure.[23]

Both Kantian and Humean accounts eschew psychologies with such novel categories as 'besires', 'self-executing representations', and 'desires (or beliefs) as normative judgments'. They can sit within a familiar belief-desire framework for intentional action, each motivated in part by their author's explicit awareness of the acute character of problems of regress. Both require belief *and* desire operating jointly in order for genuinely intentional action or 'action for a reason' to proceed. So, indeed, did Aristotle, writing in the *Eudemian Ethics* (1227a3–5):

---

[22] As it happened, Kant also thought that only a *noumenal* self could have direct non-personal goals. The *empirical* self he saw as irredeemably 'solipsistic' and 'hedonistic', so 'moral feeling' required something that freed the agent from merely empirical determination of the will, i.e., a noumenal self. This feature of his philosophical psychology is, however, as optional as the thesis of psychological hedonism. For a comparison with Hume, see P. Railton, 'Normative Force and Normative Freedom: Hume and Kant but not Hume *versus* Kant', *Ratio* 12 (1999), 320–53.

[23] On the direct character of trust, see A. Adolphs, 'Trust in the Brain', and J. S. Winston *et al.*, 'Automatic and Intentional Brain Responses during the Evaluation of Trustworthiness of Faces', *Nature Neuroscience* 5 (2002), 192–3 and 277–83. The default character of belief is shown in the so-called frame problem; for discussion, see Eric Lormand, 'Framing the Frame Problem', *Synthese* 82 (1990), 353–74. On default self-credence, see Daniel T. Gilbert, 'How Mental Systems Believe', *American Psychologist* 46 (1991), 107–19. On the structure of belief, see R. J. Bogdan (ed.), *Belief: Form, Content, and Function* (Oxford: Oxford University Press, 1986). On learning and evaluating in dynamic relation to action and experience, see R. B. Zajonc, 'Feeling and Thinking: Preferences Need no Inferences', *American Psychologist* 35 (1980), 151–75; Richard E. Petty, *et al.*, 'Attitudes and Attitude Change', *Annual Review of Psychology* 48 (1997), 609–42; and (especially on the possibility of layering multiple sources of action within the self) J. T. Cacioppo and G. G. Berntson, 'Relationship between Attitudes and Evaluative Space: A Critical Review, with Emphasis on the Separability of Positive and Negative Substrates', *Psychological Bulletin* 115 (1994), 401–23.

But it is evident that choice is neither simply desire (*boulesis*) nor opinion (*doxa*), but opinion *together with* inclination (*orexis*), whenever as a result of deliberation they are brought to a conclusion. (1139b4)

A view sharpened in the *Nicomachean Ethics*, in a phrase Raz endorses (P. 10): 'Choice is either desiderative reason or ratiocinative desire.'

Raz points out that many philosophers have asserted that action requires both belief and desire, but few have given any argument for this. We can see here a possible reason for it, if not exactly an argument. If trusting an idea were enough to provide and sustain that idea's motivational efficacy, then such worthwhile practical constraints as arise from natural and acquired human motivational dispositions (sympathy, empathy, pain withdrawal, dissatisfaction, fear, fatigue, etc.) could always be countered by a convincing line of chat that persuaded belief. The inability of theoretical reasoning to bring motivational force automatically in its wake may be a real asset in our ability to respond aptly to reasons. A tyrant might convince me of a horrible duty, but fear and empathy can stop my carrying it out. The mutual independence in the functional architecture of belief and desire, combined with their need to have each other's collaboration for action to occur, is probably quite healthy: the need to recruit actual motivational dispositions is a practical constraint on enthusiastic pursuit of attractive-sounding ideas or on resigned acceptance of some regrettable conditions wrongly deemed 'necessary' or 'inevitable'.

Belief and desire can operate without regress to yield intention if intentions can form and operate 'automatically' (as Raz put it), through a kind of self-organization around ideas. Just as molecules with a certain architecture and composition can *crystallize* into large-scale, regular geometric forms by clustering around an inclusion, without needing any guiding hand, so beliefs and desires with the right architecture and composition can crystallize into action-guiding intentions by clustering around an idea produced by thought or perception without any guiding hand. Indeed, any sort of a *guiding* hand shaping the process of intention formation would itself have to be an intentional process. Agency, then, also confronts a regress problem: we cannot posit a higher-order agent or agency within the agent, guiding an agent's deliberation and deciding upon its conclusion, for this sort of guiding and directing are themselves intentional activities, and would require yet another, higher-order agent inside this one. It had better be possible for intentions to emerge without being intended, their formation guided directly by beliefs and desires themselves.

Where am I in All This?

One might well be suspicious of this functionalist way of talking, this 'chemistry of intention', in which intentions spontaneously emerge within us. For where am *I* in all this? Doesn't rational action require, if it is to be *my* act, an exercise of judgement or decision on my part? Surely intentions can't just 'happen' to me through the chemistry of belief and desire. Raz claims that we are only ourselves when we are active, and a process of emergent intentions seems a form of passivity or receptiveness to influence. He writes:

Here we can see the central advantage of the approach I have been recommending. Its central notion is that activity is related to the proper functioning of the processes which govern our mental lives, our beliefs, moods, emotions, desires. That proper functioning consists in responsiveness to reasons. That provides the key to the account of what it is for people to live their lives as they lead them. (P. 19)

With this I can only agree, and I hope to have shown how something like this sort of government by proper functioning of 'beliefs, moods, emotions, desires' is possible. But Raz also continues:

We do so to the extent that we believe that our thoughts, beliefs, emotions, and desires are properly responsive to reason.... [W]e are ourselves so long as, as we see it, we are responsive to reason.... We are ourselves and we lead our own life so long as we see ourselves as rational agents, so long as we conduct our life under the semblance of rationality. (ibid.)

Regress threatens once again—beliefs, for example, can only be *our* beliefs if we see them 'under the semblance of' proper responses to reasons. That is yet another, higher-order belief, with a definite conceptual content different from the content of the first-order belief itself.[24] So *it* can be my belief only if I can see it 'under the semblance of' being properly responsive to yet further reasons. And so on.

[24] That is:

(1) *p*

as opposed to:

(2) Belief that *p* is a proper response to available reasons.

Neither entails the other, and the concepts sufficient to grasp the content of (1) typically are not sufficient to grasp the content of (2). In a psychological setting, we might say that a young child can understand and answer appropriately the question 'Is the food on your plate peas?' before being able to understand or answer appropriately the question 'Is believing that the food on your plate is peas a proper response to reasons available to you?'

The answer to where I am in all this, however, can be provided more briefly, and in a way friendly to Raz's first statement, above, of what it is for a person to lead his life. I *am* this self-organized complex that exhibits the proper functioning of thoughts, beliefs, emotions, and desires. The crystallizing of intentions from my beliefs and desires, and the subsequent shaping of my conduct—what I expect, what I am motivated to pursue, what I find rewarding or disappointing—that *is* me in action. The 'real me' is no subpart of this or internal manager of it, guiding it from within. The real me—the theory-forming, goal-seeking agent we hope manages to be rational—is the very organism itself. Yet that organism is no mere *bundle* of states. It is a structured, functional whole.

I close with a picture of myself, holding forth in a taut voice at an intense meeting of the college faculty. At one and the same time, I am presenting a report, trying to control my voice, struggling to hold the audience's interest, racking my mind to recall my third main point before I reach the end of the second, and worrying about the look that is growing on the dean's face. My colleagues might be saying to themselves—not without truth—that delivering the summary is barely half of what I am doing. I am also trying to win over allies from the natural sciences, to walk on eggshells with humanities colleagues, and to refight a fight I lost with the dean last year. A psychoanalyst might say—not without truth—that I am still refighting a fight with my father from many years before, and, above all, still trying to be loved.

How can all this intentionality and meaning-saturated purpose, explicit and implicit, conscious and unconscious,[25] be at work at the same time, each element contributing to the shaping of my thoughts, feelings, words, and gestures, even as I keep up a constant stream of near-coherent words? And how can the way I feel when I sit down be such a complex mixture of relief, doubt, half-satisfaction, and disappointment with myself? All these

---

[25] Because intentions are self-organizing, and to a considerable extent self-monitoring and self-policing (via the feedback of surprise, frustration, and satisfaction), they can operate in us at various levels without our conscious awareness, much less conscious permission. An image or idea or thought to which we are susceptible can recruit affect and trust, and in turn recruit motivation and expectation, which in turn shape our conduct in purposive and meaning-laden ways. (See references in n. 23.) Consolidation and operation of subconscious intention—like consolidation and operation of conscious intention—does not require a tiny, secretive agent within us, scheming away. For an empirically sophisticated discussion of dynamic unconscious processes that is sympathetic to Freudian 'depth psychology', see Howard Shervin, *et al.*, *Conscious and Unconscious Processes* (New York: Guilford Press, 1996).

intentions and sub-intentions can emerge spontaneously as I talk, rapidly crystallizing around images and ideas in my mind—ideas and images arising both from immediate perception and thought, and from the course of my life to date. All this self-organization will dramatically shape what I do, how I do it, and how I feel about it. These ideas and images, objects of some element of trust and some element of affect, can supply competing or collaborating guidance, producing in me conflict and uncertainty, or resolution and inventiveness. Each gives some meaning and purpose to what I do, and each leaves as well a distinctive signature in my manner of acting and in the residue of feelings that stir within me as I sit back down and wonder what's next. Which of these intentions are mine, where in the whir of organism is the agent who acts, what is the true reason for my action, and who is the real me—the person you (or I) would know if you really knew me? The answer can only be: the whole lot, of course.[26]

[26] I wish to thank my colleagues Allan Gibbard, Stephen Darwall, and David Velleman for helpful, sceptical conversation and encouragement. Thanks, too, to co-participants in the conference in honour of Joseph Raz—including Joseph Raz himself—who also provided helpful scepticism and encouragement. In psychology, Kent Berridge, Randy Nesse, and Oliver Schulteiss have done their best to educate and tame my amateur psychologizing. I thank Linda Braekel for guidance concerning concepts of the unconscious. The writing of this paper was partly supported by a fellowship grant from the Guggenheim Foundation, which is gratefully acknowledged.

9

Why am I My Brother's Keeper?

Donald H. Regan

I

I want to cast doubt on a proposition which many people would regard as the first axiom of moral theory. Joseph Raz has stated the proposition thus: 'Morality is . . . concerned with the advancement of the well-being of individuals.'[1] Actually, Raz includes a qualifier—the full quote says that morality 'is thought to be concerned with' advancing the well-being of individuals. But the whole tenor of his ensuing discussion suggests that Raz generally shares this view of what morality is about.

As I say, I want to cast doubt on this axiom, but I shall not take issue with any particular judgement that the axiom might entail about how to act in a concrete case. My focus in this essay is not on what should be done, but on why we should do it. Hence my question, '*Why* am I my brother's keeper?' I do not ask, like Cain, *whether* I am my brother's keeper, with the rhetorical implication that what goes on in others' lives is no concern of mine. I accept that each of us should be concerned (intrinsically) with what goes on in others' lives. The question is how best to account for or understand that obligation. Is it best understood as an obligation to promote others' well-being, or as an obligation of some other sort?

It must be emphasized (because it is easy to forget) that 'well-being' as it is used in the supposed first axiom is a normative concept. One could have

---

[1] Joseph Raz, *The Morality of Freedom* (Oxford: Oxford University Press, 1986), 267.

a purely naturalistic concept of well-being that merely picked out a range of states and events in individuals' lives and that purported to capture some empirical common-sense notion or some scientifically useful category. But then just saying that something was part of Abel's well-being would not be to assert that anyone, even including Abel, should promote it. Obviously, the proponent of the axiom (whom I shall refer to as the well-being theorist) *does* mean, when he says some state or event is part of Abel's well-being, that that state or event is to be promoted.[2] Indeed, he means something more specific still. As I have noted, I may agree perfectly with some well-being theorists about what states or events in people's lives are to be promoted.[3] But we still disagree about the nature of the values and reasons involved. The well-being theorist thinks those states or events matter because they are part of the well-being or welfare *of Abel*, because they are good *for Abel*, because they are valuable *to or for some particular valuing being*. That is what I doubt. So far as I can see, well-being as a normative concept does not figure in the best account of why we are obligated to care about what happens in others' lives (or, for that matter, in our own).

As it happens, Raz himself provides the materials for a very simple and straightforward argument against the significance of well-being. First, Raz denies that there is any deep divide within practical reason between morality and prudence. (Questions about well-being and welfare and the like are often referred to as questions about 'prudential value'.) Raz refers to 'the essential identity of people's responsiveness to their own well-being and to morality',[4] and he denies 'that there is a logical difference between a conflict of reasons which affect only the well-being of the agent, and such a conflict where the well-being of the agent is in conflict with that of others. Both types of conflict are rooted in values on which the well-being of the agent is founded, and their resolution depends on the guidance which these same values provide.'[5] These remarks by themselves hardly seem to undercut the significance of well-being, even though they indicate that well-being is founded on other values. But elsewhere Raz says, 'it is neither

[2] Stephen Darwall, *Welfare and Rational Care* (Princeton: Princeton University Press, 2002), 10–11, has a very nice argument that welfare (his version of well-being) is a normative concept.

[3] As we shall see in section V, I agree more in this way with James Griffin and Joseph Raz than with Wayne Sumner.

[4] Raz, *Morality of Freedom*, 319.

[5] Ibid. 320.

tautological nor true that we pursue our well-being,'[6] and 'it is false that we pursue our goals because their pursuit serves our well-being'.[7] Raz believes that success in our goals serves our well-being (provided the goals are valuable ones),[8] but he denies that concern for our well-being is our reason for pursuing our goals. In the realm of prudence, then, well-being seems to be epiphenomenal. But if well-being is epiphenomenal in the realm of prudence, and if the values that underlie well-being figure in moral decision making in the same way they figure in prudential decision making, why is not well-being epiphenomenal for morality as well?

There is more to say about Raz, and I shall come back to him. But for my larger purposes, starting from these Razian theses would be making things too easy for myself. Precisely because he sees that there is no deep divide between prudence and morality, and that individuals aim at their goals because they regard the goals themselves as valuable, Raz is already much closer to the full truth (as I see it) than most moral philosophers.

II

So, let us begin again. The question is why each of us should be concerned with what goes on in others' lives. What is the best account of that obligation (and does it involve the notion of well-being)? So far as I can see, there are three principal schemata for an account, which it will be useful to sketch before we look at each in detail.

First, there is what I shall refer to as the Moorean approach. On this approach, any agent's fundamental obligation is to bring about the existence of as much good as possible. The 'good' asserted here is an agent-neutral good, not tied conceptually to any person's interests. But in fact the most important goods are certain kinds of events or experiences that occur within individual lives. Therefore, an important part of promoting the good turns out to be promoting certain events or experiences in individuals' lives. Since, from any particular agent's point of view, most individuals are 'others', promoting the good requires us to promote goods in others' lives, and thus to be concerned with what goes on in others' lives.

---

[6] Ibid. 316.   [7] Ibid. 317   [8] Ibid.

The *second* principal schema reflects one source of unease with the Moorean approach. A standard objection to the Moorean view is that the notion of agent-neutral value makes no sense—that all value must be value 'for' some agent, or at least for some valuing being. This suggests that the basic category of the 'to be promoted' is not an agent-neutral good that just happens to occur primarily in people's lives. Rather, what is to be promoted is *essentially* the welfare, or the well-being, or the good *of individuals*—which I shall mostly refer to as the 'good for' individuals. So, on the second schema, what is to be promoted is what is good for various individuals, and each of us should be concerned, not just with what is good for himself, but with what is good for his fellows as well.

The *third* schema grows out of the feeling that even the second schema is too crude. Proponents of the third schema would say that the other's 'good for' does not make its claim directly on me as something to be promoted. Rather, the claim is indirect. In the first instance, I should respect or care for others because they are persons; and that respect or caring for others entails a concern for their welfare, for the good for them.

III

Let us start with the Moorean view. It is the simplest; in the end it seems to me the most plausible; and, as we shall see, it turns out to be a sort of 'strange attractor' that the other views gravitate towards for various reasons of coherence and plausibility, but that the other views must distinguish themselves from if they are to maintain a separate identity. So far as stating the Moorean view, it is not necessary to add anything to what I said in the sketch. In a nutshell, the Moorean says that we should be concerned with others' lives because we are concerned to promote the good wherever it occurs, and one of the places the good occurs is in others' lives.

There are a number of standard objections to the Moorean view. Two of them, as we have seen, lead to the two principal alternative schemata, and I shall discuss those objections in connection with the alternative schemata in later sections. But two other standard objections deserve mention. One is an objection to Moore's thoroughgoing consequentialism, according to which the *only* fundamental moral principle is that we should bring about as much good as possible. This objection, whether well founded or not, is not germane to the present discussion. We are not considering Moore's overall view, but rather a Moorean approach to justifying one quasi-consequentialist obligation that every plausible theory must recognize in some form.

The other standard objection to the Moorean view, which is germane, is the claim that Moorean 'good' has insuperable metaphysical and epistemological problems—Moore has no account of the ontological or metaphysical status of his 'good' and no account of how we have epistemological access to it. The truth of this assertion must be conceded, but not its force as an objection. There is no objection here to 'good' that does not apply equally to 'well-being' or 'welfare' or 'good for' or whatever, in the sense that is relevant to our enquiry. As I have already noted, the concept of welfare is irreducibly normative. Stephen Darwall, himself a welfare theorist, gives a very nice argument for this proposition. He imagines a debate between two people who agree completely on the empirical facts about how a third person's life is going in some respect, but who disagree about whether that respect contributes positively to his welfare or not. (His example involves the perennial problem of whether it is better to know the truth about one's life or to suffer pleasing illusion.) As Darwall points out, what these two are disagreeing about is the application of a normative concept.[9] Furthermore, it should be clear that the concept Darwall's controversialists are disagreeing about gives rise to exactly the same metaphysical and epistemological puzzles as Moore's 'good'. We may often find ourselves debating the relative importance to an agent's welfare of her desires and her needs and her health; and because these are all (more or less) empirical concepts that seem to have an intimate connection with welfare, we may be seduced into thinking that, whatever our disagreements about the content of 'welfare', it is at least a metaphysically unproblematic concept. But this is an illusion, as Darwall's example establishes.[10]

We can reinforce this point with two other observations. First, remember Moore's distinction between the questions 'What is "good"?' and 'What is "the good"?' The answer to the second question will be some complex

---

[9] Darwall, *Welfare and Rational Care*, 11.

[10] Another way to see the normativity of the concept of welfare is to observe that the welfare theorist's objection to Moorean good is not just that it gets the *extension* of the to-be-promoted wrong, but that it misconceives the nature of the *normativity* involved. But if this is the welfare theorist's objection to Moorean good, then whatever he offers as an alternative must be supposed to get the normativity right; in other words, it must be a normative concept.

disjunctive natural property; 'the good' can be identified in naturalistic terms. But the question remains what it is we are saying of 'the good' when we say it is 'good' (and how we know what to say that of). That is the question that creates the philosophical difficulties. But that question arises equally with 'good for' (or 'welfare' or whatever). Darwall's controversialists are arguing in effect about a particular instance of the question 'What is "*the* good for"?' But the question I want to press is the other question, 'What is "good for"?' What are we saying about '*the* good for Abel' when we say it is 'good for Abel' (and how do we know what to say that of)? Most theorists of 'good for' have given all too little attention to this question;[11] once we raise it, we see that 'good for' raises the very same puzzles as Moore's 'good'. I have conceded that Moore has little by way of an answer to these puzzles. He says 'good' is a simple, non-natural concept that we all in fact possess as part of our common-sense endowment, if we can just clarify our thinking enough to recognize that fact.[12] But it would be useful if the 'good for' theorists said even this much about their favoured concept; their saying this would reveal clearly that their concept has no metaphysical and epistemological advantage over Moore's 'good'.

The second observation is just that the most plausible recent theories of the 'good for' (or welfare or whatever) all give an important role to what Derek Parfit called an 'objective list'.[13] James Griffin,[14] Joseph Raz,[15] and Stephen Darwall,[16] for example, all agree that part of what is good for an agent is engaging in activities or being in states or relationships that are not picked out simply by the agent's desires, but have some sort of objective value. But the metaphysical and epistemological status of the 'objective list' of relevant values is as problematic as the metaphysical and epistemological status of Moore's 'good'.

In the remainder of this essay I shall often refer to 'welfare' or 'well-being' or 'good of', and so on, by the phrase 'good for'. There are expository advantages to the phrase 'good for', because it allows a natural contrast

---

[11] If this seems unjust to a few careful theorists who have written extended discussions of welfare or well-being, note that I shall discuss the views of Wayne Sumner, James Griffin, and Joseph Raz in section V and of Stephen Darwall in section VII.

[12] G. E. Moore, *Principia Ethica* (Cambridge: Cambridge University Press, 1962), §13.

[13] Derek Parfit, *Reasons and Persons* (Oxford: Oxford University Press, 1984), 499–501.

[14] James Griffin, *Well-being: Its Meaning, Measurement and Moral Importance* (Oxford: Clarendon Press, 1986), 64–72.

[15] Raz, *Morality of Freedom*, ch. 12.

[16] Darwall, *Welfare and Rational Care*, 17, 94–102.

between 'good' and 'good for' as the basic conceptions of to-be-promoted-ness. It is worth emphasizing that in this usage 'good for' is a normative concept, just like 'good' and 'welfare'. Purely naturalistic explications of 'good for', which would equate 'good for' with 'desired', or even 'desired under specified ideal conditions', or 'pleasurable', or the like, are excluded. These are candidates for explications of 'the good for', but not of 'good for' itself. Similarly for 'being an exemplary member of a species', along the lines suggested by Philippa Foot.[17] There is one other genuinely normative possibility for the 'good for Brown': we might take it to mean just 'what Brown ought to promote'. The most interesting development of this idea is Michael Smith's,[18] although Smith sensibly prefers not to refer to his concept as a version of 'good for', but rather as a subscripted 'good$_{agent}$'. Interesting though this possibility is, it is clearly remote from any concept of welfare. The good$_{Brown}$ in this sense may include any number of states of affairs outside Brown's life; and furthermore there is no plausibility at all in suggesting that the good$_{Brown}$ as such makes any claim on Jones. It may be, of course, that the good$_{Brown}$ and the good$_{Jones}$ overlap, or are even identical in extension, but it will not be the goodness$_{Brown}$, the fact that Brown should promote it, that accounts for anything's being good$_{Jones}$. So we can ignore this subscripted good. 'Good for', as used in this essay, is a normative concept, and a synonym for the other normative concepts of 'welfare', 'well-being', and 'good of'.

IV

Let us turn now to the second schema for explaining why I am my brother's keeper, the schema that says that the basic category of the to-be-promoted is realized not in an agent-neutral 'good', but in an agent-relative 'good for', and that each of us must promote the good for every other. This schema is suggested, as we saw, by an objection to the Moorean view—the objection that value must be value 'for' some valuing person or being.

---

[17] Philippa Foot, *Natural Goodness* (Oxford: Oxford University Press, 2001). I would construe this as a naturalistic concept. We might manage to construe it as a normative concept, but if so, it would be subject to the general dilemma I develop below: if the value of being an exemplary member of a species is really a value *for* the individual exemplar, then it is not clear how that value for the exemplar creates a reason for anyone else.

[18] Michael Smith, 'Neutral and Relative Value after Moore', *Ethics* 113 (2003), 576–98.

I admit that the 'good for' theorist seems to have a point. We come to the idea of value through our experiences of wanting and desiring and feeling needs, and so it may seem that when we ascribe value to something, we are necessarily ascribing value 'for' ourselves. On the other hand, the 'good for' theorist ought similarly to be able to understand the intuitive pull of the Moorean view. The issue of what is to-be-promoted, even what is to-be-promoted in people's lives, is a normative issue. It is not settled by anyone's desires or drives. Darwall's question of whether someone is better off knowing the truth about his life or being contentedly deceived is not to be answered just by knowing what the person wants, or even by knowing what he would want under idealized circumstances. Even if we think that what we should promote in any person's life is his always having just what he wants, or would ideally want, the fact that that *is* what we should promote in his life is not a fact about, or determined by, his desires. So it is not clear why we should think that the essence of 'goodness'—even of the goodness of pure desire-satisfaction, if pure desire-satisfaction is good—is a 'goodness for'.

It may seem that this focus on desire is beside the point. In principle, one could believe that value is completely objective, not determined by anyone's desires, and still think that the essence of value is 'value for' as opposed to 'value "from the point of view of the universe"', or 'value *simpliciter*'. True enough. One could try to understand 'value for' in terms of desire-independent 'interests', or some such (though that generates a problem of how to understand one's 'interests' as something other than having what is 'valuable for' one). I focus on desire only because it seems to me that it is implicated in the aetiology, and to some extent the continuing plausibility, of the idea that value is essentially 'value for'. Once we step resolutely into the realm of purely objective value, and then ask the fundamental question whether value is essentially 'for' certain value-supporting entities or whether it is essentially non-relative, it is hard to come up with any *arguments* at all (though I shall attempt to offer a general argument for non-relative value in section VIB and a special-purpose argument later in this section).

The situation is made more difficult by the fact that on the best versions of each theory of value, '*the* good' and '*the* good for' may have the same extension. For example, the Moorean thinks that pain is bad (*simpliciter*); the 'good for' theorist thinks that pain is bad for the subject who experiences it. They agree that pain is negatively valenced. With regard to positive values, the Moorean of today (I can speak with authority, because I am a large fraction of the relevant population, perhaps the unique member) believes that the good is pleasurable experiences of objectively appropriate activities and relationships; so everything the Moorean recognizes as good will seem a 'good for' to most 'good for' theorists, because of the pleasure involved.[19] Similarly, more and more 'good for' theorists are becoming 'objective list' theorists; they are coming to the view that what is good for people is engagement in objectively valuable pursuits. So we are approaching the point, if we are not there already, where the extensions of the Moorean's 'good' and the 'good for' theorist's 'good for' are effectively indistinguishable. In such a situation, we will not be able to decide between the concepts by adducing counterexamples to one theory or the other—states or events which the proponents of one theory can claim the other theory attaches the wrong valence to. What we need is conceptual arguments, but it is not easy to find arguments that have any purchase on such a fundamental disagreement.

Moore's own discussion of 'good for', in the course of his famous 'refutation of Egoism', suggests an argument which I think is very powerful in the present context, although for reasons that will appear, it is not an argument Moore himself makes.[20] Moore thought that the notion of a *normatively fundamental* 'good for', which could compete with 'good' for the central role in the account of to-be-promoted-ness, was incoherent; but he acknowledged that there were a number of other things that one could coherently mean by 'good for Jones'. One might mean, for example, 'what Jones ought to aim at, for instrumental reasons', or alternatively, 'what Jones *thinks* is good', or else, 'something which is good, and which occurs, or would occur, in Jones's life'. None of these, of course, establishes a sense of 'good for' which is logically independent of 'good'—that is Moore's point. But the idea that 'good for Jones' might mean 'good, and occurring in Jones's life' suggests a further argument, in the form of a dilemma for the 'good for' theorist.[21]

---

[19] I shall explain why this does not make 'good' a ruse for covert concern with 'good for' in section VIA.

[20] Moore, *Principia Ethica* §§59–60.

[21] Although I make my own use of the possibility Moore raises that 'good for' might mean 'good, and occurring in the life of', I do not suggest, and I think it would be a mistake to suggest, that this is Moore's own theory of 'good for' or 'welfare'. Moore has no theory of these concepts. He has no use for them. And in the end I agree with Moore about this too.

Clearly no 'good for' theorist can accept that 'good for' means 'good, and occurring in the life of'. That would amount to abandoning 'good for' as an independent concept. Still, accepting that definition would have one definite advantage for the 'good for' theorist. It would explain why Cain should concern himself with the good for Abel. If 'good for' meant simply 'good, and occurring in the life of', then Cain would be required to care about the good for Abel because the good for Abel would be just a part of the good *simpliciter*.[22]

As I say, this move will not do for the 'good for' theorist. For the 'good for' theorist, the relativization of goodness signalled by the 'for' must somehow appeal to each individual's interests, or desires, or point of view, or valuations, or something of that sort. The good for Abel must be peculiarly Abel's—the *goodness* or the *value* must be peculiarly Abel's—in a way that the mere occurrence of universal good in Abel's life does not necessarily satisfy. But if the good for Abel is peculiarly Abel's—if its *value* is somehow essentially a value *for Abel*—then why indeed should Cain care? We think there is a deep connection between value and reasons. That suggests precisely that if the good for Abel is a matter only of value *for Abel*, then it creates reasons *for Abel*, and for no one else.

Hence the dilemma: any understanding of 'good for' which distinguishes it clearly from 'good, occurring in the life of' also undercuts the possibility that one individual's 'good for' should make a claim on any other

---

[22] The 'good for' theorist might ask how I can so casually assert that *if* the 'good for Abel' were 'good, occurring in Abel's life', then Cain ought to care about it because he ought to care about the good *simpliciter*. Why so? What reason has any agent to care about this free-floating good? Obviously a complete answer to this question would take us deep into the debate about internal and external reasons. (I am of course an externalist.) For purposes of argument, I am prepared to concede that there is an ordinary language usage in which Cain does not 'have' a reason to promote the good *simpliciter* unless he somehow takes an interest in it; but then the question before us is not what reasons Cain 'has', but what reasons there *are* for him to behave in certain ways. What I said in the text was not that if the 'good for Abel' were 'good, occurring in Abel's life', then Cain would 'have' reason to promote it; I said he would be *required* to care about it—in other words, there would be a reason for him to care about it, and hence to promote it. The best credential for this desire-independent sense of what reasons there *are* is the fact that this is the sense involved in the question the agent asks himself when deciding what to do. At the most fundamental level, the agent does not ask himself what reasons he 'has'—he does not ask himself what he takes an interest in. Rather, he asks himself what he *should* take an interest in, or in other words, what reasons there *are*. See the further brief discussion of agency and the 'desire-transcending question' in section VI B below.

individual.[23] In effect, the problem is 'What does the "for" in "good for" mean?' If 'for' means 'occurring in the life of', this gives us an *empirical* relativization to the agent, but the normativity involved is still the universal normativity of 'good'. We need some other understanding of the 'for' to give us a concept of 'good for' that is distinct from 'good, occurring in the life of' and independent of 'good'. The relativization signalled by the 'for' must be a relativization of the *normativity*. But that is precisely the move that undercuts the possibility of Abel's 'good for' making a claim on Cain.[24]

I hope it is clear by now that we cannot escape the dilemma by saying that the 'for' means something like 'desired by'. Imagine that there is some activity Abel wants to engage in, and imagine further that we are all agreed that Cain ought to promote Abel's opportunity for engaging in that activity. Still there is the problem of how to account for this obligation of Cain's. Is the correct account that Abel's engaging in this activity, or perhaps his engaging in any activity he wants to engage in, is good *simpliciter*, and that Cain should promote that good? This account makes sense, but of course it operates without any normative 'good for Abel'. Or is the correct account that Abel's engaging in an activity he wants to engage in is (normatively) good for Abel, and that Cain should promote the good for Abel? This account simply raises again the question why. How is a value for Abel a reason for Cain?

We could of course say that (1) Abel's engaging in an activity he wants to engage in is good for Abel, and (2) Abel's having the 'good for Abel' is a good *simpliciter*. And then of course, (3) Cain should promote that good *simpliciter*. (2) is the significant new bridging premiss. I suspect that many 'good for' theorists actually operate unconsciously with some such schema as this. But this does not eliminate 'good *simpliciter*', so it is no use to those who think that 'good *simpliciter*' is incoherent and who want to eliminate it

---

[23] This is no problem of course for the 'good for' theorist who is prepared to abandon the idea that Abel's 'good for' makes a claim on Cain—in particular, it is no problem for the Egoist that Moore was arguing against. That is why this is not Moore's argument. But today there are even fewer Egoists than there are Mooreans. Present-day 'good for' (welfare, well-being) theorists do want Abel's 'good for' to make a claim on Cain. And they face the dilemma.

[24] Although I find it revealing to pose the question as 'What does the "for" mean?', I would emphasize that the dilemma is not just an artefact of a particular locution. If we were talking about well-being, for example, the corresponding question would be, 'In what sense precisely is Abel's well-being *Abel's*?' Merely that it occurs in Abel's life is not enough to distinguish 'his' well-being from the occurrence of good *simpliciter*, but a thicker relationship to Abel threatens to undercut the claim on Cain.

in favour of 'good for'. And worse, this schema invites us to apply Occam's razor and eliminate the 'good for'. Instead of saying first that a certain state is good for Abel, and then that Abel's having what is good for him is good *simpliciter*, why not just say that the state in question is good *simpliciter*? It is not clear that the reference to 'good for' is doing anything significant.[25]

V

The dilemma argument is an argument about why the good for Abel cannot make a claim on Cain if the concept of 'good for' is genuinely independent of Moorean good. It is not a general argument for the incoherence of 'good for'; it leaves open the possibility that there is a coherent, independent concept of 'good for', the significance of which is that each agent is either required or permitted to give special attention to the good for herself. (I shall suggest a broader argument against 'good for' in section VIB.) But in connection with our central question—why one agent should be concerned with what happens to others—it seems to me that the dilemma argument is a powerful argument against the usefulness of 'good for'. In this section I want to consider how the dilemma manifests itself in connection with three contemporary theories based on well-being.

A

In *Welfare, Happiness, and Ethics*, Wayne Sumner's primary project is to define 'welfare'. His conclusion is that welfare is informed and autonomous happiness; and happiness is satisfaction with the way one's own life is going or has gone for oneself.[26] The crux of happiness is thus a doubly subjective evaluation—subjective *first* because it focuses on how the subject's life is 'for him', and *second* because Sumner tells us there is no right answer to this question beyond the subject's own judgement.[27] In the last chapter of

---

[25] I have suggested in the text that we need to bring in good *simpliciter* to link up the good for Abel with a reason for Cain. The need for good *simpliciter* seems even clearer when we consider the problem of how to balance the (reasons created by the) good for Abel and the good for Seth. Balance we must, and that seems to require a 'good' (explicit or implicit) which is not a 'good for'.

[26] L. W. Sumner, *Welfare, Happiness, and Ethics* (Oxford: Oxford University Press, 1996), 172.

[27] Ibid. 153–71.

the book, Sumner argues that 'prudential value [welfare] is the sole ultimate bearer of ethical value'.[28] In other words, in so far as we make choices that bear on others' lives, our ultimate concern should be with their welfare, as Sumner defines it. But why exactly should each agent care about others' welfare? Does Sumner have any argument that avoids the dilemma I posed for the 'good for' theorist? So far as I can see, he does not.

At the most fundamental level, I do not think Sumner squarely addresses the *meaning* of the concept 'welfare', or equivalently 'good for'. This criticism may seem unjust; Sumner certainly deserves credit for a serious attempt to give a general account of welfare (his account in terms of authentic happiness), as opposed to just listing standard sources of welfare, such as achievement and rich personal relationships. Even so, Sumner seems to be offering an answer to the question 'What is "*the* good for"?' rather than to the question 'What is "good for"?' A symptom of the uncertainty about the latter is Sumner's treatment of perfectionist value as an element of welfare. This is an issue he confronts in a variety of contexts, and his conclusion is always that perfectionist value has no independent significance beyond its possible contribution to happiness as Sumner defines it. But sometimes Sumner speaks as if there is conceptual room for a genuine substantive question about the role of perfectionist value in welfare;[29] and sometimes he speaks as if claiming a role for perfectionism in the specification of welfare is just a fallacy, a bald mistake in conceptual analysis, which consists of failing to distinguish between how well a life is going and how well it is going for the subject of it.[30] These different arguments seem to reflect different implicit answers to 'What is "good for"?' As I have noted before, I cannot criticize Sumner for not *defining* 'good for'. The 'good for' theorist can claim about 'good for' what Moore claims about 'good'—that it is a simple, non-natural concept we all have. But saying this explicitly would make it clear that authentic happiness is not determined as the content of welfare by mere conceptual analysis.

Leaving aside the uncertain status of the concept of welfare, Sumner tells us that welfare is constituted by an agent's feelings of satisfaction with his life, so long as those feelings are informed and autonomous. Hence, a life devoted to trivial or even demeaning pursuits could be a good one,

---

[28] Ibid. 25. (It may seem odd that I cite p. 25 for a proposition I say Sumner discusses in his last chapter. The full discussion is in the last chapter, but the most succinct statement is in the first chapter.)

[29] Ibid. 140 n. 1.   [30] Ibid. 78–9.

provided the subject is satisfied with it.[31] But why should other agents have any positive obligation to facilitate such a trivial or demeaning life? Why, in other words, should welfare, as Sumner understands it, be the sole bearer, or even *a* bearer, of 'ethical value'? When it comes to explaining this, Sumner seems just to beg the question. Thus: 'The fact that a course of action would make someone better off counts in favour of it, and the fact that it would make someone worse off counts against it.'[32] 'Our ethical sensibilities seem to have much to do with our ability to see things from the point of view of potential victims and beneficiaries.'[33] '[H]ow well the lives of other creatures are going must matter to us *because* it matters (from the inside) to those creatures.'[34] Now, no one would deny that some facts about how a life is going from inside can make a claim on others. Even for the Moorean, pain is intrinsically bad, for example. But Sumner is claiming much more than that. He is claiming in effect that each of us has some positive obligation to facilitate others' engagement in trivial or demeaning pursuits, if that is what they find satisfaction in (and not just on the ground of their painful frustration if they are deprived of these pursuits). This seems problematic. Perhaps those pursuits are indeed what we should regard as good *for them*; but if so, it is hard to see why the good for them, so understood, makes a claim on anyone else. Sumner has neither given us a conceptual scheme from which this would follow, nor made it plausible in the concrete case.

B

James Griffin has a theory of prudential value (his favoured term is 'well-being') that is some degrees more perfectionist than Sumner's. Griffin offers a list of 'the ends of life' that he thinks are values in anyone's life: accomplishment, the components of human existence (autonomy, physical integrity, mental composure, liberty), understanding, enjoyment, and deep personal relations.[35] Sumner would agree that most or all of these things would contribute to most people's welfare; but he objects, with some justice, that theories like Griffin's provide no general theory that accounts

---

[31] Ibid. 182.
[32] Ibid. 191.
[33] Ibid. 211.
[34] Ibid. 217.
[35] Griffin, *Well-being*, 67–8.

for what is on the list and what is not.[36] If there is any general theory suggested by Griffin's discussion, it is that these various goods respond to universal and relatively stable human motivations. In any event, Griffin does not give pure subjective satisfaction the role Sumner does. Indeed, while Sumner says that a life of trivial or demeaning pursuits could be a perfectly good life if the informed, autonomous subject is satisfied with it, Griffin explicitly denies that.[37] To be sure, Griffin rejects a perfectionism which would posit one ideal form of life for all individuals. Griffin's moderate perfectionism gives us rather a list of basic elements. But even in discussing which elements from the list each individual should concentrate on, Griffin seems to de-emphasize pure preference and emphasize instead individuals' divergent capacities for different sorts of pursuit.

Moderate perfectionist or not, Griffin regards himself as setting out a theory of prudential value—a theory of the value of a life *for the subject of it*. And he insists that morality needs prudential value as a base.[38] But why this is so—indeed, why prudential value as such matters at all to morality—is much less clear. The only argument I can find to explain why one person should care about another's prudential value is roughly that because anyone's prudential value is composed of the sort of universal elements Griffin has identified, it makes a claim on others too.

That it is my, or any one individual's, pain or accomplishment is not a constituent of my, or anyone's, conception of prudential value. How well a person's life goes matters—matters immediately to that person, of course, but also matters generally in this sense: depending upon what happens to him, his life will be more or less valuable.... That value has the role in a life of point and direction that it does, and that the locus of value is not just oneself, brings one to a certain sort of impartiality.... [I am required to be concerned for your interests because] one's concerns have to be responsive to how worthy of concern its possible objects are.[39]

Griffin says that in thinking this way, an agent is neither looking at things from the other's point of view nor viewing them *sub specie aeternitatis*.[40] But the viewpoint embodied in the quoted remarks seems quite 'aeternitatist' to me. Perhaps Griffin's idea is that if the driving force is impartiality, then

---

[36] Sumner, *Welfare, Happiness, and Ethics*, 164–5.
[37] Griffin, *Well-being*, 34 n. 29, discussing the grass-counter.
[38] Ibid. 69–70.
[39] Ibid. 157–8.
[40] Ibid. 157.

the agent is just extending to the other's prudential value the concern he naturally has for his own. But that raises both the question (1) what is the nature of the agent's concern for his own prudential value (whether even that is not *sub specie aeternitatis* for the agent who has fully recognized the inadequacy of his natural motivational system for grounding genuinely justifying reasons),[41] and the question (2) why does it not make all the difference that the agent's own prudential value is his own and the other's is the other's. One would think that an agent is required to be concerned only with what is valuable for him—which does not include a prudential value that is essentially for another.

It may seem that my last remarks do not sufficiently acknowledge the force of impartiality. To clear things up a bit, we must observe that there are two possible *modes* of my concern for 'value for me'. My remarks at the end of the last paragraph assume implicitly that my concern is direct: value for me translates directly into reasons for me, and that is why, or how, I care about it. In this mode, value for others translates into reasons for them, which simply do not engage me in the same way. Impartiality has no purchase. In contrast, my concern for value for me might be indirect: it might be that I am concerned in the first instance for myself, and this leads to a concern for value for me. But now, if impartiality means that I ought to be concerned for others in the same way as I am concerned for myself, then it would follow that I ought to care about what is valuable for them in the same indirect way that I care about what is valuable for me. I shall explain why I reject this second possibility, which involves my responding to value for X (myself or another) through the mediation of a concern for X, in section VII.

I do not mean to deny the intuitive force of Griffin's argument about why we should be concerned for others' welfare. But it seems to me that what intuitive force there is militates against the idea that what we are concerned with is really prudential value. The intuitive force depends on the universal value of the perfectionist elements of good lives that Griffin has identified; and what the possession of those elements most obviously leads to is lives that are better *simpliciter*, not lives that are in any distinct sense better *for* the subject. It is interesting that a few pages further on, when Griffin is addressing the issue of conflict between our own prudential value and our moral obligations (apparently grounded in others'

---

[41] See the discussion in section VIB below.

prudential value), he says that we transcend the distinction by appealing to 'values, neither expressly prudential nor expressly moral but values taken at a higher level of abstraction...: the notion of what, all things considered is worth our concern'.[42] But once we introduce this non-relativized notion of 'worth our concern', the idea that we were dealing with a 'good for' in any stronger sense than 'good, occurring in the life of' seems to have vanished. And if this is where we finish in hard cases, this is where, in principle, we might have started.

The lesson from this discussion of Griffin is *not* that a significant concept of prudential value must not contain a perfectionist element. That would be to forget what we learned in discussing Sumner. Rather, the joint lesson of the discussions of Sumner and Griffin is that 'good for' is a chimera. If we take seriously the dependence on the agent's subjective evaluation, which Sumner plausibly claims is the best realization of the 'for', we get the very implausible conclusion that a life spent in trivial pursuits can be as valuable as Bach's life or Darwin's if the subject is as satisfied, and that the life of trivial pursuits can make as strong a claim on others to be promoted, so far as intrinsic prudential value is concerned. This is not plausible; the 'for', in Sumner's account, undermines the 'good'. In contrast, emphasizing the perfectionist element, as Griffin does, seems to attenuate the 'for' to the point where it is a mere empirical accident ('occurring in the life of') rather than an aspect of the normative concept. In Griffin's account, the 'for'-ness is totally unrelated to the nature of the value.

We could of course just stipulate that the good for a subject must be perfectionistically valuable activity which the subject himself enjoys or approves of.[43] But to my mind, this produces a conceptual monster, unmotivated by anything except the desire to avoid counterexamples from two directions. There's nothing wrong with the *extension* of the suggested chimeric concept. As I have said, I think this is pretty much the extension of the Moorean good. But, as I shall explain in section VIA, the Moorean has a way of making sense of the joint requirement of objectively valuable activity and enjoyment by the subject, in the notion of appreciative engagement with appropriate objects. By contrast, the 'good for' theorist's gerrymandering of the extension of 'good for' to avoid counterexamples does nothing to help the 'for' aspect, which is meant to involve normative

---

[42] Griffin, *Well-being*, 161.

[43] Cf. Parfit, *Reasons and Persons*, 501–2.

relativization, and the 'good' aspect, which requires normative neutrality if it is to account for claims on others, fit together in an intelligible unity.

C

The most interesting approach to fitting these aspects together into an intelligible whole is Joseph Raz's. Raz starts from the idea that well-being is (largely) a matter of success in one's goals.[44] That sounds like it emphasizes the subject-relative 'for' side of 'good for'. But Raz points out that agents want their projects to be valuable. We choose our projects because we think they are valuable; and our allegiance to them is conditioned on our belief in their value.[45] So, if my goal, loosely described, is to count the blades of grass in the Law School quadrangle, my fully described goal is to engage in the valuable activity of counting those blades of grass. If counting them is not in fact valuable, then even if I complete a perfectly accurate enumeration, I have not achieved my goal, and the 'success', which is only apparent, does not contribute to my well-being. Raz combines the neutralist and relativist aspects of 'good for' by building a concern for non-relativized value into the agent's desires.

This move of Raz's is not just *ad hoc* counterexample blocking. I think Raz is right that we intend to have valuable goals, and that if we are mistaken about the value of our goals, then even empirical 'success' does not amount to achieving what we intended. Hence, *if* well-being is a matter of achieving our goals, it follows that well-being depends on achieving genuinely valuable goals. But it seems to me that Raz's move just highlights the question why we should think in terms of well-being at all. Raz directs our attention to the agent's own view of his goals. But, as we noted right at the start, Raz recognizes that the agent does not aim at his own well-being at all.[46] If the agent does not pursue his goals with an eye to his well-being, why should we use his success at his goals to measure his well-being? Indeed, why does the problematic notion of 'well-being' even enter the picture? Why should we not just promote all agents' valuable activity, without worrying about anyone's well-being? Of course there will be trade-offs to be made between different people's valuable activity, as

---

[44] Raz, *Morality of Freedom*, 305–7, 317.

[45] Ibid. 299, 316–17. My reasons for agreeing with this claim of Raz's are suggested in section VIB below.

[46] Ibid. 316–17.

there are trade-offs to be made between different valuable activities in our own lives. But Raz has also told us that the same values are involved in these interpersonal trade-offs as in the intra-personal ones.[47] We can make the trade-offs without thinking about well-being, so why not do so?

To be sure, we cannot relate to others' projects *exactly* as we relate to our own, for two main reasons. First, even if both I and my colleague are doing analytic number theory, I *do* my own research activity, but I cannot *do* his. I can support his activity, and encourage it, and provide resources, and eliminate obstacles; I cannot actually do his doing. But I do not see how this difference lends any support to the idea that I should value his activity as a contribution to his well-being even though that is not how I value my own. The reason I do not value my own activity as a contribution to my well-being is that I value the activity directly. But I can value his activity directly in the same way, even though I do not engage in it. (In the case of my own activity, the valuing explains the engagement and partly constitutes it; but the engagement does not constitute the valuing.) I see no reason why the activity's being his and not mine means I must value it as a contribution to his well-being. The idea of his well-being does not force itself on me any more than the idea of my own does.

It may seem that the plausibility of the argument in the last paragraph depends on the fact that my colleague and I are both doing analytic number theory, which we know I value precisely because I have chosen to do it. Suppose I, the number theorist, am considering the life of an acquaintance who is a jazz saxophonist, or a construction worker, or a full-time stay-at-home parent. Now it might seem that if I do not value the other's activity for itself, I have no choice but to value it as contributing to his well-being. But this is a mistake. Recall that on Raz's view no activity contributes to anyone's well-being unless it is valuable. So I cannot even decide that the activity contributes to the other's well-being without first deciding that it is valuable (even though for whatever reason I have not pursued it in my own life); and if I recognize it as valuable, then I can value it directly. My lack of personal engagement with the value in question may increase the chance of my making a mistake, but that is true whether I think in terms of well-being or in terms of the value of the activity for itself.

---

[47] Ibid. 319–20.

VI

In this section I shall redeem two promissory notes from earlier sections. First, I shall respond to the suggestion that the Moorean view, because it regards only pleasurable experiences as valuable, must really be driven by 'good for' impulses. Then I shall offer an argument against the whole concept of 'good for' from first principles.

A

It may seem that by restricting the good to pleasurable experiences, the Moorean reveals that his real concern, like the 'good for' theorist's, is with value *for* the subjects of these experiences. Why else should an experience of a beautiful sunset, or a great mathematical theorem, or a Bach cantata, need to be enjoyable in order to be valuable? I cannot answer this point fully here. The short answer is that what is really valuable (non-relatively) is the appreciative engagement of the subject with a worthy object. The subject's pleasure is relevant because pleasure is an inevitable concomitant, and therefore a sign, of the right sort of engagement. But it is the engagement of subject and appropriate object that is valuable. To my mind, when there is the right sort of engagement, we could as well say that the value created is value 'for' the sunset, or the theorem, or the cantata, as insist that the value is 'for' the subject. The object of appreciation is brought to life by being attended to and appreciated. But in fact, the real value is neither 'for' the subject nor 'for' the object. The value is just there, in a whole to which both subject and object make an indispensable contribution.

In support of this, notice that when I am *fully* engaged in either listening to or performing a Bach cantata (for example), there is no thought in my mind of any value 'for me'; indeed, there is no thought in my mind of *me*. My consciousness is occupied with the music, and the beauty of the music and the texts, and the singing. I am fully present; I am, as an integral aspect of the activity, recognizing the value of the activity and choosing continuously to go on with it. But I am present only as *subject*, as appreciator and agent. I am not present as an object for my own thinking or feeling or choosing. The paradoxical truth is that the very sort of activity which many philosophers view as paradigmatically 'good for' an agent does not present itself to that agent, when he is engaged in it, as a 'good for' at all, because it does not present itself in conjunction with any thought about the subject of the activity. The subject is indispensably present, but only as subject, not as object of an additional thought beyond the thought internal to the activity. Thus the experience presents itself as 'good *simpliciter*'.

My argument here extends an argument that Thomas Nagel makes in *The View from Nowhere*.[48] Arguing for the claim that severe pain is a neutral disvalue, which anyone has reason to alleviate even when the pain is another's, Nagel says in a variety of ways: 'The pain can be detached in thought from the fact that it is mine without losing any of its dreadfulness.' '[The agent's] awareness of how bad [pain] is doesn't essentially involve the thought of it as his.' 'In its most primitive form, the fact that it is mine—the concept of myself—doesn't come into my perception of the badness of pain.' This all seems to me exactly right, and it justifies Nagel's continuation after the first quote above: '[The pain] has, so to speak, a life of its own. That is why it is natural to ascribe to it a value of its own.' I am suggesting that the argument has much broader application than Nagel allows it. When I am fully engaged in hearing or performing a Bach cantata, the concept of myself also doesn't come into it. If the 'selflessness' of great pain means that the disvalue of pain is agent-neutral, so does the 'selflessness' of experiences with great positive value mean that their value is agent-neutral also. The self disappears at our best moments as well as our worst.[49]

B

I turn now to the argument against 'good for' as the (or a) fundamental 'to-be-promoted-ness' concept. I said in section IV that we come to the idea of value through our experiences of wanting, and desiring, and feeling needs; and that may account for our intuition that value must be relative to a valuing agent. But if we in fact develop into fully competent agents, then we come to realize that we must look beyond our desires and needs for the full truth about value—even for the full truth about value in our

---

[48] Thomas Nagel, *The View from Nowhere* (New York: Oxford University Press, 1986), 160–1.

[49] Paradoxically, even when I am writing a philosophy paper, which I hope is a valuable activity, and speaking in the first person, the concept of myself doesn't really come into it. When things are going smoothly, the authorial 'I' is more a literary device than a self-conscious personal obtrusion.

lives. In the course of developing towards full-fledged agency, we learn first to limit some desires in light of conflicting desires, and then to criticize lower-order desires in light of higher-order desires. Eventually, inevitably, it occurs to us to ask ourselves whether our most fundamental desires (either our highest-order desires if the structure is essentially hierarchical, or the entire complex of our desires if we are more coherentist) are justified and directed at worthy ends. This is the step, raising what I have elsewhere called the 'desire-transcending question', that makes us agents.[50] When we ask this question, we are asking for a standard for our desires, a standard that cannot be grounded in our desires themselves. It is this desire-transcending question, of course, that gives rise to the metaphysical and epistemological problems that 'good' suffers from and that I have claimed 'good for' (or indeed any fundamental normative concept) suffers from as well. Still, acknowledging this question and confronting it—not in every individual decision we make, but sometimes, at crucial junctures—is the crucial passage to agency.

If it is the connection of valuing with desiring that initially makes it seem plausible that value is 'value for', what happens when we come to the point of realizing that we must at least try to transcend our desires completely as we seek to identify the to-be-promoted?[51] Does the agent who has reached the desire-transcending question and who is deliberating ideally about what to promote think in terms of 'good' or in terms of 'good for'? Remember that the issue here is about the choice between the *concepts* 'good' and 'good for'. As we have seen, it is perfectly possible that '*the* good' and '*the* good for' should be identical, in the sense that the things which are actually good, if the Moorean view is correct, are the very same things that are actually good *for* some agent or other, if the 'good for' theorist is correct. But the question remains, which is the proper fundamental concept?

Now, it seems to me that saying the fundamental concept is 'good for' amounts to imposing an unexplained a priori constraint on the agent's deliberation. The agent has realized he needs a standard to guide his choice which transcends his naturalistically given motivational system. He is looking at the world and asking what things are *truly* to-be-promoted. So

---

[50] See Donald H. Regan, 'How to Be a Moorean', *Ethics* 113 (2003), 651–77, §I.

[51] Of course, once we have identified the to-be-promoted in general terms, our desires will be highly relevant, in a variety of ways, to figuring out how we can best promote it. But our desires do not figure in the specification of what matters ultimately.

far as I can see, there is no reason why he should assume at this stage, when he first begins his survey of the world and his search for the to-be-promoted, that the to-be-promoted is necessarily limited to occurrences within people's lives—and even less reason why he should assume that the to-be-promoted is necessarily limited to occurrences within people's lives that might seem in some intuitive sense to involve benefit 'for' them. But these limitations are what would correspond to the claim that the question the agent asks himself should be understood as a question about the 'good for'. If the agent does not begin with these a priori limitations, then we should understand him as asking about the 'good'. Even if it turns out that 'the good' is entirely constituted by things in people's lives, and even things that might be thought of as 'benefiting' them in some sense, still, the agent's question is about 'the good'.[52]

It might be said that the agent's question is about 'good for' in a different sense. The agent is faced with the problem what *she* should do— simply because it is only her own actions that she does. It might be suggested that the agent is therefore enquiring in effect into what is to-be-promoted-by-her. Notice that even if we accept this suggestion, it does not lead us to a concept of 'good for' that is equivalent to the concept of 'welfare' or 'well-being'. Rather, it leads us to the sort of good$_{agent}$ posited by Michael Smith.[53] But I am inclined to reject the suggestion, for reasons like those that figured in my argument in section VIA for the neutral good of valuable activities. There is nothing in the agent's situation that compels

[52] This is as good a place as any (there is no really good place) to mention a quite particular argument for the necessity of a concept of 'good for' that is made by Darwall, *Welfare and Rational Care*, 3, 53, following Mark Overvold, 'Self-Interest and the Concept of Self-Sacrifice', *Canadian Journal of Philosophy* 10 (1980), 105–18. The argument is that if we have no concept of the good for an agent, then self-sacrifice, which is sacrificing one's own good for another's or for some universal good, becomes impossible. This is logically correct, of course, if we define 'self-sacrifice' as the sacrifice of one's own good. But why must self-sacrifice so defined be possible? What would we lose if it were not? The idea, plainly, is that self-sacrifice is praiseworthy or admirable, and we would be poorer if we lost an occasion for justified praise because our concepts made it impossible to recognize the occasion. True. But it seems to me that any action we would be tempted to identify as 'self-sacrifice' in ordinary usage will involve the agent ending up with significantly less of some natural good—less pleasure or enjoyment, less physical integrity or freedom or life. And therefore the self-sacrificing agent will have had to act against strong natural impulses in the service of (what he saw as) the overall good. Surely we can praise and admire this self-control, this ability to resist strong natural impulses in the service of the good, whether or not we see the agent as sacrificing some 'good of her own'.

[53] See the last paragraph of section III above.

her to attend to the fact of her own particularity as an agent. To be sure, the empirical circumstances in which she acts are particular, and when it comes to deciding precisely how best to promote whatever is to be promoted, she will need to take her circumstances into account. But at the stage of formulating the general theory of the to-be-promoted, there is simply nothing to suggest that there is a special to-be-promoted-*by-her*. Just as appreciative activity is transparent to particular personal identity, so, I suggest, is action in general, at least ideally (and it is the ideal situation that gives us the fundamental concepts).[54]

VII

The third schema for arguing that I am required to care about what happens in others' lives involves the claim that I must care about others, or that I must respect them as persons. Remember the problem with the second schema was that it was not clear how another's 'good for', if it was normatively relativized enough to distinguish it from 'good, occurring in the life of', could make any claim on me. The advantage of the care/respect approach is that it might seem to explain why I must take others' point of view, at least to some extent. And in so far as I take their point of view, I arguably put myself within the scope of the normativity of their 'good for'. Hence, if I am required to manifest care or respect for them, I am required to be moved by their 'good for'.

Of course, the care/respect approach may still trip over another point we have developed above—that agents do not aim at their own well-being. If Abel does not aim at his own well-being, then even when Cain takes Abel's point of view, Cain will not aim at Abel's well-being. Abel does of course care what happens in his life, and therefore if Cain takes Abel's point of view, Cain must care what happens in Abel's life. But we have suggested that Abel's own concern about his life is that it should contain valuable activity; in which case that is also Cain's concern when Cain takes Abel's point of view. Practically speaking, this brings us back to the Moorean view: Cain cares about Abel's life because he cares about the good wherever it may occur.

---

[54] For a similar point about the transparency of action, in the context of a discussion of the right and the good, see Regan, 'How to Be a Moorean'.

As it happens, the most interesting recent discussion of care and caring side-steps this difficulty, at least on the face of things. Stephen Darwall does not say that in caring for others we take their point of view, nor that we care about their (independently identifiable) welfare. Rather, he *defines* a person's welfare as what someone who cares about that person ought to want for him.[55] But the essential difficulty noted in the previous paragraph—the tendency of the care-based approach to collapse into the Moorean approach—reproduces itself within Darwall's framework. Remember that the Moorean and the 'good for' theorist (second schema) agreed that we should want and promote valuable activities both in our own lives and in others'. The question that divided them was whether we want those activities just as the valuable activities they are, or as components of the subjects' welfare. Is our focus on the good *simpliciter* or on the good *for individuals*? Analogously, what is necessary for the care-based approach to be distinctive, as Darwall fully recognizes, is that it involve caring about what happens in a person's life *for that person's sake*.

So, what is it to care about someone *for his sake*? Darwall eschews any definition of such caring. As I have made clear already, I have no objection in principle if someone wants to claim that some fundamental moral concept is indefinable; the only issue then is the plausibility of the concept and the system built on it. But Darwall takes a slightly different route. He claims that the attitude of caring about others for their own sake is a natural kind, and *therefore* needs no definition. This appeal to a natural kind seems to me problematic for two basic reasons. First of all, if the relevant attitude of caring is a natural kind, then it seems that its objects—the things that one who cares wants intrinsically for the cared-for individual—are just whatever they are naturally. The question of what the objects ought to be, or what they are rationally required to be, simply does not arise. It seems quite implausible to suggest that we can usefully *pick out* a normative concept ('welfare') by defining it as the proper object of a natural-kind attitude. There may be no difficulty about saying that some *independently given* normative concept is the required object of a very general

---

[55] Darwall, *Welfare and Rational Care*, 7. The point of this surprising move is to avoid defining the individual's welfare in terms of her own concerns. An individual may not have the relevant sort of care for herself if, say, she is depressed. And even if she does care for herself, she may have other concerns that are not generated by that self-caring. Hence there are possible discrepancies, in both directions, between an individual's own concerns and her welfare.

natural-kind attitude; we often say that one should desire the good. But we do not ordinarily propose to *pick out* the good as the proper object of some particular naturally given desire, as Darwall proposes to pick out welfare as the proper object of care for another.

Secondly, I am not persuaded that there is a natural-kind attitude of the sort Darwall posits. One way to establish the existence of such a natural-kind attitude would be by psychological experimentation, and Darwall tries to find evidence for his sort of caring in the psychological literature. The experiment that Darwall puts most reliance on shows that subjects are more likely to help someone out of a difficult situation if they are invited to attend to how the other *feels*, as opposed to just attending to the crude facts of the situation. Darwall admits that the experiment does not distinguish clearly between caring about what happens to the other (which of course includes her feelings as a crucial element) and caring about it *for her sake*, but to him the experiment more strongly suggests caring for her sake.[56] So far as I can see, that just reflects the view he began with.

Of course, the fact that we cannot clearly isolate the attitude of 'caring for another for her sake' experimentally doesn't mean it doesn't exist. It could be that we all just experience it and can recognize it in ourselves. But I don't think I recognize the attitude as Darwall describes it in myself. The main stumbling-block is a further claim Darwall makes about 'caring for another for her sake'. Darwall tells us that one who cares for another in the relevant way believes in the 'worth' of the other, and believes that this worth should be recognized by all.[57] My wanting something 'for Carol's sake' necessarily involves my viewing Carol as having such worth. I am sceptical about such 'worth', and therefore about Darwall's version of caring.

Since my scepticism about the worth of persons runs against the grain of all contemporary philosophical rhetoric, let me ease into the topic, beginning not with the worth of persons but with the worth of animals. Animals appear in Darwall's discussion only in passing, but he does speak of 'caring... for every sentient creature' as a possibility,[58] and he refers to 'the worth of living beings'.[59] I have trouble identifying such a core 'worth' in an animal, even a loved pet. I have had pets; I have cared for them, and

---

[56] Ibid. 66–8.
[57] Ibid. 8, 48, 83.
[58] Ibid. 16.
[59] Ibid. 75.

about them, and I have made sacrifices for them. I have been saddened more than I ever expected when it was necessary to put them to sleep. I have no doubt that they were 'worth caring about' in the sense that my relationship with them was a good in my life (and probably in theirs), and also that they were 'worth caring for' in the sense that it was appropriate to take measures to improve their lives. But I do not see that all of this adds up to, or is grounded in, or requires, any further distinctive claim about *their* intrinsic worth.

The point applies to people as well. Lest I offend anyone else by doubting their worth, let me begin by doubting my own. I am not depressed; I think I have an adequate sense of self by standard psychological criteria; I think I am not deficient in ordinary self-esteem; I am certainly not deficient in everyday self-centredness and selfishness. And yet, if I ask myself in a cool hour whether I have some deep intrinsic 'worth' that grounds the importance of what happens to me, or that justifies anyone, myself or another, in caring about things for my sake, I do not find it. Much that goes on in my life is important (in a small way); much of it has intrinsic value, both positive and negative. And those facts matter to how I should be treated. But the idea that they either depend on or manifest my personal 'worth' is what escapes me. Similarly, I hope I can now decently say, with regard to other people, I think I am not markedly deficient in ordinary natural impulses to improve others' lives in various ways—to do things we would refer to in everyday parlance as 'for' other people. I also regard some of my relationships with others as great goods in my life and, I hope, in theirs. But I do not see that either these impulses or these beliefs are based on a perception of others' 'worth'.

One natural response to scepticism such as mine is to focus on intimate relations, and to ask, rhetorically, 'Don't you do things *for the sake of* your spouse, or your children, or your siblings or closest friends?' But if such intimate relations seem to provide the best evidence for 'caring for another for her sake', that should also make us pause to consider closely just what sort of attitude such cases are evidence for. I take it that, on the welfare theorist's view, I can act, and I even have some obligation to act, to promote the welfare of starving or oppressed people in distant countries that I have never seen and can barely imagine in any concrete way. So I have some obligation to act to bring about the results in those people's lives that people who cared for them for their own sake would want. It does not quite follow that I must care for them for their own sake; but such an inference is certainly suggested. Now, I do not argue against the logical possibility of such caring; but it seems much less obvious what such distant caring involves than the (supposedly clear) case of caring for an intimate. This ought to make us wonder whether the case of caring for the intimate is as perspicuous as it seems. Similarly, there is a good dose of partiality for our friends and intimates built into our natural dispositions (and philosophers argue about whether such partiality is reflected in the most fundamental structure of our moral obligations). But surely no one would say he cares specially for his child or spouse because they are of greater 'worth' than someone less favoured; if we believe in this sort of worth, one of its essential features is that all persons possess it equally. Again, this does not refute the possibility of 'caring for another for her sake'; but it does suggest to me that whatever the attitude is that we see most clearly in our dealings with intimates, it is less moralized, and therefore less interesting for morality, than Darwall suggests.[60]

My scepticism about 'worth' extends also to 'dignity', which is thought to require respect as worth requires caring.[61] I resent what I perceive as affronts as thoroughly as the next person, and I am as quick as the next person to see affronts even when they exist nowhere but in my imagination; I care about my status in various groups; I always want at least my share of any good that is being distributed; I do not want to be manipulated or sacrificed for goals I do not endorse. And yet, if I ask myself in a cool hour whether this is all a manifestation of my Kantian dignity as an agent—once again, I see no such dignity. It might be said that some of these attitudes cannot be normatively justified except on the assumption of my Kantian dignity. Perhaps in so far as the attitudes are fundamentally *self*-centred that is true. But then, is the correct further inference by *modus ponens* to Kantian dignity, or by *modus tollens* to a lack of normative justification for attitudes of precisely such a form and content?[62]

---

[60] Almost the only case that Darwall discusses that does not involve an intimate involves someone seeing a child on the verge of falling into a well (ibid. 69). Here the child may be a stranger, but the child's plight is extreme and immediate and vividly presented, and it is a *child*, so the situation seems likely to provoke a strong and quite unmoralized natural reaction.

[61] Ibid. 14.

[62] For further discussion of why we cannot get a duty to promote others' well-being from a Kantian approach, see Donald H. Regan, 'The Value of Rational Nature', *Ethics* 112 (2002), 267–91, especially 276–8.

It may be, of course, that the final product of reflection on all our moral intuitions, general and specific, will be a structure in which some notions of worth and dignity are fundamental. This seems to me unlikely, but it could be the case. But Darwall's view, which he shares with many others, seems to be that our perceptions of worth and dignity are immediately given in a form that makes their moral significance manifest. That is what I do not see. Perhaps I am revealing my moral blindness, but it seems to me more likely that believers in 'worth' and 'dignity' have partly misconstrued and partly transposed too quickly into the moral sphere certain undeniably important and deep-seated (purely) natural attitudes.

VIII

When one is operating at such a high level of abstraction, there is the danger that one will see only what one is inclined to see. Perhaps that is what has happened to me. It is presumably no accident that, to my mind, both the 'good for' (well-being, welfare) theory and the care-based theory threaten to collapse into the Moorean view. The 'good for' theorist needs some equivalent of Moorean good to forge a link between any genuinely independent normative concept of 'good for Abel' and reasons for Cain. The care-based theory would seemingly collapse into Mooreanism if it required each agent to take the other's point of view (if we remember that the other, *qua* agent, herself aims at the good); to avoid this, the care theorist needs the problematic notion of caring for another for her own sake, on the basis of her worth.

It's not as if Moorean good is unproblematic. It is the worst imaginable foundation for a moral theory—except for the alternatives.[63]

[63] I am grateful for the very helpful comments, in response to this or earlier versions, of Joseph Raz, Connie Rosati, Tim Scanlon, and Michael Smith.

10

Reasons: A Puzzling Duality?

T. M. Scanlon

It would seem that our choices can affect the reasons we have. If I adopt a certain end, then it would seem that I have reason to do what is required to pursue it, a reason that I otherwise would not have had. On the other hand, many of us believe that we have other reasons that are not dependent on our choices. If accelerating my car and driving straight ahead would seriously injure a pedestrian, this is a reason for me not to do that. And it seems, to me at least, that this is a reason I would have whatever ends I may have chosen. Its being a reason is something I discover rather than create.

This gives rise to a puzzle about what it is to be a reason—that is to say, a consideration that counts in favour of some action or attitude. If the normative status of counting in favour of acting a certain way is something that certain considerations can just *have*, how can it also be something that we can *confer* on certain considerations by our choice of ends?

This puzzle arises for anyone who, like me, is inclined to be a realist about some reasons but also recognizes an agent's ends and intentions as having special normative significance. But it arises in a particularly clear form for what Joseph Raz calls the classical conception of human agency.[1] This conception distinguishes sharply between reason and the will. The function of reason, according to this conception, is to assess various reasons for action and arrive at conclusions about which actions there is sufficient reason to perform. The function of the will is then to determine which of

[1] Raz discusses this view in *Engaging Reason: On the Theory of Value and Action* (Oxford: Oxford University Press, 1999), esp. chs. 2 and 3.

these eligible actions we will in fact do. Raz believes that in many cases there will be more than one eligible action: that is to say, that available reasons will not fully determine what we should do. It follows that the activity of the will goes beyond reason and is not determined by it.

Raz's conception of rational action fits the pattern I described above. First, his view of reasons is, at least in many cases, a realist view in the respect I mentioned. He writes: 'The core idea is that rationality is the ability to realize the normative significance of the normative features of the world, and the ability to act accordingly.'[2] He also holds, as I have just said, that by the exercise of the will we choose actions from among those that reason determines to be eligible. It may not follow immediately that this activity of the will gives us new reasons beyond those that reason discovers. If a rational agent has willed a certain action, then (absent a change of mind) he or she will perform that action. Indeed, a failure to do so (again, absent a change of mind) would be irrational. But this may just be a fact about the way that rationality requires an agent's attitudes and actions to be related. It may not depend on the idea that an additional reason is generated by the agent's act of will.

Whatever one may say about this particular case, however, the puzzle I have described seems to remain when we shift from choices of actions to choices of goals. Raz mentions as typical goals such things as 'success in one's career, success in one's relationships, possessing the entire set of nineteenth-century French stamps, or qualifying as an International Master in chess'.[3] I assume he would say that reason recognizes such things as worthwhile, and that we then choose among these eligible alternative goals and adopt certain ones as *our* goals. He takes this to result in a difference in the reasons we have, since, as he goes on to say, 'We have reason to do whatever will facilitate the pursuit of our worthwhile goals.'[4] If we do not have similar reason to do what will facilitate the pursuit of other worthwhile goals (I will return to this question later), then this leaves us with the apparently puzzling duality I described above: the status of being a reason for an agent is something that a consideration can just have, and also something it can acquire through the exercise of the agent's will.

There are a number of different ways of responding to this apparent puzzle. One would be to deny that a person who chooses a goal or action

---

[2] Raz discusses this view in *Engaging Reason: On the Theory of Value and Action* (Oxford: Oxford University Press, 1999), esp. 68.

[3] Ibid. 63.   [4] Ibid. 64.

thereby comes to have a reason to do what promotes it, over and above those reasons he or she would have had without having made that choice. A second response would be to admit that an agent acquires such a reason but to deny that this amounts to a duality in the sources of reasons. This might be maintained in several different ways. The first would be to hold that *all* reasons depend, ultimately, on the nature or activity of rational willing. Christine Korsgaard, for example, argues not only that the grounds of the principle of instrumental reason lie in the fact that it is constitutive of rational willing, but also that a consideration counts in favour of our adopting an end only if we have given it that status.[5] Like me, Raz does not take this view. We could, however, deny the duality in another way, by going to the opposite extreme and holding that the *source* of all reasons is independent of the will, although the exercise of our wills may sometimes change our situation in ways that change the reasons that apply to us. In the remainder of this paper I will explore this alternative, and consider Raz's account of how decisions affect the reasons we have. I will tentatively conclude that the apparent duality in reasons is only apparent, and should not trouble us.

It will be helpful at the outset to distinguish two different ways in which an agent's judgement or decision can have normative consequences. One is by changing what the agent can do, or what attitudes he or she can hold, without being irrational.[6] The other is by changing the reasons that the agent has. These are not the same. Suppose, for example, that an agent concludes that tomatoes are dangerous to his health, and that he therefore has reason to avoid food containing tomatoes. This does not change the reasons that he has. If he is mistaken about the health risks of eating tomatoes, then he still has no reason not to eat them, even though he thinks he does. But, whether he is mistaken or not, as long as he judges that he has reason not to eat food containing tomatoes, he would be irrational if, when he is deciding what to eat, he did not treat the fact that a food contains tomatoes as a reason not to eat it. The claim that an agent must, in so far as he is not irrational, treat a certain consideration as a reason can fall short of the claim that this consideration *is* a reason for that agent. This is so because that claim need not involve an endorsement

---

[5] See Christine Korsgaard, 'The Normativity of Instrumental Reason,' in Garrett Cullity and Berys Gaut (eds.), *Ethics and Practical Reason* (Oxford: Oxford University Press, 1997), 253.

[6] Claims about what a person must, unless he or she is irrational, count as a reason invoke what John Broome calls "normative requirements". See his "Reasons" in this volume, pp. 28–55.

of the attitudes that make it irrational for the agent to fail to treat that consideration as a reason. But a claim of the former sort can be turned into a claim about the reasons that the agent in fact has by adding an endorsement of these attitudes.

This distinction suggests a strategy for explaining the puzzle I have been discussing. Since irrationality is, at least in some cases, a matter of conflict between an agent's judgement and his or her other attitudes,[7] it is not at all surprising that an agent's choices and decisions can make a difference to what he or she can do without being irrational. What would be more surprising, and raise the question of a duality of the kind I have described, is the possibility that an agent's choices and decisions could affect the reasons he or she has. What we should do, then, is to consider whether what seemed at first to be instances of the latter are really only instances of the former. If this turns out to be true in every case, it will solve the problem. If it does not, then we can consider how best to explain the residual cases in which choices and decisions make a difference to an agent's reasons.

I will begin by considering what seems to me to be an analogous question about belief. Coming to believe something, or judging that there is compelling reason to believe it, makes a difference to what one must, in so far as one is not irrational, count as a reason. Someone who judges that there is compelling reason to conclude that p is the case, but continues to reason as if p were not the case, or as if it were an open question whether p is so, is being irrational. More specifically, a person who believes p must, in so far as he continues to hold this belief and is not irrational, take the fact that q follows from p as a reason for believing q. By contrast, a person who does not believe p need not see the fact that q follows from it as having any particular significance.

But a person who comes to believe p should not see this change in the considerations she must, in so far as she is rational, take to be reasons as flowing from her adoption of that belief. Rather, the reasons she must take herself to have to rely on p in further reasoning are just those considerations that she has judged to support her conclusion that p.

This dependence is shown in the fact that a person who believes p should not *necessarily* take the fact that q follows from p as a reason for

---

[7] I have advocated using the term 'irrational' in what I called a 'narrow' sense, in which it applies only to cases in which there is such a conflict. See my *What We Owe to Each Other* (Cambridge, Mass.: Harvard University Press, 1998), 25–30. But one need not accept that recommendation in order to agree with the claim made here.

believing q. It may be that q is so implausible that she should take the fact that q follows from p as a reason for rejecting p. (q might be $0 = 1$, for example, or a contradiction.) Alternatively, she might have independent grounds for reconsidering her belief in p, if, for example, she learns that what she had taken as evidence for p was in fact mistaken. The most we can say is that someone who believes p should take the fact that q follows from p as a reason for believing q *unless she knows or believes something that gives her reason to reconsider her belief in* p. Supposing that she does not have such reasons, however, the fact that she believes p adds nothing to *her reasons* for believing q, or for taking the fact that q follows from p as counting in favour of q. Her reasons for these attitudes are, as I have said, just the considerations that she takes to support belief in q (considerations which, we are supposing, she judges to be sufficient).

Now consider the case of instrumental practical reasoning. Here we can say, in a fashion parallel to the case of belief, that adopting a goal gives rise to a difference in what an agent must, in so far as he has that goal and is not irrational, see as reasons. Someone who has adopted G as a goal, believes that x-ing is a necessary means to G, and (while continuing to have G as a goal) does not count this as a reason for x-ing, is being irrational. This difference follows simply from principles that are constitutive of practical reasoning. Since adopting a goal involves taking oneself to have reason to do what advances it, a failure to take oneself to have a reason to advance a goal one has adopted, and continues to hold, is irrational. Should we say, then, that an agent need not see his adoption of G as constituting or giving rise to a new reason, and that he should, on the contrary, see the reasons he has as flowing entirely from the considerations that he takes to support adopting G as a goal?

I defended a positive answer to the parallel question in the case of belief, and it may seem that we should give the same answer here. The principle of instrumental reasoning does contain a qualification parallel to the one I discussed in the case of conditional theoretical reasoning. A person who has G as an end should not necessarily take the fact that doing x would promote G as a reason to do x. If x is the only way of achieving G, and is morally repugnant, then it may be that the person should abandon G (or at least suspend pursuit of it until some other means becomes available). And she might have other reasons for reconsidering whether G is in fact worthy of pursuit. So the most we can say is that a person who has G as an end should take the fact that doing x would promote G as a reason to do x, *unless he knows or believes something that gives him reason to reconsider his adoption of* G.

The need for this qualification indicates that an instrumental reason for doing what advances one's goal continues to depend on the reasons for having that goal. But in at least some cases the fact that the person has adopted G seems also to be doing some normative work. Suppose that Jones reasonably believes the following:

1. There are a number of ends, call them G, H, and K, which he has sufficient reason to adopt (they are all *eligible*, to use Raz's phrase).
2. He has good reason not to adopt more than one of these goals.

If Jones, believing (1) and (2), has adopted G as a goal, then he must, if he is not irrational, take the fact that x-ing would promote G as a reason for him to x. But he need not, similarly, take the fact that y-ing would promote H as a reason for him to y, which he should balance against his reasons for doing x. So he must, in so far as he is not irrational, take the fact that he has adopted G as a goal as itself making a difference in what he should treat as a reason—as itself a reason why the fact that x-ing would promote G is a reason for him to x.

So far, this is just a claim about what Jones must, in so far as he is not irrational, take to be a reason. But if we add that Jones not only reasonably believes (1) and (2) but that these claims about the reasons he has are correct, then we are committed to the stronger claim that the things he must, in so far as he is not irrational, take to be reasons are in fact reasons. In particular, we are committed to the claim that the fact that Jones has adopted G as a goal is a reason for him to take the fact that x-ing would advance G as a reason to x, and hence to the claim that the fact that an agent has adopted a goal can make a difference to the reasons he has, not merely to what he must see as a reason, in so far as he is not irrational.

In cases of this kind, the normative significance of an agent's having adopted G as an end seems to derive from the element of free play involved—that is to say, from the fact that, in Raz's terms, the adoption of G as a goal is an exercise of the will, not required by reason. One might maintain that there can be a similar element of free play in the case of belief. Raz seems to suggest something of the kind.[8] He argues that there can be evidence making a belief rational but leaving it none the less 'optional'. The apparent evidence may be such that a very trusting person

---

[8] Raz, *Engaging Reason*, 95–6.

would take it as grounds for believing p, while someone of a more sceptical turn of mind would not. But it may be that neither response would be irrational. Should we say in this case that the first person's decision to believe p leads to a difference in the epistemic reasons he subsequently has? This decision does seem to make a difference in what he must treat as a reason if he is not to be open to a charge of irrationality. If he refuses to see the fact that q follows from p as sufficient reason for believing q (absent reasons for reconsidering his belief in p), then he is being irrational. The more sceptical person is in a different situation. She should take the fact that q follows from p as counting in favour of q to the degree that, in her judgement, the available evidence supports p, but no more than this. However, the less sceptical person need not see the fact that he believes p as making a difference to what he must take to be a reason. The difference in what the two must see as reasons in so far as they are not irrational results simply from a difference in their assessments of the underlying reasons supporting p.

There seems, then, to be a difference between the cases of theoretical and practical reasoning. In the case of practical reasoning, the fact that someone has adopted G as an end may make a difference in what she must treat as a reason in so far as she is not irrational. But it also may itself be something that she must (in so far as she is not irrational) treat as a reason, and it may even *be* a reason for her—namely, a (second-order) reason to treat the fact that x-ing would promote G as a reason for her to x. In the case of theoretical reasoning, by contrast, the analogues of the latter two claims do not hold.

The next question is whether this amounts to a troubling duality in the sources of practical reasons. As I have said, a constructivist who holds that the rational will is the source of all reasons would see no duality here. I will not explore this alternative. I want to examine the options available within a view that is at least partly realist in the way that both Raz's and mine seem to be. Given such a view, one possibility would be to offer a realist account of the additional reasons that a person comes to have as a result of adopting a goal.

Here I must begin with a few remarks about how realism about reasons is to be understood. Realism may seem an odd view if it is taken to hold that facts about reasons are just facts 'in the world' that we can discover but that, in their nature, have nothing to do with us. This way of understanding the matter fails to take account of the relational character of claims about reasons. To claim that some consideration 'is a reason' is to claim that it counts in favour (or against) an agent in certain circumstances holding a certain attitude, such as, for example, a certain belief or intention.

Making this relational aspect of reasons explicit may make realism seem even stranger. How, it may be asked, can there be such facts 'in the world' about the relations between our attitudes and various possible states of affairs? I believe, however, that this worry results from giving normative realism an unnecessary and unwarranted ontological reading. We all believe that there is a difference between good reasons for a belief and bad ones. And whether we are internalists or externalists about reasons for action, if we believe in practical normativity at all, we believe that some considerations are good reasons for a person to act in a certain way, and other considerations are not. The most natural construal of these beliefs takes them to involve commitment to relational truths of the sort I have described. There would be reason to withhold this commitment, and to seek a revisionist understanding of our beliefs, only if it involved some further commitment that is properly deemed implausible. But the naïve reading of our beliefs about reasons commits us only to what needs to be the case if they are to have the kind of significance we attribute to them. This significance—normative significance—does not depend on these truths having any special ontological status; nor would it be enhanced or supported by such status.

Returning now to what I called the relational character of claims about reasons, suppose that a certain feature of some goal—for example, that achieving it would increase the educational level of children in some city—is a good reason to adopt it. More explicitly, this is a good reason for someone to adopt it if he or she is in the right situation, for example has the right skills and opportunities to promote the goal, and perhaps only if he or she stands in the right relation to the children, or the city, in question. For someone else, who was not in this position, the same consideration might only be a reason to encourage someone who was in this position to adopt the goal and a reason for him not to interfere with her pursuit of it. So the same consideration can be a reason for different people to do different things, depending on their relation to the goal in question.

To adopt a goal is to set oneself to pursue it, and to take the fact that certain actions would be means to that end as counting in favour of those actions. So if the fact that this goal would increase the educational level of the children in a certain city is a good reason for someone in my situation to adopt it, it is also a good reason for me to pursue it *if* I adopt it, and if I adopt it, for me to take the fact that some action would promote that goal as a reason for that action. But what is the force of this conditional? How is it that adopting the goal makes a difference?[9]

Here it is important to remember the kind of situation we are considering (the kind in which, as I argued above, the fact that an agent has adopted a goal can make a difference to the reasons the agent has). This is a situation in which there is more than one goal which the person has sufficient reason to adopt, but in which the person also has compelling reason not to adopt more than one of them, perhaps because they cannot be effectively pursued at the same time. What a person has reason to do in such a situation is to pursue one of these eligible goals. To do this, she must employ some procedure for selecting one of the goals and then pursue that goal, rather than any of the others. Once she has selected a goal, she is no longer in this situation.

This might be put by saying that adopting the goal puts one in a different relation to that goal, and this makes a difference to what a given consideration gives one reason to do, just as having the opportunity or skills to advance it, or standing in the relevant relation to the city in question, can make this kind of difference. It is therefore unnecessary, and a mistake, to suppose that adopting an end can make a difference in the reasons one has only if, when we adopt an end, we *generate* new reasons by an act of will. By adopting an end, we do come to have reasons that we otherwise would not have had. But these reasons are not different in their source from our reasons for adopting the goal in the first place.

We may be misled into thinking that they have a different source by confusing claims about reasons with claims about irrationality. As I have noted, the fact that someone has adopted a certain goal makes it the case that he is irrational if, absent a change of mind, he denies that the fact that some action would advance this goal is a prima-facie reason for performing it. This particular species of irrationality is independent of the reasons the person may have for adopting the goal in the first place, and is therefore created by the person's adoption of the goal in a way that the reasons I have just been discussing are not.[10]

---

[9] I am grateful to Samuel Scheffler for raising this question in discussion at the Raz conference.

[10] Nomy Arpaly advances some reasons for doubting this claim about rationality in 'On Acting Rationally Against One's Best Judgment', *Ethics* 110 (2000), 488–513.

What I am calling the relational character of reasons amounts to this: considerations that are reasons are not reasons in the abstract, but reasons for agents in particular circumstances.[11] Defensible claims about the reasons we have must take into account various facts about our situation, such as the fact that we can't do everything worth doing, or adopt every goal. This seems to be built into the notion of an eligible action (or goal), which Raz invokes. To claim that a goal is an eligible one, for an agent in certain circumstances, is to make a claim about the reasons supporting that goal considered in relation to the reasons supporting other goals that that agent could choose. It is to claim that there is good enough reason for the agent to adopt that goal rather than others and, once having chosen it, to pursue it. If a goal is an eligible one for a given agent, and she adopts it, then she has no reason to reconsider that decision unless she has reason to believe that her circumstances have changed or that new information about the merits of these goals has become available to her. All of this, it seems to me, is part of the normative content of the idea of an eligible goal. If this is correct, then an agent's decision to adopt one eligible goal among others makes it the case that she has reason to pursue that goal rather than others even though that decision does not *create* this reason by a kind of self-legislation.

I have so far been supposing that if the adoption of a goal makes a difference to the reasons we subsequently have, it does this by making it the case, in one way or another, that we have a new positive reason to do what will promote that goal. An alternative view would hold that a decision to perform an eligible action or adopt an eligible goal changes our normative situation in a different way, by changing the normative status of reasons for doing other actions or for doing what would promote other goals. Rather than providing a new reason to do the act one has chosen, a decision among alternative eligible actions gives one a reason to regard the considerations that might have counted in favour of performing alternative actions as no longer relevant.

One might put this is in terms of a purely pragmatic second-order reason. As I have said in the preceding paragraph, if an agent has decided to do A after carefully considering the matter and weighing what seem to her to be the relevant reasons, then she has no reason to reconsider this decision unless she comes to have some reason to think that circumstances

[11] This is not to deny that some considerations might give *anyone* a reason, regardless of that person's circumstances.

have changed, or that she has overlooked some relevant factor. One might add that an agent in this situation has a positive second-order reason *not* to reconsider her earlier decision. Doing so would be costly. It would be, at the least, a waste of time. Worse, a general policy of reconsidering one's decisions in such circumstances would be a serious impediment to doing anything at all.

This is a second-order reason because it is a reason to ignore the first-order reasons favouring courses of action other than the one chosen. I call it a purely pragmatic reason because it concerns the costs and effectiveness of the process of deliberation, rather than the substantive relevance of the reasons it instructs an agent to ignore. Its pragmatic character can be seen from the fact that if the agent's circumstances were to change in a way that would eliminate the costs of reconsideration, then these particular reasons against reconsidering the merits of alternative actions would disappear. Suppose that I am about to attend a meeting at the start of which I will have to vote for one of two job candidates. After deliberating about their merits for some time, I decide, just before the meeting, to vote for Smith rather than Jones. But as I am on my way to the meeting, there is a power failure, and I am stuck in the elevator. Given that I don't have anything else to do while I am waiting for the power to come back on, I would seem to have no reason not to revisit the merits of the candidates and consider whether Smith is indeed the one to choose.[12]

Not all second-order reasons are purely pragmatic. If I am on a committee considering revisions in the undergraduate curriculum, then I have reason to disregard the effects that new requirements would have on the number of teaching fellow positions available to graduate students in my department. This is a second-order reason, since it bears on the status of other considerations as reasons for or against the policies I am considering. But it is not purely pragmatic. Rather, it is based on the substantive view that considerations of graduate funding are not relevant to the question of what undergraduates should be required to study in order to get a good education.

It is uncontroversial, I believe, that a decision, taken after deliberation, to do one of several eligible actions, or to adopt one among several eligible goals, can give rise to a purely pragmatic reason to subsequently ignore,

---

[12] This example is a modification of one suggested to me by Derek Parfit, who credits it to John Broome.

and not reconsider, the reasons for choosing alternative courses of action or alternative goals. A stronger and more interesting claim would be that such a decision gives rise to a reason of this kind that is not purely pragmatic. With this question in mind I want to examine Raz's important idea of an exclusionary reason.

Raz's account of the normative significance of decisions takes this significance to involve, in part, the exclusion of reasons the agent would otherwise have had. He writes: 'A decision is always for the agent a reason for performing the act he decided to perform and for disregarding further reasons and arguments. It is always both a first order and an exclusionary reason.'[13] Raz's category of exclusionary reasons is defined quite broadly, in a way that seems to include both what I have just called purely pragmatic reasons and reasons that are not purely pragmatic. Thus he writes: 'A second order reason is any reason to act for a reason or refrain from acting for a reason. An exclusionary reason is a second order reason to refrain from acting for some reason.'[14] The question I want to consider is whether the exclusionary reasons that a decision generates, according to Raz, are all purely pragmatic reasons.

Here we should begin by recalling what Raz takes a decision to be. In his view, to decide is to form an intention after deliberation. And he says that a decision is reached 'only when the agent (1) reaches a conclusion as to what he ought to do and (2) forms the belief that it is time to terminate his deliberation'.[15] Raz's reason for including this second clause is that even if a person has 'formed the view that the proper decision is to do A', if he also believes that he should consider some further evidence, then we would not say that he has decided to do A.[16]

But 'belief that it is time to terminate his deliberation' may not be the best way to formulate the condition Raz has in mind. For he goes on to say that 'a person can decide knowing that he should not'.[17] One might wonder how a person could believe that it is time to terminate his deliberation while knowing that he should not. One way of avoiding this problem would be to restate the second of Raz's two components of decision as an *intention* to terminate his deliberation. This would avoid the problem, since a person could form the intention to terminate

---

[13] Raz, 'Reasons for Action, Decisions, and Norms', as reprinted in Raz (ed.), *Practical Reasoning* (Oxford: Oxford University Press, 1978), 135.

[14] Ibid. 132.   [15] Ibid. 134.

[16] Ibid.   [17] Ibid. 136.

deliberation even while knowing that this is premature. Doing this might be irrational, but it is still a possible thing to do. This formulation still fits with the rationale Raz offers for the condition, since it seems natural to say that what is lacking in the case of the person who has formed a view about what he should do but wants to consider some further evidence is an intention to terminate deliberation rather than a belief that he should do so.

Raz believes that it is the decision itself, rather than the considerations that provide reasons for that decision, that provides the exclusionary reason he is describing. More exactly, he holds (indeed, holds that it is 'logically true') that a person who has made a decision to do A must regard this decision as an exclusionary reason to disregard further reasons for alternative actions. He believes that a person may be mistaken in deciding to do A, and that when this is so, the person may not have a *valid* reason for excluding reasons for other courses of action. But he maintains that the person must regard his decision as such a reason. Raz argues that even if a person comes to believe that a decision that he has made was premature, this decision itself still provides an exclusionary reason not to reconsider the matter, and continues to do so as long as the person does not unmake the decision by deciding to reopen the matter. He takes this to support the conclusion that it is the decision itself, and not the reasons supporting it, or even the agent's own assessment of those reasons, that the agent must take as providing an exclusionary reason.

It does not seem quite right to say that an agent must take his own decision as providing a reason not to reconsider it, in the way that Raz maintains. I want to suggest, however, that much the same point can plausibly be made by making use of the distinction discussed above, between a claim about the reasons that an agent has and a claim about what that agent must do in so far as he or she is not irrational. Suppose, for simplicity, that we modify Raz's conditions in the way I described above, replacing his requirement that a person who makes a decision must form the belief that it is time to terminate his deliberations with the requirement that a person who makes a decision must form the intention not to deliberate further. I believe, as I suggested earlier in this paper, that a person who forms an intention to do something but then does not do it (without abandoning or modifying that intention) is being irrational. Moreover, as I argued there, this irrationality seems to be a matter simply of the incompatibility between such a person's attitudes. It persists whether or not the person had good reason, or now judges that he had good reason, to form the intention in the first place. Nor does it need to be explained by claiming that a person who forms an intention to do something thereby acquires a new *reason* to do it. So, in the present case, if deciding involves forming an intention not to deliberate further, then a person who has reached a decision would be behaving irrationally if (without abandoning that decision) he were to consider further the reasons for taking a different course of action. That this would be irrational follows (logically, one might say) from the decision itself, regardless of the soundness of the grounds for making it and regardless of the agent's assessment of these grounds (as long as this assessment does not lead him to abandon the decision and reopen the matter). But there is no need, in order to explain this phenomenon, to say that the decision itself provides the agent with a *reason* not to reconsider.

If we accept this analysis, then we can say two things about a person who has decided to do a certain eligible action or to adopt a certain eligible goal. First, this decision (as long as it is not abandoned) makes it irrational for her to consider further the reasons favouring alternative actions or goals. Second, she has purely pragmatic reasons of the kind described above not to abandon the decision unless she comes to believe that her situation has changed or that there are further considerations that must be taken into account.

On this account, a decision to do A does not give rise to a new positive reason to do A, apart from purely pragmatic reasons we have not to reconsider that decision. Raz's claim that the opposite is true—that a decision to do A is a positive reason to do it—is supported by an appeal to an alleged similarity between decisions and promises. So in closing I want to consider that similarity, to see whether it suggests that the reason a decision provides is not purely pragmatic.

A person who promises to do A normally comes thereby to have a new reason to do A (as well as certain exclusionary reasons). This reason is not generated by a decision or the formation of an intention on the part of the agent, since it exists even if the promise is entirely insincere. In normal cases, promising creates a reason because it changes the agent's situation in a way that gives her a reason. A person who promises to do A leads the promisee to expect that she will do A unless the promisee consents to her not doing so, and she creates this expectation in a situation in which she has reason to believe that the promisee wants reliable assurance of this kind and understands her to be intending to provide it.[18] If a person has done this, then it would be wrong of her not to do *A* (absent special justification). Thus, by changing her circumstances in this way, she comes to have a moral reason to do *A*. (She could also do the same thing—create similar expectations in similar circumstances—without using the words 'I promise', in which case, I would argue, she would have created the same moral reason.[19])

Raz says that while a decision is 'materially' different from a promise, the two have the same formal features.[20] Central to this formal similarity is the fact that a person who promises, like a person who makes a decision, 'must regard this as a reason for him to behave in a certain way', and this reason is independent of the content of the promise or decision. For the reason just mentioned, I have doubts as to whether a person who promises must see the promise as providing a reason. But what interests me here is whether the parallel with promises casts light on the kind of reason that Raz takes a decision to provide. Promises generate reasons because we need to be able to give and receive reliable assurance about what we will do. The suggestion, then, is that decisions provide reasons because we need to be able to rely on ourselves—to be able to bind ourselves to particular courses of action, as it were.

But in the case of decisions, this 'binding' is weaker than in the case of a promise. If a decision to do *A* constitutes a positive reason to do *A*, it does so only so long as the person has not unmade this decision by deciding to reopen the matter. And the only reasons not to do this are purely pragmatic ones. The only thing like a 'need to rely' that is playing a role in this picture is the fact, which I mentioned among the pragmatic considerations counting against reconsideration, that if one keeps reopening a decision without grounds for believing that one's circumstances have changed or that new relevant information has become available, this will make it impossible to act. But the force of this consideration in any particular case will depend on the costliness of reconsideration, and the costs of postponing action in that particular case.

---

[18] In abnormal cases the promise may fail to create his expectation, or the promisor may be mistaken in believing that the promisee wants it. But as long as it is reasonable for the promisor to believe that the normal conditions obtain, she should *believe* that she has come to have a reason to do the thing promised.

[19] I describe this account of promises in more detail in *What We Owe to Each Other*, ch. 7.

[20] Raz, 'Reasons for Action, Decisions and Norms', 137.

I am therefore inclined to accept the account sketched above, according to which the exclusionary *reasons* generated by a decision are purely pragmatic ones. Beyond that, what a decision does is not to generate a new reason but to change what one can do without being irrational.

To sum up, I have argued for the following claims:

1. An agent's decision can change what she must, in so far as she is not irrational, treat as a reason. But it need not do this by being or giving rise to a new reason.

2. In some cases, the fact that an agent has adopted a certain goal is itself a reason for her to regard the fact that an action would advance that goal as a reason for that action. But this is not because the decision to adopt that goal creates a new reason.

3. The fact that a person has decided to follow a certain course of action can make it irrational for him (as long as he does not reconsider that decision) to consider further the reasons for alternative courses of action.

4. A person who has decided, after due reflection, to adopt a certain course of action, has a purely pragmatic second-order reason not to reconsider that decision.

Taken together, these points seem to me to account for the observed facts about the normative significance of decisions without suggesting any troubling duality in the sources of reasons.[21]

[21] For helpful comments at the conference, or on drafts of this paper, I am indebted to Frances Kamm, Derek Parfit, Philip Pettit, Joseph Raz, Samuel Scheffler, and Michael Smith.

11

Projects, Relationships, and Reasons

Samuel Scheffler

The relation between values and reasons has been the subject of much discussion in recent moral philosophy, but few people have explored the topic with as much insight and sensitivity as Joseph Raz. In this essay, I will discuss one aspect of what Raz calls 'the value–reason nexus':[1] namely, the relation between valuing certain kinds of things and the recognition of reasons for action. Elsewhere I have argued that to value one's relationship to another person non-instrumentally just is, in part, to be disposed to treat that person's needs, interests, and desires as providing one with reasons for action, reasons that one would not have had in the absence of the relationship. This is part of what valuing a relationship non-instrumentally involves. In this essay, I want to extend the argument from interpersonal relationships to personal projects. I will argue that, just as valuing one's relationships non-instrumentally involves seeing oneself as having what I will call *relationship-dependent reasons*, so too valuing one's projects non-instrumentally involves seeing oneself as having *project-dependent reasons*. I take this argument to support Raz's claim that a focus on the 'value–reason nexus' not only does not support a maximizing conception either of ethics or of practical reason, but in fact has significant anti-maximizing implications. I also agree with Raz when he holds, in effect, that both relationship-dependent and project-dependent reasons embody

---

[1] Joseph Raz, *Value, Respect, and Attachment* (Cambridge: Cambridge University Press, 2001), 5.

forms of legitimate partiality, but that neither is incompatible with any reasonable understanding of the universality of ethics or value. However, there is also one important asymmetry between relationship-dependent reasons and project-dependent reasons, and I will argue that Raz's formulations are not helpful in explaining this asymmetry.

As I have said, to value one's relationship to another person non-instrumentally just is, in part, to be disposed to treat that person's needs, interests, and desires as providing one with reasons for action, reasons that one would not have had in the absence of the relationship. If I attach non-instrumental value to my relationship with you, then I will be disposed to see your needs and interests as providing me, in contexts of certain kinds, with reasons of a sort that I would not otherwise have had, and with which the interests of other people do not provide me. This means that I will see myself both as having reason to do things on your behalf that I have no comparable reason to do for others, and as having reason to give your interests priority over theirs in at least some cases of conflict.

To be sure, these reasons will normally be seen as defeasible or over-ridable. But if I have no tendency at all to see any of your needs and interests as providing me with reasons for action of this kind, then it ceases to make sense to say that I value my relationship with you. This is a conceptual truth, in the sense that it is part of our best understanding of what it means to value one's relationship with another person. If I tell you that I care deeply about our relationship, but I never treat your needs and interests as any more capable than anyone else's of impinging on my practical deliberations, then my claim to care is bound to ring false or hollow. If I value a relationship in which I am a participant, then that relationship must have the capacity to affect the way I choose to live. To value one's relationships is to treat them as reason-giving.

In other writings I have elaborated on this argument and qualified it in various respects, and I do not want to repeat here what I have said else-where.[2] But there is one point that I do want to emphasize. If one values one's relationship to another person non-instrumentally, then one will recognize distinctive reasons for attending to the interests of that person. But it does not follow that one must regard the person as more valuable

---

[2] See my 'Relationships and Responsibilities', *Philosophy and Public Affairs* 26 (1997), 189–209, and 'Conceptions of Cosmopolitanism', *Utilitas* 11 (1999), 255–76. Both of these essays are reprinted in my *Boundaries and Allegiances* (Oxford: Oxford University Press, 2001), 97–110 and 111–30 respectively.

than other people. What is significant about my interpersonal relationships is not that they are unusually valuable relationships or that my intimates and associates are people of greater than normal worth or value. It is rather that, so long as I value my relationships non-instrumentally, I will see them as providing me with reasons for action of a distinctive kind. Other people's friendships, and other people's friends, may be just as valuable as mine. Not only can I recognize the value of those people and those friendships, but their value can have important effects on my reasons for action. There are many norms of conduct that govern my treatment of other human beings with whom I myself have no special relationship. Moreover, if other people have a valuable relationship, then it would be wrong of me gratuitously to seek to undermine or disrupt that relationship. Thus, it would be a mistake to suppose that, if I value my own friendships, then I cannot recognize the value of other people's friendships, or even to suppose that I cannot see their friendships as giving me reasons for action.

What follows from the connection between valuing one's relationships and the recognition of special reasons arising out of those relationships is not that, if we value our relationships, then we are committed to repudiating the equal worth of persons or to regarding our relationships as more valuable than other people's. What follows, instead, is that there is an important difference between recognizing the value of a relationship in which one is not a participant and valuing a relationship of one's own. The value of the relationships may be—and may be seen to be—the same. But they will affect one's perceived reasons for action in different ways. If I value a relationship in which I am a participant, then I will treat that relationship as presenting me with reasons that differ from the reasons generated by other relationships of the same type in which I am not a participant. And, of course, the participants in those other relationships will take a reciprocal view of my relationship and the reasons it generates. In general, then, one will see one's own relationships as giving one reasons for action of a kind that other relationships do not. That is simply what is involved in valuing a relationship of one's own.

Viewed in a certain light, this may seem surprising. It may seem that, if we acknowledge the equal value of all people, then the interests of all people should generate reasons of equal strength and content. Indeed, this line of thought has led some philosophers to question the legitimacy of any form of partiality toward one's intimates and associates. But the argument I have presented demonstrates that this way of thinking about the connections between our values and our reasons is too simple. Some of our reasons for treating people in certain ways arise in the context of personal relationships with those people; others do not. The fact that we have a relationship with someone does not affect that person's value, but it may well affect the strength and content of our reasons. To put it another way: when we value our relationship with someone, that does not make him a more valuable person, but it does affect the strength and content of the reasons with which his interests will be seen as providing us.

There may be some temptation to express this point by saying that, although the fact that we have a valued relationship with him does not increase his *impersonal* value, it does increase his *personal* value—the value that he has for us. Many philosophers, including Raz,[3] have drawn a distinction between personal and impersonal value, and I have sometimes talked in similar ways myself. In the present context, distinguishing between personal and impersonal value can be a natural enough way of trying to register the obvious facts that we care in special ways about the people with whom we have valued relationships, and that those relationships affect our practical orientation: they affect the reasons that we recognize in deliberation. However, the distinction between two putative categories of value—personal and impersonal—can be misleading if taken too seriously. For one thing, it tends to obscure the fact that it is our relationships with other people that affect our reasons. If we locate these effects within the category of 'personal value', we tend to make the reasons in question seem private or subjective when what they are is precisely interpersonal and social. We also recast as an ontological or axiological distinction what is partly an insight into the way social relations structure individual deliberation: the way in which our relationships affect our reasons.

In addition, the distinction between personal and impersonal value can be misleading if it is taken to suggest that the values that fall on the impersonal side of the divide are values that can be appreciated only from a detached, 'impersonal' standpoint, and are not values that we ourselves recognize or accept. But the fact that my friend is no more valuable than other people is something that I myself recognize; I do not merely acknowledge that this is the way things look from an impersonal standpoint. In other words, it is not as if my actual view of the matter is that my friend

---

[3] See, e.g., Raz, *Value, Respect, and Attachment*, 83–4.

really is more valuable than other people. Such a view would of course be unstable, since I can recognize that other people also have friends and that, if I regard my friend as being more valuable than other people, then they presumably regard their friends as being more valuable than other people too. On the slightly idealized assumption that everyone is the friend of someone, this would then raise the spectre of what might be called 'the Lake Wobegon problem', in honour of Garrison Keillor's fictional community in which all the children are above average. Here the problem is that all people may turn out to be worth more than other people. In fact, however, I do not regard my friend as being more valuable than other people. I believe that all people, friends and strangers alike, are of equal value. Of course, my friend matters more to me, in many very important ways, than strangers do, and I see myself as having all kinds of reasons to treat my friend differently than I treat them. That is the upshot of our friendship, however. It is not a hypothesis about my friend's relative worth.

Another distinction that is often employed in discussions of these issues is the distinction between agent-neutral and agent-relative reasons. As this distinction is usually understood, agent-neutral reasons are reasons for everyone, whereas agent-relative reasons are reasons for a particular agent only. In the present context, it might be suggested that, in addition to the agent-neutral reasons that I have for respecting the interests of all people, I have agent-relative reasons for attending to the interests of my own friends and associates. Furthermore, it might be said, in so far as we see ourselves as having reason to give the interests of our intimates and associates priority over the interests of other equally worthy people, what this shows is that we regard agent-relative reasons as capable of taking priority over agent-neutral reasons.

The distinction between agent-relative and agent-neutral reasons does not seem to me as misleading as the distinction between personal and impersonal value, but it too is liable to be misunderstood in some of the same ways. Thus, if one wishes to use this distinction, it is important to emphasize that to describe reasons as agent-relative is not to say that they are subjective or unreal or mere appearances. Nor is it to suggest that they are private or asocial in character, or that they are, in Christine Korsgaard's phrase, 'the personal property of individual agents'.[4] Agent-relative reasons

---

[4] Christine Korsgaard, 'The Reasons We Can Share: An Attack on the Distinction between Agent-Relative and Agent-Neutral Values,' *Social Philosophy and Policy* 10 (1993), 24–51, at 48. Korsgaard's essay is reprinted in her *Creating the Kingdom of Ends* (Cambridge: Cambridge University Press, 1996), 275–310.

are social in the sense that they universalize over all agents in relevantly similar positions, and can therefore be understood and respected by people other than the agent who has them. At least some of them are also social in the sense that they are generated by participation in human relationships of various kinds. Indeed, the very point I have been making concerns the way in which certain kinds of 'agent-relative' reasons for action arise in the context of human interpersonal relationships. Later I will emphasize that the reasons that arise in this way are also social in an even stronger sense: namely, that the agent to whom they are ascribed lacks the unilateral authority to disregard them. Although there need be nothing wrong with describing reasons of this kind as agent-relative, provided all of the qualifications I have mentioned are borne in mind, it is at least as important to note that they are *relationship-dependent reasons*. For the purposes of this paper, in other words, it is important to distinguish between those agent-relative reasons that an individual acquires by participating in an interpersonal relationship and those that arise in some other way.

This affects the way we describe the implications of the argument I have offered up to this point. I have argued that if we attach non-instrumental value to our interpersonal relationships, then in some contexts we will see ourselves as having reason to give the interests of our intimates and associates priority over the interests of other equally worthy people. Sometimes, in other words, we should attend to the interests of our associates, even if doing so means that the comparable interests of other equally worthy people will go unsatisfied. As I have said, this could be taken to show that valuing one's relationships commits one to the idea that agent-relative reasons sometimes take priority over agent-neutral reasons. However, it is important to note that the priority to which one is thus committed is the priority of *relationship-dependent* relative reasons over neutral reasons. It is a further question whether we have similar commitments with respect to relationship-independent relative reasons. I want now to consider one such class of reasons, which I will refer to as *project-dependent reasons*.

We may begin by considering what is involved in valuing (non-instrumentally) a project or activity in which one is engaged. I take it for granted that people value an enormously varied range of activities and pursuits. In part, of course, to value one of one's pursuits non-instrumentally is to see that pursuit as valuable or worthwhile. But it is also quite possible to regard pursuits in which one is not oneself engaged as valuable or worthwhile. Indeed, most people, at least in liberal societies, subscribe to what might be thought of as a sort of common-sense pluralism about value, according to which there are many different kinds of projects and activities that are valuable. Yet valuing a project or activity of one's own seems to involve something more. That is, it seems to involve something more than just believing that the project is one's own and that it is valuable.

One way of explaining what else is involved would be to suggest that there is a special kind of pleasure or satisfaction associated with participation in an activity or project that one values. Yet it would be wrong to suppose that the distinctiveness of valuing one's own projects can be understood in purely hedonistic terms. Deriving pleasure from one's pursuits is neither necessary nor sufficient for valuing them. One may derive pleasure from an activity without valuing it non-instrumentally, and one may value a project non-instrumentally without finding it especially pleasant. It may be suggested that, if one values an activity non-instrumentally despite not finding it pleasant, then one must at least find it a source of satisfaction in another, non-hedonistic sense. But even if this is true, it is not clear what it adds to the idea that one is engaged in an activity that one judges to be valuable or worthwhile. So this suggestion does not do much to advance our understanding of what valuing one's projects non-instrumentally amounts to.

Of course, this is not to deny that there are feelings and emotions that are normally associated with the pursuit of valued projects and goals. Even those feelings and emotions, however, cannot be adequately described in purely hedonistic terms. And valuing a project cannot be adequately understood solely by reference to those feelings and emotions. Each of these points deserves some elaboration.

As I have already said, it is a mistake to suppose that if one values one's engagement with a particular project or one's pursuit of a particular goal, then one's experience of pursuing that project or goal will be characterized by an undifferentiated sensation of pleasure or enjoyment. The psychological truth is considerably more complex. If one values a project of one's own non-instrumentally, then one will normally be subject to a wide array of emotions, not all of them pleasant, depending on the circumstances and on how the project fares. To take only some obvious examples: one may feel anxious about whether the project will be successful, frustrated or angry if it encounters obstacles, depressed at not having as much time as one would like to devote to it, ambivalent if forced to choose between it and other valued pursuits, defensive if other people do not regard the project as worthwhile, exhilarated if things go better than expected, and miserable or empty if the project fails. We could sum this up by saying that the project will assume a certain emotional importance in one's life. But this is simply a re-description, in emotional shorthand, of the more complex reality at which I have just gestured; 'importance' is not a common psychological metric to which the feelings of anxiety, depression, ambivalence, exhilaration, and emptiness can be reduced. There is no such metric, and it is only the continuing influence of hedonism and certain simple forms of subjectivism that might tempt one to suppose otherwise. The emotional importance of the projects that one values is revealed in the whole complex array of feelings to which one becomes vulnerable by virtue of one's engagement with them. To value one's projects—or, equally, one's relationships—is always to be made emotionally vulnerable. It is, in other words, to be made susceptible, depending on circumstances that are never fully under one's control, to a whole gamut of emotions from elation to despair. Everyone knows this; only the temptations of bad theory lead people occasionally to find ways of forgetting it.

Even if we accept this, however, the distinctiveness of valuing one's own projects or goals non-instrumentally is not exhausted by the emotional importance those projects and goals assume in one's life. Just as significant is the way they affect one's perceived reasons for action. If I value my projects non-instrumentally, then I will see them as providing me with reasons for action in a way that the projects of other people do not, and in a way that other activities now open to me do not. I need not suppose that my projects are more valuable or worthwhile than anyone else's projects, or than the other activities in which I might now engage. Indeed, if I am inclined to think in such terms at all, I am far likelier to suppose that there are many other people whose projects are just as valuable or more valuable than mine, and many other activities in which I might engage that are just as valuable as the ones in which I do engage. But the capacity of my projects to provide me with reasons for action is not dependent on a conviction that they are worth more than other people's projects or than other available pursuits. To value my own projects just is, among other things, to see them as providing me with reasons for action in a way that other activities and other people's projects do not. Of course, these reasons can be overridden in various circumstances by reasons of other kinds. The reasons with which my projects provide me are not absolute or incapable of being outweighed by other considerations. But if I do not see myself as having any more reason to pursue my own projects and goals than I do to engage in other comparable activities, then it no longer makes sense to say that I value those projects and goals. Indeed, it no longer makes sense to describe them as my projects and goals at all.[5]

If this is correct, then people will see the projects and goals that they value as sources of reasons for action that differ in character from, and can within limits take priority over, their reasons for engaging in other valuable activities. In particular, they will see themselves as having reasons to pursue their own projects and goals even if that means forgoing opportunities to assist other people with the pursuit of their equally valuable projects and goals. To be sure, there are in any case conceptual limits on our ability to help other people achieve their goals or succeed in their projects, since to have a project or goal is to aspire to accomplish certain things oneself.[6] If my goal is to play the piano well, nobody else can do that for me. Nevertheless, there are frequently ways in which it is possible to assist other people in the pursuit of their projects: for example, by helping to provide them with resources and opportunities that they need if they are to be successful. Furthermore, there are many contexts in which we feel moved to provide such assistance. However, in so far as we ourselves have projects and goals that we value non-instrumentally, we will also see it as appropriate, within limits, to devote energy and attention to those projects even if doing so means passing up opportunities to provide assistance to others. This does not mean, of course, that our own projects must have an individualistic or self-interested character. It goes without saying that there are all kinds of projects that themselves involve working collaboratively with and helping other people. But agents who have and value such projects will see those projects too as generating reasons for action that

---

[5] Compare Raz: 'I believe that writing poetry and teaching are both valuable activities. But as a teacher who has never taken up poetry, I have reasons for teaching that arise out of my commitment to teaching, and I do not have similar reasons for writing poetry.' As Raz goes on to observe, this 'suggests a certain complexity in the relations between value and reason' (*Engaging Reason: On the Theory of Value and Action* (Oxford: Oxford University Press, 1999), 64). Raz's own account of that complexity is often cast in highly voluntaristic language, as is suggested by his use of the term 'commitment' in the passage just quoted. In *The Morality of Freedom* (Oxford: Oxford University Press, 1986), he speaks of the choice to pursue one valuable goal rather than another as 'creating new reasons which were not there before' (p. 389). The view that the choice of goals *creates* reasons is criticized by T. M. Scanlon in his contribution to this volume.

[6] This is emphasized by Raz in his essay 'Duties of Well-Being', which is included in his *Ethics in the Public Domain* (Oxford: Oxford University Press, 1994), 3–28.

take priority over other worthy pursuits. If my project is to help establish
and maintain a homeless shelter in my community, then I will see myself
as having reason to pursue that project even if doing so means forgoing
opportunities to help other people with their equally valuable projects.

It may seem that there is at least one exception to this rule. If my
project is simply the second-order project of providing assistance to those
people whose first-order projects are of the greatest value, then, it may be
argued, it cannot be true that I will see myself as having reason to pursue
my project, even if that means forgoing opportunities to assist other people
with the pursuit of their equally valuable projects. For, by hypothesis, if I
am indeed pursuing my project, then I will also be assisting the people
whose projects are of the greatest value. Thus, my particular project is
logically incapable of providing me with reasons that take priority over the
reasons generated by other people's equally valuable projects. In fact, however, the second-order project just described makes no sense. At the risk of
belabouring the obvious: even if, *per impossibile*, some person had complete
information about the projects of every single human being on the face of
the planet, there is no remotely credible way of ranking the value of
different projects that would enable that person to identify some particular
project or projects, out of all the billions being pursued at any time, as the
most valuable. The most that such a person could say, and the most that
any of us can in fact say, is that there are many valuable projects, of many
different kinds, being pursued by many different people.[7] I might, perhaps,
have the second-order project of helping some of these people with some
of their projects. If that really is my project, however, then two things will
be true. The first is that the project's capacity to provide me with what I

---

[7] This is in keeping with what I referred to above as 'common-sense pluralism about
value'. I take it as evident, though I will make no attempt to argue the point here, that no
attempt to reduce all of our diverse values to a single master value can succeed; all forms of
value monism are false. However, pluralism about the good admits of different philosophical
interpretations, among which I shall make no attempt to adjudicate. To support the claims
that I make in the text, it is not necessary to go beyond the common-sense pluralism upon
which I rely. Two important but very different contemporary philosophical accounts are
those of Joseph Raz, in *The Morality of Freedom*, esp. chs. 13 and 14, and John Rawls, *A Theory of
Justice* (Cambridge, Mass.: Harvard University Press, 1971), esp. chs. 7 and 9. See also Rawls,
'Social Unity and Primary Goods', in Amartya Sen and Bernard Williams (eds.), *Utilitarianism
and Beyond* (Cambridge: Cambridge University Press, 1982), 159–85. I have discussed Rawls's
pluralism about the good in 'Rawls and Utilitarianism', in Samuel Freeman (ed.), *The Cambridge
Companion to Rawls* (Cambridge: Cambridge University Press, 2003), 426–59; reprinted (with slight
revisions) in *Boundaries and Allegiances*, 149–72.

take to be reasons will in part derive not from the worthiness of the other people's pursuits, but from the fact that helping them is *my project*. The second is that I will indeed see myself as having reasons to pursue my project, even if that means forgoing opportunities to assist other people with their equally worthy projects.

Clearly, there is a strong parallel between the argument for *project-dependent reasons* that I have just been giving and the argument given earlier for *relationship-dependent reasons*. If one values one's relationship with another person non-instrumentally, then one will see oneself as having reason to devote special attention to that person's needs and interests. Similarly, if one values a personal project non-instrumentally, then one will see oneself as having reason to devote special attention to the flourishing of that project.[8] To value one's relationships to other people is to treat those relationships as reason-giving; so too, to value one's projects and goals is to treat them as reason-giving. The relationships and projects that we value are among the most important sources of our reasons for action.

As Raz has noted,[9] another important parallel between project-dependent reasons and relationship-dependent reasons is that both of them have significant anti-maximizing and anti-consequentialist implications. In so far as we have relationship-dependent reasons to give the interests of our intimates and associates priority over the interests of other equally worthy people, we have reasons not to maximize net aggregate value. And in so far as we have project-dependent reasons to give the pursuit of our own aims and ambitions priority over assisting other people with their equally valuable projects, we again have reasons not to maximize aggregate value. Moreover, both relationship-dependent and project-dependent reasons also have anti-maximizing implications of a deeper and less formal kind. Both flow from independent sources of reasons that have nothing to do with the maximization of aggregate value. Our projects and our human relationships are what give our lives much of their shape. They are among the most basic and enduring sources of reasons for action that we have, and among the most important factors influencing our thinking about how to

---

[8] It is worth emphasizing that the precise character of the reasons that a valued project or relationship is seen as providing will appropriately vary depending on the context and also on the nature of the particular project or relationship in question. The generic characterizations of such reasons that I rely on in the text are meant to allow for this sort of diversity and should not be taken to exclude it.

[9] Raz, *Value, Respect, and Attachment*, 4–8.

live. No account of the norms governing human conduct can be credible unless it gives a credible account of the role played by the reasons they generate. At the level of normative guidance, the role of those reasons is not merely to establish certain formal limits on the maximization of aggregate value. They are independent normative factors with at least as fundamental a role to play as the idea of aggregate value itself.[10]

Despite the strong parallels between relationship-dependent reasons and project-dependent reasons, there appears to be one important difference between them. We normally suppose that many of our relationship-dependent reasons are reasons on which we are morally required or obligated to act, at least in so far as they are not outweighed or otherwise defeated by competing considerations. By contrast, we do not normally think that we are obligated to act on our project-dependent reasons, but merely that we are permitted or entitled to do so, even when they are the strongest reasons we have.[11] To use Raz's terminology, relationship-dependent reasons seem to be unlike project-dependent reasons in being 'wrong-making', that is, in being reasons it is wrong to ignore. The point might also be expressed by saying that, while we have the right to pursue

[10] This seems an appropriate point at which to acknowledge the existence of two different strands in the argument I have been developing. For the most part, I have emphasized the connection between valuing a project or relationship and taking oneself to have reasons of certain kinds. But at times, and particularly in the last two paragraphs, I have asserted, not merely that people who value their projects and relationships will take themselves to have such reasons, but also that projects and relationships really do give people reasons. There is of course a gap between the first, 'phenomenological' strand of argument, and the second, 'realist' strand. I have not provided any direct defence in this paper of the realist strand, nor have I explained how exactly the realist strand is related to the phenomenological strand. These tasks must await another occasion, although I have made a start on them in 'Relationships and Responsibilities'.

[11] It is not clear how sharp this contrast is. On the one hand, as implied in the text, there seem to be some relationship-dependent reasons on which we think we are permitted but not obligated to act. On the other hand, there may be some projects that we are morally required to undertake, in which case the reasons generated by those projects may be reasons on which we are required and not merely permitted to act. Still, even relationships on which we have no obligation to embark routinely generate reasons on which we are obligated to act, once we have indeed embarked on those relationships. The same does not seem to be true of personal projects (except in cases covered by the qualification noted in the next paragraph of text). Of course, some people may wish to deny that there is any asymmetry of this kind at all. In this paper, I will assume that the asymmetry is genuine, though I will not try to defend that assumption or to characterize the asymmetry precisely, and for ease of exposition I will hereafter omit the various qualifications I have mentioned. If anyone is inclined to challenge the existence of such an asymmetry, nothing I say in this paper will count as a rebuttal.

our projects, we have special duties or obligations arising out of our relationships. In view of the parallels we have noted between relationship-dependent and project-dependent reasons, it may be wondered why there should be such a contrast. If one values one's relationship with another person non-instrumentally, then one will see oneself as having reason to give special attention to that person's needs and interests. Similarly, if one values a personal project non-instrumentally, then one will see oneself as having reason to devote special attention to that project. Why, then, should we be morally required to act on relationship-dependent reasons but merely permitted to act on project-dependent reasons?

The issue is complicated by the fact that personal projects and interpersonal relationships can be intertwined in various ways. Sometimes people's relationships lead to the development of shared projects, and sometimes their projects are constituted in part by relationships with other people. We might say that people's project-dependent reasons can overlap with their relationship-dependent reasons, either because they have relationship-dependent projects or because they have project-dependent relationships. In cases of either of these types, the reasons generated by one's projects may be impossible to distinguish from the reasons generated by one's relationships, and in such cases we may be morally required, rather than merely permitted, to act on our project-dependent reasons. Still, project-dependent reasons are separable, at least conceptually, from relationship-dependent reasons, and they do not always overlap with them in practice. Sometimes, in other words, we have purely project-dependent reasons and, when we do, it seems that we are permitted but not required to act on them. Why should this be so, given that we are required to act on our relationship-dependent reasons? It will not help to say that we are required to act on our relationship-dependent reasons because our failure to do so may have effects on other people, for the same is true of purely project-dependent reasons. Even the failure to cultivate one's own garden may deprive others of a source of pleasure, instruction, or inspiration. Yet we do not normally suppose that we are morally obligated to act on our purely project-dependent reasons.

The puzzle is only deepened when we observe that, at the level of phenomenology, there need be no introspectible difference in the way the two sorts of reasons present themselves to the agent. In other words, there need be no difference between the quality of people's experience when they see reasons to pursue their projects and the quality of their experience when they see reasons to attend to the interests of their intimates and associates. To be sure, if one values one's relationships non-instrumentally, then one's reasons for attending to the interests of one's intimates will present themselves, in some circumstances at least, as reasons that must take priority over considerations of other kinds. However, it is also true that if one values one's personal projects non-instrumentally, then one's reasons for attending to those projects may, in some circumstances at least, present themselves as reasons that must take priority over other considerations. In both sorts of cases, the reasons may present themselves as decisive reasons for acting in one way rather than another, and there need be no experiential difference between seeing a reason of one type as decisive and seeing a reason of the other type as decisive. This makes the asymmetry between relationship-dependent reasons and project-dependent reasons seem even more puzzling. Why, to frame the question using a mixture of Raz's terminology and my own, are decisive relationship-dependent reasons normally thought of as wrong-making while decisive project-dependent reasons are not?

In *Value, Respect, and Attachment*, Raz proposes an explanation of why some conclusive or decisive reasons are wrong-making while others are not. His proposal rests on a distinction between *respecting* a value and *engaging with* it. He summarizes his proposal as follows:

We must respect what is valuable and it is wrong not to do so. We have reason to engage with what is valuable, and it is intelligible that we should do so. Sometimes it is foolish, rash, weak, defective in some other specific way, or even irrational to fail to engage with what is of greater value than available alternatives, or to engage with what is of lesser value. But it is not, generally speaking, wrong to do so.[12]

Raz's idea is that there are many different values, and that although nobody can 'engage with' everything that is valuable, 'there is a universal reason for everyone to respect'[13] whatever is of value. Reasons of respect

---

[12] Raz, *Value, Respect, and Attachment*, 6. Raz is not entirely clear about whether he is understanding 'wrong' as a moral notion here, and in other writings he has frequently expressed scepticism about the distinctiveness of morality as a form of normative assessment. However, if he is not understanding 'wrong' as a distinctively moral notion, but instead as a more general term of normative appraisal, then it is unclear why he thinks it inappropriate to apply the term to acts that are foolish, rash, weak, defective, and irrational, and which the agent has conclusive reasons not to perform. In my discussion, I do treat 'wrong' and 'wrong-making' as moral notions.

[13] Ibid. 164.

are reasons not to destroy, and perhaps even to preserve, valuable things. They are also, Raz says, reasons to think about such things 'in ways consistent with their value'.[14] Reasons of respect are categorical 'in the sense that their weight or stringency does not depend on our goals, tastes, and desires', but their stringency and importance varies, and they can be defeated by reasons of other kinds.[15] Still, 'in being categorical reasons of respect are also reasons the flouting of which, when they predominate (that is when they defeat other reasons), is wrong'.[16] Reasons for engaging with values are different. Although we are fulfilled and our lives are rewarding only if we engage with some values or other, the weight and stringency of our reasons for engaging with any particular value must appropriately depend on our goals and tastes. Thus reasons for engaging with values are non-categorical. Accordingly, even when such reasons are conclusive, acting against them is not wrong.

In view of these contrasts, Raz concludes that 'while in one way ultimately our lives are about engaging with value, the rest being mere preliminaries, in another way the reasons for respect are more basic'.[17] He also says that '[t]he doctrine of respect, with the difference it assumes between respecting what is valuable and engaging with it, is meant to explain the limits of partiality, that is, that partiality [e.g. toward one's family, friends, and projects] is permissible so long as it does not conflict with respect for what is valuable, respect being...within the domain of reasons whose violation is wrong. The discussion of respect explains the contours and limits of partiality in one's own cause.'[18]

In short, the core of Raz's proposal is as follows. Reasons for respecting values are categorical, whereas reasons for engaging with values are not. Acting against conclusive categorical reasons is wrong, whereas acting against conclusive non-categorical reasons is not. Accordingly, acting against conclusive reasons of respect is wrong, whereas acting against conclusive reasons for engagement is not.

Although the distinction between respecting a value and engaging with it is of undoubted interest and significance, Raz's proposal does not help to answer the question of why relationship-dependent reasons are wrong-making whereas project-dependent reasons are not. Indeed, on the face of it, his proposal is difficult to reconcile with the existence of such an

---

[14] Ibid. 161.   [15] Ibid. 168.   [16] Ibid.
[17] Ibid. 164.   [18] Ibid. 8.

asymmetry. The basic difficulty is that, in Raz's terms, both project-dependent and relationship-dependent reasons derive from our engagement with particular values. Both represent forms of partiality. Thus, on the face of it, neither would appear to qualify as wrong-making by his lights.

Let us examine this difficulty in somewhat greater detail. We may note, to begin with, that there is a tension between Raz's suggestion that respect defines the limits of permissible partiality and his claim that reasons of respect can be defeated by reasons of other kinds. As I said, Raz holds that the categorical status of reasons of respect does not mean that they are always weightier or more stringent than other reasons. This seems to imply that, although reasons of respect sometimes defeat reasons for engagement, at other times the reverse may be true. If that is correct, however, then it is unclear how reasons of respect define the limits of permissible partiality, in any sense in which it is not equally true that legitimate partiality defines the limits of respect.

As we have seen, Raz's argument to the contrary depends on the idea that reasons of respect lie 'within the domain of reasons whose violation is wrong'. That is what gives respect the capacity to limit permissible partiality, for partiality is said to involve responsiveness to reasons that are not similarly wrong-making. There are at least two difficulties with this suggestion, however. The first is the one just noted: namely, that the suggestion is difficult to square with the idea that reasons of respect can sometimes be defeated by reasons for engagement. The second difficulty, which is closely related, is that one of the canonical forms of legitimate partiality involves responsiveness to relationship-dependent reasons, and these reasons too can be wrong-making. Raz himself implicitly acknowledges this. He says that the duty of respect 'is less extensive than the duties of a friend, a lover, a parent, or an employer. They all value, or ought to value, the person they are so related to. The bulk of humanity need only respect him or her.'[19] This implies (a) that we have duties arising out of our partial engagements with particular people, (b) that these duties are not duties of respect, and, presumably, (c) that violation of these duties can be wrong. If this is correct, then the mere fact that duties of respect 'lie within the domain of reasons whose violation is wrong' does not by itself show that respect defines the limits of partiality, for we have duties arising out of our partial engagements which also lie within that domain. More importantly,

---

[19] Raz, *Value, Respect, and Attachment*, 170.

for our purposes, the distinction between respect and engagement does not suffice to distinguish wrong-making reasons from others. Relationship-dependent reasons are reasons generated by our particular engagements, and yet they too can be wrong-making. Raz's proposal neglects the asymmetry, within the realm of our engagements, between project-dependent and relationship-dependent reasons.

The same point can be brought out in another way. In speaking of 'reasons for engaging' with particular values, it is important to distinguish between the reasons we have for initially engaging with one value rather than another, and the reasons that arise out of those engagements on which we have already embarked.[20] If one focuses solely on the former, then it may indeed seem that partiality and engagement always involve responsiveness to non-wrong-making reasons. But if one attends to the latter, the inadequacy of this position becomes clear. There is nothing wrong with deciding not to have children—the reasons for having children are not 'within the domain of reasons whose violation is wrong'—but once one has children, one has special responsibilities toward them. In other words, one has relationship-dependent reasons for attending in certain ways to their interests, and the neglect of these reasons is, other things equal, wrong. Yet these reasons arise out of particular engagements, and they represent a form of partiality if anything does.

There is a passage in which Raz attempts, in effect, to turn this argument on its head. The fact that special responsibilities arise out of optional engagements, he suggests, shows that they themselves are to some degree optional. He puts the point as follows: 'Most forms of legitimate partiality are more or less optional. We may be required to favour our children or friends, but it is up to us whether to have children or friends. We may have to be partial to our country, or city, but we may emigrate to another country, or choose where to live, and so on. Even more clearly, we may choose whether to devote much time and resources to music or to golf, etc.'[21] The fact that this argument is said to apply only to 'most' forms of partiality is of course crucial to its plausibility; it may be up to us whether

[20] This is a distinction whose importance Raz has often emphasized in other writings. In *The Morality of Freedom*, e.g., he writes: 'In embracing goals and commitments, in coming to care about one thing or another, one...generates, through one's developing commitments and pursuits, reasons which transcend the reasons one had for undertaking one's commitments and pursuits' (p. 387). See also *Engaging Reason*, 64.

[21] Raz, *Value, Respect, and Attachment*, 4.

to have children or friends, but it is not up to us whether to have parents or siblings. Even when its scope is understood to be restricted, however, the argument seems misleading, for it can easily be taken to suggest that, in virtue of their 'optional' character, our special responsibilities to family and friends are less than full-fledged requirements. That is clearly not true. It is up to us whether to make promises, but we are required to keep the promises that we make; our reasons to keep our promises are 'wrong-making' reasons. Similarly, it is up to us whether to have children or friends, but, once we have them, we have responsibilities to attend to their interests. The reasons arising out of close personal relationships are wrong-making reasons. In this respect, there is a fundamental difference between such reasons and the project-dependent reasons we may have to devote resources to music or golf. Those project-dependent reasons differ from relationship-dependent reasons not in being 'even more clearly' optional in character, but in being reasons we can neglect without doing anything wrong.[22]

It might be suggested that the distinction between respect and engagement can be interpreted in such a way as to accommodate the wrong-making character of relationship-dependent reasons. Recall that reasons of respect, as Raz understands them, are reasons not to destroy, and perhaps even to preserve, valuable things. It might be argued that, once one has developed a valuable interpersonal relationship, one's neglect of the relationship-dependent reasons to which it gives rise may tend to undermine or even destroy the relationship. Thus, despite their source in an optional engagement, those relationship-dependent reasons actually count as reasons of respect. I need not engage in a friendship with Frank, but once I do, my failure to act on the reasons to which it gives rise would

---

[22] In *The Morality of Freedom*, Raz himself draws an analogy between the way in which making a promise generates a new duty and the way in which engaging with particular 'relationships and projects' changes 'one's normative situation'(p. 387). The point I have been emphasizing, however, is that participation in a personal relationship produces a different sort of change in one's 'normative situation' than does engagement with a personal project. In an earlier paper, Raz had argued that, because promises create 'special relationships between people', the analysis of promises 'can serve as the model for the analysis of all kinds of obligations, for all depend for their validity on the value of special bonds and many of them are, like promises, constituent elements of special human relations (husband–wife, parent–child, leader–led, etc.)' ('Promises and Obligations', in P. M. S. Hacker and Joseph Raz (eds.), *Law, Morality, and Society: Essays in Honour of H. L. A. Hart* (Oxford: Oxford University Press, 1977), 210–28, at 228). If one takes this view, however, then one cannot also maintain that respect, rather than engagement, is the source of all wrong-making reasons.

constitute a failure to respect the value of the friendship. Those reasons, like other reasons of respect, are categorical—even though the reasons for engaging in the friendship in the first place were not—and so neglecting them would be wrong. More generally, once one has engaged with a particular value, one may have to do more, in order to preserve or to avoid destroying that value, than do people who have not engaged with the value at all. In other words, respect and engagement are not mutually exclusive categories; the effect of engaging with a particular value is to raise the standard that one's conduct must meet if it is to count as respecting that value. If this is correct, then relationship-dependent reasons *are* reasons of respect, and so their wrong-making character can be reconciled with the idea that 'wrong-makingness' derives from the categorical status of reasons of respect.

One peripheral difficulty with this proposal is that it is often wrong to neglect one's special responsibilities even when doing so will *not* destroy the relationship giving rise to those responsibilities. But the more fundamental difficulty is that the proposal still provides no basis for distinguishing between relationship-dependent reasons and project-dependent reasons. It implies that relationship-dependent reasons are wrong-making reasons of respect only if it also implies the same thing about project-dependent reasons. After all, once I have engaged in a project, my neglect of the project-dependent reasons to which it gives rise may tend to undermine or destroy the project, just as my neglect of my relationship-dependent reasons may tend to undermine or destroy my relationships. Yet project-dependent reasons, in so far as they are independent of relationship-dependent reasons, are not, in general, wrong-making. Thus, even as we have reinterpreted it, the distinction between respect and engagement cannot account for the asymmetry between project-dependent and relationship-dependent reasons.[23]

An alternative proposal might be that the correct explanation of the asymmetry lies not in Raz's distinction between respect and engagement,

---

[23] As I observed in n. 11 above, it would of course be possible to deny that there really is such an asymmetry. One might argue either that it is wrong to neglect project-dependent reasons or that it is not wrong to neglect relationship-dependent reasons. I doubt whether Raz himself would want to defend either of these positions. His emphasis on the optional character of legitimate partiality counts against attributing the first position to him, and his reference to the special duties of 'a friend, a lover, a parent, or an employer' counts against attributing the second position to him.

but rather in the distinction between categorical and non-categorical reasons itself. As we have seen, a person's reasons are categorical, in Raz's sense, if their weight or stringency does not depend on the person's goals, tastes, and desires. Otherwise, the reasons are non-categorical. The lesson to be drawn from our discussion to this point, it may be said, is that it is a mistake to associate the distinction between respect and engagement with the distinction between categorical and non-categorical reasons, for some reasons deriving from personal engagements can also be categorical. In recognizing this, however, we should not lose sight of the fact that it is always the status of a reason as categorical that explains why it is wrong-making. Thus, Raz is correct to insist that reasons of respect are wrong-making because they are categorical. And in so far as relation-ship-dependent reasons are also wrong-making, that is because they too are categorical. By contrast, the reason why project-dependent reasons are not wrong-making is that they are not categorical; their weight or stringency depends on the tastes and desires of the person whose reasons they are. This difference, it may be said, suffices to explain the asymmetry between project-dependent and relationship-dependent reasons.

The difficulty with this proposal is not that it is wrong, but that it is incomplete, for it does not explain why exactly relationship-dependent reasons are categorical whereas project-dependent reasons are not; nor does it explain why decisive categorical reasons are wrong-making while decisive non-categorical reasons are not. In effect, then, it offers a re-description rather than an explanation of the asymmetry. Having said that, however, I should also add that re-descriptions can often be illuminating, and that re-describing a problem is often the first step toward solving it. In that spirit, I want to conclude the paper by offering what amounts to yet another description of the asymmetry between relationship-dependent and project-dependent reasons—a description that is not inconsistent with the one just proposed, and which seems to me to point us in the right direction.

When my participation in an interpersonal relationship gives me reasons to act on behalf of the person or persons with whom I have the relationship, there is a sense in which those relationship-dependent reasons are not mine alone. Of course, they are still reasons for me alone to act, and in that sense they are agent-relative. But the very fact that I have those reasons is itself a reason for the other parties to the relationship to form normative expectations of certain kinds about my conduct. In other words, they may reasonably regard themselves as entitled to rely on me to act in certain ways on their behalf. And if I fail to do so, they may reasonably hold me to account, by treating me as an appropriate object of reactive attitudes like resentment.[24] In effect, then, my reasons are also their reasons, in two related senses. First, the very fact that I have relationship-dependent reasons to act on their behalf is itself a reason for them to form normative expectations of me. Second, the fact that they may hold me to account for breaches of those expectations means that I do not have the authority unilaterally to disregard the reasons in question. In these respects, my relationship-dependent reasons are shared with them. By contrast, my purely project-dependent reasons are not in the same respects shared with others, even when there are others who stand to benefit from my pursuit of my projects. I may have decisive reasons to finish my novel, but—to be intolerably pedantic—that fact could not possibly give *the novel* reasons to form expectations of me or to hold me accountable for breaches of expectations. Nor, in the absence of any contractual or other relevant relationships, does it license the formation of normative expectations by the bookstore operators who might profit from selling the novel, or by the audience that might gain pleasure and insight from reading it, or by the scriptwriters who might benefit from adapting it for the movies.[25]

---

[24] The idea of holding agents to a set of normative expectations is central to the account of responsibility developed by R. Jay Wallace in *Responsibility and the Moral Sentiments* (Cambridge, Mass.: Harvard University Press, 1996). Here I focus on the expectations that may be generated by participation in a particular interpersonal relationship.

[25] Christine Korsgaard argues that 'all neutral reasons for action arise from ... the category of personal relationships' ('The Reasons We Can Share', 49), and that 'the only reasons that are possible are the reasons we can share' (ibid. 51). Although there may be a way of understanding the second claim that makes it true, it is not the case that all reasons are shared reasons in the specific respects that I have identified. As I have argued, for example, project-dependent reasons are not shared in those ways. I should also note in passing that there is a difficulty in interpreting Korsgaard's first claim—the claim that all neutral reasons arise from personal relationships. Korsgaard is especially concerned to demonstrate that this is true of deontological constraints. But which personal relationships are the ones that give rise to such constraints? Sometimes the idea seems to be that deontological constraints arise from our shared membership in the human community, and that the claims to which they give rise are 'claims springing from an acknowledgment of our common humanity' (ibid. 32). On this view, membership in the human community is one important type—in some ways the most important type—of personal relationship, and it is this relationship that gives rise to deontological constraints. In effect, then, deontological reasons are seen as relationship-dependent reasons of a certain kind. At other times, Korsgaard appears to endorse a view defended by Thomas Nagel, who suggests that a deontological constraint '"operates through the relation" between agent and victim'

The fact that relationship-dependent reasons are shared, whereas purely project-dependent reasons are not, may provide some support for the suggestion that the former are categorical whereas the latter are not. In so far as our relationship-dependent reasons are shared with others, they do not simply disappear once they cease to conform to our goals, tastes, and preferences. Still, as I have said, the appeal to shared reasons does not really explain the asymmetry between project-dependent and relationship-dependent reasons; it merely re-describes it. It does not explain the asymmetry because it does not answer the question of *why* relationship-dependent reasons, but not project-dependent reasons, are shared—why the people with whom I have interpersonal relationships may legitimately hold me accountable when I neglect my relationship-dependent reasons to act on their behalf. The natural answer is that they may hold me accountable because, in neglecting those relationship-dependent reasons, I have done something wrong. But the wrongness of neglecting relationship-dependent reasons is the very thing we are trying to explain. Thus, the appeal to shared reasons does not, by itself, explain the asymmetry, for it simply presupposes, rather than explains, the wrong-making character of relationship-dependent reasons.[26]

(ibid. 48). Korsgaard expresses the point by saying that 'the relationship of agents and victims, like that of love or friendship, is a *personal* relationship' (ibid.). In this spirit, she cites with approval the idea that shooting at someone 'establishes' (Ibid. 48 n.) a relationship with that person. Nagel, similarly, says that the source of deontological constraints lies in the fact that 'to treat someone else horribly puts you in a special relation to him' (Thomas Nagel, 'War and Massacre', as reprinted in S. Scheffler (ed.), *Consequentialism and its Critics* (Oxford: Oxford University Press, 1988), 51–73, at 66). And Korsgaard suggests that deontological reasons are '*created* in personal interaction' ('The Reasons We Can Share', 48). But these formulations elide the difference between valuable, ongoing interpersonal relationships of the sort that give rise to relationship-dependent reasons and discrete interactions consisting in instances of mistreatment. Only a pun on the word 'relationship' makes it possible to suppose that grounding deontological constraints in discrete interactions between agents and victims is equivalent to grounding them in the relationship of common humanity. Note, moreover, that, if we take seriously the idea that mistreating a person 'establishes' the kind of relationship on which deontological reasons supervene, this implies that no such relationship exists at all between the agent who respects a deontological constraint and the person who would otherwise have been his victim. In the absence of mistreatment, there is no victim and hence no 'relationship' between agent and victim. So it is unclear how the deontological reason the agent respects could have its source in such a relationship. In any case, the idea that the reason has its source in such a relationship is not the same as the idea that it arises from the relationship of common humanity. (Niko Kolodny has made a similar observation in his as yet unpublished work on relationships as the sources of reasons.)

[26] This is a point that Niko Kolodny has emphasized in discussion and in the unpublished work referred to in the previous footnote.

Nevertheless, I think that the appeal provides an illuminating re-description of the asymmetry. It is an illuminating re-description because it directs our attention toward the structures of interlocking reasons that are generated by valued human relationships. In so doing, it suggests that, in order to explain the asymmetry between project-dependent and relationship-dependent reasons, we will need to look behind the deontic categories of requirement and permissibility, and to investigate the differing roles that reasons and values of the two types play in human social life. It may seem at first that this is the wrong lesson to draw from the re-description I have given. The correct lesson, it may seem, is that whereas relationship-dependent reasons play an important role in human social life, purely project-dependent reasons have no social dimension at all. Yet, as we have already seen, one's decision whether or not to act on one's purely project-dependent reasons can certainly have effects on other people, so it is misleading to characterize such reasons as having no social dimension at all. Furthermore, this characterization overlooks one of the central themes of Joseph Raz's work, which is that valuable projects and activities, no less than valuable relationships, depend on social practices and forms. It is Raz who has urged us to remember 'not merely that companionship and friendship are among the most important goods one can realise in one's life, but that all the others, careers, leisure activities, cultural interests, and the rest, are the products of people interacting with each other, against the background of existing social practices, ever in a state of flux'.[27] If we take this lesson to heart, then, as I have said, what the re-description I have given suggests is not that relationship-dependent reasons have a social dimension while project-dependent reasons do not, but rather that reasons and values of the two types play very different roles within human social life. This seems to me a promising suggestion about where to look for an explanation of the asymmetry between relationship-dependent and project-dependent reasons, and perhaps it is also a suggestion with which Joseph Raz himself could agree.[28]

[27] Raz, *Ethics in the Public Domain*, 10.

[28] I am grateful to Jay Wallace and Niko Kolodny for helpful comments on an earlier draft of this paper.

12

Egalitarianism, Choice-Sensitivity, and Accommodation

Seana Valentine Shiffrin

Introduction

Many contemporary liberal egalitarians construe egalitarianism to require resource distributions that are designed to be insensitive to features of people that are due to luck but sensitive to their choices.[1] While many disagree about how to interpret this aim, there is a surprising degree of consensus among egalitarians and many non-egalitarians that a fair distributive scheme would require individuals to internalize the costs of their voluntary choices. Many egalitarians not only contend that egalitarianism is fully compatible with respect for freedom and autonomy, but further regard the concern to ensure conditions of equal freedom as an important motivation behind egalitarianism and its emphasis on choice-sensitivity.

---

[1] See, e.g., Richard Arneson, 'Equality and Equality of Opportunity for Welfare', *Philosophical Studies* 56 (1989), 77–93; G. A. Cohen, 'On the Currency of Egalitarian Justice', *Ethics* 99 (1989), 906–44; Ronald Dworkin, 'Equality of Resources', *Philosophy and Public Affairs* 10 (1981), 283–345; *idem*, *Sovereign Virtue* (Cambridge, Mass.: Harvard University Press, 2000), 287 and *passim*; William Kymlicka, *Contemporary Political Philosophy: An Introduction* (Oxford: Oxford University Press, 2001); Eric Rakowski, *Equal Justice*, (Oxford: Oxford University Press, 1991), 1–2 and *passim*.

In this essay, I want to raise a problem for this construal of egalitarianism. The problem emerges from thinking about some actual legal and social practices of protecting freedom through accommodation, practices that most liberal egalitarians support. Many important forms of accommodation seem difficult to reconcile with this understanding of egalitarianism.

The difficulty I identify for this interpretation of egalitarianism arises from one of its less scrutinized features: its stress on choice-sensitivity.[2] While there has been vigorous discussion of whether luck-insensitivity is compatible with freedom, I will bypass that controversy. I will assume that resource distributions that enforce luck-insensitivity do not (unjustifiably) interfere with individuals' legitimate sphere of freedom. Instead, I will question whether choice-sensitivity, if it is understood as strict cost-internalization, is an attractive ideal. I will argue that strict cost-internalization is less supportive of freedom than less thoroughgoing alternatives, and that this is a reason to reconsider strict cost-internalization as an ideal.[3]

Although my focal point is the underlying structure of egalitarian theory, the paper's scope encompasses a wider terrain. Many non-egalitarian political and legal theories stress the importance of holding individuals responsible for their choices. The difficulties I identify for strict choice-sensitivity directly pertain to how such theories should interpret the value of individual responsibility. Further, in developing this criticism of strict choice-sensitivity, I aim to articulate a distinctive defence for some of these contemporary practices of accommodation. This defence also provides a critical perspective on some contemporary American methods of structuring accommodation, specifically the approaches taken by Title VII and the Family and Medical Leave Act.

---

[2] A new critical literature on choice-sensitivity is emerging. See e.g., Elizabeth Anderson, 'What is the Point of Equality?', *Ethics* 109 (1999), 287–337; Jules Coleman, and Arthur Ripstein, 'Mischief and Misfortune', *McGill Law Journal* 41 (1995), 91–130; Timothy Hinton, 'Must Egalitarians Choose between Fairness and Respect?', *Philosophy and Public Affairs* 30 (2001), 72–87; Samuel Scheffler, 'What is Egalitarianism?', *Philosophy and Public Affairs* 31 (2003), 5–39. Some of the arguments and examples of this paper are introduced in a truncated form and in a different argumentative context in my 'Paternalism, Unconscionability Doctrine, and Accommodation', *Philosophy and Public Affairs* 29 (2000), 205–50.

[3] My approach here is strongly influenced by what I take to be among the implications of Joseph Raz's *The Morality of Freedom* (Oxford: Oxford University Press, 1986): namely, that liberal theorists should investigate how liberal social institutions may be arranged to facilitate and promote individual autonomy.

The Formula

Before introducing the problem for strict choice-sensitivity, I should say more about the egalitarian *formula* and its motivations. By 'the formula', I mean the claim that egalitarianism requires resources to be distributed according to luck-insensitive, but choice-sensitive criteria. A just system would aim to ensure that the distribution of resources, as carried out and mediated by social institutions, was not propelled by factors due to luck, because luck is morally arbitrary and ought not to influence one's prospects. We together should bear the costs of each other's involuntary misfortunes. It is unfair for distributions to be guided by morally arbitrary factors and for some individuals to benefit, and others to suffer, disproportionately because of them. However, on this view, the choices individuals make within the context of such a luck-insensitive distributive scheme are not morally arbitrary. It is perfectly reasonable for individuals to bear the costs of their choices within this fair context. It would be unfair to expect others to do so for them.

As I mentioned earlier, there is some consensus about the general formula and its motivations. Unsurprisingly, there is also active disagreement about its interpretation. Egalitarians differ about whether equality demands merely that social distributions be insensitive to the influence of factors attributable to natural misfortune, such as congenital disabilities, or whether, further, unlucky individuals should be compensated for the negative, intrinsic consequences associated with such conditions.[4] Further disagreement arises about what features properly fall under the luck-insensitive umbrella, and what features should be attributed to choice. This disagreement is reflected in the disputes over the proper metric of equality: that is, whether equality of welfare, resources, primary goods, access to advantage, capabilities, or something else captures the aim of nullifying the influence of morally arbitrary factors.

---

[4] For various approaches, see John Rawls, *A Theory of Justice*, (Cambridge, Mass.: Harvard University Press, 1971), §17; Jonathan Wolff, 'Fairness, Respect, and the Egalitarian Ethos', *Philosophy and Public Affairs* 27 (1998), 97–122; Anderson, 'What is the Point of Equality?'; Cohen, 'On the Currency'; Dworkin, *Sovereign Virtue*, 73–83. In 'Wrongful Life, Parental Responsibility, and the Significance of Harm', *Legal Theory* 5 (1999), 117–48, I argue that it may be appropriate to assign liability to parents for the disabilities their children suffer, if children bring a cause of action. These arguments are made in a non-ideal context in which there is insufficient provision of state medical care. I believe, though, that justice requires adequate provision of medical care for the disabled, and this might obviate, partly or entirely, the need for finding private agents liable.

Even in beginning to describe the fault lines, it is apparent how rough and loaded the luck-insensitive/choice-sensitive terminology is. What seems germane is that resource outlays should not be influenced by morally arbitrary factors. But what is morally arbitrary, on some views, may encompass more than what results from luck, strictly construed. Many egalitarians believe that, in whole or in part, one's natural and social talents are morally arbitrary with respect to one's needs or claims on social resources, but yet are not a matter of luck. Reasonable views about personal identity, character, and the conditions necessary to develop one's talents may render it implausible to regard one's talents or other personal features, like sex, gender, race, or ethnicity, as attributable to *luck*, even if they should not affect one's claims over the products of social co-operation. It is also unnecessary that what registers as morally arbitrary, necessarily, be due to factors beyond one's influence. Many believe that even were sexual orientation controllable, one's orientation should be regarded as morally arbitrary with respect to how social resources such as medical care, employment under fair terms, or housing, are distributed. None the less, despite 'luck''s limitations, given its brevity, I will use the term to abbreviate the real underlying notion of insensitivity to a possibly wider range of morally arbitrary factors.

Notwithstanding these disagreements, there is a powerful sense that so long as morally arbitrary factors (however understood) do not influence the social distribution, justice requires that individuals bear the costs of their own chosen endeavours. It is this idea that I want to challenge. I believe there is a problem associated with strict choice-sensitivity, at least if that notion is taken in natural ways, a problem that is largely independent of these disputes about the proper interpretation of the formula.[5]

I will advance a modest conclusion. I will not argue for the general rejection of choice-sensitivity. To be sure, the ideal of choice-sensitivity exerts a strong appeal. But, there are intuitions that pull against its universal application, and important values underlie this resistance.

The criticisms I will advance lend support to three different, alternate conclusions: (1) that the choice-sensitivity some egalitarians celebrate

---

[5] The view I develop might be taken as an argument for, or elaboration of, the view that egalitarianism involves the provision of equal opportunity for meaningful freedom. I do not, however, defend the claim that this is the only component of the metric of equality. Further, to the extent that my argument can be reasonably construed this way, it none the less cannot be comfortably or helpfully construed as an interpretation of the luck-insensitive/choice-sensitive formula, however broadly it is understood.

should be understood as involving something other than strict cost-internalization; or (2) that egalitarianism is not, in fact, compatible with the achievement and maintenance of the social conditions of full, meaningful freedom; or (3) that an egalitarianism that aims to provide fair access to the social conditions of such freedom must relax its commitment to strict choice-sensitivity: to protect and maintain a valuable sort of freedom, it must temper choice-sensitive measures of resource distribution with accommodation, that is social practices in which we absorb some of the costs of others' free, morally relevant choices.

I will argue for the third conclusion: egalitarianism is compatible with meaningful freedom, but that this compatibility depends on revising the luck-insensitive/choice-sensitive formula.[6] I hope to cast doubt upon the alternative, second conclusion of incompatibility by showing that practices of accommodation are not inconsistent with egalitarian methods or motivations. I will not try directly to refute the first possible conclusion. Rather, I hope to show that natural understandings of strict choice-sensitivity are unattractive. I suspect that the reinterpretation of choice-sensitivity that would be required to make it attractive would be so substantial and unnatural that the label 'choice-sensitivity' would be more of a theory-driven designation than an illuminating characterization or guide to practice.

I will present the problem in two mutually supporting, but independent stages. First, I will begin by offering a set of examples of legal, social, and interpersonal practices, typically supported by liberal egalitarians, in which strict choice-sensitivity does not seem attractive. These examples involve complex social phenomena that may reflect the conjunction of a number of moral aims and are susceptible to a variety of different, overlapping explanations. Still, in substantial measure, they reflect a latent resistance to

---

[6] This too might be taken in various ways. First, the argument might be taken as showing that the formula misrepresents or incompletely renders the egalitarian commitment. Second, the argument might be taken to show that the formula incompletely renders the aims of a theory of justice. It is one component, but a full theory would temper its egalitarian measures with accommodation. Or, third, the conclusion might be taken to suggest that the formula represents what justice requires, but that justice should sometimes be overridden. I reject the third understanding and mean to be arguing about what justice requires. I favour the first understanding because I believe the egalitarian commitment encompasses, at least in part, a commitment to provide equal access to the social conditions for the exercise of freedom. But no part of the argument hinges upon resolving the difference between the first and second understandings. Its resolution would depend, in part, on issues about what figures in the metric of equality.

a strict choice-sensitivity scheme. Second, I will offer a more general argument to support this resistance and to defend accommodation. At the end of the paper, I will return to the question of how to reconcile this defence of accommodation with the underlying motivations of egalitarianism.

The Problem: Stage One—Accommodation Practices

We practise a fair amount of accommodation. By 'accommodation', I mean a social practice in which agents absorb some of the costs of others' behaviour, even if this behaviour is voluntary and the cost-absorption is not necessary in order to achieve luck-insensitivity.[7] Of course, the examples I will discuss involve social practices within a contemporary context of

---

[7] This notion of accommodation is narrower than the ordinary legal notion in American law. First, it is limited to the assumption of costs connected to others' voluntary activity. Much of the accommodation required by the Americans with Disabilities Act (ADA) falls outside the scope of my discussion because it is triggered by accidental or congenital conditions and would probably be required by the luck-insensitivity component of egalitarianism. Significantly, though, the ADA's protections typically cover all disabilities, not only accidentally or involuntarily caused ones (Americans with Disabilities Act 1990, 42 U.S.C. §§12102 (2001)). Second, not all forms of legal accommodation involve burden shifting. Some familiar legal examples involve exemptions from legal requirements, exemptions that do not create significant externalities. For example, a federal law protects Native Americans' ability to engage in traditional ceremonies (42 U.S.C. §1996a (2000)). This law was passed, in part, to exempt the religious use of peyote from federal and state narcotics laws. It is unlikely that sacramental peyote use shifts burdens on to others, nor, given the fairly private nature and relatively rare pattern of consumption, that it detracts from the achievement of the (putative) social aims associated with drug control. But see *Employment Division* v. *Smith*, 494 U.S. 872, 906 (1990) (J. O'Connor, concurring) (citing state concern that isolated exceptions might impede drug control efforts). The ability to wear non-conforming attire *may* represent another form of non-burden-shifting accommodation, depending upon whether exceptions pose a threat to uniformity and whether its non-achievement would represent a cost to each of us. The right of military personnel to wear non-conforming attire for religious reasons is not constitutionally protected, but it is protected, to some degree, by statute. See *Goldman* v. *Weinberger*, 475 U.S. 503 (1986); 10 U.S.C. § 774 (2000). In other work places, Title VII protects some employees' choice to wear non-conforming attire for religious reasons (42 U.S.C. §2000(e)). See *Carter* v. *Bruce Oakley Inc.*, 849 F. Supp. 673 (E.D. Ark. 1993) (protecting employee's religiously driven decision to wear a beard when no special reason provided for no-beard policy); but see *E.E O.C.* v. *Sambo's of Georgia, Inc.*, 530 F. Supp. 86 (N.D. Ga. 1981) (no Title VII violation in restaurant's refusal to hire a Sikh applicant with a beard when the restaurant had a health-related interest for its no-beard policy). See also *Francis* v. *Keane*, 888 F. Supp. 568 (S.D.N.Y. 1995) (entertaining First Amendment claim that Rastafarian prison employees had a

inequality. I concede straightaway that what is attractive in a non-ideal situation may be less acceptable under more just conditions. None the less, I believe that these practices would remain attractive even in conditions of greater luck-insensitivity. Some examples concern practices that fall into a more narrowly defined class of moral, rather than political, behaviour. Examples from interpersonal relations do not always bear critically on political philosophy, of course. But these seem relevant because I suspect that the intuitions driving endorsement of the formula arise partly from intuitions about personal responsibility and moral character. These intuitions are powerful, but only partially explanatory. Reflecting on the more complex nature of our interpersonal relations may help us to reconsider their shape and force.

Religious accommodation provides perhaps the most familiar example of accommodation. Traditionally, we have granted limited exemptions of conscience to the military draft. Those who do not make claims of conscience have a greater chance of being drafted, and bear the costs of those who assume certain religious affiliations. Employment-related accommodations provide another example. Efforts, albeit sometimes limited ones, are made to exempt certain religious observers from having to work on their Sabbath and holidays.[8] Where that is not possible, those who lose their jobs because they refuse to work on their Sabbath are eligible for unemploy-

---

right to wear dreadlocks). See also *Grant v. Canada*, 125 D.L.R. (4th) 556 (1995) (defending Canadian Mounties' decision to permit Sikh Mounties to wear turbans against a challenge that this violated religious neutrality).

[8] See, e.g., *Sherbert v. Verner*, 374 U.S. 398 (1963); *Thomas v. Review Board*, 450 U.S. 707 (1981); *Hobbie v. Unemployment Appeals Commission*, 480 U.S. 136 (1987); Title VII §2000(e) and a variety of state accommodation laws. An excellent critical overview of current Title VII law on religious discrimination and accommodation may be found in Kent Greenawalt, 'Title VII and Religious Liberty', *Loyola University Chicago Law Journal* 33 (2001), 1–56. But see *Employment Division v. Smith*, 494 U.S. 872 (1990) (holding it constitutional to refuse unemployment benefits to a drug counsellor fired for sacramental peyote consumption); *Thorton v. Calder*, 472 U.S. 703 (1985) (finding unconstitutional a state statute that guaranteed an absolute right not to work on one's Sabbath); *T.W.A. v. Hardison*, 432 U.S. 63 (1977) (Title VII does not require accommodation efforts that pose more than *de minimis* costs for employers and non-observing employees); *Ansonia Board of Education v. Philbrook*, 479 U.S. 60 (1986) (Title VII employers must offer reasonable accommodation, not the least burdensome option to employees); *In re Harvey* 689 N.Y.S. 789 (1999) (worker's proselytizing against employer's direction is misconduct). Title VII's accommodation provisions are less demanding for employers than the ADA's. This may serve as some evidence that, even though we try to accommodate some chosen activity, we make greater efforts to accommodate involuntary conditions. On the other hand, the Family and Medical Leave Act's provisions are in some respects more generous than either the ADA or Title VII. See discussion *infra*.

ment insurance. The non-observant bear extra costs as a consequence of
the observants' choice to affiliate with and practise a certain religion. The
non-observant may be asked to volunteer for more rigid schedules and to
work a greater number of what are otherwise desirable days to have off
(generally weekend days).[9] And the greater costs of the unemployment
scheme are shared by all of us, whether we volunteer to bear them or not.

Increasingly, similar forms of accommodation are emerging around
child, parent, and spousal care practices.[10] Through formal means (benefits,
time off, and more flexible schedules) and informal means (e.g., different
expectations of what entertainment responsibilities are expected from
married versus unmarried workers and from workers who are parents and
those who are not), workers who choose relationships involving these
forms of care are sometimes relieved of certain responsibilities and may
enjoy certain benefits. The costs of these practices are shared, or sometimes
fully borne, by workers who are not similarly situated.

One may offer explanations of these practices that compete with the
diagnosis that accommodation, in my sense, is going on. Active, religious
observance can provide the community with many public goods: it may
help to foster community ties, it may promote appreciation of and compliance with moral norms, and it may spark contemplation about philosophical and theistic subjects. There is also an aspect in which children are, to
put it crudely, public goods. They make possible the community's continued existence and flourishing. These accommodation practices may

---

[9] See, e.g., *Opuku-Boetang v. State*, 95 F.3d 1461, 1471 (1996), certiorari denied 520 U.S. 1228
(1997) (employer must try to find volunteers to trade shifts). Although employers must try to
find volunteers to cover shifts, they rarely impose swaps on unwilling employees. Michael
Wolf and Daniel Sutherland, *Religion in the Workplace* (Chicago: American Bar Association, 1998).

[10] See, e.g., Family Medical and Leave Act, 29 U.S.C. §§ 2601–54 (1993). Eligible workers
may take up to twelve weeks of unpaid leave to care for a newly born or newly adopted
child, or to care for an ill spouse, parent, child, or oneself. Around half of the work-force is
covered by the Act. See Commission on Family and Medical Leave, *A Workable Balance: Report to
Congress on Family and Medical Leave* (Washington: U.S. Dept. of Labor, 1996), *http://www.dol.govt/esa/
public/regs/compliance/whd/fmla/summary.html*. Some states offer more expansive protection, including
some wage replacement. Preliminary research on compliance indicates that the most common
way employers cover the work of employees who take the leave is to assign their work to
other, current employees. Joseph Willis, 'FMLA: A Progress Report', *Brandeis Journal of Family Law*
36 (1998), 95–108, at 99 (67.5 per cent of employers temporarily assigned the work of leave-
taking employees to non-leave-taking employees). See also *Workable Balance* and Department of
Labor, 'Balancing the Needs of Families and Employers: The Family and Medical Leave Surveys
2000 Update' (2001), *http://www.dol.gov/asp/fmla* (98.3 per cent of employers reassign some work to
non-leave-takers).

represent a way to recoup some of the costs of these public goods. And the manner of recouping makes some sense. As many feminists have observed, the traditional work place is structured around the unreasonable and exclusionary assumption that the typical worker is not a primary caretaker. Some forms of work-place release represent attempts to compensate for a biased structure without engaging in full-scale organizational revolution.[11]

Even so, the public goods argument seems an overly blunt and incomplete explanation. For it is not at all clear that the accommodation-related burdens on the non-observant or the childless are meaningfully calibrated to the costs they should absorb for these public goods. Moreover, there would be good grounds to accommodate even if it turned out that, all things considered, children were not a public good. To illustrate this point, consider what should be done if the situation were reversed and non-parents needed accommodation. Suppose that children are a public good but that choosing *not* to procreate produced health costs that caused people to miss work or to need flexible schedules.[12] We would still have good reason to accommodate the choice not to procreate, even if this choice does not contribute to a public good.

To turn to some other examples: we also practise some forms of accommodation in the medical arena. It is still infrequent for those with medical insurance to be charged higher premiums for engaging in relatively unhealthy behaviours, such as smoking, heavy drinking, or abstention from regular exercise, that place extra stress on the medical care system.[13] Admittedly, our practices are mixed. Extra taxes are charged on cigarettes and

---

[11] This is part of the explicit purpose of the FMLA. See 29 U.S.C. §2601(a)(5–6). The Act's findings also articulate an interest in facilitating parental care opportunities and concern about parents having to choose between job security and parenting. See 29 U.S.C. §2901(a)(2–3). I say these are 'attempts' to compensate for bias advisedly. Some argue that laws of this kind, involving non-comprehensive, piecemeal reforms, may create incentives to discriminate against those who might seem likely to take advantage of the Act's benefits. See n. 45 *infra*. I do not here try to argue that these laws, on their own, or in the current context, succeed in making the work place more hospitable to women. Accommodation efforts may require (or better achieve their aims in) a more comprehensive regulatory and institutional framework, including supplementary funding to avoid the creation of adverse incentives in hiring and wage levels. In what follows, I mean only to articulate some of the value of accommodation, on the assumption that accommodation laws do not work to the overall disadvantage of those they aim to protect.

[12] Women who do not bear children have a higher risk of contracting ovarian cancer. See, e.g., U.S. Dept. of Health and Human Services, The National Women's Health Information Center Website, *http://www.4woman.gov/faq/ovarian.htm#5*.

[13] Some employers do, however, charge employees higher insurance costs for legal but unhealthy behaviour. See Terry Morehead Dworkin, 'It's My Life—Leave Me Alone: Off-the-

liquor for a number of reasons—partly to raise revenue, partly to deter consumption, and partly to collect some of the behaviours' costs.[14] But we tend not to collect costs through premiums and not to deny access to health care because of past behaviour. Most significantly, we tend not to treat past behaviour as relevant in contexts of scarcity. Those with congenital diseases do not get priority for bypass surgery over those whose indulgent behaviour has caused their heart disease. Currently abstinent alcoholics are eligible for liver transplants, even if their behaviour gave rise to their liver failure.[15]

To a degree, our practices of medical accommodation reflect rough efforts to achieve luck-insensitivity. We may worry that the behaviour of smokers and drinkers is not voluntary but, rather, results from an addiction that may have genetic and environmental contributory causes. But, worries about voluntariness cannot provide the full explanation of these practices. We do not treat as relevant whether the cause of the liver failure was a genetically caused addiction to alcohol, initiated before the agent was fully responsible, or whether it was just the result of heavy, non-addicted drinking. Further, we regularly hold people responsible for other consequences of their drinking: for examples poor job performance and dangerous driving.[16] For some purposes, we expect people to take responsibility for these behaviours or for avoiding and controlling their addictions. And we do not, typically, regard poor eating or exercise habits as involuntary.

Job Employee Associational Privacy Rights', *American Business Law Journal* 37 (1997), 47–98, at 52 n. 31 (citing Johnson & Johnson and N.Y. Lab. Law §201 (d) (6) permitting employers to charge employees for behaviour that increases group insurance premiums). But see discussion of lifestyle statutes *infra*.

[14] See Frank Chaloupka, Melanie Wakefield, and Christina Czart, 'Taxing Tobacco: The Impact of Tobacco Taxes on Cigarette Smoking and Other Tobacco Use', in Robert Rabin and Stephen Sugarman (eds.), *Regulating Tobacco* (Oxford: Oxford University Press, 2001), 39–71.

[15] The general policy of the United Network for Organ Sharing, the umbrella organization that co-ordinates US organ transplantation, is that past behaviour, so long as it is not also an indicator of transplant success, is not a permissible criterion for candidacy for organ transplants. See 'UNOS Ethics Committee General Considerations in Assessment for Transplant Candidacy', *http://www.unos.org/*, and James Neuberger, David Adams, Paul MacMaster, Anita Maidment, and Mark Speed, 'Assessing Priorities for Allocation of Donor Liver Grafts: Survey of Public and Clinicians', *British Medical Journal* 317 (1998), 172–5 (American Medical Association and the World Health Organization guide-lines exclude past conduct as a relevant criterion).

[16] The ADA extends work-place protection to non-using addicts who seek or have sought rehabilitation. The protection does not extend to those whose alcoholism or addiction interferes with performance of the job (42 U.S.C. § 12114(c); 28 C.F.R. 36.104; 28 C.F.R. 36 (app. B)).

So, if these practices are efforts to achieve luck-insensitivity, they are rather crude and ill-fitting devices. Of course, it may be that this is just as precise as we can get. Heavy but non-addicted drinkers enjoy a windfall because the rule cannot be further refined yet remain practicable. But, although this is a possible explanation, it does not ring true to me as the full explanation—partly because we often do collect information about the origins of disease, showing that it isn't impracticable, and partly because many addictions stem from initial choices to consume substances, even in light of the risk that they may have long-term, addictive, and destructive consequences.

Some appeal to the involuntary nature of religious affiliation to explain religious accommodation.[17] The sense that religious affiliation is involuntary may stem from the idea that one's religious beliefs are inherited from one's parents or one's culture or from the idea that religious belief and practice are compelled by truth or by God. I do not see how these claims about the unchosen nature of religious belief distinguish religious beliefs from others sorts of practical belief. Our beliefs generally are influenced by our surroundings, and in a sense, all belief is compelled by its perceived truth; belief, famously, is not the direct object of choice.[18] Is religious belief especially impervious to deliberation and reflection? In any case, the unchosen nature of religious belief does not show that religious *actions* in conformance with beliefs are unchosen. Further, I worry that this explanation undervalues the efforts of the range of religious adherents who regard themselves as choosing, sometimes with great difficulty or with strength of will, to behave compliantly. Moreover, while this story may represent the situation of children and some adults as a general account, I think it grossly underestimates the degree to which, sociologically, much religious affiliation and practice reflect voluntary choices and commitments. Although many grow up within a religious environment, most

---

Some state provisions also partially accommodate some behaviour related to addiction. See also *Independent School District* v. *Hansen*, 412 N.W.2d 320 (Minn. App., 1987) (on-duty drinking due to alcoholism may be sufficient reason to terminate but insufficient reason to deny unemployment benefits); *Portland* v. *Employment Division* 765 P.2d 222 (1988) (distinguishing between alcoholism which might be activated by innocent act and cocaine addiction whose activation would require initial illegal act).

[17] See, e.g., Cohen, 'On the Currency', 936.

[18] See, e.g., Bernard Williams, 'Deciding to Believe', as reprinted in his *Problems of the Self* (Cambridge: Cambridge University Press, 1973), 136–51; Joseph Raz, 'When We Are Ourselves: The Active and the Passive', in *Engaging Reason: On the Theory and Value of Action* (Oxford: Oxford University Press, 1999), 5–21. For similar criticisms, see Rakowski, *Equal Justice*, 61–3.

adults are able to assess whether they endorse the beliefs to which they were acculturated and whether they wish to continue to practise.

The crux of the matter may be the claim that to the believer, religious practice is compelled by God. This characterization, though, is not true of all creeds or all practitioners. Some people consciously engage in religious practices for social reasons and for reasons of custom, without a sense of compulsion and often with an openness to coming to religious belief. Some even engage in religious practices consciously as a way to cultivate belief or to explore the grounds for belief. Likewise, not all creeds regard membership or belief in their creed as compulsory on members. Moreover, this characterization does not hold of all religious activity that we might wish to accommodate. There may be good reason to accommodate observant practices that facilitate or enhance religious life but which are not regarded, by the creed or the practitioner, as compulsory (e.g., undertaking leadership roles, engaging in conscientious objection, wearing symbols of faith, attending regular services).

Finally, I do not see how the idea that religious activity is involuntary could fuel a *liberal* account of religious accommodation practices. It is difficult to see how liberals could take such a view: it seems incompatible with a public stance of neutrality on religion to accept the view that religious activity really is compelled.

One might further object that the cases, and in particular, the medical care cases, illustrate another factor at work—that accommodation often seems appropriate where the consequence seems disproportionate to the significance of the choice.[19] Some may think that the imprudence involved in heavy drinking or smoking does not merit the refusal to provide aid necessary for life.[20] Concern about proportionality may be partly explanatory

---

[19] We might draw an analogy between this defence of accommodation and Frances Kamm's principle of irrelevant utilities. See Frances Kamm, *Morality, Mortality*, vol. 1 (Oxford: Oxford University Press, 1993), 146. Kamm's principle suggests that if a trolley must be diverted toward one person or another, it should not count as a reason to prefer one track that diversion down it will save a flower-bed or eliminate a sore throat in addition to saving a life. Life-and-death decisions should not turn on something so small as the relief of a sore throat. Similarly, one may think that the decision between candidates for livers should not rest on imprudence or weakness of the will; the consequence of death is too profound a response to that behaviour.

[20] The consequence that one's life is endangered and one needs a scarce resource, unlike some others I discuss, is not artificially created. The behaviour compounds true resource scarcity. Our medical practices, on this line, would have to be understood as making up for a

here, but it is incomplete. We often hold people responsible for predictable, major consequences of other lapses, some of which, by contrast, are shorter and irregular. For example, we imprison for reckless behaviour that sometimes amounts to a momentary failure of self-control or results from a single bout of drinking.

More example: Some privacy protections represent examples of accommodation. Not all privacy protections obscure irrelevant, though intriguing, information. Many advocates hold that we should enjoy privacy rights about whether we consume drugs and alcohol off-duty,[21] our medical status, our relationship status, our sexual practices, our contraceptive use, and our credit rating.[22] We also object to intrusive methods of investigation, such as polygraph testing.[23] This is partly because the information or the methods of eliciting it may be overvalued. But it is hard to deny, I think, that the information can reasonably matter to employers. Relationships, family plans, and off-duty consumption patterns may affect job performance, signal the likelihood of retention issues, affect workers' moods, create schedule pressures, or affect group insurance rates. Thus, some privacy rights allow individuals to make choices in an insulated way. Others are deprived of the ability to

naturally generated disproportionate response. This defence then would involve substantially revising the understanding of choice-sensitivity so that it involves responsibility not for foreseeable consequences but for foreseeable, *reasonable* consequences.

[21] The legality of drug-testing requirements varies by jurisdiction and purpose. Compare *Chandler* v. *Miller*, 520 U.S. 305 (1997) (finding unconstitutional a state law requiring candidates for public office to pass drug urinalysis) and *Borse* v. *Piece Good Shop, Inc.* 963 F.2d 611 (3d Cir. 1992) (Pennsylvania privacy law permits a private employee to sue for wrongful discharge for refusing testing) with *National Treasury Employees* v. *Von Raab*, 489 U.S. 656 (1989) (upholding tests of state employees who engaged in drug enforcement, carried arms, or handled very sensitive classified information), *Skinner* v. *Railway Labor Executives Association*, 489 U.S. 602 (1989) (upholding drug testing of state railroad employees for safety concerns), *Board of Education of Pottawatomie County* v. *Earls*, 122 S. Ct. 2559 (2002) (upholding drug tests of students participating in extracurricular activities), *Twigg* v. *Hercules Corp.*, 406 S.E. 2d 52 (W.Va. 1990) (limiting private employers' right to require testing to employees whose work involves others' safety and about whom there is reasonable suspicion of drug use), *Wilkinson* v. *Times Mirror Corp.*, 215 Cal. App.3d 1034 (Cal. 1989) (upholding a private company's testing of job applicants).

[22] See, e.g., Colo. Rev. Stat. §24–34–402.5 (Supp. 1995) (protecting employees, but not applicants, from termination for off-duty behaviour); N.D. Cent. Code §14–02.4–.1 (1993) (protecting applicants and employees); N.Y. Lab. Law § 201–d (McKinney Supp. 1995) (protecting applicants and employees from discrimination for certain sorts of legal off-duty behaviour). See T. M. Dworkin, 'It's My Life—Leave Me Alone', 51 (a majority of states have some privacy protection for off-duty employee behaviour).

[23] The Employee Polygraph Protection Act, 29 U.S.C.A. §§ 2001–9 prohibits covered employers from imposing mandatory polygraph tests on applicants or employees.

respond to relevant information about these choices, and may therefore bear costs that they otherwise could have chosen to avoid.[24]

A social, non-legal arena in which we tend to practise accommodation is that of supererogation. We often absorb costs associated with others' supererogation. Non-vegetarians will adjust their menu plans as hosts, go to different restaurants, and sometimes eat vegetarian when they are with vegetarians.[25] Most vegetarians do not regard themselves as acting supererogatorily,[26] but their companions often do. They often regard it as an optional stance (sometimes goofy or precious, sometimes admirable). Nevertheless they will absorb costs to accommodate it. Other examples may include the tax stance toward charitable donations: some of them we regard as supererogatory, and some of them we regard as directed toward causes we find deeply misguided.[27] Yet, to facilitate others' giving, the tax system, through deductions, tends to spread their costs among us.

[24] I am not advancing a version of the claim that the formulaic versions of egalitarianism violate privacy because they require shameful revelations that undermine one's self-respect. Wolff and Anderson have voiced concerns that some egalitarian schemes, especially those that attempt to compensate for natural inequalities, would require invasive investigations into people's shortcomings and insulting forms of compensation for them. These complaints seem directed more at the luck-insensitive branch of the formula than the choice-sensitive branch, the object of my concern. See Anderson, 'What is the Point of Equality?', and Wolff, 'Fairness, Respect, and the Egalitarian Ethos'. I am not entirely convinced by these concerns. The criticism seems to assume a heavy social ambivalence towards things like talents—that it is agreed that their distribution is morally arbitrary, but still, to have fewer than others is shameful and destructive of self-respect. My primary concern is not that investigations will reveal shameful or embarrassing information (although that may happen). It is rather that the process of tracking choices affects those choices: the scrutiny and the knowledge of the purpose behind it introduce reasons that affect people's deliberations, and may alter the sorts and feelings of the choices that are made.

[25] See also Justice Souter's notice of social, non-legal religious accommodation in *Lee* v. *Weisman*, 505 U.S. 577, 628 (1992) (noting cases in which Christians choose kosher restaurants when dining with observant Jews and atheists yield to Amish carriages).

[26] Many who habitually perform supererogatory action come to see it as obligatory. This may seem counter-intuitive: doing something as supererogatory might garner admiration, and would distance oneself from appearing to suggest, through one's behaviour, that one's peers were doing wrong. But some come to see supererogatory activities as required. Some of this may be a motivational boost. Also, the behaviour, although morally voluntary, often becomes an integral part of one's life. Identity-based reasons may emerge that have some of the feel of moral structure.

[27] Contributions to the Heritage Foundation are tax-deductible. So are contributions to Amnesty International, People for the American Way Foundation, and the Brookings Institution. Organizations representing opposing sides of the euthanasia issue also qualify for deductible donations. See, e.g., *www.irs.ustreas.gov/prod/bus_info/*.

Another example is the social practice of 'being supportive'. Many declare to friends and family that they will support their intimates—whatever decision they make—even when it is clear that a particular option is patently superior. Being supportive can incur real costs. If the colleague with the relevant information does not whistle-blow, we will both have to endure the intolerable supervisor. If one's friend continues with the plainly unsuitable lover and gives the cad one more chance, one will have to endure more insufferable dinners with the unworthy partner and then cancel plans to give comfort when the inevitable further betrayal occurs. Sometimes all that supportiveness involves is refraining from criticism of what clearly is a bad choice. This social practice has its detractions. Over-use of this stance can resemble the worst sort of relativism activated by loyalty: it can lead one to turn a blind eye to bad or seriously imprudent behaviour and to resist imparting the critical perspective that good friends share. But, in moderation, it does not represent a base form of relativism. It reflects an understanding that others will make choices one disagrees with, but that in some domains, a relationship involves acceptance and even refraining from articulating the criticism that both parties know is lurking. To return to the culinary arena, ethical vegetarians rarely cook animals for omnivorous friends; but, they do dine out with them, frequently refrain from initiating discussion of the topic, and often split the tab. (This usually involves vegetarians subsidizing those who ordered (what are usually more expensive) dishes with meat.)

These are some examples of the phenomenon of accommodation to which I mean to draw our attention. Concerns about voluntariness, public goods, anti-free-riding norms, and disproportionality partially explain these practices. But I do not believe they provide a full explanation. We have fashioned a range of practices that involve subsidizing others' voluntary choices. These practices are, by and large, attractive ones, I'd submit, but I do not think they can be fully explained by our commitment to luck-insensitivity. In the next section, I aim to provide a different argument for the limited relaxation of choice-sensitivity norms: namely, an argument for accommodation.

Stage Two—An Explanation

The theoretical argument for accommodation has a negative and a positive dimension. Negatively, strict choice-sensitivity in contexts of social co-operation may not support, and may even compromise, a certain sort of freedom. Positively, accommodation practices often facilitate this sort of freedom.

The general, negative argument goes as follows. Liberal egalitarians champion high levels of social co-operation that involve inter-personal co-ordination and interdependence. Indeed, insurance is both a favoured egalitarian metaphor and an actual tool. In sharing the costs and benefits of each others' good and bad fortune, we are in essence creating an insurance pool to manage exigencies fairly and more efficiently. Other co-operative enterprises involve interconnection—we live close together, our work and social lives involve co-ordination and close affiliation. Sometimes we choose the particular people with whom we have such close ties, but often not. We rarely exert direct control over who our colleagues are (academics are unusual) or who our neighbours are (although indirect control of their class is often achieved through zoning laws). We depend on a daily basis on the good will and care of complete strangers. These co-operative systems bring increased productivity, social cohesion, new ways of life, and other forms of common welfare—goods that, among other things, often enhance our freedom and create important, different opportunities for its exercise.

But such collective enterprises can also impinge upon freedom. When people become interdependent, choices that would otherwise be self-regarding come to have more and more other-regarding components. The more intertwined we become, the more this effect is enhanced. Absent social interconnection, your heavy drinking would be predominantly self-regarding. But, if we are part of a medical group plan, it may take on other-regarding aspects. It may place a burden on the medical care system and increase our premiums or, worse, contribute to scarcity or competition for scarce medical resources.[28] In dense quarters, your smoking will generate second-hand smoke. Noise will become noise pollution, if one's neighbours are in close enough proximity. If we share the fruits of our economic enterprise, then occupational choices, which seem self-regarding in many respects, will have serious other-regarding effects. If I choose less productive, but more rewarding employment, it is not just that I lose extra

---

[28] This is a contested claim. Compare J. J. Barendregt, L. Bonneux, and P. J. Van Der Maas, 'The Health Care Costs of Smoking', New England Journal of Medicine 337 (1997), 1052–7, with competing studies discussed in Chaloupka et al., 'Taxing Tobacco', 61–2. For my purposes, I will assume the claim to be true.

income, but others enjoy a lesser standard of living than they would if I undertook more productive work. If the distributive system is roughly egalitarian, what others lose is roughly comparable to what I lose.

Since my behaviour has other-regarding effects, it may fall under the jurisdiction of the harm principle. As it is typically understood, the harm principle permits behaviour to be prohibited or restricted if it issues in harm to others. Depending on its interpretation, the principle can embody an especially strong conception of choice-sensitivity. One is permitted to make decisions whose significant effects lie mostly with oneself, but not those that have significant, detrimental effects on other, non-consenting persons. If I persist in such behaviour, others may object to having to endure the effects of my choices. They may be able to claim that my behaviour harms them and so feel entitled to interfere with my behaviour. How serious a claim of harm may be made will depend partly on the depth of our interconnection and partly on the interpretation of the harm principle. Some interpretations tend to count any diminishment of position or opportunity cost as a form of harm; others enact significance thresholds before concluding that harm has transpired. At least some significant range of behaviour that is generally associated with the exercise of autonomy will, in contexts of social co-operation, generate externalities that render it vulnerable to restrictions underwritten by the harm principle (although the degree of vulnerability will depend on the interpretation of the harm principle).[29]

This is not meant as an objection to the harm principle. Its basic insight is correct. Still, there is a problem here for the proponent of autonomy. The formation of collective, co-operative enterprises is critical to the successful pursuit of the egalitarian agenda. But their formation, coupled with the harm principle, may threaten the existence of some arenas in which people can freely make and exercise certain valuable choices without vulnerability to significant interference.

One may object that the harm principle is a rather blunt instrument to wield in the name of choice-sensitivity. Instead of implementing Draconian measures such as prohibiting smoking or eliminating occupational choice, one could devise less restrictive means to extract the costs that individuals

---

[29] I do not mean to appeal to a non-co-operative, libertarian-style state as a baseline for freedom or self-regarding activity. Rather, I mean to be pointing to certain activities that we generally associate with autonomous activity and self-sovereignty, including decisions about how to care for oneself and what practices and relationships to pursue.

impose by pricing them. Often, this is an appropriate response. But, a full-fledged pricing system, implemented at every opportunity and in every context, can be wearing. Very thorough schemes of choice-sensitivity involve the collection and possession of detailed information about individuals by others. Even supposing the information could be obtained without invasive scrutiny, its mere possession and use by other community members may compromise feelings of privacy and freedom. The sense of being watched and scrutinized often has an inhibiting and chilling effect on choice. In certain contexts, people will make less authentic choices just because they are being watched, because they feel the pressure of the reasons that motivate the scrutiny, or simply to avoid scrutiny and others' judgement.

Furthermore, such practices may detract significantly from the feelings of community that are generated by such co-operation and part of their impetus. It isn't merely that pricing every action feels petty and nitpicking. It may affect and skew the experience of freedom. In contexts driven by the impetus to exact individuals' costs thoroughly, agents may feel constrained by the sense that everything they do impacts on others and is subject to accounting. This may constrain or dominate the experience of choice. Cost-internalization schemes may also seem to deliver the message that certain behaviour is costly to the community and even disapproved of. The message of disapproval may exert a powerful effect on the socially sensitive recipient. It may over-influence or skew her deliberation. But even apart from the phenomenon of over-reaction, there are disadvantages to the persistent and systematic presentation of these messages that nearly every action displaces costs on others. A reasonably responsive citizen may get past concerns about being the object of disapproval but still be stymied by the nagging sense that he is disadvantaging others, and that the cost-internalization scheme may not fully compensate, since not every burden is monetizable.[30] The goods of purely free choice may be overly compromised. Some of the more important goods of self-expression

---

[30] Sensitivity to this phenomenon does not always cut against schemes of cost-internalization. As Paula Casal pointed out to me, some practices of cost-internalization make deliberation freer. When companies internalize the full costs of their production, it renders choices between products freer for morally conscientious agents. In such an environment, their choices may be based purely on consumer criteria without having to investigate or worry that some products are environmentally dangerous or the product of exploitative labour. Such examples do not run counter to the case I want to make for accommodation. As I later argue, whether we should accommodate should depend on how the context of choice actually frames the deliberative field.

may be sacrificed, particularly in arenas in which agents feel especially susceptible to social pressure. So, it may be important to preserve some social domains in which one's choices are deliberately not monitored, so that responsive agents feel psychologically, as well as morally, free to choose as they see fit.

Strict accounting and pricing procedures may also threaten to place community members in untenable interpersonal situations. As with cigarette sales, we can tax some behaviour as it occurs. But other taxes are difficult to impose when risky decisions are made. It is difficult to tax sexually risky behaviour. Or, suppose individuals evade the taxes, refuse to pay them, or lack the means to (because they have spent their resources on other goods). Although it may not violate the autonomy rights of patients to enact treatment preferences against those who voluntarily incurred risks of disease, at some point this will feel cruel and merciless—the more so the more we have cultivated relations of co-operation and interdependence. A thoroughgoing choice-sensitive system would unreasonably require health-care workers to suppress their reactions of care and compassion.

I have been making broadly two sorts of points about the ways in which thorough cost-internalization measures may affect individual freedom. The first concerns certain phenomenological effects on individuals' experiences of freedom—they may feel intimidated, surveilled, chilled, etc. from making authentic choices. The second concerns a different sort of constraint, namely the way a choice-sensitive system may impose obstacles to individuals' rationally responding to certain sorts of reasons and values more or less directly and discretely. This latter point is the more unusual one, and may be better fleshed out by turning to the positive argument for accommodation.

Accommodation practices provide a way to mitigate these effects by insulating people's deliberations from certain sorts of pressures. It may help to delineate the argument I wish to pursue by distinguishing it from a common justificatory explanation for accommodation, especially religious accommodation. On the common justification, accommodation practices protect people from having to make wrenching, difficult choices between comparably weighty, central values. It protects them from having to choose between livelihood on the one hand and the compulsions of conscience on the other.[31] On this explanation, accommodation serves to enhance

[31] See, e.g., *Employment Division* v. *Smith*, 494 U.S. 872, 895 (J. O'Connor, concurring); Michael McConnell, 'Free Exercise Revisionism and the *Smith* Decision', *University of Chicago Law Review*, 57 (1991), 1109–53.

people's welfare by insulating them from particularly costly choices.[32] There is much to be said for this explanation. Still, I do not think it is a complete or deep enough one. It does not explain, for one thing, accommodation practices around consumption choices. Moreover, this characterization overemphasizes welfare: the *costs* of a difficult choice and the *cost* of the loss of the forgone good. By doing so, it neglects the way in which the absence of accommodation practices tends to alter the nature of the deliberations involved with respect to the goods at stake. Their absence affects detrimentally the experience and the choice, even of the option that is chosen, even when the particular choice is a clear one. I think that accommodation plays a more direct role in enhancing freedom by facilitating certain sorts of purer deliberation that themselves represent a kind of valuable freedom.

To clarify, I will return to an earlier example. Suppose Sabbatarianism does displace costs on to other workers and on to the work-force generally. Sometimes, we should reorganize the structure of work so that the Sabbatarian can keep her job. In other cases, it may be impractical to reorganize, but we should ensure that unemployment benefits and other forms of work are available. A different justification for shouldering these burdens on behalf of another person's choice to engage in religious practice is that we want to insulate the person's deliberations. We may think it important that a person's deliberations about whether to be observant should not be clouded by considerations about whether she will lose her job or access to benefits, whether others will suffer inconvenience as a result of her decisions, or whether others disapprove of her religious beliefs and practices. With some of these considerations, there may be the fear that they would dominate the decision-making process. These considerations would be so strong that they would eclipse the possibility of choosing certain sorts of goods, like adherence to faith. With respect to some of the others, we may just think that the decision should be free of that sort of pressure—*that* sort of reason should not be forced on her as a grounds for not adhering to a purported requirement of conscience. Considerations

---

[32] A powerful, critical discussion of defences of religious accommodation that appeal to the flourishing of religious adherents appears in Christopher Eisgruber, and Lawrence Sager, 'The Vulnerability of Conscience: The Constitutional Basis for Protecting Religious Conduct', *University of Chicago Law Review* 61 (1994), 1245–1315, at 1254–67. See also Eisgruber and Sager, 'Religious Liberty and the Moral Structure of Constitutional Rights', *Legal Theory* 6 (2000), 253–68, and Eisgruber and Sager, 'Equal Regard', in Stephen Feldman (ed.), *Law and Religion: A Critical Anthology* (New York: New York University Press, 2000), 200–25.

about the reactions of others and the impact on others may intrude. They may make the decision more one between one's commitment to God versus one's commitment to others, rather than more directly about whether one believes in God, what one believes is an appropriate response to that belief, and whether one accepts the putatively associated commitments and sacrifices as binding on oneself.

Similar characterizations fit other examples. Good friendship requires a lively and honest exchange of ideas and opinions. But, at some point, once that has occurred and differences remain, on some occasions it is appropriate for friends not only to withhold criticism but, to some degree, to participate in activities of which they disapprove. Vegetarians will split the tab with omnivores. Feminists and gay activists of certain bents will attend weddings despite their disapproval of the intrinsic or contingent properties of the marriage institution.[33] One reason for participation of this sort is that while we may disapprove of each other's stances or activities, we do not want friends to desist merely because of our disapproval; nor, really, do we want our disapproval to function prominently in their deliberations. That is to say, we do not want disapproval as such to exert influence over our friends, although we do want the reasons driving the disapproval to have sway. Their decision should be based on the reasons relating to animal treatment, in the one case, and in the other, to their relationship, the qualities of the marriage institution, and their best judgement about the need and possibilities for change and the appropriate fora in which to pursue it. But the nature of our connection to each other makes us naturally and understandably sensitive to each other. We are quite likely to be reasonably and admirably responsive and reactive to each other's disapproval, disappointment, and detriment *as such*. Being responsive in this way is not, essentially, a kind of over-reaction. Rather, it is how a friend, a colleague, or an intimate should be. (There is, of course, variation in the nature of this responsiveness, and it may become corrupted or distorted. Some are overly eager to please and to avoid disapproval. Others over-react with stubborn, perverse resistance.) To avoid transforming the nature of the decision, we may actively support a person's endeavour because abstinence would make our disapproval evident and salient. We support endeav-

---

[33] I was prompted to think harder about this question by a talk given by my colleague William Rubenstein: 'Why Do Straight Couples Invite their Gay Friends to their Weddings? And Why Do We Go? Research into the Politics of Resistance', Faculty Research Colloquium, LGBT Studies Program and Center for the Study of Women, UCLA, 3 November 1998.

ours we disagree with, in some contexts, to ensure that the reasons reasonably salient to the deliberator are predominantly those most closely connected to the worth of the activity.

What does this have to do with meaningful freedom? One concern is purely prophylactic. In certain contexts, people are especially vulnerable to considerations of cost or expressions of disapproval. They will shy away from some decisions even if the result is an inauthentic expression of their convictions. They will be intimidated in ways that are disproportionate to the social cost or disapproval. But that is not all.

The other aspect of freedom I have in mind has to do with the experience of responding to reasons. In another context, concerning responsibility and identity, Joseph Raz has recently argued that we are ourselves, active as opposed to passive, when we are responsive to reason—as opposed to acting in ways that are unintelligible to ourselves.[34] It is something like this idea I want to draw on. Deliberate action in response to reason is the central form of self-expression. The ability and opportunity to react to reason is a sort of freedom. It is not merely valuable to have the opportunity to respond to reason generally and to that which there is all-things-considered reason to do. It is, moreover, valuable to be able to respond to particular sorts of reasons, and in a more or less direct way. If responding to reasons is roughly connected to responding to values, what I am suggesting is that it is important and desirable to have the opportunity to respond to and to engage with particular values or goods in purer, more direct ways. It is valuable to have the opportunity to engage with a particular value, in some degree of isolation, to determine its significance to oneself and to respond appropriately to the reasons it presents. It is important to be able to appreciate that value in particular, to assess its relation to oneself, and to have this evaluation exert palpable influence over one's activity and experience. Likewise, it is valuable to have opportunities to develop and exercise one's capacities for choice with respect to these disparate values. These distinct aspects of oneself should, on occasion, have room to develop and some space in which to be dominant.[35]

[34] Raz, 'When We are Ourselves'.

[35] Joseph Raz draws on similar values in characterizing the set of options necessary for autonomous choice in *Morality of Freedom*, ch. 14. I argue that these considerations may also provide an independent ground for justifying agent-centred options in 'Morality and Agent-Centred Options', *Analysis* 51 (1991), 244–54.

If all situations present a multiplicity of mixed reasons, especially some strong ones, this may interfere with the achievement of this form of responsiveness. The familiar cases are those where values conflict. Without accommodation, one may have to choose between being observant (which one believes one has reason to be) and making a livelihood or being self-sufficient. One's situation may dictate that one sacrifice the former, and so one will not have an open, salient opportunity to engage fully with the values associated with resolving how and if one should be observant and in what way. Although one is responsive to reason A in one sense when one sees that reason B outweighs it and acts accordingly (follows B), one will not have been fully responsive to A. One will not have had the chance to act, reasonably, in appreciative, positive response to its good. One will only have *acted* in light of its relative deficiency.

In other cases, the choices will be overdetermined yet have a similar, regrettable consequence. The course of action recommended by reason A and reason B may be the same, but one reason is so strong that it clearly determines what one should do. But situations with this structure may mean that one does not really respond to some of the contributory, fellow-travelling values. Because A is so much stronger and would dictate the course of action whether or not reason B pointed in the same direction, the reasonable agent need not engage fully with B's significance and meaning. Consequently, there will not be a salient opportunity to have engagement with B's significance determine one's action. For example, it may be clear (and reasonably so) that one does not want to introduce conflict into a relationship with a close friend or partner who is an adamant, non-accommodating vegetarian. One may refrain from eating meat for that reason—to maintain harmony and to avoid threatening the relationship. Consequently, the ethical reasons will not be salient to one, and one will not confront, in as vivid and practically relevant a way, the reasons for and against vegetarianism. Their resolution will not guide one's conduct. One will not act out of appreciative response to one's assessment that vegetarianism is a gentler way of life. Or consider a variation on the case in which employment conditions and conditions of religious observance conflict. For the atheist or the doubter, this may represent a case of overdetermination. The trumping power of reasons of livelihood may render questions about religion moot. Deliberation about the existence of God and what significance his or her existence should have on one's action need not go beyond abstract reflection. The atheist may not have a salient deliberative situation in which it really mattered for her conduct to resolve the challenges associated with the (putative) reasons to believe in God.

In some contexts (like many economic markets) whose architecture is not shaped by an interest in protecting freedom as such, choice situations of these problematic sorts may arise. They arise not because we value them and aim to create them as such, but often just as an arbitrary by-product of an efficient or convenient mode of organization. In such situations (and some others), strong choice-sensitivity may sometimes eclipse or overly narrow the range of opportunities to respond directly to certain reasons and to develop and exercise the associated capacities for choice.

These problems associated with strict choice-sensitivity hold true both for those vulnerable to the enforcement and for those who would have to do the policing. Accommodation permits people some aspects of their lives in which they do not have to police themselves and others so hard or so comprehensively. This makes room for the expression and development of certain values, feelings, and relations. If we are highly interconnected, responsible agents, we may feel complicit in what others do, as when organizations and institutions to which we contribute are used to support others' projects. If we subscribe to strong views of complicity, we may feel that we must remain highly alert to others' business to avoid involvement and complicity in others' activities of which we disapprove. But if we accept the idea behind constrained practices of accommodation, this may allow us some limited space in which to relax our vigilance and scrutiny. This is freedom-enhancing and reduces what would otherwise be a form of exhausting civic anxiety. We can understand the costs we absorb, depending on how they are structured, not as forms of support for the particular activity chosen, but in furtherance of an institution that facilitates a particular sort of freedom. This may be a way for some of those morally opposed to abortion to reconcile their moral views with the public funding of abortion as an aspect of a general system of medical care. It is also a way to think about student fees that support student organizations or tax deductions that may subsidize organizations whose ends we disagree with or taxes for government activities we abhor.

The medical examples may also provide a case in point here. Non-conduct-based principles of allocation do, of course, subsidize smokers, drinkers, and the like. And they do, in one way, create a more streamlined context of choice for consumers. The consumer can select whether to drink or not without the very heavy prospect of having the community refuse available care in a pronounced expression of disapproval. This makes possible a somewhat more focused deliberation based on the values of one's health and life success versus the values of momentary pleasures and hedonism. It makes the decision not to drink more attributable to an appreciation of the former, more central values. But the consumer is not the only agent of concern here. The policies make possible a realm of purer compassionate response. Where access is insulated from choice-sensitive measures, health-care workers can respond purely to need, urgency, and outcome. They need not temper their compassion with moral judgements or withhold it pending moral investigation. Their compassionate responses are protected and permitted expression in a realm in which the pulls of compassion are quite strong.

To be sure, I have said little about when and where we should relax our choice-sensitivity norms. I certainly do not mean to suggest that we must always accommodate religious activity or that we should try to make smoking or drinking costless. As I discuss briefly below, it matters how much we would sacrifice in accommodating and how the burden would be borne. Nor do I mean to deny that it is also an important aspect of our capacity for choice that we are able to make decisions in contexts in which a variety of mixed values and reasons are relevant. I mean just to make the limited point that there is an important value to sometimes relaxing norms of choice-sensitivity to facilitate this one important sort of freedom—the freedom to engage with and react directly to discrete reasons and values.

While I take this to be an issue for those committed to individual autonomy, I should concede that the connection to freedom is not the only way in which these opportunities might be valued. One might simply think that accommodation is important because, in some contexts, it is the decent thing to do, because it allows one to express compassion, because it facilitates religious expression by believers, or because acting otherwise could be cruel. That is, one might believe it is important primarily because of the specific values it permits one to express. These may, indeed, be sufficient grounds themselves to doubt strict choice-sensitivity and to defend accommodation. I do not mean to challenge them, although an appeal to the considerations I mention may help to delineate the scope of these reasons—to determine, for example, when refusing accommodation would be cruel and when it would not.

Although there may be other grounds for accommodation, I emphasize the connection with freedom and autonomy for two reasons. First, the opportunity to act on certain reasons enhances the meaningfulness of the set of options. Having a diverse range of options enhances autonomy. This may be a value in itself that is not reducible to the value of the particular options themselves. Second, the fact that one may appeal to the conditions for meaningful freedom may serve as a public reason for accommodation even in cases where the values that accommodation facilitates response to (e.g., religious reasons) cannot themselves serve as public reasons for political action.

The Scope of Accommodation and its Relationship to Egalitarianism

I am not convinced that there are determinate formulas for when and where arenas of accommodation should be formed. This presents a challenge, to put it lightly, for the development of a positive theory. Much will depend on the composition of the entire social structure and the specific contexts for deliberation. I also suspect that it is no accident that our accommodation practices occur in areas where many values and aims overlap. For reasons of efficiency, convenience, and perhaps to avoid having to resolve hard cases, we may locate accommodation practices where we also have concerns about discrimination, avoiding luck-sensitivity, and providing public goods. Still, something more can be said about how to approach accommodation. This will return us to the question of the compatibility of accommodation with egalitarianism.

The argument for accommodation suggests that we should attend to valuable aspects of our capacity for choice. People should have some, limited, opportunities to engage with these values more directly and to make decisions in response to them. With respect to the goods that merit some insulation, I am sceptical that a definitive list could be generated, since so much reasonably depends on the context and structure of social organization. None the less, I would hasten to note that the right approach would not involve merely ticking off the central goods or aspects of choice that are crucial to individual identity. It is a mistake to conceive of the value of autonomous activity as nested solely in certain core, central activities that define one's character. One suffers a (minor) insult to one's autonomy when somebody prevents one from selecting one's preferred, available chocolate bar, although I believe (even in the face of contrary pressure from commercial advertisers), that this choice is not central to, or even on the periphery of, forming or performing one's character or identity. All the same, having the space to make even trivial choices purely on the basis of the small, specific reasons that trivial options provide seems like an important component of being an individual who exercises sovereignty over her environment. There is a certain sort of freedom in making decisions that reflect little of substance and involve responding to and forming preferences or judgements about even small details. There is something to be said for a modicum of insulation, somewhere, even for these choices.

At least in the American context, I suspect, though I will not defend the claim, that the areas of decision around which there should be some accommodation should include decisions relating to personal relationships and their place within one's life; decisions relating to the content and demandingness of one's work; decisions and deliberations relating to the requirements on individual conscience and other important areas of practical and theoretical enquiry, including, but not limited to, the demands, if any, of religion; decisions relating to the development and exercise of significant, individuating virtues—such as charity, compassion, mercy, honesty, integrity; and decisions relating to one's body and one's physical experiences.

Decisions about accommodation should also pay attention to who will bear the costs and how. We should consider what sort of support or involvement by others is required: whether it involves mere financial support or other sorts of involvement that more directly engage with considerations regarding autonomy; whether the support is direct or indirect; whether the support appears to communicate personal agreement or affiliation; whether the degree of support or involvement required of others seriously implicates their integrity or interferes with their capacities to pursue their own aims; and whether the burdens fall disproportionately hard on certain individuals or groups. We should also consider whether, given the nature of the goods at issue, a practice of accommodation in this domain would itself provide perverse incentives to choose particular goods just to benefit from accommodation. That is, we should bear in mind whether some practices would not serve the aim of facilitating more direct response to particular values, but would instead be especially subject to free-riding or perverse adaptation.[36]

[36] A useful cautionary discussion of perverse but subtle incentive effects of accommodation on religious groups and their internal doctrine may be found in Mark V. Tushnet, 'Questioning the Value of Accommodating Religion', in Stephen M. Feldman (ed.), *Law and Religion: A*

Although I hope sometime to say something more concrete about what to accommodate and to what degree, I want to return briefly here to the subject of egalitarianism. Briefly, I want to address two, opposing questions. First, how, if at all, is my view different from the theories of leading egalitarians? Don't most egalitarians, one way or another, acknowledge the need for the protection of the basic liberties and, to varying extents, their priority over distributive aims? Second, if the argument does represent a departure from contemporary egalitarian theories, does this suggest that there is a conflict among accommodation, freedom, and egalitarianism, and that something should be sacrificed?

In one respect I agree with the thrust of the first question, that I have been elaborating upon a commitment of liberal egalitarian theories. But the rehearsal of the argument for accommodation has brought out more explicitly that the affirmation of the priority of the basic liberties may be in some tension with an understanding of egalitarianism that describes itself as strictly choice-sensitive.[37]

In another respect, though, I should emphasize that there is more to the view than a mere re-description of the priority of the basic liberties. First, some forms of accommodation, such as the accommodation of

---

Critical Anthology (New York: New York University Press, 2000), 245–57. While accommodation may be susceptible to exploitation by some bad faith actors, it seems an over-reaction to refuse accommodation merely because of the risk of some inauthentic behaviour. For a longer discussion, see my 'Paternalism, Unconscionability', 248 n. 52.

[37] I take choice-sensitivity theorists to task for not providing a strong enough foundation for the protection of freedom. But one might object that these liberties are presupposed by any system that relies on choice-sensitivity norms. To assess fairly what counts as a choice and what does not, we must assess what people want and choose against a backdrop of liberty. Choice-sensitivity is to be enforced only in a context of liberty-provision; it does not tell us what liberties are to be protected. (This may be Ronald Dworkin's position. See Ronald Dworkin, 'What is Equality? Part 3: The Place of Liberty', *Iowa Law Review* 73 (1987), 1–54, and *idem, Sovereign Virtue*, ch. 3.) This seems to be a version of the claim that choice-sensitivity is not captured by methods of cost-internalization. This approach requires an independent way to understand what the background structure of liberty should look like, and what values should drive this structure. One will have to decide whether religious liberty principles should require accommodation or not, and the ideal of choice-sensitivity cannot be used to settle the question. So something distinct must still be added to the formula of eliminating luck-insensitivity and enforcing choice-sensitivity. While I may, in the end, agree with the prescriptions of such a scheme, I believe this defence eviscerates the power of 'choice-sensitivity' as either an organizing principle or an illuminating characterization of the underlying structure of egalitarianism.

consumption choices, are not clearly or necessarily connected to the standard list of the basic liberties. They may lack the special, trumping powers of
the standard basic liberties. Although I generally favour personal autonomy in matters of individual consumption, I do not mean to elevate this
to the importance of freedom of speech or to deny that the values of
accommodation might be overcome if the externalities were great enough.

More important, recognizing the value of accommodation may inform
our interpretation of the basic liberties. On a popular conception of the
basic liberties, they amount merely to negative rights: strict protections
against state prohibitions on certain sorts of behaviour. Congress may not
ban or criminalize speech. The view of basic liberties as negative rights,
though, is consistent (to a point) with aiming as much as possible to
recoup the costs of the exercise of the right (or at least not to subsidize its
exercise any further than is necessary to tolerate it). For example, some
take this view about the Free Exercise Clause of the First Amendment.
On this view, so long as Congress does not ban a religion or target it
for special burdens, an otherwise well-motivated law that incidentally
places special burdens on religious groups or practice is not suspect.[38]
These burdens may represent costs of otherwise well-motivated activity.
Further, some argue that granting exceptions to such groups may be
problematic—it may represent a deviation from our commitment to religious neutrality and an endorsement of religious practice.[39] To take another example, some believe that the constitutional right of privacy
demands only that we permit reproduction and abortion. If we disagree
with the practices, we should not have to subsidize them through the
welfare system, because subsidizing them may represent an endorsement of
these practices, and it would be unfair for us to have to bear those sorts of
costs. If the argument for the value of accommodation succeeds, though, it
exposes a difficulty with *this* argument for purely negative interpretations
of the basic liberties. It provides a positive, non-instrumental account of

[38] See, e.g., *Employment Division* v. *Smith*, 494 U.S. 872, 877–80 (1990); Eisgruber and Sager,
'Vulnerability of Conscience', 1285. Eisgruber and Sager have an admirably capacious interpretation of the anti-discrimination test: a law must not discriminate between sects; nor may
it privilege other sorts of fundamental, secular concerns over religious concerns.

[39] Although, if other accommodation practices are in place (such as accommodation of
family choice), there may then be anti-discrimination reasons to accommodate religious
behaviour. Given the range of accommodation practices in place, my position and the anti-
discrimination theorists' position may converge. What anti-discrimination theories lack,
though, is the positive account for accommodating in the first place.

why we might offer fuller protections and forms of support for the exercise of the basic liberties that does not depend upon an endorsement of the actual choices that rights-bearers select.[40]

Whether more positive support in the form of accommodation should be provided depends also on how the accommodation practices are structured. When the burdens of accommodation are heavy and are displaced on to discrete individuals, the objection that those individuals do not endorse the chosen behaviours has greater force than when the costs are smaller and more dispersed. It may also depend on there being reciprocity of accommodation across different activities—for example, that spousal, family, and significant-other care is accommodated as well as religious activity. A criterion of reciprocity should not be taken as a disguised way to achieve choice-sensitivity through equally calibrated exchanges. What matters for reciprocity is the mutual willingness to share burdens to facilitate a meaningful sense of freedom in, and access to, the pursuit of a variety of practices that engage with diverse values. The mutuality seems crucial for maintaining the social bases of self-respect: one may be willing to shoulder the burdens of activities in which one does not partake or that one does not value, but it matters that others would do the same for you.

This notion of reciprocity differs in two ways from choice-sensitivity. First, what matters is the mutual *willingness* to shoulder burdens for each other. Willingness may be manifest even if it is never activated—that is, even if one is never called upon to do what one is willing to do. So, reciprocity may be present between parties even if only one of them is actually ever called upon to accommodate. Second, reciprocity obtains even if the size of the burdens borne by reciprocating parties differs due to

[40] Hence, religious accommodation may be defended without relying on the claim that religious views are correct or religious practice facilitates (or especially facilitates) well-being. It would also serve as a partial reply to arguments that the legal (and social) system unfairly assumes the special value of child-bearing and so unfairly shifts (some) costs of reproduction on to non-parents. See, e.g., Katherine Franke, 'Theorizing Yes: An Essay on Feminism, Law and Desire', *Columbia Law Review* 101 (2000), 181–203; Mary Anne Case, 'How High the Apple Pie? A Few Troubling Questions about Where, Why, and How the Burden of Care for Children Should be Shifted', *Chicago–Kent Law Review* 76 (2001), 1753–86. The answer is only partial, because these critiques also suggest a different criticism with which I substantially agree: namely, that to be fair, accommodation regimes should exhibit reciprocity. If child-bearing practices are accommodated, so should other choices of substantial import, such as decisions not to bear children, to care for other dependents (e.g., parents and life-partners), and decisions concerning religious activity. Further, they should ensure that heavy burdens of accommodations are not clustered on to a discrete, over-burdened group as I discuss *infra*.

the different nature of the activities accommodated and their contexts. In either of these two cases, reciprocity may obtain, though one party bears greater burdens than another that are not the result of his voluntary choices.

To be sure, reciprocity is not sufficient, and there are better and worse ways to accommodate. The approaches of Title VII and of the Family and Medical Leave Act provide instructive examples of two different approaches, both of which are flawed in different respects. Title VII aims to prevent religious discrimination, and uses accommodation as an instrument to achieve anti-discrimination goals. It requires employers to make some accommodation efforts, but none that represent an 'undue burden'. (Ironically, in this context, by contrast with the term's use in the constitutional law governing abortion rights, an undue burden is anything greater than a *de minimis* cost.[41]) Even large employers need not incur costs to offer flexible schedules, to hire temporary workers to cover, or to offer overtime pay to employees willing to cover. Employers also may not require, though they must ask, other workers to cover the shifts of the observant. The motivations for this approach seem twofold. First, so long as there is some good reason for the organizational structure and for the refusal to alter it, such as that it would be costly, a failure to accommodate is not discriminatory. Second, requiring other, specific employees (and perhaps the employer) to carry significant burdens for another employee would amount to religious discrimination.

The FMLA provides an instructive contrast. It also aims to prevent discrimination (against women), but it has an explicit, distinct accommodation aim as well. Unsurprisingly, then, it levies greater burdens on employers and, seemingly, on employees. Employers must grant leave for the rather large class of qualifying employees. This places pressure on employers to hire temporary covering workers or to reassign work to other employees.[42] Unlike Title VII, nothing prohibits transferring work to

---

[41] See *TWA v. Hardison*, 432 U.S. 63, 84 (1977); *Planned Parenthood v. Casey*, 505 U.S. 833, 837 (1992).

[42] Under the FMLA, employers must reinstate leave-taking employees to their original position (including status, wages, and benefits) unless they fall within the top 10 per cent of the pay scale and reinstatement would cause the employer grievous injury (FMLA §2614). Employers under Title VII need not accommodate if accommodation would impose a greater than negligible cost. So, employers do not have to hire temporary replacement workers under Title VII, but they may have to to meet FMLA requirements. See Department of Labor, 'Balancing the Needs' (41 per cent of employers hire temporary workers to cover the work of FMLA leave-takers).

other employees. So far, it is the most common way employers cover the work of leave-takers.[43]

I think something in between these is appropriate. Title VII falls short, I think, by excusing employers from incurring more than the most minimal burdens.[44] This follows in part from a narrow view of what constitutes discrimination, but in part from a narrow view of accommodation—seeing it only as serving anti-discrimination goals and not as serving other purposes. The FMLA goes too far, on the other hand, by permitting the burdens of accommodation to fall particularly hard on specific individuals. A more egalitarian approach would aim to place the burden on the company and have mechanisms to protect against the burden falling disproportionately hard on particular, individual shoulders or groups. These are costs we should attempt to share together, roughly, within a larger system exhibiting reciprocity.[45]

These suggestions convey the flavour of my answer to the second question: Is a distributive system that makes room for accommodation still egalitarian? Why doesn't the argument for accommodation show that egalitarianism should be rejected or trumped in some circumstances?

The short answer is this: A system that distributes resources on criteria that are luck-insensitive, but that also incorporates accommodation measures, is none the less egalitarian, because it aims to eliminate the influence of factors that are arbitrary from a moral point of view and irrelevant to our status as equals. Second, its departures from choice-sensitivity are in the service of providing an equal opportunity for freedom.

---

[43] See n. 10.

[44] See also Greenawalt, 'Title VII and Religious Liberty', 21.

[45] Some legal commentators raise even broader concerns that contemporary approaches to accommodation may yield reduced job opportunities or reduced wages for discrete groups—often, broadly speaking, the groups the law aims to protect. Samuel Issacharoff and Elyse Rosenblum, 'Women and the Workplace: Accommodating the Demands of Pregnancy', Columbia Law Review 94 (1994), 2154–2220, at 2192 (by putting the burdens of leave on firms, the FMLA may create adverse incentives against hiring women). But see Christine Jolls, 'Accommodation Mandates', Stanford Law Review 53 (2000), 223–306, at 285 and 292 (arguing that in certain markets, accommodation mandates may be more likely to result in wage reductions than hiring discrimination, and that analysis of accommodation laws must also look to the interaction with anti-discrimination statutes). See also Case, 'How High the Apple Pie?' My argument is consistent with suggestions for broader regulatory reforms that preserve accommodation but aim to spread its costs to a larger population. Whether such suggestions should be implemented depends on further facts, such as the pattern of burdens imposed by other accommodation schemes and whether their combined effect is to achieve reciprocity.

A slightly longer answer to the question would return us to the initial motivations for the inclusion of choice-sensitivity in the formula: first, that the distributive system aims not to reflect morally arbitrary factors, but choice is a morally relevant factor; second, lapses in choice-sensitivity threaten to put one person to work for another, serving her purposes, and this generates hierarchy.

Systems including accommodation need not run afoul of either motivation. Accommodation practices serve the purpose of facilitating a certain sort of freedom. In this respect, they are not driven by a morally arbitrary feature. They do not violate the primarily negative aim that the distributive system's features and outcomes should not reflect morally arbitrary factors. Second, if suitably general and diverse, accommodation practices need not subordinate one person to another or put one person to work for another. Well-designed structures of accommodation can manifest reciprocity by spreading costs among many of us and accommodating a diverse range of activities. The purpose of accommodating is also relevant. The point of accommodation is to provide a certain sort of access to freedom, not to support particular choices or outcomes. These features make it difficult to view accommodation practices as putting one group to work for another's purposes. Rather, we together share burdens for the purpose of facilitating meaningful freedom.[46]

---

[46] I am grateful to many friends and colleagues for help and criticism, especially Paula Casal, G. A. Cohen, Michael Dorf, Ronald Dworkin, Kent Greenawalt, Barbara Herman, Samuel Issacharoff, Christopher Kutz, Gillian Lester, Samuel Scheffler, Steven Shiffrin, Judith Jarvis Thomson, Jonathan Wilwerding, and the members of the Los Angeles Law and Philosophy Group. I have benefited enormously from research assistance from Alissa Kolek and Dustin Osborn. I have also benefited from the reactions of accommodating audiences at Boston University School of Law; MIT; the NYU Philosophy Department and the NYU Colloquium on Law, Philosophy, and Political Theory; Princeton; the University of California at Berkeley; the University of San Diego School of Law; the University of Southern California; and the University of Virginia School of Law.

13

Raz on the Intelligibility of Bad Acts

Michael Stocker

One of the central unifying themes of Joseph Raz's *Engaging Reason: On the Theory of Value and Action* is a presentation and defence of what he calls the *classical* as opposed to the *rationalist* conception of human agency.[1] Raz likens the classical view to the views held by Plato and Aristotle, crediting Elizabeth Anscombe's *Intention* with its modern formulation and interest.[2] A central issue of the debate between classical and rationalist accounts is whether desire in itself, mere desire, provides a reason for action, or whether reasons have to do with what is good (independently, that is, of desire). As Anscombe says in *Intention*, § 38, 'the question "What do you want that for?" arises—until at last we reach the desirability characterization, about which "What do you want that for?" does not arise, or if it is asked has not the same point.' An alternative, general form of Anscombe's question, 'What do you want that for?' is 'What's the *good* of that?' According to the classical view, if there is no good in doing that, there is no reason to do it, and thus, it cannot be done for a reason, and only what is done for a reason is intelligible. This great set of issues in ethics and theories of agency finds Aristotelians and Kantians on one side and Humeans on the other. (Perhaps strangely, Humeans are rationalists,

---

[1] Joseph Raz, *Engaging Reason: On the Theory of Value and Action* (Oxford: Oxford University Press, 1999).

[2] Ibid. 22; G. E. M. Anscombe, *Intention* (Oxford: Blackwell, 1957).

and Kantians are not rationalists but, with Platonists and Aristotelians, classicists.)

I count myself as a follower of Aristotle, and someone who has been strongly influenced by Anscombe, but I think I disagree with Raz—both in his interpretation of Aristotle and Anscombe and also in some of his claims about the nature of reasons for action. I certainly disagree with one of his general claims, since I hold, and he denies, that we can intelligibly desire the bad.[3] I say I *think* I disagree with him on other points because I am often unsure what his positions are. In what follows, when I say I disagree with him, that can be taken as advancing various interpretations and asking whether they are correct.

The area of dispute concerns whether reasons for action must 'have to do with', be 'aimed at', the good, that we always act *sub specie boni*, or whether what is bad or neutral or something outside the realm of value can provide reasons for action. Raz's view can be summarized by the conjoint claim that acts are intelligible only if they are done for reasons, and that only what is good provides reasons. It is hard to explicate his claim. In part, this is because his accounts are given in terms of a cluster of tightly interconnected notions: intelligibility, reason, goodness, activity, people as active (versus passive), and what one identifies with. To understand any of these, the others must be understood; but for that, that first one must be understood.

By the same token, questions about any of these may allow us to break into this cluster, leading us to questions, and perhaps answers, about the others. In what follows, I will focus on intelligibility. I do not claim a full understanding of how Raz understands intelligibility, and I realize that I may often use that notion where he would not. My hope is that my discussion of intelligibility will be a useful way to break into that cluster of terms, to illuminate and test them and Raz's uses of them.

One of the main concerns of chapter 2 of *Engaging Reason*, 'Agency, Reason, and the Good', is the objection that what is, and is seen as, bad can serve as reasons—reasons that make for intelligibility. For simplicity I will call these reasons or 'reasons' *reasons*$_{bad}$, similarly for *reasons*$_{good}$. Raz considers whether, as an opponent to the classical view might hold, a person can intend to harm another person—not because he thinks this

---

[3] See my 'Desiring the Bad: An Essay in Moral Psychology', *Journal of Philosophy* 76 (1979), 738–53.

would be good, nor because he thinks justice requires it, nor for the pleasure of seeing it, but just for the harm. 'The objection ... is aimed at the classical approach, while accepting the common assumption, that is, the assumption that reasons make actions eligible by making their choice intelligible from the point of view of their agents.'[4]

Before commenting on the relations between eligibility and intelligibility, some clarification is needed about the agent's point of view. When concerned with the agent's point of view, we are concerned with how the agent sees the act, with how the act is identified by the agent, and, according to Raz, with considerations which the agent identifies him- or herself with. (The last is brought out most clearly in chapter 1 of *Engaging Reason*, 'When We Are Ourselves'.) Further, Raz holds, these are considerations which, if they held, would show the act good—in the present case show that the harming is good, by showing, for example, that the other person deserves to be hurt or that hurting him restores the balance.

Raz does not require that the harm *is* deserved or restorative of balance. Rather, the agent must *believe* that this is so. Now, we may well agree that the agent's believing the harming deserved or restorative of balance makes the harming intelligible. But, as will be argued below, we need not think, as Raz seems to, that what the agent believes deserved or believes restorative of balance is good or believed good. Thus, we need not agree that goodness is needed for intelligibility.

Before taking this up, however, we should ask how Raz's intelligible agent believes the act good. One question this asks is, 'What, on Raz's view, is the agent's *evaluative* point of view?' One possible understanding that goes well with a view that intelligible acts are always *sub specie boni* is that the agent believes the act to be good. However, as I now understand Raz, this is not his view. (This is all to the good, for that requirement is implausible on its face and for many reasons given below.) His view is that the agent believes the act to be of a certain sort, which sort is good, whether or not the agent believes it good. Commenting on my Conference presentation, Raz writes,

Stocker is mistaken to think that I attribute a kind of high order reflectiveness to people: for example that they not only think of their actions as pleasurable or thrilling or beneficial to X or Y, etc. but also think of them as good in virtue of possessing those properties. All I ever claimed is that people act for

---

[4] Raz, *Engaging Reason*, 26–7.

considerations which we classify as a belief in the possession of a good making property.[5]

Using brackets to mark the scope of the belief, the view he rejects is that the agent must believe <the act is good>. His view is that the agent must believe <the act to be of a given sort, F> and Fs are good. The latter is satisfied whether or not the agent believes that this F or Fs in general are good. Were that belief required, goodness would, once again, be within the scope of the belief. As I will argue, this moving of the evaluation outside the scope of the belief has the consequence of either making goodness unnecessary for intelligibility, or of making us call unintelligible much of what is intelligible.

It also has the further consequence of suggesting a mysterious relation between goodness, on the one hand, and reasons, reasoning, and intelligibility, on the other. If the goodness is outside the scope of the agent's belief—if, that is, it is irrelevant whether the agent takes account of, even takes note of, the goodness—how does the goodness make for intelligibility? (This assumes that intelligibility is *available* to the agent, and is not, in this way, like truth: a belief can be true whether or not the agent takes account of, or even takes note of, that.)

To show these problems, let us start in a way that seems to justify or at least motivate moving the goodness outside the scope of the belief. In good practical reasoning we often see no need to advert to an act's goodness in deciding whether or not to do it. Often enough, it is sufficient to advert to what makes for the goodness. For example, in deciding whether to read a particular book, it may be sufficient to advert to how important it is to my area of interest. I do not mean that that is all that need be considered—that, for example, I do not have to consider how reading it will preclude my fulfilling pressing obligations—but only that I need not go further and note that its importance makes it good.

Continuing this line of thought—and omitting many steps—we come to something like the following view: an act is intelligible only if the agent believes <the act to be an F and thus to have certain features> which features are good-making. As indicated by the brackets, the agent need not believe the features to be good-making. If the agent must believe <the act to be an F and thus to have certain features *which features are good-making*>, goodness has, once again, been moved within the scope of the belief.

<hr />

[5] p. 7 n. 7 of his reply to the Conference presentations.

This leaves us with many issues about the dispensability of explicit evaluative thoughts—including for comparisons, 'this is *better* than that'. But that is not our present problem.

Our present problem concerns these *F*s, in particular their nature and existence. The *F*s are such that to believe that they are instantiated is to believe that certain features, which are good-making features (whether or not conceived of as good-making), are thus instantiated. Are there any such *F*s? And if there are, are they necessary for intelligibility?

These questions are very like traditional questions about naturalism. For what we need is a characterization of the act which the agent believes and which, if it does obtain, ensures that the act is good; but where, following Raz's stricture, the belief that the act is good is not or need not be included in that characterization. For the sake of argument, let us assume that there are some such characterizations. The question for us is whether characterizations which do not in this way ensure goodness also allow for intelligibility.

To answer this, let us assume that harming someone can be intelligible if it is done to effect an equitable resolution of a conflict—if, that is, our agent harms another person because, as he believes, so doing will effect an equitable resolution of a conflict. Let us further assume that there is a non-evaluative, perhaps naturalistic, characterization of the act such that if the act is as characterized, it is equitable and thus good. (Our issue is whether Raz is correct, not whether, for example, naturalism is correct.) For simplicity, let us further assume that (at least some) correct characterizations, correct understandings, of equitable resolutions are such characterizations. To see whether Raz is right that intelligibility requires goodness—that only acts that are *sub specie boni* are intelligible—we can ask whether only such characterizations of equitable resolutions make for intelligibility.

As I see matters, the answer is No. Those are not the only sorts of characterizations of equitable resolutions that make for intelligibility. To start with, it should be clear that there are other sorts of intentions to effect an equitable resolution—made *other* by the contents of the intention. I have in mind cases where the agents have a mistaken, perhaps a deformed, conception of what an equitable resolution is. From these agents' points of view, they are intending to effect an equitable resolution. But what they intend is not, in fact, equitable. By this last, I mean that if they effect exactly what they have in mind, they may well think they have effected an equitable resolution, but what they have in fact effected will not be equitable, and perhaps not good. None the less, as I see matters, their acts can be intelligible.

As put, my argument requires that, despite being mistaken, their misconceptions are close enough to correct conceptions—close enough that their misconceptions of equitability are accurate enough to count as conceptions of equitability. As an example, we could consider people who are like the agents with correct understandings of equitability, with the exception that they will defer to their elders in cases of dispute. I think we can assume that in at least many of the cases where the elders get things wrong, what is intended is, in fact, not equitable and not good. Here we have a characterization or mischaracterization of an act as equitable where, if an act is as characterized, it may well not be equitable and not good. (I say 'may well not be', not 'are', since elders can be right, and even where wrong, they may be wrong in harmless ways.)

None the less, I think that acts with such characterizations—whether or not they are equitable and good—are intelligible. Indeed, to suggest that they must be unintelligible is to suggest that much of traditional or tradition-bound thought and action is unintelligible. It is one thing to hold that such thought is mistaken, precisely because of its reliance on tradition. It is quite another thing to hold, implausibly, that it must be unintelligible—much less that it is unintelligible because it relies on tradition.

I am here taking it that to be concerned with agents' points of view is to be concerned with their understandings—here *mis*understandings—of the category, the *F*, in question. This is to say that in these cases we cannot substitute correct understandings of what *F*s are for the mistaken understandings agents have. Where we do make such a substitution, it is unclear to what extent we are still concerned with the agent's point of view.

Some might object that this makes intentions too subjective, too much a matter of what is in the agent's head or mind (to invoke Putnam). The objection would be that if a person does intend to achieve an equitable resolution, then what the person intends to achieve is an equitable resolution, and what that is, is determined by the correct, the public, meaning of 'equitable resolution', and not by what the person incorrectly or even correctly thinks an equitable resolution is.

I am unsure of the force of this objection when applied, as it is here, to intentions, not meanings. There is, however, no need to pursue it. All that need be done to accommodate it is to hold that, in so far as it is correct, we should simply recast the argument. Instead of considering a person who has a misunderstanding of Fs, we should consider a person who is intending something else, an F*, where the agent's mistaken conception of F is a correct conception of F*. Keeping with the aim of the argument, we can also require that F* is close enough to F. So, some might want to say that the people just considered do not have a conception of equitability, but only of traditional-equitability. (For simplicity, I will continue to write as if we can consider people who have some mistaken conceptions of F none the less to have conceptions of F. Those who are bothered by this should recast the argument in terms of appropriate F*s.)

I want now to turn away from Fs that are explicitly good, like equitable resolutions, and consider Fs which are conditionally good, good in certain circumstances or given certain conditions. Let us consider agents who mistake what those circumstances are, or who do not care whether or not relevant circumstances obtain. As above, my argument against Raz would have us consider cases where these mistakes are small enough to allow that the agents do, in fact, believe their act to be an F, but large enough so that its instantiation as conceived by them may well not be good. (The above worry has less bite here. But again, we can recast the argument in terms of the appropriate F*s.) None the less, the acts, even when not good, can be intelligible.

For examples here, we can start with our case of harming another person. Harming another person can be good, given certain conditions: for example, it is a deserved punishment, it is proportional to the offence, it is done at the right time, in the right manner, and so on. Absent those conditions, it can be bad. Yet it can be intelligible, for example, on account of hatred. Indeed, hatred can explain why the agent did not care that or whether the good-making conditions failed to obtain.

For other examples, we can consider doing what one thinks good, or following one's conscience, or seeking pleasure, or acting out of love. As I see matters, each of these can be good or bad, depending on the circumstances. On my view, acting from an evil or even a seriously mistaken conscience or conception of the good can be bad, not good. Indeed, I think it can be entirely bad, with no redeeming features, not even that it was thought good or was conscientious. Consider here people who think it only fair that if they suffer, then everyone deserves to suffer; or consider people whose consciences dictate killing non-believers.

Similarly, I think that sadistic pleasure is bad. It, too, can be through and through bad, with no redeeming features, not even that of being a pleasure. Examples are, unfortunately, too easy to come by. So too, I think that some acts done from, and characteristic of, deformed senses of love, such as cases of violent possessiveness, are bad. They, too, need have no good features, not even that of being done from love. Consider here someone who batters or kills his beloved, rather than let her leave him.

I mention these *Fs* because they are often enough cited as making for intelligibility. I have in mind such claims as 'I did that because I thought justice required it', 'I did that because my elders told me to', 'I did that because my conscience required it of me', 'I did that because I thought it good', 'I did that because it was pleasant', and 'I did that because I love her'.

Many steps of the argument are left unarticulated and unargued. I have not argued that we cannot substitute a more accurate understanding of the *Fs* for the mistaken ones. Nor have I argued that these acts—intending $<Fs>$ that are mistakenly understood, or intending $<Fs>$ absent the conditions in which they are good, or intending $<F^*s>$—are, none the less, intelligible. Some of what I say below, especially about Aristotelian teleology and bad second natures, bears on these issues.

To aid our understanding of these and related issues, some other points should be mentioned. The first is that when I say that the agent believes the act good (or bad or neutral), I do not restrict my claim to, nor do I exclude, *moral* goodness (or badness or neutrality). I leave it open, as Raz does, how we understand goodness. We are both concerned with such high-level categories as doing, having, and being—with what it is good to do or to have or to be. Neither of us is concerned with such questions as whether an intelligible desire for a table, say, must be a desire for a good table—unless that bears on the goodness or intelligibility of, say, having or keeping a table.

Second, I see it as an open and important question whether the intelligibility of an act can depend on its actual or believed evaluative or moral status, including its actual or believed moral goodness, badness, or neutrality. So, for example, if people want to do their duty, that may, as such, make for intelligibility. More generally, some acts are clearly intelligible in virtue of their explicit concern with value, not with some other sort, F. For example, I might want to do something that will benefit you, without having yet come to any more specific or concrete view of what to do in order to accomplish that goal.

This raises again, but in a different way, the issue of when and how, especially on Raz's view, explicit evaluative beliefs are relevant for intelligibility. Here we would have to consider whether there are different intelligibility considerations for (i) John believes his act <to be F> and Fs are good, and (i′) John believes his act <to be F and bad> and Fs are good, or for (ii) John believes his act <to be F> and Fs are bad, and (ii′) John believes his act <to be F and good> and Fs are bad.

Third, and finally, although I sometimes write in ways suggesting that the goodness is or is not within the scope of the agent's belief, those claims can be easily modified to take account of the issues just discussed.

I turn now to *eligibility*. As Raz uses the term, an act is eligible just in case it may justifiably be done. Quite generally, an eligible act will be one among many acts any one of which may, with justification, be done. The issue for us is how Raz moves between intelligibility and eligibility, how he holds that only what makes for eligibility makes for intelligibility.

Even if we agree that reasons$_{bad}$ do not make for eligibility, why should we think that they do not make for intelligibility? And even if we agree that reasons$_{good}$ do make for eligibility, why should we think that they make for intelligibility? We find one of Raz's answers in the following:

The difficulty in explaining the eligibility of actions in ways other than by reference to good-making qualities may make one doubt the objection. But is it just failure of imagination which makes the classical approach seem the only coherent account to have? I do not think so. The problem is of finding conceptual room for an alternative. Suppose we concede the objection and allow that one has reason to hurt others. It would seem to follow that those who do not hurt others, or who deny the fact that an action would hurt others is in and of itself a reason to perform it, are irrational or at least imperfectly rational, for they fail to acknowledge such reasons. If cogent this argument constitutes a refutation of the objection, its *reductio ad absurdam*.[6]

Making a related point, he writes:

But does this way of explaining reasons independently of value preserve the normativity of reasons? Does it account for the fact that defying reasons is irrational, that one may disregard a reason only to follow a more stringent one? The problem is not in the reality of the example the objector produces in support. The problem is in providing a coherent account of reasons, which allows for agents (a) believing that possession of properties other than good-making properties can provide

[6] Raz, *Engaging Reason*, 28.

reasons for actions, and (b) allow for the normative force of reasons, i.e., for the fact that failure to conform to them is a fault.[7]

I agree with the general claim that acting on a reason$_{bad}$ is bad. I am uncertain that it is always foolish. I disagree with the general claim that it is a fault, that it is bad or foolish, not to act on a reason$_{good}$ (unless acting on a better and incompossible reason$_{good}$).[8]

I also disagree with the general claim that it is irrational, or imperfectly rational, to act on a reason$_{bad}$ or not to act on a reason$_{good}$ (again, un$_{less}$ acting on a better and incompossible reason$_{good}$). To make only one point here, not all moral changes, or even all moral advances, are changes or improvements in rationality. This holds whether the moral change or advance is discovering new reasons, or coming to accept, or coming to accept and act on, previously recognized reasons. For example, I may think that equal schooling for boys and girls is a moral requirement—that I have a reason$_{good}$ to provide my daughter with the same education as I provide my son—but not think that those who, several hundred years ago, did not see this are irrational or imperfectly rational. But they did not acknowledge such reasons. Much the same holds for people nowadays who do not accept or do not act on this principle. I need not think them irrational or imperfectly rational. I can think they have other defects.

Put in terms of the example in question, my claim is that people who think harming another is a reason need not hold that anyone who disagrees is irrational or imperfectly rational. They might charge only a lack of imagination, or being too innocent or naïve or 'too good' or too simple.

Taking another tack, they might suggest that this reason, like many reasons, is a reason only for those who are inclined in certain ways. It would be like the beauty of Paris giving me a reason to visit it. It does, but I need not be irrational in not going to Paris—now or at any time. I may not be inclined to visit it or seek out that sort of beauty—now or at any time.

Against the latter, Raz says, 'The refutation cannot be avoided by claiming that bad-making properties are permissive reasons. They are not, and it is wrong to follow them.'[9] I wish Raz had said more on this—if only

---

[7] Ibid.

[8] See my *Plural and Conflicting Values* (Oxford: Oxford University Press, 1990) for arguments that quite generally we may faultlessly not do what is best or what we have most and strongest reason to do.

[9] Raz, *Engaging Reason*, 28.

to avoid seeming to miss the point. After all, the discussion starts with the knowledge that it is wrong or at least bad to act on those reasons$_{bad}$. But the question is whether they make for intelligibility.

So, I do not agree that all reasons, including reasons$_{bad}$, must have normative force in the sense of being aimed at the good. None the less, I think they can have normative force in other ways. Here are some of these ways. The person with that reason$_{bad}$ may regret, and think he deserves being chided or mocked for, not having the courage of his convictions when he acts against it or when he simply fails to act on it. Similarly, he may congratulate himself when, despite pressure to the contrary, he acts on it. He may, in this sense, show that he thinks the reason$_{bad}$ is *to be acted on*.

Further, a reason$_{bad}$ can play the role of a standard of what will be attempted. It can (help) show whether the person or act succeeded or failed. It can serve in or as a prelude to the deliberations typical of practical reasoning. It can be pursued with tact, intelligence, nuance, critical assessment of alternative means, and so on. As R. Jay Wallace comments, 'People sometimes exhibit great intelligence and skill in executing plans that they view as dubious or questionable—think, for instance, of the extraordinary talent many of us display at procrastinating when it comes to tasks that we regard as worthy but difficult.'[10]

So far I have been offering some worries about particular claims Raz makes. I want now to offer some more general views which underlie those criticisms. My overall aim here will be to show that what makes for intelligibility in action is being able to answer Anscombe's question, 'What do you want that for?' in a certain way. Raz holds that this way is, or includes, that, according to the agent's lights, it is good. I will argue that although sometimes that does provide a satisfactory answer, often it does not. I will also argue that citing what is bad or is seen as bad can sometimes suffice. It will take some time to establish these points, so I ask for a bit of patience while a number of seemingly disparate issues are raised.

I start with a commonplace. If I hate you, it may well be intelligible that I want to harm you—not to restore the balance or because you deserve it,

---

[10] 'Normativity, Commitment, and Instrumental Reason', R. Jay Wallace, *Philosophers' Imprint* vol. 1, no. 3 (2001), 1 <*www.philosophersimprint.org/001003*>. This is directed against a claim made by Christine Korsgaard that, in effect anyway, is very similar to Raz's present claim. As Wallace puts it, this is 'a moralizing tendency ... [to hold] that instrumental requirements come on the scene only in relation to ends that have themselves been endorsed in some way by the agent, as ends that it would be good or desirable to achieve' (p. 1).

nor for the pleasure of it, but simply because I hate you. To my mind, wanting to harm what one hates is as intelligible as wanting to benefit what one loves. Further, in order for my hate-inspired harm to be intelligible, I need not believe that the harm or my hate is good. In saying this, I allow that some cases of hate are unintelligible. And I also allow that any such unintelligibility might be transferred to pursuing that harm. My claim is only that enough cases of hate and harming on account of hate are intelligible.

Much the same can be argued for by focusing on pleasure and pain; but the case seems easier to make with hate. Let me explain both parts of this claim. I start with the thought that it is relatively easy to make hate intelligible. 'Mere history' or happenstance can often enough make hate intelligible. Indeed, 'I have always hated him' or 'Our family has always hated his' may be sufficient. But more seems required for intelligible pleasure and pain.

This last can be shown by noting that many pleasures and pains must be understood in terms of values and disvalues: my pleasure at the English victory at Waterloo can be understood only in terms of my valuing that victory or something associated with it. Without some such valuing, that pleasure is unintelligible (or misdescribed). And if, as may be, it is unintelligible for me to have certain values, my (real or supposed) pleasure involving those values may also be unintelligible; so too for a supposed reason based on that pleasure.

Further, some pleasures, including pleasure taken in harm, may be difficult to understand. As Anscombe writes in *Intention*,

Hobbes [*Leviathan*, Part 1, ch. VI] believed, perhaps wrongly, that there could be no such thing as pleasure in mere cruelty, simply in another's suffering; but he was not *so* wrong as we are likely to think. He was wrong in suggesting that cruelty had to have an end, but it does have to have a point. To depict this pleasure, people evoke notions of power, or perhaps of getting one's own back on the world, or perhaps of sexual excitement. No one needs to surround the pleasures of food and drink with such explanations.[11]

Her claim might seem to support Raz. But, as I will argue below, it does not. Rather it supports my claim about what can answer the Anscombian question 'What do you want that for?' In any case, my point in citing this passage is simply to support my claim that there can be a need to show the

---

[11] Anscombe, *Intention*, § 38.

intelligibility of many (supposed or alleged) pleasures and pains, especially if they are to show the intelligibility of acts or reasons.

To show how that passage does support my claim about what can answer the Anscombian question, and to further my criticism of Raz, I want to consider a related case and issue. Suppose that John is well known, both to himself and to others, to be a xenophobe. This, I want to suggest, is sufficient to make intelligible his throwing out Oxfam mailings, not pursuing the goods they put forward. But suppose that one day he responds generously, with a $500 cheque. Does the goodness of this or his believing it good make his response intelligible? My question must be taken as assuming that his evaluative views can be taken as remaining constant: he always thought it good to alleviate hunger, whether near or far; he just did not like, could not abide, foreigners.

The question for us is not 'Why did he contribute?', but 'Is his contributing intelligible?', or 'Is it made intelligible by his seeing it as good?' As I see matters, his contributing is not intelligible, not even though he sees it as good. As I also see matters, his hating foreigners makes his earlier non-contributions intelligible. Here I may be able to answer 'Why was it intelligible?' The answer is already given: he hates the recipients. For that reason, aiding them does not attract him. He does not desire it. It goes against his settled custom. It does not suit him. If something along these lines is correct, then at least in this and similar cases, we need something, perhaps like care and interest, to make for intelligibility.

Sometimes care and interest can simply be assumed. On the assumption that I am well brought up, with adequate love and care for others, my caring for and responding appropriately to the well-being of others can be assumed, so the intelligibility of my contributing to Oxfam can be assumed. That is why my story had it that John is a xenophobe.

My goal here is not to argue that in every case where pursuing something—whether good or bad—is intelligible, there must be a concomitant or underlying care and interest. To modify a point made by Christine Korsgaard, it might well be foolish to think that we need such care or interest to explain why people adding $2 + 2$ come up with 4. But perhaps it is not so foolish. Perhaps we need to exclude people who do not care whether they get things right.[12]

---

[12] My thanks to Daniel Nolan for discussion here.

I do not think that goodness or badness, or all goods and bads, must engage or repel all agents. As just suggested, I do not think that benefit or harm must engage agents. Indeed, contrary to what might be thought, I am strongly inclined to agree with Raz, and, we should note, with Anscombe on Hobbes, that 'He did it just for the sake of the harm' in certain cases may be unintelligible. That, I suggest, is why it is so natural to make the harming intelligible by assuming hatred: 'I hate him, that's why I want to harm him.'

But on my view, this does not show an asymmetry between bads and goods; nor does it support Raz's classical account. It does not do either, because even if it does show that this bad requires something like hatred, it leaves untouched the issue of whether a good, such as that provided by supporting Oxfam, requires something similar, too. And, to repeat, just as I find it difficult to understand the 'bare' pursuit of harm—without hate, for example—I find at least some cases of the bare pursuit of benefit equally hard to understand.

If this is right, the difficulties in understanding the bare pursuit of harm need not be taken as showing that reasons$_{bad}$ fail to make for intelligibility. To be sure, pursuing harm may well be unintelligible. But what makes for unintelligibility here may not to be the badness of the harm. What makes for unintelligibility may be its unconnectedness with the agents, their not caring about it. When goods, or at least some goods, are similarly cut loose from care, they too may well not make for intelligibility. When connected with care, both harm and benefit may make for intelligibility.

This line of thought would also go some way toward answering a very probing question which Raz asks his objector: If on your view, bads, not just goods, can make for intelligibility, why cannot what is neutral also make for intelligibility?[13] Better put, my line of thought would not so much answer that question as it would transform it into a question about why we care about only what is good or bad, and not also about what is neutral.

But I think there are desires for what is neutral that can make for intelligibility. Consider the desire that an obsessive compulsive person has to put all the items on his desk in a rigid, regular order. That order, though better than wild disorder, seems neutral, neither good nor bad. And turning now to evaluative beliefs, it may well seem neutral, both to

---

[13] Raz, *Engaging Reason*, 29, section (d).

us and to that person. However, once we know what sort of person that person is, we can find his work on his desk intelligible. Perhaps we should find it odd, neurotic, unfortunate, even bad. We can put this in terms of care: he cares about what he should not care about, or he cares too much about order, or he cares about what even he recognizes is of no value or not worth caring about. But it is intelligible.

I have been arguing that at least certain goods and bads are symmetrical in their need for further desire or care or interest to make for intelligibility. In section 6, 'On What One Need Not Explain about Normativity' of chapter 5 of *Engaging Reason*, 'Reason and the Will', Raz offers an argument that might seem to reject this claim of symmetry. (I say 'might seem' since it is concerned with a different, albeit related, issue.) He summarizes the claim of this section thus: 'But to the extent that the question is merely of why we followed reason the answer is simply that we are rational.'[14]

Perhaps transforming, perhaps misapplying, his argument to present concerns, I think that he holds that the intelligibility of doing what is bad always requires recourse to some further consideration, which consideration makes for goodness, but that the intelligibility of doing what is good requires no further consideration. We are rational beings, and to be rational is simply to respond appropriately to circumstances, without the need for further considerations. To respond appropriately, to have the appropriate intention, is, in Raz's view, to have all the desire that is needed to explain doing the act. He calls this *thin* desire, which is shown and in fact constituted by, simply, intending.[15]

Central to Raz's claim is his understanding of a capacity and its exercise. If someone has a capacity, he says, we do not need an account of that person's exercising it correctly. So, if Mary can see—has that capacity—we do not need a further account of how or why in broad daylight she sees the tree that is thirty feet away from her. But given her capacity and those conditions, we would need an account of her not seeing it. By not needing a further account, I mean that we have already explained her seeing the tree when we said that she has the capacity to see and exercises it appropriately on appropriate objects in appropriate circumstances.

Without going into the complexities of capacities and their exercise, I hope the following is an adequate reply to Raz. Perhaps it is true that if a

---

[14] Raz, *Engaging Reason*, 117.

[15] See, e.g., Raz, *Engaging Reason*, 115–16.

being is necessarily rational, then citing that being's rationality is sufficient to explain its doing what is rational. But matters seem different when concerned with beings that, though rational, are not necessarily rational. Here it can be important, even essential, to explain why it was then and there doing what is rational. So, if John is only sometimes rational, but has the capacity to be rational—in these two ways, he is a typical humanly rational animal—I do not see that 'doing that was rational' need explain or make intelligible why he did it. It can leave unanswered the pressing question of why then and there he exercised that capacity. This, I suggest, is our position in regard to our xenophobe who contributed to Oxfam.

There is another theme—which I will call the *Aristotelian teleological* theme—and line of argument that may help tie together some themes I find in Raz. Its main claims are that in an important sense of 'natural' (and thus of 'necessary'), it is natural for a being of a certain sort—for example, human or wolf or orchid—to do what is good for it. Indeed, we can identify what is natural for it to do, and how it is natural for it to be, only by understanding what it is for it to live well and be a good human, wolf, or orchid.

As Philippa Foot puts it in *Natural Goodness*:

We start from the fact that it is the particular life form of a species of plant or animal that determines how an individual plant or animal should be.... And all the truths about what this or that characteristic does, what its purpose or point is, and in suitable cases its function, must be related to this life cycle. The way an individual *should be* is determined by what is needed for development, self-maintenance, and reproduction[16]

And '*Goodness* in plants and animals nests in an interlocking set of general concepts such as *species, life, death, reproduction*, and *nourishment*.'[17]

And, finally,

In spite of the diversity of human goods—the elements that can make up good human lives—it is therefore possible that the concept of a good human life plays the same part in determining goodness of human characteristics and operations

---

[16] Philippa Foot, *Natural Goodness* (Oxford: Oxford University Press, 2001), 32–3, emphasis in original. See also two works Foot cites: Rosalind Hursthouse, *On Virtue Ethics* (Oxford: Oxford University Press, 1999), and Michael Thompson, 'The Representation of Life', in Rosalind Hursthouse, Warrey Quinn, and Gavin Lawrence (eds.), *Virtues and Reasons* (Oxford: Oxford University Press, 1995), 246–96.

[17] Foot, *Natural Goodness*, 36, emphasis in original.

that the concept of flourishing plays in the determination of goodness in plants and animals.[18]

Of central importance to us is the conjoint claim that we understand what is good for a being by understanding its species being, and also that it is natural for any being to seek its good. When the being does not seek its good, that can often be understood only in terms of its being in unnatural circumstances or its being defective—not defective in general, if that even has a meaning, but defective in ways specific to, and understandable only in terms of, that sort of being. The last holds that there are specifically human ways for humans to be defective: for example, to have certain neuroses.

Using Foot, we can advance a claim similar to Raz's, if it is not Raz's: all we need do to explain a human seeking a human good is to see that it is a human doing the seeking. But to explain a human seeking what is a human bad, we need to cite both that it is a human and that it is defective (perhaps in a certain way). Thus, we cannot understand how just on its own a human bad can attract a human. But we can understand how just on its own a human good can attract a human.

I find this line of thought powerful and attractive. But I do not want to defend or criticize it. I want to comment on how it fits with Raz's claims.

It may be that we get the fullest, best understanding—perhaps the only adequate understanding—of humans in terms of good humans, living good lives. None the less, Aristotelian-influenced theorists can hold that to understand people, we must understand how people develop, in particular the earlier stages from which humans develop, both well and poorly. This, too, may require starting with good humans. For it may well be that we can identify those multi-potential earlier stages only by starting our investigations with good humans, with humans whose second nature is good, and identifying and examining their developmentally earlier stages.

But once we understand those earlier stages and how development can go well or poorly, and thus how a person's second nature can be good or bad, we can understand as intelligible many bad acts as natural, that is, second natural, for a human who has developed in a relevant defective way. Perhaps the Aristotelian—as opposed to the Platonic—claim to make is that we can understand pursuing the good on its own, that is, without

---

[18] Ibid. 44.

further desire; but similarly, we can understand pursuing the bad on its own. 'All' that is required in both cases is that we be concerned with a person whose second nature is of the relevant sort.

This allows, but does not require, that we can understand how a bad second nature works—how it provides goals and how its reasoning proceeds—by likening it to a good second nature. So taken, we would understand how, say, greed works by understanding how liberality works—in particular, how a deformed sort of liberality works. This also allows, but does not require, that we can understand how a bad second nature works only if it is not too different from a good second nature. A second nature which is too bad, or too different from a good one, may force us to see the person as a beast or otherwise inhuman.

As incomplete as these comments are, I want to draw some tentative conclusions from them. First, it may be that the classical view is correct for and about good people, but another view, perhaps the rationalist view, is correct for and about other sorts of people. So, it might turn out that to explain why Jack, who is not a good person, does what is good, we do need to posit some desire that goes beyond the goodness or believed goodness of that act. None the less, to explain why Jane, who is a good person, does what is good, we might not need to posit a desire that goes beyond the goodness or believed goodness of the act.

We find this disparity in some of Aristotle's descriptions when we extend our consideration beyond good people to people who are not so good. So, for example, it is a characterizing feature of *enkratics* acting *enkratically* that an account of their doing what is good may make essential use of further desire.

Second, it may be that we understand people who are less than good in terms developed from our understanding of good people. None the less, we may be unable to understand people who are less than good *directly* in terms of good people, as failed-good-people. By the last, I mean that we may not be able to apply to bad people what we can to good people simply plus or minus some corrections. Each sort of person might have to be understood on its own terms, according to it own laws and principles. By analogy, we may be able to understand a particular bad heart, a poorly functioning heart, as a good heart that has gone somewhat bad, or as a good heart with certain difficulties. But we may have to understand another bad heart as a heart which never developed well, perhaps never developed into a real heart.

Third, Aristotelians will think it a mistake to locate the difference between good and bad people in terms of whether or not desire is present and needed to understand action. To be sure, there is a different view (sometimes suggested by Stoics and Kantians) that badness can be ascribed to desire, as such. But for Aristotelians, the sorts and roles of desire, not the presence of just any desire, are relevant.

Aristotelians reject the view that to understand the good person, we do not have to posit desire, especially not desire for the good. True, they will hold that we do not have to posit a further desire. If Jane is a good person and she sees that this would be good, she does not need a further desire to do this. But this is not because desire for the good is unimportant for people like Jane. It is rather that essential to a person's being an Aristotelian good person is having this sort of desire. The Aristotelian good and rational person is a person of desire—again, only certain desires deployed in certain ways, but desire, none the less.

Raz might be willing to accept all or some of these three last claims. He can hold that at least so long as these less-than-good people act—so long as what they do is intelligible to themselves and perhaps to others—they will have to understand their actions in the same, or pretty much the same, terms as good people understand their action. So the less-than-good people will see—mis-see—their acts as just, liberal, and so on. They can accept the question, 'What's the good of that?' And they can answer it in terms of justice, liberality, and so on.

A complete argument against Raz might seem to require explaining—perhaps explaining away—why 'good' comes to be used here. Even if it includes, it goes well beyond, the instrumentally good. Perhaps it is simply a stand-in for 'point' as in 'What's the point of that?' But why is *it* an appropriate stand-in? Perhaps it is that it plays the roles for agents played by human goods in good agents—where, perhaps further, we cannot understand bad reasoning except as a failure of good reasoning.

Taking a different, even if related, tack, perhaps the common applicability of 'What's the good of that?' is tied up with the fact that few of us are willing to see ourselves as not good. This last has to do with the duality of being both social beings and individual beings. As Simon Blackburn notes in his 'How Emotional is the Virtuous Person?', we must take account of the fact that 'What's the good of that?' is often a challenge made to an agent by someone else—a challenge that agents may understandably try to answer in ways acceptable to the challenger.[19] It is also tied up with serious personal and psychological problems people have in believing that they are bad or of little or no worth.

As important as these issues about 'good' in 'What's the good of that?' are, there is another way to complete the argument against Raz. Those of us who think that Anscombe is on the right track in her claims about the need for desirability characterizations would like, perhaps need, a general account of desirability characterizations or a list of at least many of them. I want to locate at least some of them in basic human concerns. As put, this says too little and too much. It may help to note that I would include curiosity, knowledge, understanding, pleasure, power, self-protection, narcissistic concerns, love and hate, acceptance by others. To continue the list, we can examine the traditional virtues and vices and see what are the goals to be achieved or avoided in them, and also the goods characteristic of different lives as traditionally conceived—for example, the life of pleasure, of honour, of knowledge, of spirituality.

I do not want now to pursue a general characterization of desirability characteristics, nor do I want to attempt to list them. I want, rather, to make what I take Anscombe's point to be, and incidentally, say why I think her comments on Hobbes support me, not Raz. We have succeeded in making an act intelligible when we answer 'What's the good of that?' with a desirability characteristic. That something is pleasing, or exciting, or interesting, or a show of power, or...makes for intelligibility from the agent's point of view.

To repeat a point made early in this chapter, I agree with Raz's antirationalist claim that not just any and every desire makes for intelligibility. I think we need desirability characteristics for that. Here we might consider Anscombe's suggestions about the intelligibility of claiming to want a pin. To 'Why do you ask for it?', 'Just to carry it about' seems not to provide intelligibility. But 'To see if you will cater to my every whim' does; so may 'To have something, no matter how small, that I can call my own'. Neither the second nor the third needs to be good or thought good for it to make for intelligibility.

---

[19] Simon Blackburn, 'How Emotional is the Virtuous Person?', in Peter Goldie (ed.), *Understanding Emotions* (Aldershot: Ashgate, 2002), 81–96; e.g., at 87. Blackburn has an extended and very useful discussion of intelligibility and desirability characteristics. My work has benefited from his, both as printed and as heard at the conference 'Understanding Emotions', held in Spring 2000 at London University.

My claim here is not that beliefs in goodness must be irrelevant. Nor is it that such beliefs are always one belief too many. Some people—perhaps good people, or well-socialized people—may not find desirable anything they believe bad. Indeed, some people may not find anything desirable unless they believe it good. And some people will find things desirable in virtue of the things' goodness or believed goodness.

I do not deny the possibility of such people. Rather, I hold that what they find necessary or sufficient for desirability is not necessary or sufficient for intelligibility for all people. Many people find intelligibility just by finding desirability characteristics that are independent of those evaluations.

I now want to bring together the claims that desirability characteristics can make for intelligibility, even if they do not depend on evaluations, and the earlier claims about second natures. This will give us yet another way to question Raz's conjoint claim that acts are intelligible only if they are done for reasons, and that only what is good provides reasons.

Above, I suggested that one reason why his claim might seem correct has to do with difficulties in thinking oneself not good or difficulties in answering the challenging 'What's the good of that?' These difficulties are difficulties of people who want or need to rationalize, want or need to show that their acts are acceptable. They are concerned to show that what they did and they, for doing it, are not really so bad, if bad at all. They thus try to show themselves to be members in good standing of the society of good and well-socialized people, who see that they have something to answer for if they pursue what is bad, and who see that these answers have to take a particular form and have a certain content.

But there are other ways of seeing the world and one's role in it. Here we might consider people who see themselves as out for number one; or who see themselves as tough guys, as ruthless; or who see the world in terms of constant struggle, with people pitted against each other as in the Social Darwinism of the captain in Jack London's *Sea Wolf*; or who see justice as imposed on us by the danger of retaliation, and who would jump at the chance to have Gyges' ring; or who see others more or less as objects to be used and disposed of or to be played with, as we might imagine an absolute tyrant to be; or who, for narcissistic reasons, require being the centre of love and attention; or who believe that striking back is the natural response to being struck; or people given to spite, malice, and contempt.

These people, in larger or smaller areas—perhaps only in regard to the act in question—are not concerned to moralize or rationalize their actions. For them, 'I could get away with it' or 'I thus gained an advantage over him' or 'He harmed me, so I harmed him in return' or 'I was bored' or 'I wasn't getting enough attention' all make for intelligibility. But many of them involve reasons$_{bad}$, and none need involve reasons$_{good}$.

Here I might add that, as I read him, Aristotle accepts this for spite, malice, and contempt (see *Rhetoric* II. 2). And I think he may well be right. Consider a dialogue on spite with one's child.[20]

Child (1): 'I won't go, because then you won't be able to go.'

Parent (1): 'But you'll make yourself unhappy, by not going.'

Child (2): 'At least I'll stop you from going, and that will make you unhappy.'

Parent (2): 'You must think it a matter of justice that we not get what we want. Otherwise you'd not be willing to spite your face by cutting off your nose.'

Child (3): 'No, I just want you to suffer. Justice never entered my thoughts.'

Why is citing justice, as in Parent (2), so natural for *us*? Is it that we—that is, we good people; we parents, trying to socialize our child—try to imagine what would lead us to give up something we want, and we think of a high moral principle, such as justice? Is it also, perhaps, that we are trying to get the child to think in socially approved ways? I think the answer is some combination of these and similar ideas. I am certain it is not, as I think Raz would have it, that absent this, we could not find the child's spiteful act intelligible. Indeed, if the child did act out of a sense of justice, there would be difficulty in understanding the act as spiteful. At most, we could see the child's sense of justice as, itself, spiteful.

To sum up this last line of thought, we do believe many of our acts to be eligible. But that need not be because intelligibility requires that. It can rather be because we explain by justifying in particular ways, ways that require such beliefs. My claim, thus, might be put that good people or people who take themselves to be certain sorts of social beings—people like us or the sorts of people we would like to think we are—are given to rationalizing, perhaps even to moralizing. (This may well be necessary for having the sorts of lives and societies we have and want.)

---

[20] My thanks are owed to Jonathan Adler here.

To extend this line of thinking, I want to suggest that I find a number of disturbing features in Raz's conception of the person—especially the person as active, as differentiated from passive—as presented in chapter 1 of *Engaging Reason*, 'When We Are Ourselves', and his correlative view about reasons. On his view, there is a demand—when put in terms of reasons, a conceptual demand—that agents see their actions as good: people must identify with their reasons, and people can identify, or identify fully, only with what they see as good. (This claim must be in terms of what they *believe* good, not what *is* good.)

To my mind, this suggests a requirement that can too easily involve self-righteousness, idealization of the self, obsessiveness, or split-off fragmentation—all of which are ways to attempt to purify the self, to rid it of what is seen by the agent as not good, to deny wilful, dark, or even demonic aspects of the self.[21] It fails to recognize that many people are not bothered, not conflicted, by seeing themselves as, in part, bad. They have little, if any, difficulty in identifying with their neutral or bad aspects.

To put a related, though milder, objection, this fails to recognize that many people are not so concerned with value as Raz requires. It fails to recognize that many people are not bothered, and certainly not conflicted, by having neutral or bad aspects. It should be noted that not all such people are bad, uncaring, indifferent to value, and the like. Even good people can be more accepting of their less-than-good aspects—that is, more accepting than Raz suggests. They can treat themselves the way many people, whether good or not, treat their less-than-good friends and acquaintances.

So, for example, at least some—I would say many—people identify with thrill seeking and excitement, without thinking, further, that this is good, or that this is a good way for them to be. Somewhat more strongly, at least some—again, I would say many—identify themselves as being out for excitement even when they see that here and now, or more generally, this is not good or is even bad. Not everyone is so good, or so concerned with the good, or so uneasy about the bad, that they would cease being attracted to excitement upon seeing that what is exciting or being out for excitement is generally, or here and now, not good or even bad.[22]

[21] My thanks are owed to Elizabeth Hegeman here.

[22] My thanks are owed to Ruth Chang for discussion here. See also J. David Velleman, 'The Guise of the Good', *Nous* 26 (1992), 3–26.

Putting the matter this way is to allow for a split between what is good or believed good and what is attractive. It is also to allow that what is merely attractive, whether or not it is also good or believed good, can be intelligibly desired. This gives us another way to show that, contrary to the classical conception, what is bad or believed bad can be intelligibly desired. And since what is merely attractive need not be thought good, bad, or neutral—it need not be evaluated at all—it gives us yet another reason to reject the classical conception's claim that intelligible desire, reason, and action are always *sub specie boni*.[23]

I do not here have space, nor is this the place, to argue that what I call a purified view of the self is a defective and inaccurate view of the self. To do this would involve defending a psychoanalytically informed view of the self and, correlatively, criticizing the rationalistic, all-good view of the self so familiar in philosophy and suggested by Raz. Put in a related way, this would involve arguing for the real existence, now within our psyches, of bad, even evil, aspects, as well as uncaring, self-indulgent, selfish, narcissistic, etc. aspects. Put in terms of the history of philosophy, the argument against Raz's account of identification and reasons parallels the arguments against Kant's early account of reasons, arguments which led him to posit both *Wille* and *Willkür*. It is also an argument against Raz's Socratic attempt to explain all seekings of what is bad in terms of mistakes.[24]

I want now to combine two of my last claims, the one about bad second natures and the one about people whose intentions are not cast in evaluative terms. It is of the utmost importance for present concerns to recognize that some intelligible acts are so clearly bad—and some are also so clearly so bad—that we have to ascribe near-lunacy, and certainly absolutely incredible, preposterous evaluative views to agents of these acts for us to claim that they see them as good or to accept their claims that they saw them as good.[25] Their 'mistakes' cannot be accepted as mistakes. Rather, following another of Anscombe's suggestions, now from 'Modern

---

[23] Allowing for such a split is needed to understand akrasia and many other sorts of conflict. This is argued in my *Plural and Conflicting Values*, esp. ch. 7, 'Akrasia: The Unity of the Good, Commensurability, and Comparability'. As also argued there, the failure to recognize such a split led Wiggins, Nussbaum, and others to think that akrasia, and other forms of conflict, require plural *values*, not just plural *attractions*.

[24] See Raz, *Engaging Reason*, 28.

[25] My thanks are owed to Elizabeth Hegeman here.

Moral Philosophy', these mistakes show these people to be corrupt or evil.[26]

Consider this dialogue:

Police interrogator (1): 'Did you see hitting your five-year old child to be good?'

Suspect (1): 'Well, her screaming was upsetting me and hitting her was the only way to shut her up.'

Police interrogator (2): 'Did you see that as good, or did you just not think or not care whether it was good or not?'

How could a parent think quieting the child that way was good? How could, and why should, we credit a person with understanding the sentence 'This is good' who says that hitting the child to stop her crying was good? For all that, I do think we can see the act as intelligible from the inside. But to do this, it seems better to hold that the accused did not bother to evaluate the act, that all the person thought about was getting peace and quiet.

Do we think that criminals, when acting intelligibly and criminally, think what they do is good? Some may, as in the case of ideologically motivated criminals and terrorists. But the average housebreaker? Need we think that sadists not only enjoy what they are doing but also think that this enjoyment is good—say, because it is enjoyment? Here we might consider the case of a philosopher or a cleric whose pleasures include sex with children, and who not only enjoy these relations but offer philosophical arguments for the acceptability of such activities. I think they would do better just to shut up. It is bad enough that they engage in and enjoy those practices. They only compound the wrong and show themselves more vice-ridden and corrupt by arguing that they are really good or even all right.

To be sure, many wrongdoers do claim, 'I thought it a good thing to do at the time'. But rather than accept this as literally true, I think we should often interpret it as an attempt to cover up, to rationalize, to make appropriate noises.

Some, perhaps to defend the classical view, may suggest that I have missed the point. The father need not believe that hitting the child is good. Rather, he aims at peace and quiet, and he believes that good. Housebreakers need not think stealing is good. Rather, they aim at an easy

---

[26] G. E. M. Anscombe, 'Modern Moral Philosophy', *Philosophy* 33 (1958), 1–19.

life—one with the advantages of theft over hard work—and they think that that is good.

I have not missed that point. Rather, it is not in question here. I have no doubt that some child abusers think that what they do is to some extent good; I have no doubt that some housebreakers think that their ease is good; and so on. I was not concerned to deny or affirm that. I was concerned with people who do not think in terms of such evaluative views. I was also concerned to ask why it is held that people who do these clearly bad acts must be seen as having those evaluative views.

My question is: Given their evident lack of regard for evaluative concerns, why do we need or even want to ascribe those evaluative views to them? The answer cannot be that we need to do this in order to see their acts and reasons as intelligible. As argued, we can do that in light of their non-evaluative concerns, in terms of what they find attractive and compelling, in terms of their character and desires. Further, we have good reason not to ascribe such evaluative views to them: the best accounts of their thinking and planning, their character and intentions, do not involve such views.

It might now be suggested that I have fallen into an error encouraged by a simplistic understanding of evaluative beliefs, as discussed early on in this chapter. The charge can be put as follows: Even if the father does not think in explicitly evaluative terms about hitting his child, he does think about, indeed aims at, peace and quiet, and peace and quiet is good. But I do not think I have fallen into such an error.

The most plausible understanding I have reached of Raz's understanding of acting *sub specie boni* is in terms of an act category, *F*, such that to believe it instantiated is to believe features instantiated which—going outside the scope of the belief—are good-making. Now, I certainly agree that in many circumstances, peace and quiet is such an *F*. But our question is whether the *F* in the mind of the just-described father is such a category.

For my part, I think that here it is not such a category. I do not think peace and quiet is necessarily such a category. I think that whether it is depends on the circumstances, perhaps as believed or perhaps as they are. Turning to extreme circumstances, I would deny that the peace and quiet of the aftermath of a nuclear holocaust is good. And certainly, if a person instigated that holocaust in order to have peace and quiet, I would deny that *that* peace and quiet is good.

I do not put much faith in arguments from extreme cases. But I think we can accept this one to show that circumstances can be relevant for goodness. I do not know how, and to what extent, circumstances are to be taken into account in assessing the goodness or otherwise of an item occurring in those circumstances. And I have serious reservations about any general view that holds that items cannot be assessed on their own. But I also have deep reservations about any general view which holds that we can always assess an item's value independently of its circumstances. I do not know how to proceed in general here. But I think it at least plausible to hold that in the cases just considered, the items in question are not good: contrary to what happens in other, better circumstances, their instantiation in those circumstances does not involve the instantiation of good-making features.

These last comments, and much of the earlier discussion, raise serious issues about conditional or circumstantial goodness. As I see matters, peace and quiet is good in certain circumstances, and in other circumstances it is bad. In this, peace and quiet is like pleasure, hate, harm, and much else that makes or allows for intelligibility. On my view, many pleasures are good, but sadistic pleasures are bad. Hate, which can make a desire to harm intelligible, can be bad, but it can also be good—for example, where the hated object is, itself, bad. And so on for much of what has been discussed above. These obvious facts about conditional goods and bads, especially when conjoined with the obvious fact that so many goods and bads are conditional, raise serious questions for Raz.

We must ask why he thinks that showing that an act is aimed at a conditional good, such as pleasure, shows that the act is *sub specie boni*. To show the latter, it seems to me that one must show that the act is aimed at good or perhaps neutral pleasure, rather than bad pleasure, or at pleasure no matter whether good, neutral, or bad. I do not think that this last is shown by showing that what is aimed at, pleasure, gives an answer to 'What's the good of that?'—that is, that what is aimed at has a desirability characterization. For, again as I see things, pleasures of any of those evaluative sorts can provide a desirability characterization. So too, for peace and quiet, excitement, and many of the other goals of the less-than-good people discussed throughout this chapter, especially in its later parts.

As said earlier about a similar issue, these problems do not arise for Aristotelian good people. But, as I have been urging, they most assuredly do arise for people whose second nature is not so good. This is to say that

Raz's classical programme may work for good people. But it may work only vacuously or accidentally, if it works at all, for people who are not so good. It is not that these latter people aim at what is *conditionally* good in so far as they aim at what is good. For that is generally true of good people, too. Rather, people who are not so good, unlike good people, aim at what is conditionally good *without sufficient care that the conditions for the goodness obtain*. Thus, as I understand Raz, he will have to hold that in so far as people who are not so good act in their characterizing ways, their acts are unintelligible—or at the most, that it will be an accident relative to their character and their point of view if, as may happen, their acts are intelligible.

As significant as these various discussions have been, a nagging, perhaps exasperated, question may still remain: Is there any substantive issue dividing my claim denying that intelligibility requires goodness or believed goodness and Raz's claim asserting that it does? Why couldn't Raz agree with my comments on desirability characteristics, but hold that they provide all the goodness he says is required for intelligibility? So, for example, why couldn't he focus on and use the appropriateness of someone who answers, say, 'It is exciting' to 'What's the good of what you are doing?' Or even 'To stop being bothered' as an answer to 'What's the good of hitting your child?'

Would I have anything to offer in reply to Raz except the appropriateness of that person also saying, or saying instead, 'This excitement isn't really good, but it is attractive', and 'Peace and quiet were then and there the only things that attracted me; they may well not have been good, but they were attractive'? Is there anything to decide between these two views, these two intuitions, about how 'good' may be used?

I think there is something to decide between these two views—not so much about the proper or appropriate uses of 'good' as there is in regard to some theoretical, systematic relations among the cluster of concepts deployed by Raz.

First, to accept this view, Raz will have to allow for a certain sort of mistake that troubles some philosophers. He writes:

The classical approach allows that a gap may open between what is good and what attracts agents. But it accounts for the gap by the fact that agents can make mistakes. Certain actions appear to them attractive because they appear to them to possess good-making properties, but in fact they do not possess them.[27]

---

[27] Raz, *Engaging Reason*, 28.

In some cases, the possibility of mistake seems easy enough to accept. For example, an agent can all too easily be mistaken in seeing an act as just. But in other cases, where *percipi* comes close to *esse*, some find mistakes less easy to accept. I am thinking here of such desirability characteristics as being interesting, exciting, or pleasant. Now, I do think mistakes can be made here—'As I was having it, I thought the experience pleasant, but it wasn't.'

Raz will also have to abandon his Socratic account of mistakes in favour of an Aristotelian one. For he will have to accept as mistakes, for example, the deformed conceptions of people with bad second natures. The 'mistakes' that allow such people to believe mistakenly that something has good-making properties—for example, that the conditions for goodness are satisfied—are mistakes in the way they were raised and in their character, not or not just mistakes in their beliefs.

Second, there are people who do not think in evaluative terms. To 'What's the good of that?', they may well answer: 'There was nothing *good* about it, but it was *attractive*.' I do not mean only that they do not explicitly think, for example, 'This is good'. Rather, I also have in mind the following sorts of things: they may well deny thinking this; they cannot be (easily) brought to see that they do think this; and, most importantly, the best accounts of their thinking and planning, of their character and intentions, do not involve such views. It should be noted that these considerations can apply even if the agents think they do have those evaluative views, or indeed do think in terms of them: people can be mistaken in thinking that they have those views or think in terms of them.

Third, there are other consequences of holding that the goodness required by the classical account can be supplied by desirability characteristics. Perhaps of most importance is that this allows for a disjunction, even a rupture, between intelligibility and justification. For clearly, many desirability characteristics do not help justify their associated acts, and many help show them bad. But as I understand the classical approach, it is supposed to show an intimate connection between intelligibility and justification.

My point here is not that what is good in one respect may well not be overall good. It is that what is good in the present sense—given just by being or having a desirability characteristic—does not make the act good at all in any way whatsoever; or, not to beg the question, in any other way whatsoever.

Another way to put this, perhaps more strongly, is that desirability characterizations can be given by what is conditionally good, even when the conditions for the goodness do not obtain. Indeed, what is conditionally bad can be good, in the presently relevant sense: a desirability characterization can be given by what is conditionally bad, where the conditions for its badness obtain.

Further, holding that the goodness required by the classical account can be supplied by desirability characteristics seems to decrease the distance between the classical and the rationalist accounts. For both accounts will agree that intelligible desires are (or concern what are), in this sense, good.

They may disagree about *un*intelligible desires. But I do not think they need do so. I do not think that rationalists would give up all that much by restricting their claims to intelligible desires, to desires backed by desirability characteristics. This does allow that goodness is prior to desire, or value-giving desire. But that goodness and that priority are not sufficient for the classical view.

To sum up, I have argued for three interrelated theses: that reasons$_{good}$ are neither necessary nor sufficient for intelligibility; that reasons$_{bad}$ can make for intelligibility; that desirability characteristics, not goodness or badness, make for intelligibility. Unless Raz thinks that desirability characteristics give the required goodness for his classical account, we disagree on many of these points. If he does think this, we may agree on just about everything.[28]

---

[28] My warmest thanks are owed to discussants at the Conference on the Moral Philosophy of Joseph Raz (22–4 March, 2002, Columbia University), especially Joseph Raz and Michael Smith. My thanks also to Erik Schmidt, whose help was essential, and to Jonathan Adler, Jeffrey Blustein, Ruth Chang, Christopher Gowans, and Elizabeth Hegeman.

14

What is it to Wrong Someone? A Puzzle about Justice

Michael Thompson

This will be the best way of explaining 'Paris is the lover of Helen', that
is, 'Paris loves, *and by that very fact* [*et eo ipso*] Helen is loved'. Here, therefore, two propositions have been brought together and abbreviated as
one. Or, 'Paris is a lover, and by that very fact Helen is a loved one'.

—Leibniz, 'Grammaticae cogitationes'[1]

Definition: 'X has a right [against Y]' if and only if X can have rights,
and, other things being equal, an aspect of X's well-being (his interest)
is a sufficient reason for holding [Y] to be under a duty.

—Joseph Raz, *The Morality of Freedom*[2]

1. The Normativity of Considerations of Justice is an Intrinsically Relational, or 'Bipolar', Normativity

Consider some one human being. Let us adopt the manner of contemporary academic moralists and give her a name: let us call her 'Sylvia'. Now,

---

[1] G. W. Leibniz, *Logical Papers*, ed. G. H. R. Parkinson (Oxford: Oxford University Press, 1966),
12. See also a passage from a letter to Des Bosses: 'You will not, I believe, admit an accident
which is in two subjects at once. Thus I hold as regards relations, that paternity in David is
one thing, and filiation in Solomon is another', quoted in Bertrand Russell, *A Critical Exposition
of the Philosophy of Leibniz* (Cambridge: Cambridge University Press, 1900), 201.

[2] *The Morality of Freedom* (Oxford: Oxford University Press, 1986), 166; the second bracketed
expression replaces Raz's 'some other person(s)'.

even the coarsest utilitarian consequentialist, the scary monster of modern moral philosophy, will side with common sense on this one point: that it would be wrong for you or me or anyone to kill Sylvia on any ordinary prudential ground. For example, it would be wrong for *you* to kill *Sylvia* on the ground that she is just ahead of you on the waiting list for admission to law school. But, unlike that coarse consequentialist (who may in any case be imaginary), common sense will also insist that we do not really alter the case if we replace the prudent hope of law school with some more exalted charitable aim. For example, it changes nothing in the moral equation that you are proposing to harvest Sylvia's internal organs in the hope of saving five transplant patients with suitably diverse organ needs. And this is not, we affirm, because the occurrence of one murder, or one death-by-murder, or one 'active' killing, is somehow a worse sort of happening than the occurrence of several purely natural deaths. For common sense also teaches that the case remains unaltered even if your killing Sylvia is aimed at saving several other people precisely from being murdered—perhaps by a perverse tyrant who has forced this choice upon you.[3]

Your moral relation to Sylvia seems to survive intact in all of these cases; it has a certain robustness; there is, we think, something there. Sylvia and you have fallen into a peculiar nexus which limits your pursuit of objectives of any kind, even the beautiful objectives of charity and the love of justice. The consideration operates pairwise, and the rest of the world is, at least to a certain extent, closed out.

You have, as we sometimes say, a duty 'to Sylvia' not to kill her. You 'owe' it to her not to kill her. Such language is perhaps a bit stiff, but we can put the same point more colloquially. We can say, for example, that in killing Sylvia *you* would wrong *her*: you would do wrong precisely 'to' her, or do wrong 'by' her. And, though it opens something of a Pandora's box, we might reverse terms in the relation, saying, I think quite aptly, that Sylvia has a *right*, morally speaking, precisely *against you*. She has a right, namely, not to be killed by you, and a claim to something better. You, on the other hand, have *no right*, in respect of her, to do what will kill her. What we have said of the ordered pair of you and Sylvia, we might equally have said of the ordered pair of Sylvia and you, of course, or of the ordered

---

[3] These examples are taken from Philippa Foot's 1968 paper 'Abortion and the Doctrine of Double Effect', reprinted in *Virtues and Vices* (Berkeley: University of California Press, 1978), 19–32.

pair of either of you and anyone else, and so on. The class of pairs of potential mutual wrongers is unlimited or indefinitely extensible.

Common-sense meditation on our murderous materials thus seems, upon reflection, to trigger deployment of a collection of abstract forms of judgement. These forms of judgement express what we might call *forms of bipolar normativity*, or *forms of relation of right*. Counting internal negations as distinct types, we might tabulate them as follows:

X wronged Y by doing A	X wronged Y by not doing A
X has a duty to Y to do A	X has a duty to Y not to do A
X has a right against Y	X has a right against Y
—that he do A	—that he not do A
—to do A	—not to do A

The propositions in the first row express forms of Aristotle's 'X *adikei* Y'; those in the last two rows express Hohfeldian 'claim' and 'privilege' respectively. The concrete judgements that come under these abstract headings can be quite various. Murdering and maiming people and breaking promises made to them are among the traditionally accredited content-providers under the heading in the upper left, suitable readings of 'doing A'; they are specific 'wrongs' or concrete ways of wronging someone.

But I am interested in the form that is, I believe, shared by all of the tabulated judgements, irrespective of the particular heading (and in the corresponding form of fact). A further act of reflection ought, I think, to bring us to see that a special way of coupling representations of agents runs throughout our table. In all such judging, whatever the determinate form, I may be said to view a pair of distinct agents as joined and opposed in a formally distinctive type of practical nexus. They are for me like the opposing poles of an electrical apparatus: in filling one of these forms with concrete content, I represent an arc of normative current as passing between the agent-poles, and as taking a certain path. My aim in this paper is to think out some of the peculiarities of this form of representation.

The 'bipolarity', as I will sometimes call it, of the judgements that come under these several headings is something more determinate than the form of coupling of singular terms in a Fregean two-place relational judgement. Merely relational judgements like *Everest is taller than McKinley* and *143 is divisible by 11* contain two singular representations; if we remove each of them in sequence, viewing its position in the judgement as replaceable by other singular representations, we arrive at the relational judgement-types

ξ *is taller than* ζ and ξ *is divisible by* ζ. If, then, we similarly remove the relational material that at the outset joined those singular representations, we arrive at a form that the two original judgements share—the general form of a two-place relational judgement, $\Phi(\xi, \zeta)$, as Frege would write it, or $\xi\Phi\zeta$.[4] This arrangement of schematic letters captures a certain fundamental 'posture of the mind', in Locke's phrase, a posture that is adopted in the framing of any given relational judgement.[5] It is plain, then, that any concrete judgement that exhibits a form found on our table must exhibit this merely Fregean 'relationality' as well: a 'bipolar' practical judgement will after all always contain two singular representations—representations, namely, of two agents, substituends for 'X' and 'Y'.

But note that any concrete judgement that exhibits Fregean relational form must exhibit Fregean *subject–predicate form* as well, and in at least two different ways. For what can be viewed as bearing the form $\Phi(\xi, \zeta)$ can equally be viewed as bearing either the form $\Psi(\xi)$ or the form $\theta(\zeta)$. In thinking that Everest is taller than McKinley, I think *of* Everest (as I think of K2) that *it is taller than McKinley* and of McKinley (as again of K2) that *Everest is taller than it*. But the reverse is not the case: reflection will find subject–predicate form, $\Psi(\xi)$, in the judgement that *Everest is a mountain*, but not relational form. The relational form of a given relational judgment is thus *more determinate* than the subject–predicate form it inevitably also exhibits.

My thought, then, is that there is something still more determinate, but something belonging nevertheless to the form of thought, or to the 'posture of the mind' in judging, that any instance of the tabulated judgement-type X *wrongs* Y has in common with any instance of X *has a right against* Y, or X *has a duty to* Y, or indeed X *promised* Y and a number of other judgement-types. This is the practical-bipolar form, $J(X,Y)$ or XJY, as we might write it (switching from Greek to Latin, as suits our incipiently juridical material). This practical bipolarity is something that judgements coming under these headings do *not* share with instances of, say, ξ *is taller than* ζ, much less ξ *is divisible by* ζ. The instruments devised by Frege will obviously not distinguish the former class from the latter; if then, by the 'logical'

---

[4] See G. Frege, *Grundgesetze der Arithmetik*, vol. 1, part 1, §§ 1–4, trans. in Michael Beaney (ed.), *The Frege Reader* (Oxford: Blackwell, 1997), 211–15. See also the essays 'Function and Concept' and 'Concept and Object' in the same collection.

[5] John Locke, *An Essay concerning Human Understanding*, ed. P. Nidditch (Oxford: Oxford University Press, 1975), 472 (bk. III, ch. VII).

form of a judgement we mean its 'Fregean' form—a very reasonable use of the honorific term 'logical'—then we will speak of the practical bipolarity of a judgement as a matter of, say, 'categorial' or 'intellectual' form. For, as I will argue, thought takes a distinctive turn here, a turn which cannot simply be reduced to its taking a certain body of concrete relations, practical ones, as its theme—and still less by making reference to a special class of objects: namely, agents. Such thought has, among other things, a novel and particular relation to what it is about.[6]

This special posture of the mind in coupling certain representations of agents marks the resulting judgements as belonging to the element of *justice*.[7] Here 'justice' bears its traditional sense, naming a virtue of individual humans like you and me, and not a feature of the larger social structures into which we fall. The mark of this special virtue of human agents, as Aristotle says, is that it is 'toward another', *pros heteron* or *pros allon*;[8] it is, as St Thomas says, *ad alterum*,[9] or as Kant says, *gegen einen Anderen*.[10] It is characteristic of the individual bearer of justice, in this traditional sense, to apprehend this order of thought and to deliberate with *first-person* judgements of the bipolar types found on our table—and thus to view *herself* as related to others, and as other to others, in this peculiar way.

My chief aim in this paper will be to find where this genuinely just agent, our heroine, locates herself in the 'space of reasons' as she thinks these thoughts of justice. How are we to understand this being-toward-another of her thoughts? The 'puzzle' I mean to identify is a difficulty in saying what could make her bipolar moral thoughts *true*.

---

[6] Elizabeth Anscombe, thinking of propositions like 'You can't take that, it's for N' or 'You can't do that, it's N's to do', writes: 'We have here a very special use of the name of a person, or a very special way of relating something to a person, which explains (not is explained by) the general term "right".... The general term "right" is constructed because, as it were, our language feels the need for it. As for example, a general term "relation" was invented' 'The Source of the Authority of the State', in *Collected Philosophical Papers*, vol. 1 (Minneapolis: University of Minnesota Press, 1981), 130–55, at 142.

[7] Or, more precisely, they belong under this heading given the 'moral' atmosphere my remarks have so far generated. I will suggest in section 5 that practical bipolarity, or relational 'deonticity', is found in extra-moral departments of thought.

[8] Aristotle, *Nicomachean Ethics*, book V, ch. 1.

[9] Aquinas, *Summa Theologiae*, IIa, IIae, q. 57.

[10] *Metaphysics of Morals*, e.g. *Doctrine of Virtue*, § 16, (*Akademie*, 442) in M. Gregor (ed.), *Practical Philosophy* (Cambridge: Cambridge University Press, 1996).

2. Bipolar Normativity may be Distinguished from Merely Monadic Normativity

We can sharpen the idea that these many types of judgement exhibit a single practical 'bipolar' form, distinct from, but subordinate to, the general form of a Fregean relational judgement, if we oppose our table of forms of judgement to a parallel array of *non-relational*, *monopolar*, or, as I will mostly say, *merely monadic* forms:

X did wrong in doing A	X did wrong in not doing A
X has a duty to do A	X has a duty not to do A
X has a right to do A	X has a right not to do A

These propositional forms provide the usual theme of ethics and meta-ethics, and are typically assigned a distinctive status within the totality of propositions. But tradition and intuition alike assign them a place very different from that occupied by our bipolar forms. Aristotle and St Thomas would, if I understand them, place the categories of this merely monadic table under the general heading of *to nomimon* or *lex*—that is, 'what is lawful' or 'law'. (Here, the idea of law is, I think, to be taken very broadly, as covering *inter alia* any principles of what we would call morality.) The categories of our properly bipolar table they would place under a heading of *to dikaion* or *ius*—that is, of 'what is just' or 'fair', or of 'right'. Thomas's discussion of *ius*, or bipolar normativity, appears several hundred octavo pages after his famous discussion of merely monadic *lex*.[11] Aristotle expends much thought distinguishing the 'unjust' man in the thin, 'general', monadic sense of the lawless, unruly, unprincipled, unrighteous, immoral man—the *paranomos*—from the unjust man in the properly bipolar sense of the unequal, unfair, and grasping man—the *anisos* or *pleonektēs*.[12] The latter and his virtuous opposite—our heroine, the bearer of justice properly so-called—are the principal theme of book V of the *Nicomachean Ethics*. If, following Bentham, we call moral judgements of the monadic sort 'deontological', we might, in homage to Aristotle, call those of our bipolar sort 'dikaiological'. If the study of the monadic type of judgement is meta-ethics, the study of the bipolar type is the little practised meta-dikaiology.

---

[11] The question on *lex* is IaIIae, q. 90; the question on *ius* is IIaIIae, q. 57.
[12] Aristotle, *Nicomachean Ethics*, book V, chs. 1 and 2.

In the course of objecting to it, Kant dignifies what amounts to the conflation of our two tables with the title of the 'amphiboly of the moral concepts of reflection'.[13] This amphibolical assimilation might run in either direction, and it seems to appear in even the most intuitively hostile environments. A. I. Melden and T. M. Scanlon have, for example, found it in John Rawls's theory of the obligation of promises. Rawls's account clearly puts *every* bearer of a 'practice' of promising into the position of *the one to whom the promise is made*. All alike are positioned to charge the promisor with a violation of merely monadic 'moral duty' should he fail to carry through. The account does not single out the unhappy promisee as one who is *wronged* in a way others are not—or, equivalently, as the one *to whom* the promisor had a duty. Rawls, according to these writers, misperceives the merely monadic requirement that his theory is equipped to explain as amounting to the evidently bipolar obligation of promises, which thus remains unexplained. His uniformly monadic vocabulary seems to leave something out.[14]

It seems equally plain, to consider the other direction of possible assimilation, that our monadic table of moral categories is not reducible to the bipolar in any straightforward way. It is presumably true that I 'act wrongly', monadically, whenever I wrong another. But justice isn't the *only* virtue, and so I can intelligibly be said to do wrong or go wrong or act wrongly, morally speaking, even when no one is wronged. If, for example, you are making an unjustly intrusive enquiry, and I tell you a lie in response, it certainly doesn't seem that *I* wrong *you*. But a lie would cover me with shame nevertheless. The claims of honesty thus seem to outrun

---

[13] Kant, *Metaphysics of Morals*, §16.

[14] John Rawls, *A Theory of Justice* (Cambridge, Mass.: Harvard University Press, 1971), § 52. The source of the trouble is Rawls's reliance on H. L. A. Hart's 'Principle of Fairness' (or of 'Fair Play'). This principle assimilates practices which intuitively bind us to one another to practices which, like recycling, bind us to the production of some public good. The principle says that, where I have voluntarily accepted the benefits of a fair practice of any kind, I am 'morally required' to do 'what the practice requires'. It is in the nature of the case, then, that the form of moral requirement that figures in the principle is merely monadic. Rawls thus misses the directed character of the obligation of promises. See A. I. Melden, *Rights and Persons* (Berkeley: University of California Press, 1977), 87–104, and T. M. Scanlon, 'Promising', in the *Routledge Encyclopedia of Philosophy*, vol. 7 (London: Routledge, 1998), 740–2. These writers seem to think that their objection runs against any 'social practice' conception of the obligation of promises. But it seems plain that Rawls could easily meet it by distinguishing two types of practice, one type merely monadic and the other directed or bipolar, and two corresponding 'principles of fairness'.

those of justice. The intellectual content of my feeling of shame is a deontological, not a dikaiological, judgement. 'I did wrong in that I lied to you' contains representations of a pair of agents, indeed, but the combination is not properly bipolar: the representation of *you* falls inside the scope of the action description that is fitted into this monadic normative form; it does not go to characterize the form of normativity itself. You are the occasion, not the victim, of my fall.

Perhaps I would be mistaken to think and feel these things in the case I have imagined. But, as Joseph Raz forcefully argues, a blanket denial of the possibility of acting wrongly, or 'immorally', where no one is wronged, would be a strong and implausible *substantive* claim, amounting, I suppose, to a sort of moral libertarianism.[15]

3. The Opposition between Bipolar and Merely Monadic Deonticity Extends beyond Morality

My suggestion has been that the opposition between our two tables is a matter of the form of thought, of categorial or intellectual form. We reached those tables by framing and reflecting on judgements with a 'specifically moral' content, as I will put it. We imagined certain killings and certain lies, and then let our moral intuition take them where it would. But, having come upon our second, merely monadic, table, we can see, I think, that we have latched on to a distinction that transcends the purely ethical sphere and the particular locutions we have chosen to express the contrast. Meditation on this fact should make the purely formal character of the opposition quite plain.

Wherever a philosopher is inclined to speak of normativity or deonticity and of practical or deontic 'norms', 'standards', or 'principles', we will have an interpretation of our merely monadic forms of judgement. The *specifically moral* interpretation of our six monadic forms is just an example: on this interpretation, the relevant 'norms' are, let's suppose, the so-called principles of the various true virtues taken together as one body. But the standards that give sense to a merely monadic employment of deontic vocabulary might instead be purely instrumental or technical. They might be the broader counsels of prudence. They might belong to a system of

---

[15] Raz, *Morality of Freedom*, ch. 5.

criminal legislation or to a logical calculus. They might be the rules of a game or the canons of etiquette.

It would of course be a bit strange to use the *words* 'duty' or 'right' in some of these connections—for example, in issuing counsels of prudence. But the common underlying logical structure is clear and familiar, whatever words we may use to decorate it. A merely monadic 'duty' is simply the deontic necessity or requirement or 'must' that is constituted by the underlying norms or standards, whatever they are. A merely monadic 'right' is what these requirements leave open, a deontic possibility or permission or 'can'. They are thus respectively what deontic logicians express by their operators O and P, which they grant have innumerably many interpretations and enter into many different departments of thought. 'X O to do A' means that X is required to do A or is committed to doing it—or has a 'duty' to do it; 'X P to do A' means that X is permitted or entitled to do it—or has a 'right' to do it.

Once we see that our 'merely monadic' forms of deontic judgement may be read as empty logical forms admitting many radically different interpretations or schematizations, only one of them specifically moral—that the O's and P's are apt to receive numerous indices or subscripts, so to speak (as they do in some attempted formalizations)—we will, I think, see that the same holds of their dikaiological or bipolar counterparts.

We speak, as we saw, of your moral duty 'to' Sylvia. But we can also speak of your *legal* duties 'to' her. These might arise from a valid contract with her, for example. Moreover, legal duties binding one agent to another can be judged according to different and even overlapping legal systems. You may be bound to Sylvia in one way under the laws of the United States, for example, and in another way under the laws of Pennsylvania. Each legal system is associated with a different rendering of our tabulated bipolar judgements, a *different* way of schematizing the abstract relational O's and P's of the bipolar deontic logic we are implicitly imagining. Where the 'subscript' needs to be made explicit, it will be by use of such an expression as 'under L', 'according to L', 'at L', or 'in L', where L is the legal system in question.

But the contrast between *properly bipolar* and *merely monadic* deonticity is a precipitate of other conceptual atmospheres, not merely those of morals and law. Customs, practices, and institutions of quite various sorts can give sense to our bipolar linkages.

Think, for example, of an absurdly exploitative pre-legal system of property relations. The pairwise linkages it constitutes are not legal, for there is no institution of appeal to an independent judge. And they are not moral linkages because morals, by hypothesis, say something different. As a fellow 'free' man under this system, perhaps you 'wrong' me and my house, if you kill my brother or take our cattle or burn down our dwelling-place—but not if I've been found helping your slaves to liberate themselves.

And if there can be such a thing as a system of *etiquette*, why should there not be a *petite justice*—a space within which even etiquette reaches intelligibly for our bipolar deontic grammar? *Petite justice* would seem to be most of what etiquette is.

And David Hume, in the course of making what is essentially my present point, argues that *competitive games* like chess and chequers may be said to attract thoughts in these same logical shapes.[16]

The tabulated forms of dikaiological judgement are thus no different from the merely monadic forms in this one central respect: if we are to get anywhere with them in thought—if they are to register truth or even falsehood—then they must first be shifted into a particular gear. Or, if you prefer, they must be sung in a particular key. In addition to a pair of relata, our *relational* O's and P's must always at least implicitly be supplied with an index or subscript. One of these is specifically moral, or, as we might say, directly normative: namely, the one with which our heroine the just agent distinctively operates.[17]

---

[16] David Hume, *An Enquiry concerning the Principles of Morals*, ed. P. A. Nidditch, 3rd edn. (Oxford: Oxford University Press, 1975), 210.

[17] Let us leave aside the question of indices, gears, and keys. If we use 'X P to do A' and 'X O to do A' to symbolize the usual monadic cases—respectively permission and obligation, 'may' and 'must', monadic right and duty—then '$<X,Y>$ P to do A' and '$<X,Y>$ O to do A' could symbolize the properly bipolar cases: respectively Hohfeldian privilege and directed duty or owing. A substitution instance of the latter would be '$<$Jones, Smith$>$ O to mow Smith's lawn': i.e., 'Jones owes it to Smith to mow his lawn'. An advantage of taking both forms, 'O' and 'P', as primitive in the monadic and relational cases alike is that we then need not take either the idea of omission or that of an 'internal' negation, as basic: 'X P not to do A' would be defined as 'Not X O to do A', and 'X O not to do A' would be defined as 'Not X P to do A' (and similarly for the relational cases).

Notice that if we fix the second variable in '$<X,Y>$ O to do A', so that we have, say, '$<X$, Sylvia$>$ O to do A', then we are left with an ordinary monadic deontic operator which needs one agent-term and one action-term for completion. It is thus in the nature of a form of bipolar deonticity to constitute a type or form of merely monadic duty or requirement associated with each agent in the system. Where our bipolar categories get a grip, each agent

What particular acts count as wronging someone, what things may be called duties to him, will of course depend on the particular gear into which the dikaiological conceptual machinery is shifted. Private law and true justice do not much concern themselves with modes of greeting people or the movements of very small pieces of wood. On the other hand, chequers, chess, and etiquette do not have much to say about killing people—unless perhaps duelling rules count as a sort of etiquette.

4. Positive Law Encodes our Opposition in the Distinction between Private Law and Criminal Law

In order to develop the contrast between *properly bipolar* and *merely monadic* forms of deonticity, let us tarry briefly with the narrowly legal material.

The zone in which juridical practices *paradigmatically* generate bipolar deonticity—'legal relations' as Wesley Hohfeld called them, translating the *Rechtsverhältnisse* of Kant, Fichte, and the German legal tradition—is of course so-called private law, the sort carried on under headings of contract, property, tort, and so forth. Indeed, in our system the names of particular private-legal proceedings already exhibit the peculiar nexus of representations that interests us: *Mr X* v. *Ms Y*, we call them, or [*your name here*] v. *Sylvia*. The atmosphere of a lawsuit is saturated with judgements of our type: 'She's done me wrong,' we say, 'She owes me,' and so forth. Wherever customs and institutions take this turn—which is of course much more ancient and simple than our lawyers are likely to let on—all of our abstract bipolar forms of judgement are given a sense and thrown into a particular gear.

is as it were a law, a monadic *lex*, for all the others. This thought suggests a possible response to the difficulties Samuel Scheffler has raised about one of the moral intuitions with which we began: namely, that you would wrong Sylvia in killing her, even if it were to save several others from being killed. If a form of deontic requirement sets its face against killing, Scheffler suggests, surely it does so incoherently and self-defeatingly if it makes no exceptions for killings that save numerous others precisely from being killed.

But in a bipolar conceptual scheme, we have in a sense not one but many parallel forms of monadic deontic requirement, one for each agent. It doesn't seem that a properly Schefflerian incoherence can be found in connection with any *one* of these—for example, the one 'indexed' by Sylvia. Our obligations-to-Sylvia are easily made coherent with each other by appeal to Sylvia's interest and will. (See especially Scheffler's helpfully clarifying response to the arguments of Philippa Foot in 'Agent-Centred Restrictions, Rationality and the Virtues', in S. Scheffler (ed.), *Consequentialism and its Critics* (Oxford: Oxford University Press, 1988), 243–60.)

The interpretation of 'X wrongs Y' forged by these customs is precisely that attached to the words of the plaintiff, 'He's done me wrong.' And in recognizing a particular collection of grounds for such complaint, or 'causes of action'—*dikai*, as they were called in Athens—private-legal institutions must at the same time implicitly generate a collection of directed or bipolar duties and rights. The violation of such a duty or right is the plaintiff's theme. And, of course, the result of a successful complaint is itself to be described in our terms: the plaintiff gains a right against the defendant to receive restitution, perhaps, and the defendant acquires a correlative duty to 'make her whole'.[18]

The zone in which juridical institutions paradigmatically generate merely *monadic* deonticity, by contrast, is of course criminal law—that is, in institutions of punishment and sanction, not those of restitution and compensation. The verdict of the jury, 'Guilty!', expresses a property of one agent, not a relation of agents. If another agent comes into the matter—if there is, as we say, a 'victim'—it is, so to speak, as raw material in respect of which one might do wrong. The position occupied by other agents in the associated legal facts might equally be held by rare birds or old buildings. Much criminal law pertains after all to acts involving no other agent at all. Though the criminalization of murder in ancient Athens kept each Athenian off the rest of them to a certain extent, it turned their specifically

---

[18] The relational character of private law is emphasized by Evgeny Pashukanis, *General Theory of Law [i.e., Right] and Marxism* (London: Pluto Press, 1983), in which the legal equivalent of Kant's amphiboly is attacked under the title of 'normativism', or, as we might call it, monadicism or lexism. It is also emphasized in Giorgio del Vecchio, *Justice* (Edinburgh: University of Edinburgh Press, 1955), and more recently by Ernest Weinrib, *The Idea of Private Law* (Cambridge, Mass.: Harvard University Press, 1996), from whom I take the expressions 'bipolar' and 'bipolarity'.

The idea of a bipolar legal relation is so much taken for granted by Wesley Hohfeld that its opposition to monadic legal requirement is not thematized by him; monadic notions are nowhere in view in his text. It is a mistake to use Hohfeld's notion of correlativity as if it involved any substantive idea; if he had read Russell, he would have used the idea of a logical converse to express his ideas. The thought that one kind of right 'correlates' with duty means that the two general relations—namely, those on the second and third lines of our first table—are logical converses, like 'less than' and 'greater than', or 'kisses' and 'is kissed by'. They are, if you like, the same concept, the same 'fundamental legal conception', the only difference being the order in which the terms are taken. Where writers say that 'some duties correlate with rights', what they seem to mean could as well be expressed by a Hohfeldian by saying that some monadic duties 'correlate' with bipolar or directed duties; they are thus using the word in a completely different sense, and expressing a form of thought nowhere present in Hohfeld, who does not use the conception of a monadic duty. See the title essay of Wesley Hohfeld, *Fundamental Legal Conceptions* (New Haven: Yale University Press, 1923), 23–114.

juridical *Achtung* toward 'the State and the Laws' themselves, as Socrates puts it in the *Crito*, and not, at least in the first instance, *toward one another*. As the Athenians distinguished *dikē* and *graphē* as forms of legal proceeding, we distinguish '*Mr X* v. *Ms Y*' from '*Mr X* v. *The State of Y*' as types of case. The form of criminalization is in this sense 'merely monadic', and criminal law is for this reason, I think, the implicit model of much philosophical discussion of normativity and deonticity.[19]

5. Excursus: Because Moral Bipolarity Extends beyond the Forms Listed on our Table, Received Reductions of that Table may not Dispense with Moral Bipolarity in General, but rather Presuppose it

I have been suggesting that the categories of our first, dikaiological or bipolar table are very abstract; they may be shifted into various gears, or

---

[19] The private-legal employment of our bipolar notions can hardly be supposed the most primitive type. The existence of such institutions evidently presupposes that the agents who meet in it also meet in exchange, in some measure, and thus also as bearers of private property; Aristotle notes that ideas of market value and equivalence must have a foothold among the bearers of such a practice (*Nicomachean Ethics*, book V, ch. 4, 1132b13). It is striking, though, that as soon as Aristotle begins to touch on our bipolar, commutative, or 'synallagmatic' ethical material, his attention is immediately absorbed in an abstract characterization of this sort of 'corrective' institution, in terms of 'arithmetical equality'. This has led some to think that the part of virtue of justice that 'corrects interactions' (*to en tois suallagmasi diorthōtikon* (1131a1), also known as *to en tois sunallagmasi dikaion* (1131b33))—i.e., the part of justice Thomas calls *commutative*—can show itself *only* in independent judicial operations correcting past disasters. But why not in the just agent's getting things right in the first place, e.g., by not killing other people, keeping agreements, returning deposits, and taking due care not to injure? She operates with a view of what's right as between herself and another, and this same view operates in the just judge where agents differ and things go awry.

That Aristotle should suddenly move to the contemplation of corrective institutions in the course of a discussion of *justice as a virtue of individual human beings* might be thought to betoken an optimistic conflation of what we distinguish as the legal and moral orders. But, like his use of mathematical analogies, it might equally be taken to express the idea we are propounding: namely, that the moral virtue that interests us operates with a very abstract collection of categories, categories that can find application elsewhere. Following Aristotle's example, I will take the peculiar yoking of agent to agent that is constituted by this sort of institution as a paradigmatic realization of the idea of a dikaiological nexus, but I will not assume that these institutions have any specifically moral significance at all. For all I pretend to know here, private law and etiquette and competitive games are all alike the devil's work. Perhaps our ideal heroine, the bearer of true justice, rejects them all.

sung in various keys, as I have put it, only one of them specifically moral. But note that once we fix upon a particular gear setting or schematization, we will be inclined to think that the forms our table tabulates are really only examples chosen from a wider class. Reflection on this fact will provide some insight into received accounts of rights.

The further untabulated elements will of course differ according to the gear setting selected—etiquette or Pennsylvania law, as it might be. For example, a developed system of private law will constitute a vast range of concepts pairing one agent off with another—for example, *X has a contract with Y* or *X has an action in trespass against Y*, and so forth. Judgements deploying these concepts will exhibit the specific form of bipolarity or pairing that is associated with the legal system in question. So it is with the specifically moral case. For example, the judgement-type *X promises Y that he'll do A* would seem to capture a more determinate form of *X has a moral duty to Y to do A*; this is more or less what Melden and Scanlon accused Rawls of missing. The former judgement-type would thus seem also to exhibit the bipolarity of the latter. In framing a representation of a promise, the mind adopts our special posture, $J(X,Y)$ or XJY, and shifts it into a specifically moral gear.[20]

And suppose I represent *you* as having, say, turned left rather than right because you knew that turning right might kill *Sylvia*. Here I link representations of *you* and *Sylvia* in another untabulated form of Fregean relational judgement. It is a representation, true or false, of an explanatory reason. But where I am amassing a record of your sterling justice, my judgement still exhibits, I think, the generic 'bipolar' form we are investigating. For in that case my account is not intended to abbreviate a more involved aetiology referring, say, to your fear of the inevitable manslaughter prosecution or wrongful death suit. Nor am I implicitly alluding to your *general* horror of moral wrongdoing or violation of God's law, though these things may be present in the case as well. My action-explanation purports rather to record the special sort of dent that Sylvia *herself* is making on your agency. Sylvia is, as I judge the matter, appearing on your practical radar in a quite particular way; current is passing between opposed prac-

---

[20] Note that in framing an instance of the judgement-type *X promises Y he'll do A*, I implicitly represent the parties themselves as operating with the same judgement-type, each putting the first person where I put a representation of her. The conceptual difficulties this fact poses for an account of promising, and of the concept of promising, provide a rough model of difficulties pertaining to dikaiological judgement generally.

tical poles. The same intuition that leads us to insist upon the distinctiveness of moral duties 'to' others thus seems implicitly to contain a conception of a special possible *mode of dependence* of the actions of one agent on facts it apprehends about another. The deployment of this conception of dependence in a particular case will exhibit Fregean relational form, indeed, but also, I think, our sub-Fregean categorial form $J(X,Y)$ or XJY, shifted, again, into a specifically moral gear.

If that is right, then this same bipolarity, and a similarly distinctive mode of dependence, must surely be exhibited in the corresponding *normative* reasons-judgement, a judgement we might have framed in advance of your heroic left turn: namely, that *you* 'had reason' to turn left rather than right, in that turning right might have killed *Sylvia*. For the reasons why a virtuous agent does what virtue requires are presumably among the reasons she has to do it. The bipolar conceptual atmosphere of the former reasons-judgement will thus also surround the latter.[21]

And it is the same where I represent *Sylvia* as, say, *consenting* to *your* turning right, perhaps despite the fact that it might kill her. This judgement is neither normative nor explanatory; it is a representation of an 'act of mind', a state of Sylvia's will, but in framing it I enter the same bipolar conceptual element that is our theme. This becomes clearer if we consider a proposition involving a third party: for example, 'Sylvia consented to your telling Meredith her secret.' If this is true, then Sylvia has indeed entered into a certain Fregean relational nexus with *Meredith*: namely, ξ *consented to your telling* ζ *her secret*. But Sylvia has entered into a formally more special nexus with *you*—one of the type, $J(Sylvia, you)$ or Sylvia-J-you, the representation of which I am calling bipolar. Current is again passing between opposed practical poles. Meredith, after all, occupies the position held by the road to the right in the other example of consent.

I said above that it is characteristic of the just agent to operate with certain first-person judgements of this bipolar form—judgements of the form $J(I,Y)$, shifted into the specifically moral gear setting. But my representation of the just agent as effecting suitable couplings in thought will

---

[21] The bare proposition 'You have reason to turn left rather than right' contains an implicit existential quantifier ranging over possible reasons or considerations; it is only in the proposition that validates it, and states what your reason is, that we see its underlying bipolarity, directedness, or orientation. Thus, just as we speak of an agent's duties *simpliciter*, but also of his duties 'to' another, we might speak of an agent's reasons *simpliciter*, but also of his reasons 'toward' or 'in relation to' another.

itself, I think, be a case of such coupling. So, for example, instances of the judgement-type *you know that Sylvia has right against you that you do A*, will exhibit our general bipolar shape, $J(X,Y)$—here, J(you, Sylvia). We will later see, I think, that the possibility of facts corresponding to such judgements—facts about people's first-person bipolar practical knowledge and judgement—is crucial to the constitution of the material we are treating, on both moral and non-moral constructions of it. That is, the possibility of such couplings in judgement, in the minds of the parties, is internally related to the possibility of such couplings in fact. Or again, what brings agents together in reality in these peculiar ways, must at the same time potentially bring representations of themselves together in their first-person thoughts. This is part of the ground for my confidence that we should speak not only of a special practical-bipolar form of fact, but should enter competition with Frege and speak of a special practical-bipolar form of thought.[22]

In all of these thoughts, tabulated and untabulated, I seem to view *you* and *Sylvia* as points or bodies moving in a special moral space. You have fallen, namely, into a space of moral *ius* or 'right', as we might say; the intrinsic geometry of this space makes possible the various specific relations that I have mentioned. The class of such 'moral relations' extends well beyond the rather rarefied class I have tabulated.

Now, let us apply this thought. I mentioned above that Joseph Raz's critique of 'rights based' moral theories may be viewed as opposing a reduction of our monadic to our bipolar table. On the other hand, though, the quotation from Raz with which I began this essay might be said to outline a sophisticated reverse reduction: a reduction of moral *ius* to *lex*, of dikaiology to deontology, of our bipolar to our merely monadic table. Raz intends, if I understand him, for the concept of a *right against someone* to be explained in terms of a merely monadic concept of duty: we are to speak of a 'right', on his account, where merely monadic duties—cases of moral requirement *simpliciter*—are apt to have a specific sort of ground. And, though Raz does not make it explicit, the associated concept of a duty 'to' someone would *a fortiori* have to be reduced to the concept of moral requirement period: the prepositional phrase would simply be used to

---

[22] The bipolarity that interests us might also be found in the representation of certain of the states of *directed feeling* that you might bear toward Sylvia, or Sylvia toward you. Judgements employing the concepts of grievance, grudge bearing, and resentment would be clear examples. A philosophical comprehension of these concepts of feeling presupposes a grasp of this formal feature of the judgements in which they are exercised.

mark off the special case in which a duty is founded on the interest of another agent. For you to wrong someone, on such an account, would be for you to cross an interest of *hers* that grounds a moral requirement attaching to *you*.

Thus, in a Razian framework, any moral fact which may be captured in our tabulated dikaiological forms may as well be represented without them. I do not mean to oppose this reduction; to prove that it fails as an account of 'right against', 'duty to', and 'wrongs' would involve delicate verbal reflection that is not to the present point. I will for the moment only pose the question whether, if such a reduction is legitimate, it amounts to a reduction of *moral bipolarity in general* to something else. This is not a matter of vocabulary, I think, but of the fundamental structure of the thoughts in question.

Certainly Leibniz's remarks, which I paired with Raz's definition at the outset, fail to provide a reduction of *Fregean relational judgements in general* to logically merely monadic ones. After all, 'ξ loves, and by that very fact (*et eo ipso*) ζ is loved' is as much a Fregean 'relation word' as 'ξ loves ζ' is; it is the result of deleting two singular representations from a complete proposition. *The propositions conjoined are (logically) monadic, but the proposition conjoining them is not.* Leibniz may thus successfully reduce other forms of relationality to that contained in his special conjunction 'ξ is F *et eo ipso* ζ is G'; but if there is some difficulty about relational propositions in general, we have clearly not evaded it. Perhaps the monadologist's conceptual knot has only been tightened.

Is Raz, then, a sort of moral monadologist? Certainly, if anything like Raz's 'X has an interest *and for that very reason* Y has a duty' is to amount to an elucidation of anything like 'X has a right against Y' or 'Y has a duty to X', then it may be wondered whether something in the use of the connective, the other element in Raz's definition, is not doing the work of importing bipolarity into the equation. The agents X and Y are brought into connection by the proposition as a whole: is it a merely Fregean relation, like that between Sylvia and Meredith in our example of consent; or is it something more, something specifically dikaiological? The propositions conjoined may be (morally) monadic, but perhaps the proposition conjoining them is not.

It does seem that Raz's definition must implicitly presuppose *a distinctive mode of dependence* of duties in one agent on facts about another. I spoke above of a distinctive bipolar mode of dependence of a just agent's action, and of his 'reasons', on facts about another agent. A similar thought must surely hold here, for in speaking of *reasons why I am morally required to do something*, we must also be speaking of *reasons for doing the thing required*, and thus also of *reasons why the morally virtuous agent does it*. The bipolarity, the form of pairing of representations of agents, that is exhibited by the complete judgement formulating either of the latter reasons must also infect any formulation of the former. As Frances Kamm notes, it is easy to generate what strike intuition as counterexamples if the notion of rational grounding that Raz presupposes is assigned an uncharitable breadth.[23]

A 'choice theory' of moral rights of the type associated with the name of H. L. A. Hart will face a similar difficulty if it too is taken in a boldly reductive spirit.[24] On such an account, to simplify, a moral duty 'to' someone, in the sense that interests us, is again held itself to be a merely monadic duty, or a moral requirement, period. The prepositional phrase merely marks the fact that this monadic duty is responsive to, or dependent on, the choice, will, or consent of the one to whom we thereby declare the duty to be directed. It is in such cases that we speak of the other, the *heteros*, as having a 'right'. Here, as with Raz, we might query the proposition expressing this dependence: if *it* exhibits the form of pairing in question, then the fly-paper of bipolarity has merely been moved from one hand to the other. But consider instead the form of choice or willing that is at stake. For surely the all-important potentially duty-cancelling state of will is a matter of *directed consent* of the type discussed above. There is an obvious intuitive difference between *Sylvia consents to your doing B* and *Sylvia doesn't mind that you're doing B*, the latter being a species of the more general

[23] Frances Kamm, 'Rights', in Jules Coleman and Scott Shapiro (eds.), *The Oxford Handbook of Jurisprudence and Philosophy of Law* (Oxford: Oxford University Press, 2002), 476–513, esp. 483–7. 'For example, if I have a duty to help you by praying to God for your recovery, you still might not have a right that I relate to God in this particular way' (p. 483). After canvassing a number of such objections, Kamm reaches the heart of the matter, noting that 'these problems arise because in both accounts of rights that Raz offers the duty is not described as a directed duty owed to the person with the right' (p. 484).

My only complaint against Kamm's discussion is that she takes the notion of 'directed duty' or 'owing' for granted, as not needing explanation or philosophical elucidation. We might boldly accuse her of lacking the general conception of practical bipolarity, just as she accuses Raz of blindness to the more specific conception of bipolar directed duty or owing. For this reason she is unable to supply a more charitable reading of Raz in which the concept of interest-dependence is taken narrowly, as itself exhibiting practical bipolarity.

[24] H. L. A. Hart, 'Bentham on Legal Rights', in A. W. B. Simpson (ed.), *Oxford Essays in Jurisprudence: Second Series* (Oxford: Oxford University Press, 1973), 171–201.

type found in *Sylvia doesn't mind that E is happening*. The contrast between these judgements is evidently an instance of the general contrast we are pursuing. It seems that no description of *what Sylvia doesn't mind* or *what she would very much like to be the case* will ever add up to your *having her consent* to your doing something. Thus, though it may supply an adequate elucidation of the particular locutions 'right against' and 'duty to', a Hartian account appears to move the larger question of bipolarity from the forms found on our table to the form of willing that is at stake.[25]

6. The Practical-Philosophical Conception of a Person must be Distinguished Formally from the Concept of an Agent

It has emerged that our topic is not just the specifically moral form of bipolarity or dikaiology, but the dikaiological character of judgement taken generally, whatever the gear setting or key, and the conditions of its possibility and truth. I want to prove various lemmas about *any* such thing, or anyway to envisage them. The point of the lemmas, though, would be in application to the specifically moral, or directly normative, case: the bipolarity or being-toward-another that we found at the outset in the thoughts of our heroine and in your self-conception as bearing certain duties to Sylvia. The 'puzzle about justice' that I mean to present will be a difficulty in the interpretation of these specifically moral pairings and of the conditions that could make *them* true.

The chief question before us in 'general meta-dikaiology' is this: what beyond a mere 'system of norms' must be in place before we can advance from merely monadic deontic propositions of the types found on our second table to properly bipolar propositions of the type found on the first? What gives this dyadic grammar a foothold? What moves Sylvia out of the worldly materials which ground a particular monadic deontic judgement, and carves out a place for a representation of her in the form of

---

[25] In a traditional Jewish wedding, the bride is not among the signatories of the *ketubah*, but she is studied for signs of despair or opposition to the advancing proceeding. If they are found, the wedding is off. Though everything depends, in a sense, on the bride's will, the arrangement seems not to give her a (Mosaic-legal) *potestas* over the groom and her father. Her will does not enter into the matter in the right sort of way, as directed consent.

deontic judgement itself (whether it belongs to morals or law or etiquette)? What makes her not just *raw materials for wrongdoing*, but *someone whom someone might 'wrong'*, in one sense or other?

Let us introduce the following terminology: wherever a couple of agents are apt to be represented in true bipolar deontic judgements of one type or other, in one gear setting or another, we will say that they stand together under a particular *dikaiological order* or a particular *order of right*—that is, a particular form of *dikaion* or *ius* (though, unlike Aristotle and Thomas, but like Hume, we will recognize ludic *iures* and an occasional *ius* of etiquette). A dikaiological order is simply the objective correlate of a particular 'gear' into which dikaiological judgement can be shifted or a particular 'key' in which it, or its language, can be sung.

We may also say, to continue with mere definitions, that where a particular agent does fall under a dikaiological order, or under a particular *ius*, the agent is thereby rendered a *person*. This is a straightforward generalization of the concept of a person forged by classical jurisprudence, in which, not to put too fine a point on it, persons are defined as possible parties to a lawsuit, possible terms of legal nexuses.

This practical-philosophical conception of a person is to be distinguished, at least notionally, from that of an agent simply, or anyway from a certain conception of an agent. An *agent*, we may say, is something that operates on the strength of practical reasons or thoughts or considerations. It is something that can be viewed as doing one thing for the sake of another, according to concepts, or equivalently, I think, simply as a realizer of concepts. I see a process as a phenomenon of agency, in this sense, when I see the concept through which I describe or represent the process as itself at work in the genesis of the process I describe or represent.

The conception of an agent as a subject of concept-realizing processes, or of concept-governed teleology, is thin in certain respects. If we suppose that communicability is a defining feature of properly conceptual representation, there would seem to be no impediment to speaking, for example, of *collective* agents in this thin sense, and of their collective practical operations. Donald Davidson can write the word 'action' by typing each letter in sequence; here the concept or conceptual structure *writing the word 'action'* is suitably in play; it is under realization. But the high school football team in Action, Arizona, might write the word 'action' on the hillside above town, in gypsum dust or chalk, each member taking a letter for himself. The conceptual structure *writing the word 'action'* is then held in common by the various members of the team, and it is here again in play in a process that falls under it, but in another way.

This notion of an agent, consequently, is thin in a further sense, and this is my present point. A couple of mere agents, a couple of 'concept-realizers', might find that their concepts are crossed a bit, that they are moving in different and incompatible directions, trapped together in a single natural world. We need only suppose that, as an agent, each is in possession of the concept of an agent or a concept-realizer, that each brings the other under it, and that each is in a position to attribute determinate conceptually apprehended objectives to the other. In such an unhappy meeting, the practical representations that either agent works with will of course differ from those it applies in interaction with non-rational animals or with minerals or vegetables; they will perhaps be, as we say, more complex. But this is *only* because the object with which it interacts moves in higher categories than animals, minerals, and vegetables do. The other agent is sunk in the materials with which either agent operates, as old buildings and rare birds are in criminal law. The other agent is something in respect of which either agent might 'mess up' instrumentally. All of the normativity in the case derives from the agent's own ends, and is thus merely monadic.

This, it seems, is how things stand if we cleave to the materials analytically contained in the thin idea of an agent or concept-realizer. If all else is left out of account, pairs of agents will at best provide materials adequate for an application of game theory. That game theory operates with something like our thin conception of agency emerges in the fact that its practitioners move indifferently from assignments of pairs of individual rational animals to the variables contained in their theories—assignments like Prisoner X and Prisoner Y, say—to assignments like X Inc. and Y Ltd., or the USA and the USSR.

So much for abstract agency; let us turn again to abstract right and to the concept of a person—which, I want to say, is formally something quite different or more. The judgement X *is a person*, as I explained it, is essentially a 'de-relativization' of the prior bipolar judgement X *is a person in relation to Y*. Similarly, X *is a sister* is a de-relativization of X *is a sister of Y*. 'Recognizing someone as a person' is registering her as a person in relation to yourself; it is the appropriation of such a proposition in the first person. Similarly, recognizing someone as a sister—saying 'Hey, sister', maybe—is registering her as your own sister.

The underlying judgement *X is a person in relation to Y* is the minimal judgement that is contained in all of the forms represented on our table. It expresses a 'determinable' of which all these dikaiological judgements express possible 'determinates'. As the Fregean judgment ξ *is an object* expresses the bare possibility of ξ's entering into facts of the form $\Psi(\xi)$, so we might say that *X is a person in relation to Y* expresses the bare possibility of X's and Y's entering into facts of the form $J(X,Y)$ or XJY.

As a de-relativization of a prior relational concept, the practical-philosophical conception of a person is formally unlike any monadic 'concept of a person' that might be found in theoretical philosophy: for example, that of Boethius, Strawson, or Frankfurt. This would be clearer if I were to replace the word 'person' with something like Aristotle's *isos*, an 'equal', or *heteros*, an 'other'—though each of these would be misleading in its own way. Nothing can be in any sense an 'equal', or an 'other' in isolation, unless perhaps prospectively or retrospectively. The concept *person* as I am explaining it is a concept of this kind. It is not attained by enriching the thin conception of an agent with further monadic properties.

But the fact of diverse and overlapping dikaiological orders (a fact upon which my whole argument will turn) shows that the present conception of a person is doubly relational: it can *itself* be shifted into various gears, or sung in different keys, or supplied with various subscripts. And, as an agent might enter as a person, *isos*, or *heteros* into several such forms of dikaiological nexus, so she might be related to a different class of 'persons' or *isoi* or *heteroi* under each of them. It will economize discussion if I introduce a concept to express this: namely, that of *the manifold of persons induced by a given dikaiological order*. This is the whole class of agents apt to be joined pairwise by concrete dikaiological relations of the type that the particular order makes available. Given a suitable gear-shift for 'X wrongs Y', they are the potential mutual wrongers in that sense.

Thus, supposing that a given system of etiquette can intelligibly be seen as constituting a *petite justice*, the induced manifold of persons will be coextensive with what is called 'polite society', the upper crust. The manifold of persons under chess, by contrast, is the class of players of chess, the possible poles of a chess game.

Our thinly defined conception of an *agent* indifferently covered individual human beings and various sorts of collective agent. The practical-philosophical conception of a *person* must also be explained so as to admit various types of collective or corporate person, depending on the order of right in question. Lawyers speak of corporations as jural or legal persons and of states as persons under international right. Kant speaks of families as 'moral persons'. And we may speak of baseball teams as ludic persons: just as a lawsuit might go by the name of X Inc. v. Y Ltd., so a baseball game might go by the name of the X Sox v. the Y Sox.[26]

7. A Modified Roman Empire Illustrates the Concepts so far Expounded

To illustrate the relativity of the concepts of a *ius*, a person, and a manifold of persons, and to prepare the ground for our principal argument and puzzle, let us consider a somewhat fantastic rendering of the Roman Empire in certain periods. Different orders of positive right were abroad in that empire, and the connection between them was peculiarly simple and clear.

In the city of Rome itself, there was the ancient civil law, or *ius civile*, some of it derived from the Twelve Tables, which bound Roman citizens with Roman citizens. No foreigner could possibly be linked with a Roman by this *ius*. At early stages, for example, no foreigner could sue a Roman in the associated tribunals with their quasi-religious procedure; none could join with a Roman to perform the picturesque ritual which inaugurated a traditional Roman contract.

Meanwhile, out in the provinces, in Palestine, say, or in Greece or Asia Minor, there were other equally traditional private-legal systems adjudicated by traditional local authorities—here again frequently with a religious coloration. No Roman citizen would sink to such a debased level, of

---

[26] Impatience with the idea of collective agents and corporate persons often parades as a sort of metaphysical hard-headedness, but I think that its real source, laudable in itself, is in intuitions belonging to the *specifically moral* case, in which individual reasoning animal agents— each with two eyes and two ears—are the real business. It is these especially whom our heroine, the bearer of the virtue of justice, herself two-eyed and two-eared, takes 'into account' or takes 'seriously'; it is these especially whom she opposes to herself, each as 'another' in thinking the thoughts of true justice. For her, unlike a lawyer or a game theorist, a corporation or state will seem to be something in the nature of a 'fiction'. It will fall off her specifically moral radar. She will meet the claims of any such thing with a certain impatience, wondering how things stand with the *people* in question. All of this is a consequence of the particular gear setting our heroine distinctively deploys, and has nothing to do with metaphysics.

course, nor would it make much sense for an Athenian to bring complaints to the authorities in Jerusalem. Most such local systems would, for example, have instituted their own equally picturesque formalities for the formation of a contract, quite different from those prevailing in Rome.

But finally, for the empire as a whole, there was the so-called *ius gentium*, the law of peoples, the private law originating under the authority of the *praetor peregrinus*. This more 'rational' and less procedurally grotesque system is the Roman law so much praised by our ancestors. It was a non-religious commercial necessity, one supposes, and a product of imperial expansion. This *ius*, this dikaiological order, indifferently bound Roman with Roman and Jew with Greek and Greek with Roman and Greek with Greek.

We may suppose, now crudely simplifying, that women and slaves fall entirely outside all of these specifically legal practical relations. But we may also suppose that a local form of etiquette exists among the upper class of citizens in Rome, and another in Athens, and so forth. Each forms a *petite justice* binding the men and women there alike with men and women. In each city the local *petite justice* allots its bearers distinct positions according to gender and age.

To complete our picture—at least for the moment—we may also suppose that some particular competitive game has overtaken the empire, a little known ancestor of chess, let's say. Its following includes members of all nations and classes: in chess, as we know, there is neither Jew nor Greek, man nor woman, freeman nor slave.

We have thus imagined a plurality of dikaiological orders and a corresponding plurality of manifolds of persons or *isoi* or mutual *heteroi*. A slave in Rome, a captive Scythian, might be a person under chess or a chess-person—a chess-player, as we say. He is apt to fall into chess-governed, or chess-indexed, bipolarity with his master or with a visiting Athenian notable, assuming they too know how to play. A Roman wife might be a 'player' and moreover also a 'lady'—a special type of person-under-the-local-*petite-justice*. A male head of a family in particular might wear many hats or crowns, and command the attention or *Achtung* of 'others' in several different ways, practically speaking. At least two of these will be private-legal: one type provincial, the other cosmopolitan.

But the class of attending 'others', the associated manifold of persons or *heteroi*, will differ according to the hat or crown worn. If he is to grasp his situation, each agent will himself have to operate our forms of judgement first-personally in several different gears and identify a suitable range of 'others' corresponding to each gear. It should be noticed that each manifold of persons we have considered is in a sense indefinitely extensible. The rules of chess do not need to be rewritten when the number of players doubles, nor does a profound understanding of Athenian private law depend on any knowledge of the number of persons who are related to one another under it.

Manifolds of persons expand and contract according to the form of dikaiology in question, but this need not just be a matter of the crowning and uncrowning of individual natural human agents, as a woman might be crowned in chess and etiquette and uncrowned in provincial and cosmopolitan private law. For we may also suppose that non-human, non-two-eared agents appear under some regimes and disappear under others. Anything we would ordinarily call a 'corporate' agent is, we may suppose, completely invisible to the traditional local systems, below their radar. But let us suppose that certain sorts of corporation do appear—through representatives—in the general courts of the empire.[27] The workings of the system involve the deployment of propositions assigning corporate agents legal duties to, and rights against, other corporate agents, and also toward individual 'natural' persons or human beings. 'Wrongs' can be committed against them, debts left unpaid, and contracts violated. Certain corporate agents, then, belong to the manifold of persons induced by that particular order. We might similarly complicate our empire by imagining, say, a cosmopolitan team sport.[28]

[27] In actual Roman antiquity there was apparently comparatively little of this, but examples are sometimes found, for instance, in the treatment of municipalities and of the burial societies as instances of which many primitive Christian churches are said to have originated. See P. W. Duff, *Personality in Roman Private Law* (New York: A. M. Kelley, 1971).

[28] If in Roman antiquity corporate 'personality' was little developed, this is presumably because such a thing awaits the development of deeper forms of market relationship than existed in antiquity. The thought might naturally form, then, that primitive legal systems look to natural persons, whereas more advanced systems recognize corporate persons. But if the notion of a corporation is taken less narrowly, something close to the reverse comes to seem the case. It is often said that in primitive legal institutions the typical term of a private-legal relation of right is a household, a *domus*, an *oikos*; the *paterfamilias* merely represents this collective. In so far as this is a reasonable interpretation of the traditional local Roman institutions, then it is not true that the *ius gentium* was the first among Roman systems to 'see' corporate agents, however obscurely; we could as well say that it was the first to see the *individual human being* or 'natural' person, and to bind one of them to another after the fashion of a private-legal system. Within the traditional system, the family or household was the real

A person is indeed *one among many, all equally real*, as the *Nagelsatz* runs,[29] but there are many 'many's, many manifolds of persons, into which concept-realizing agency of one type or other can be inserted. The existence of any such manifold, as such a manifold—its distinctness from some arbitrary set of agents of one type or other—has certain metaphysically distinctive conditions, as we will, I think, see.

8. Three Possible Theories of the 'Specifically Moral' Case: Hume, Aristotle, and Kant (Our Puzzle will be This: That None of Them Seems to Work)

Armed with these thoughts, let us remember that in our picture of this imagined empire we have left something out. We have left one type of crown undescribed, one shape of yoke unhewn, one form of pairing unconsidered, one manifold unsynthesized. A bearer of the virtue of justice, we have supposed, operates with our bipolar forms of judgement and throws them into a particular gear. Our heroine thinks '*I* can't do *A*, it might kill *Sylvia*; I have a duty to her', and she thinks it in a specific way. Or she thinks what might be made articulate in that way. She has given our bipolar forms a new, specifically moral turn. How, though, are we to interpret this intellectual phenomenon, this solid crystal buried among the coarser overlapping dikaiological strata of our imagined empire?

If our virtuous agent is lucky enough to have legal relational duties as well, and maybe ludic relational duties and duties under a *petite justice*, then representations of these might of course provide *grounds* for some of these 'specifically moral' bipolar judgements, which nevertheless should be distinguished from them. If justice is a genuine virtue, if it is not a sham or a kind of practical idiocy, then some of these *specifically moral* dikaiological thoughts must be true.

Let us pose the interpretative question in this way, approaching it perhaps a bit indirectly: Where is the new line to be drawn? What *manifold of persons* is induced by the form of bipolarity or being-toward-another and other-to-each-other that is at issue in the thoughts of our heroine, the

proprietor and could be made to answer with its property for delicts arising from the operation of father, son, daughter, slave, and cattle alike.

[29] Thomas Nagel, *The Possibility of Altruism* (Oxford: Oxford University Press, 1970), chs. 9–12.

genuinely just human being, and in our own representation of her as acting from 'reasons of justice' in a particular case? In what 'many' does our just agent implicitly locate herself as 'one' in thinking the thoughts of justice? What puts her into connection with Sylvia, thereby inducing a class of others to whom she might intelligibly be similarly linked?

Three traditionally accredited conceptions of the matter compete for our allegiance. There is, first, the doctrine of *Hume*, that justice is an artifical virtue, as he puts it. It rests on a convention, as he says, or on a 'social practice' as we might say.[30] For Hume, then, there is no great break between the sort of bipolarity our heroine distinctively registers—that is, the type of pairing of representations that she characteristically effects— and the sort found in more sophisticated later developments like private-legal institutions, in which appeal is made to an independently isolated judging agent and to a notion of market equivalence. Both alike are matters of custom, or 'artifice'—as also are the still more advanced prop-erly political institutions, in which rules of positive right are consciously altered and adjusted, and merely monadic norms adopted for the solution of large-scale collective action problems. If the Humean conception of the matter is right, then the manifold of persons into which our heroine implicitly inserts herself will at best (I will suggest) be the class of bearers of the specific historically developed right-making practice under which she falls and which she has, as we say, 'internalized'.

There is, secondly, the view of *Aristotle* and *St Thomas* and lately, I think, of *Philippa Foot*,[31] that justice is a 'natural' virtue, a 'natural' excellence: it is something that makes a human being good or excellent or sound *as a human being*—that is, as a bearer of the particular life form it bears. The formation of the associated type of representation of others as 'others', or as persons—the comprehension of 'oneself' as 'one among many' after the manner of our heroine—would on such a teaching be accounted an aspect of sound *specifically human* development. It is to be compared—but also of course in many ways contrasted—with the mastery of a language (of *some* human language), or even with the formation of eyes and optic nerves, and of the parts of the brain that figure in, say, the recognition of human faces. The individual human is seriously damaged, as a human, if it lacks

---

[30] David Hume, *A Treatise of Human Nature*, ed. L. A. Selby-Bigge (Oxford: Oxford University Press, 1988), book III, part II, §§ I–VI; *idem*, *An Enquiry concerning the Principles of Morals*, § III.

[31] Philippa Foot, *Natural Goodness* (Oxford: Oxford University Press, 2001).

any of these things. Human action and life, detached from the peculiar representation of oneself as 'one among many' that is characteristic of the just agent, might on such a view be compared, at a rather high level of abstraction, to the 'movement' of a detached frog's leg.

A teaching of this type might be developed in a number of ways. It is of course consistent with its central thought that the dictates of this virtue might, in respect of a given pair of agents, be massively affected by some of the so-called social practices under which the pair happen *together* to fall. Similarly, Hume's doctrine is consistent with the idea that some fundamental justice-inducing customs should have grown to encompass an extensive empire (non-politically speaking), but that their dictates in the case of a *given* pair might be massively affected by some of the more local and determinate justice-inducing 'practices' that the agents in question happen both to bear. On an Aristotelian account, though, every bipolarity-inducing *custom* will be understood as either determining, decorating, or competing with a deeper form of dikaiology of a categorially distinct type, not merely a more extensive form of the same basic customary type. On such a conception of the matter, it is thus intelligible to speak of relations of 'moral right' as joining pairs of individuals who share no social practices or institutions nor suffer any one common *Bildung*. In this it contrasts, I think, with the Humean doctrine, properly understood. Nevertheless, the class of individual 'persons' with whom a just agent is prepared to reckon pairwise will, on this view, at best (I will suggest) be the class of bearers of the nature or life form in question, the class of all human beings.

9. Excursus on the Concepts Life Form and Practice

Before describing the third competing conception of the manifold of persons into which our heroine inserts herself—the view, namely, of *Kant*—it may be well to emphasize three points about the leading concepts on which the Humean and Aristotelian doctrines turn. These are the concepts *practice* and *species*, respectively—or *form of life* and *life form*, as we might better call them, or again *second nature* and *first nature*, as we might equally well call them.[32]

---

[32] I discuss the concepts *life* and *life form*, and their relations, in my paper 'The Representation of Life', in Rosalind Hursthouse, Warren Quinn, and Gavin Lawrence (eds.), *Virtues and Reasons* (Oxford: Oxford University Press, 1995), 247–96. I discuss the concept *practice* or *social*

Consider first the concept *species* or *life form*. The first point to emphasize is that it is perfectly intelligible to speak of a *pair* of occupants of this category which are exactly the same in their inner constitution, but are nevertheless *distinct species* or *distinct life forms*. Such is the relation that the life form you and I share bears to the life form shared by all the exactly similar humanoids up on the philosopher's Twin Earth: they are on all accounts properly 'twin humans', not humans; their form is not human form but twin human form. The anatomical, pathological, and cardiological textbooks published up there may say exactly the same things as ours do, and the diagrams may look exactly the same, but their treatises are speaking of and diagramming something else. The distinction appears to hold despite the fact that a life form is in some sense something universal or general or indefinitely extensible, or is internally related to something that is.

Occupants of the category *social practice* may likewise be the same in their inner constitution, though they are, again, *distinct practices*. So it would be with an independently developed Twin English spoken somewhere in the South Seas: it would be a different language. If Captain Cook, overhearing the locals, mistakes them for fellow English speakers—descendants perhaps of earlier shipwrecked Englishmen—he will be wrong. And if he asks (in English), 'Do you know where I can get a shave?' and they answer (in Twin English), 'Go up Mindanao Avenue three blocks, turn left on to Fiji and you'll see it on your right,' and in the end he even gets a shave, still this will not be a conversation; nor, more obviously, will Cook be gaining testamentary knowledge about the places of things. Grammars and dictionaries of the two languages (written, let's suppose, in a third language) will say all the same things, but they will once again say them about different things. This again holds, despite the fact that an individual language is something universal or general or indefinitely extensible.

Similarly, anticipating a bit, we may suppose that on the frontiers of our empire some class of people, call them the Lombards, have a system of personal private law—a not-specifically-moral form of right-inducing 'social practice'. The system is completely decentralized and traditional; it does not put its bearers into 'political society' with one another, constituting

practice in my paper 'Two Forms of Practical Generality', in Arthur Ripstein and Christopher Morris (eds.), *Practical Rationality and Preference* (Cambridge: Cambridge University Press, 2001), 121–52, and more extensively in my forthcoming book *Life and Action* (Cambridge, Mass.: Harvard University Press).

government proper. When disputes arise, a jury of fellow Lombards is empanelled according to fixed rules, and the case is decided according to time-honoured principles which one learns along with one's language and religion.

Meanwhile, across the Alps, philosophers have arranged that by a freak accident unrecognized on either side, another people, the Schlombards, can be found working with a sub-political system of private right that is exactly the same in every respect. The formalities necessary to the formation of a contract are the same, as is the age at which the capacity to contract is acquired, etc.

Still it seems plain that the two peoples will not share a common system of personal private law. They do not appeal to the same time-honoured principles to settle disputes, but to *different principles with exactly the same content.*[33] We may suppose that the languages these peoples speak are also exactly alike, a member of either crowd calling herself (in her language) a 'Lombard'. In that case, if a pair of agents from the opposing groups meet by chance in the Alps, they would both have every reason to think that they are both (as each would put it) 'Lombards' and that they are, say, *concluding a valid contract* with this particular assemblage of song and dance. Again, though, it seems plain that they are not—no more than they are engaging in a genuine conversation in the process of 'bargaining' that leads up to the seeming contract-sealing ritual. I will try to say more about why this is so a bit later.

Another example: suppose that many of the Lombards have learned to play chess from wandering Roman soldiers, but that the Schlombards have an independently evolved game that is exactly the same—a twin chess or tzschess. Chess and tzschess are, once again, *different games with exactly the same rules.* As a result, at least on first meeting, in ignorance of these facts, there will intuitively be nothing that the ostensibly opposed players are playing.[34]

---

[33] The Turkish Ministry of Foreign Affairs writes as follows: 'In 1926, the Swiss Civil Code and the Code of Obligations were adopted by the Turkish Parliament with minor modifications as the Turkish Civil Code and Turkish Code of Obligations. The Code of Civil Procedure, brought into force in 1927, was adopted from the law of the Swiss Canton Neuchâtel' (see *http://www.mfa.gov.tr/grupe/eg/eg27/11.htm*). Here it is clear that the Turkish Republic is instituting its own laws, but that some of them are *the same in content* as some of those of the Swiss Federation and one of its cantons. It is not that the territory governed by the procedural laws of Neuchâtel was extended to cover Asia Minor.

[34] We might introduce a systematic way of representing these distinctions. Given the name of any practice or life form, we suffix an asterisk to it, writing 'English*', 'human*', 'Lombard

A second point to be emphasized is that occupants of either category supply a kind of background for the interpretation of particular phenomena pertaining to their individual bearers. Thus, for example, it is because this pair of speakers speak and are speaking *English* that the one, in saying 'Cut it out', can be read as having *told the other to cut it out*. In another language the same might be said in different sounds; in yet another, the same sounds might say something different. And it is because the players are playing *chess* that this distribution of pieces can count as *Black's king's being in check*. In an unorthodox chess some of the pieces might have different powers, so that other distributions of them count as 'check'. And it is because of its connection to the practice of playing *baseball*, as Rawls says, that this 'peculiarly shaped piece of wood' is a *bat*.[35]

On the other hand, but similarly, it is because this is a *sugar maple* that this mass of cells amounts to a *leaf*; in another form of vegetative life, any such thing would constitute a cankerous excrescence, and something quite different would count as a leaf. And so, likewise, it is because this is a *moon jellyfish* that these bits can be understood to be *tentacles*. And, finally, it is because I am a *human being* that these aggregates of flesh and bone add up to *arms*, not excrescences—and these movements to *my moving my arms*, and this pallor to *an expression of fear*. A life form is in this respect like a language that physical matter can speak.[36]

A third point to emphasize is that there is no reason to think—and it is no part of either theory, Humean or Aristotelian, to hold—that a shared practice or a shared (intelligent) life form must *be* right-inducing or justice-inducing: no more than a form of animal (i.e., sentient) life must be sighted, and no more than a language must contain an expression for *Schadenfreude*. The English language and 'solitaire' are practices or customs in the sense that Hume is using. But neither of them is intuitively right-inducing;

---

law*', 'chess*', etc.; the resulting term covers any practice or life form with exactly the same inner content as the one covered by the unasterisked name. Captain Cook's islanders speak Twin English, which is an English* and of course a Twin English*; Captain Cook speaks English, which again is an English* and a Twin English.* The exactly similar Twin Earthers are twin humans, unlike us, but they are bearers, like us, of a human* life form and a twin-human* life form. Tzschess, like chess, is a chess* and a tzschess*. In general X* and Twin X* are the same, though X and Twin X are distinct.

[35] John Rawls, 'Two Concepts of Rules', in *Collected Papers*, ed. Samuel Freeman (Cambridge, Mass.: Harvard University Press, 2000), 20–46.

[36] This feature of the concept *life form* or *species* is developed at length in my essay on 'The Representation of Life', part II: 'The representation of the living individual'.

certainly solitaire isn't. Similarly, on Foot's view, though she does not emphasize it, there is no reason a priori to say that an intelligent life form could never be one of which Hobbesianism, say, is true, and thus one for which prudence is the only really fundamental virtue. Nor does she suggest that there could not be a life form in which the arguments of Callicles—that what is praised hereabouts under the name of 'justice' in fact drags its bearers down and declaws them and renders them harmless, and so on—would be sound. Why shouldn't that be possible? It is just that it isn't so with specifically human beings, she thinks: for us there is justice.[37]

10. The Received Conception of the Manifold of Moral Persons is Abstract

But let us return to our three conceptions of the manifold of persons in which our heroine is lodged. In addition to the Humean and Aristotelian conceptions, there is, finally, the received conception, the Kantian and neo-Kantian conception (though it is not only Kantian and neo-Kantian). This should perhaps rather be called a family of conceptions. The mark of membership in this family of conceptions is that the specific 'many' of which our heroine sees herself and Sylvia each as 'one' is identified with something like the class of *all agents*, or *all rational animals*, or *all rational animals who can act on principle*, or *all 'persons' in the monadic sense of Boethius or Strawson or Frankfurt.*

One feature that all of these concepts share is that a pair of agents can come together to fall under any one of them in complete natural-causal independence of one another, without any shared dependence on *anything* we can understand as a common source. There need be no one common account of it that practical reasoning or principled action or second-order desire goes on in this two-eared animal here on Earth, say, and can also go

---

[37] Foot's book has two components. One component, which we might call formal Footianism, is an analysis of the concepts of genuine 'reasons', ultimate 'normativity', and true 'value'; all are brought into connection with 'natural goodness'. The analysis holds, if it holds, wherever in the cosmos these concepts gain a foothold in discursively thinking agents. But a different component of her theory—substantive or local Footianism—appears in her arguments that justice and prudence are, as a matter-of-fact, genuine virtues among human beings. The interest of her book does not stand or fall with these latter claims: the exposition of formal Footianism might rather have been annexed to a sort of substantive Hobbesianism in which, say, prudence alone is human virtue.

on in *that* two-eared one on Twin Earth and in that two-antennaed one up there on Mars. Developments have perchance taken this turn in each case; the capacity for the phenomenon in question has come to be on these three planets—as vision has come to be independently several times on this one planet—by familiar processes of variation and selection.

Let us elaborate the point by considering the classical definition of Boethius: a person, he says, is an 'individual substance of a rational nature'.[38] Well, *human*, *twin human*, and *Martian* are three 'rational natures', we may suppose; they are three 'forms of intelligent life'. Since the origins of these species or natures or life forms are, by hypothesis, entirely independent, the hypothetical homogeneity of the agents, as reasoning, would appear to be entirely accidental. Yet individual bearers of these several life forms will all alike be 'united' under the one concept *person* that Boethius is forging, even including Martian babies and Twin Earth idiots.

It is the same, I think, with any grand abstract concept under which a philosopher might bring herself and her friends—say, *self-constituting self-conscious subjecthood under a practical identity*. That sort of thing might chance to break out in the Andromeda galaxy quite as well as it might down here.

It cannot be so, though, with the class of co-practitioners of a single practice like *the English language*, or *Lombard law*, or *chess*. The homogeneity of the agents who come under any one of these is not an accident. Nor can it be so with co-bearers of a single genuine life form like *red oak*, *Norway rat*, *human*, *twin human*, or *Martian*. An individual object's falling under any one of the italicized concepts is always a matter of its falling into a single, naturalistically intelligible, trait-transmitting historical succession. Or rather, this is the only way we can understand these categories—life form and form of life—to be realized in nature as we know it to be. Falling into a succession of processes of *reproduction of a life form* and of *habituation into a practice* are respectively schemata of these categories, as we might say.[39] In bringing a *pair* of individual objects together under one *such* concept we bring them

---

[38] Boethius's definition is discussed and defended by Aquinas, *Summa Theologiae*, Ia, q. 29, art. 1. The concept is of course intended to cover not just people, but God and angels.

[39] Perhaps other schemata could be imagined: for example, on theological hypotheses. Perhaps God, operating in accordance with *one* divine idea, could people each of several planets with an original pair: Adam and Eve, Adam* and Eve*, etc. In that case we might perhaps speak of them all as sharers in some one single life form, interpreted as a sort of divine archetype. Similarly, God might perhaps be said to teach agents in diverse galaxies some one language, or some one game; 'the language' or 'the game', considered as something present in many, would then itself be identified with the archetypal idea. But our point about

under a common interpretative background, and we bring their homogeneity under a single common account. We can thus see this homogeneity as 'no accident' in a perfectly intelligible way. It seems plain that any concept under which I fall together with a twin human will not have these features.

There would thus appear to be a radical distinction between concepts like *animal*, *rational animal*, *Boethian person*, *agent*, and *speaker*, on the one hand, and those like *Norway rat*, *human*, *twin human*, *speaker of English*, *player of chess*, and *Lombard*, on the other. The former we might call 'abstract' class concepts, and the latter 'concrete'. The mark of a Kantian or neo-Kantian or 'received' type of account can then more clearly be stated: it uses an ostensibly abstract class concept to identify the manifold of persons in which our heroine implicitly locates herself. Just for this reason, though, received views are all very difficult to maintain once the nature of our bipolar nexuses is properly grasped; the metaphysical consequences of all such views are quite extraordinary. Of course, the other two views, the Humean and Aristotelian, face difficulties of their own. And this is my puzzle: we seem to be unable to supply an unproblematic interpretation of the thoughts that are distinctive of our heroine.

11. Apprehension an Order of Right within the Manifold of Persons it Induces: Our Chief Lemma

To see the difficulties, let us return to the question of practical bipolarity in general. Suppose that I am drifting through the empire we imagined, saturated as it was with overlapping dikaiological orders, diverse gear settings, and expanding and contracting manifolds of persons. I now overhear the words 'You've done me wrong'. The context makes it plain that this could be expanded into 'You've done me wrong, *legally* speaking'. We will not concern ourselves with the particular contents. Our abstract forms are

---

life forms and practices as supplying a common account of the homogeneity of many bearers would still, I think, have to hold. It is a central feature of a life form or practice, I think, that it should in some sense account for individual bearers' coming under it: each life form or practice is a 'concept that procures its own existence', as Hegel often says, or a 'universal that provides its own instance'. On naturalistic assumptions, it would seem that this structure can only be realized where a thing's coming under this form or universal arises through the operation of prior bearers of the form—that is, through reproduction or habituation.

being deployed, and in a specifically legal or juridical sort of way. In interpreting such words, and appraising them for truth, I must link them first with a particular order of private right. Is it the local provincial one, or the general imperial one? In which manifold of persons is he implicitly locating himself and his interlocutor?

If our speaker actually names one of these regimes of positive private right in the discourse we are trying to interpret, then that will decide the matter: 'I have a contract with you, Marcus, under the *ius civile* of our immortal Roman forefathers,' he says. Fine, he means the local system; the dikaiological thought he is expressing has been shifted into the local gear. But why does that decide the matter? It is presumably because his use of this name, '*ius civile*', bears some relation of dependence, perhaps causal dependence, on the particular regime of right named. Of course, we can say as much of the relation that the name of a lake bears to the lake it is the name of. My thoughts of Lake Michigan, are about Lake Michigan because they somehow depend on it. But it seems that an order of private-legal right is not something that just stands there like a lake. It is not something to which an agent might just happen to refer in making judge-ments about 'rights' and 'duties'. That is admittedly how things would stand with a comparative jurist or legal anthropologist who happens upon the scene. But (I want to suggest) the bearers of the system cannot intelli-gibly be supposed *generally* to relate to it in that sort of way.

I have maintained all along that a deployment of our bipolar deontic machinery is empty thought, spinning in a frictionless void, if you like, until it has been thrown into a specific gear attaching it to a definite dikaiological order, or *ius*. My present thought is that we must also hold the converse: a dikaiological order cannot exist unless the manifold of 'persons' or *isoi* or *heteroi* it joins and opposes manage to throw these abstract forms of judgement into a gear that refers to or expresses it, even if they are not in a position *explicitly* to name it with a phrase like '*ius civile*'. A *ius* and the concepts through which the associated nexuses are expressed must come into the world together.

This of course does not mean that any single agent who comes under such an order, and is a 'person' under it, is in actual possession of suitably adjusted dikaiological concepts or the associated person conception. He might be too young or too dim or too mad to grasp such things. How befuddled and ignorant an agent can be and still count as a 'person' under a given order will depend on the order in question, just as the range of potential 'wrongs' and the conditions of their imputability will. In a competitive game like chess the requirements are comparatively high. To count as a chess-player, or as a 'person under chess'—and thus to be positioned to fall into chess-governed bipolarity with another similarly positioned—an agent must know or at least be learning something about how one plays chess. She, or her teacher, must know something about the moves one 'can' and 'can't' make in a chess game played with, or rather against, another chess-player. This knowledge will deploy our directed deontic machinery in a chess-related gear: homogeneous dikaiological thought will thus appear on both sides of the chess-board. In what we are calling the 'specifically moral' gear setting, by contrast—the one distinctively deployed by our heroine—it would seem that even the dullest infant will count as a person and be wrongable in many of the ways in which Sylvia, a highly reflective grown-up, is.

We must content ourselves, then, with a rather weak proposition: the real existence of a dikaiological order, and thus of a contentful deployment of bipolar deontic concepts, presupposes this much, that the apprehension of the appropriate deployment of bipolar deontic concepts—and the same deployment, in the same gear setting—is a *typical attainment* within the associated manifold of persons. Otherwise no dikaiological nexuses can join any of them to any of them; we would have a mere set of agents, not a manifold of persons. And so too the imagined deployment of dikaiological concepts will be contentless. A manifold of persons must be a genus, an indefinitely extensible class, within which apprehension of the associated form of practical opposition holds typically or 'as for the most', *hōs epi to polu*, as Aristotle says. This weak lemma is enough, though, to introduce numerous metaphysical subtleties into our enquiry.

In fact, a parallel claim would seem to hold for all forms of deonticity, bipolar or not. Consider the classical formulae 'A law must be promulgated' and 'Ignorance of law (or of "principle", or of "the universal") does not excuse'. These propositions must no doubt be qualified, especially in their application to positive law; but we can, I think, see that they rest on deep features of deontic judgement in general, and in fact express the same fundamental idea. Each means that *deontic truth of a given type is not there to be apprehended or to bind until ignorance of it among those whom it binds is rendered exceptional.* Apprehension of it must be 'no accident' or somehow typical. This is the state of things that the Greek tyrant intuitively failed to effect—the one, namely, who is said to have placed his 'criminal legislation' on the top of a high pillar, so that it would be impossible to read. Again, though an agent's grasping his deontic situation must in some sense be the standard case, whatever form of deonticity we may have in view, it may of course be that the 'standard' case is statistically rare, and that valid excuses are very common.

What is distinctive of our bipolar deonticities is that this weak condition applies at *both* poles of the typical, or 'standard', dikaiological relation. Their relation must be something that the agents at either pole can be wrong about, of course, but it must be something upon which they can be in agreement, and in suitably *non-accidental* agreement. The fundamental question of general meta-dikaiology is this: What can put such a structure in place?

12. Illustrative Theological Application of our Lemma

We might elaborate on these ideas by again moving outside our empire and adding one more spectacular thought experiment to our collection. Suppose that God gives a positive law, a list of ten 'commandments', to all the Hebrews. All of the actions that this Law requires will be 'required by reason' as well, on ordinary theological premisses. But we can distinguish two senses of 'necessity' in the matter: only one of them, rational requirement, had application to anything before the appearance of the Law. Individual Hebrews were *rationally required* to do various things before the appearance of the Law—to brush their teeth, for example—but they were not *bound by the Law* to do anything.

Let us consider now a heretical variant in which lists of ten commandments are given *separately* to the heads of each household, as separate acts of revelation, separate cases of divine fiat. We can make the same twofold conceptual distinction in each household's case: there is what reason requires, and there is what the Law given to it requires. The latter, we piously affirm, is always included under the former. It will seem a somewhat academic question whether the forms of 'deonticity' inaugurated by these several hundred acts of divine legislation and domestic reception are the same or different. If we suppose that the different lists have different ingredients, and that each is to govern its recipient's household and the households of all its male descendants, then it is clear that we have imagined something like the inauguration of several hundred nations all with the same divine sovereign, but each with a separate divine positive law and a different theological gear setting for deontic vocabulary.

If now it perchance happens that, though they are otherwise different, several or indeed all of these lists have some one item in common—not to kill any 'reasonable creature *in rerum natura*', for example—then, in acting in obedience to this item on its own list, the members of different households will be *acting on different principles, but principles with the same content.*[40] Any 'reasonable creature *in rerum natura*', a visiting angel or a Martian, for example, will be relieved to learn that a household nearby is subject to such a constraint, and may come to reckon on the impediment. But it is no part of the constitution of that constraint and the genus of deonticity contained in it that those extra-domestic reasonable creatures should happen to know this, as it *is* part of the constitution of the divine law of a given house that it should be *no accident* if its members grasp its terms. In particular, it is no part of the constitution of the constraint attaching to any one household, that *it* is grasped or tends to be grasped by the members of other nearby *households* which live under similar such Laws. Indeed, it might be legitimate and reasonable to try to keep it a secret that one is thus bound.

So, now, though members of each household are kept from killing members of any household, as well as any 'reasonable' space aliens who might happen by, they are all operating on different principles and are under different Laws. The explanations of the apparently similar thoughts 'I'm forbidden . . .' will be different in different households, and the index of the deontic operator will be different as well: the several Laws are as different as the 'Old Law' and the 'New' are supposed to be. But just for this reason, I want to say, it is impossible to view the situation as one in which the members of the different households have fallen into relations of right.

Wesley Hohfeld, in his discussion of 'legal relations', affirms the proposition that our two forms, 'X has a duty to Y to do A' and 'Y has a right against X that he do A', in its 'claim' use, represent the same 'legal' or 'jural' relation from the different points of view of the legal persons caught up in it.[41] His implicit thought, I think, was that the possibility of such a

---

[40] I am presupposing, for purposes of argument, a 'divine command theory' positivism, which would hold that no one has any special reason to avoid this apart from divine legislation.

[41] Hohfeld, *Fundamental Legal Conceptions*, 40.

bipolar nexus *presupposes* that someone in the position of X can potentially think: *I have a duty to Y to do A*, and someone in the position of Y can think: *I have a right against X that he do A*. To speak of a 'possibility' of such convergence might perhaps be too weak, as we have already noted; rather, there must in the nature of the case be a tendency for each side to grasp the appropriate first-personal thought. This type of relational fact is generally internally related to two points of view that might be taken on it; it is such as to be registered by each of its poles. In this it differs from facts of the type X *is taller than Y*, and spatial relations generally; such relations are completely indifferent to conceptual apprehension by their terms. But, now, if there is to be such a harmony of judgement, there must be identity in the chief concepts the judgements deploy: namely, those expressed in our tabulated abstract forms, considered as shifted into a particular gear. It is the same with the deeper thought form implicit in all of these forms: X *is a person in relation to Y*, again considered as set in a particular gear. This concept, as Fichte says in *Foundations of Natural Right*, is a concept for two.[42] It cannot generally be left to the relata to grasp the appropriate gear setting, the appropriate form of pairing, through abstraction from (say) external anthropological experience—for deployment of the gear setting in question must already be present in the materials from which an external anthropological conception of it might be abstracted. Our non-external-anthropological account of a determinate dikaiological gear setting's arising in one agent, or of one agent's thoughts as set in it, must exhibit a source through the operation of which the same gear setting might figure in the thoughts of the other agent—even, and especially, if the pair now go on to conflict in the particular judgements they frame in terms of it. And because a dikaiological order is indifferent to the number of persons who fall into the manifold associated with it, and are potentially joined in the nexuses it constitutes, the source in question must potentially be such as to operate in indefinitely many agents.

---

[42] J. G. Fichte, *Foundations of Natural Right*, trans. Michael Baur (Cambridge: Cambridge University Press, 2000), 45. Using the concept 'individual' where I would use the word 'person', and exaggerating matters somewhat, Fichte writes: 'the concept of individuality [personality] is a *reciprocal concept*, i.e. a concept that can be thought only in relation to another thought, and one that (with respect to its form) is conditioned by another—indeed by an *identical*—thought. This concept can exist in a rational being only if it is posited as *completed* by another rational being. Thus this concept is never mine; rather, it is... *mine and his, his and mine*; it is a shared concept within which two consciousnesses are unified into one.'

These criteria are not met at our heretical Sinai, with its hundred separate tablets and manifold acts of domestic divine legislation and reception. But notice that they already fail at the orthodox Sinai, where a Law is put to all of the Hebrews at once, *given* the content we assigned to that law (interpreting the text a bit): namely, not to kill *any* 'reasonable creature *in rerum natura*'. It is indeed part of the constitution of the deonticity attaching to the ten common orthodox formulae that the Hebrews should come to be in regular possession of a concept of it—that is, a new gear setting for deontic judgement. Individuals who come under the Law will only lack this gear setting *per accidens*, by infancy, idiocy, stopping up of ears, forgetfulness, parental flakiness, etc. God has arranged that *Hebrew* is a genus within which such apprehension holds as a rule. But it is no part of the constitution of this form of deonticity that any non-Hebrew reasonable creatures should ever have any conception of it at all, even though they are, as we say, 'protected' by it. Alien others are in this respect formally like rare birds protected by environmental legislation: not dikaiological wrongables, but raw materials for wrongdoing. If other reasonable creatures do come to be aware of the constraint, it will be as a matter of comparative divine jurisprudence or theological anthropology. Knowledge of the Law, whether anthropological or not, is thus *per accidens* within the protected genus; and so this genus is not constituted as a manifold of persons by divine operations of the type we are imagining.

It may be, of course, that other classes of reasonable creatures have been given their own respective divine laws, and it may by chance be that each of these contains the precept not to kill other reasonable creatures. This does not affect the relation of these outsiders to the specifically Hebrew Law. *They do not act on the principle the Hebrews act on, but on another principle with the same content.* The structure of things is thus as it was at our heretical Sinai, but writ larger.

Where it is a question of constituting merely monadic duty, the distinction between a number of people acting under *common norms or principles* and a number of people acting under *norms or principles with the same content* will inevitably seem subtle and academic. Where it is a question of constituting an order of right, it is decisive. A manifold of 'persons' must together come under a genuinely common, not merely similar or parallel, form of deonticity. This is not all that is necessary to make the step from *lex* to *ius*, of course, but it is enough to make the trouble I am proposing to make about the 'specifically moral' case.

Let us return to our Lombards and Schlombards. Though hitherto there has been no connection between the different tribes, a pair of them, we supposed, might meet high in the Alps, the Lombard inevitably mistaking the Schlombard for a Lombard—after all, he calls himself by the name 'Lombard'—and the Schlombard mistaking the Lombard for a Schlombard. We asked: can such agents constitute a contract, and thus legal duties of one to the other and the other to the one? We can now see more clearly why not. When the songs and dances and handshakes have been completed, each will indeed think he has a legal obligation of some sort to the other and a legal claim of the same sort upon him. In fact, if the putative terms of the putative contract are symmetrical ('If you do A for me, I'll do A for you'), there may be no difference at all between the agents viewed physically, functionally, dispositionally, etc. But our hypothesis in this thought experiment is precisely that this homogeneity is sheer accident, and just for that reason it is not a Hohfeldian homogeneity of *thoughts*: our agents are in fact thinking different things. In assigning a determinate content to the dikaiological thoughts of either agent—that is, in seeing the pairings he frames as set into some one among the many particular gear settings the cosmos makes available—we must indeed advert to something through which we can see another agent's correlative or mirroring thought as no accident. And this is in each case the wider juridical practice of which the agent in question is a bearer, and which is in some sense the source of these thoughts and manifested in these thoughts. The existence of such an account explains why phenomena can be interpreted as containing genuinely bipolar contractual obligations of Lombard to Lombard, or of Schlombard to Schlombard, and parties who register such facts in thought. But on our high Alpine hypothesis, the account that applies to the one does not extend to thoughts of the other; a contract-admitting gear setting is available on each side, but no contract-admitting gear setting is available on both sides. If the Roman Empire had extended far enough, and our agents had performed the formalities necessary for a contact *iure gentium*, then a common account and thus a common index for dikaiological thoughts might be found at both ends of the handshake. As it stands, though, there is nothing on both sides of the handshake: the type of claim the Lombard thinks he has is a claim 'under Lombard private law', as we might say, making the gear setting explicit; the type of 'correlative' duty the Schlombard thinks he has is a duty 'under Schlombard ("Lombard") law'. They are like ships passing in a juridical night.

13. Preliminary Application of our Lemma to the Specifically Moral Case

But enough of Law Positive, divine and human alike; enough, too, of games and *petite justice*. Here again is our heroine, the bearer of true justice, acting on the strength of her recognition of a duty *to Sylvia*, a duty which she knows has no legal or ludic representation. Our *abstract* bipolar categories have thus been brought into play. But if there is to be any truth in this pairwise representation, if it is not idle thought, then it must be linked to some specific dikaiological order. We are supposing that this is the order of 'true justice', so to speak, or the order of 'moral rights'. And if there is to be any truth in this representation, then it must be linked indirectly to some specific manifold of persons, the manifold into which our heroine sees herself and Sylvia as inserted. We may suppose, if you like, that the elements of this manifold are the true or real or equally real persons, and that together they constitute what is called the moral community—or rather, that these are the 'true' persons *in relation to* our heroine, and this is the moral community *to which she belongs*.

And if there is to be any truth in this pairwise representation, there must be a possibility of a correlative representation in the agent our agent is thinking of, or rather a tendency for such thought to appear in her. Or rather, our pair must come together under an indefinitely extensible genus within which such a tendency prevails. The tendency must be for *the same thought*, modulo a reversal of first-person polarity, to appear in *the same gear setting* at both poles of the nexus in question. But, on the other hand, it is only given this tendency for suitable thought to appear at both poles of the moral relation it registers that there is any contentful thought available to appear, and any moral relation for it to register. This tendency might not often be realized, but it cannot generally be an accident that these correlative representations coincide. If this sometime community of minds *is* to be possible, there must be a possible *account* of the agents' agreement with one another, of the might-be meeting of their minds.

14. The Humean View has Intolerable Moral Commitments

The natural way of finding a determinate content for our heroine's thought is Hume's. The thoughts of co-practitioners of a single practice or custom do indeed come under a common source and a common background of interpretation: namely, the practice itself—a practice supplies a wavelength for everyone to be on, if you like. In the light of a suitably structured practice in which a pair of agents are together sunk, we can see the pairwise thoughts of either as reaching out toward completion, so to speak, by converse thoughts in the other, even if this homogeneity fails often to be realized. So a practice or custom can easily meet the criteria we have been attempting to articulate for the constitution of a determinate dikaiological gear setting and a corresponding order of right—as was plain all along from the examples of chess and *petite justice* and private law, which are all matters of custom or institution. Hume's thought is simply this: that the form of practical bipolarity with which our just agent operates has this same fundamental customary character. She has acquired her thoughts with her upbringing, her *Bildung*, on any account; why should we not characterize this upbringing as habituation into, or initiation into, a special 'moral' practice, distinct from those of chess and etiquette and private law?

But remember that if a given practice or custom 'protects' non-bearers as much as it does bearers, and in just the same way, then its dikaiological character collapses: it acquires instead the merely monadic aspect of criminal law or of the various divine commandments 'not to kill' that we considered. Possession of the associated conceptual machinery will be *per accidens* within the protected class. If the deontic thoughts in question are to be genuinely dikaiological, then the associated manifold of persons can only be the class of bearers of the practice, in whom the emergence of correlative thoughts will be non-accidental. Hume's conception of the matter entails that the manifold of persons associated with our heroine's distinctive, specifically moral form of thought can only be the class of bearers of that same practice—the class of those in whom thoughts mirroring hers are typically induced.

Hume no doubt thought that it was enough that our relation to outsiders is governed by benevolence or natural sympathy. It simply did not occur to him, as a naïve eighteenth-century writer, that apart from justice one might, out of natural sympathy, kill one person to remedy the plight of several others, or for any number of other beautiful purposes. A theory like Hume's can of course explain why *you* should not kill *Sylvia* even in order to save five others, where you and Sylvia are bearers of a single dikaiological practice; it need only be that the practice constitutes a directed duty not to kill and a claim not to be killed among its bearers. But he forgot that you might kill several recalcitrant practice-outsiders in order, from the deepest sympathy, to introduce your more advanced system of practices to their more numerous backward compatriots. And this is what we cannot bear to think; and this, we cannot help but think, is what our just agent cannot bear to think. Our heroine purports to see farther than the specific practices she bears, and views her connection with outsiders in dikaiological terms. She sees herself as bound to, and as owing something to, and as a 'person in relation to', each single one of them.

Sophisticated wisdoms will inevitably teach us that a 'common sense' that condemns our imagined benevolent imperialist is a refined product of certain sophisticated 'social practices', practices which these wisdoms may or may not feel inclined to praise. But we can now see that this same so-called common sense must reject all such accounts of itself. In seeing the practice-outsider as making as good an example of a murderable as any practice-insider, we plainly put ourselves into dikaiological connection with her and commit ourselves to the falsehood of any such account.

15. The Aristotelian View has Difficult Epistemological and Moral Commitments

We thus feel compelled to reject Hume's doctrine as immoral and wrong, though it may in the final analysis be the only account we can make any sense of. Where else can we turn? On an Aristotelian account, the generic unity of agents that makes for the possibility of 'specifically moral' bipolar nexuses is provided not by a shared practice, but by their shared specifically human life form itself. It is characteristic of the human being, on such an account, to develop the capacity to pair itself off dikaiologically with others, and others with others—even if this development is unfortunately often impeded, as the development of hands is unfortunately often also impeded. But if something like this is characteristic of the kind, then it will be no accident if a pair who come under this kind exhibit correlative forms of such thought—even if, again, this possible harmony should often break down. The non-accidentality of the convergence is underwritten by the shared life form. Thus our general criteria for genuinely dikaiological judging might be met, and there could be something for these correlative dikaiological judgements to be about. The concept of the human would be the concept of a manifold of persons.

What are we to think of such a construction of our heroine's thoughts? It is often complained that reference to the human form or 'species' or to human 'nature' will introduce an unwanted empirical element into moral philosophy. It is supposed to make things somehow 'biological', and thus to violate the autonomy of the ethical. Kant is especially alarmist on this point. The Aristotelian's first difficulty is to show that this supposed threat expresses a distorted conception of our relation to our own life form or nature. It is in fact clear, I think, that one representation of this particular form or nature is entirely a priori: namely, the representation of it as my kind, or as my form. If I am thinking a thought of it, I might think of it as *the life form manifested in this very thought, which is a bit of life*, to which I might rightly attach the predicate *has thousands of bearers*. The question who else does come under this a priori representation, and thus how many do, is indeed empirical; but so is the question what things and how many come under such plainly 'pure' concepts as *agent* or *rational being*.

But if each of us is in possession of a non-empirical, and thus non-'biological', representation of the specifically human life form, it might be doubted whether we have any substantive knowledge *about it* that is not empirical, as our knowledge of the existence and operation of the human liver is empirical. It may thus be doubted whether the substantive knowledge our heroine applies in particular dikaiological moral judgements can be given the construction we are considering. For we do not want to call this knowledge empirical. The Aristotelian's second difficulty is thus to develop an epistemology to match her conception of the matter at hand.

Let us illustrate the difficulty by contemplating a particular case. I have what we may call a 'moral intuition' that on the fateful day when Stalin ordered all of the blind wandering minstrels of the Ukraine shot, he wronged them all.[43] It was a horrible injustice. Of course, I might be wrong about this. But what does my thought contain? In so reckoning, I do not look to the laws or customs of the Soviet Union in the Thirties, if we can speak of laws and customs in such catastrophic circumstances. Nor do I contemplate the credentials of the particular further ends that Stalin had in view. I do not, for example, enquire how beautiful true

---

[43] Dmitri Shostakovich, *Testimony*, ed. Solomon Volkov (New York: Harper and Row, 1979), 214–15.

communism was going to be once the minstrel question was resolved. I view the matter in dikaiological categories, but in dikaiological categories that purport to outstrip any conventions, institutions, or laws. On the present view, then, my supposed 'intuition' is latently about the human form which Stalin and I and the minstrels all share: *in it*, I am thinking, this counts as injustice, as *in chess* moving a pawn three squares forward is cheating. In thinking this thought that is implicitly about the human form or human nature, I must further implicitly think that this thought itself is an apt expression of precisely the nature it is implicitly about, and that it would as such aptly appear at each pole of the Stalin–minstrel pairs I am considering. And thus I must implicitly think that wherever this thought is rejected, the processes typical of that form of life have been impeded. In thinking this thought, then, I must think of this thought as something other than the product of field-work or empirical investigation: where ignorance of liver function prevails, we need not suppose that processes typical or characteristic of specifically human life have been impeded. I must, that is, think of *certain* features of my life form as given to me in some other way, even if they might be given to, say, Martians by a subtle sort of field-work. But, of course, I do think this thought: Stalin did them all wrong.

The Aristotelian, I am suggesting, must articulate an epistemology according to which all of this can make sense: she must show how some life forms might be such that *some* substantive knowledge of them is non-empirical among their bearers; she must show how it can be that an intellectual life form might in certain of its aspects be known 'from the inside', if you like.

But isn't there a further difficulty? What about our practical relation to the Martians and the Twin Earthers? Can't we frame a moral complaint against an Aristotelian account that is structurally akin to the one we raised against the Humean teaching? A human and a Martian are outsiders in relation to one another in respect of life form, and someone might have the intuition that a Martian is as much wrongable by a human being as another human being is. Here there are various avenues of defence, none perhaps completely satisfying. We must first note the differential status of the two intuitions. Reflection on the twentieth century presents us, I am thinking, with a kind of established fact about inter-human right: we can now see, for example, that every human who ever thought it was a good idea for one human being to kill another human being for beautiful purposes was wrong. It is not simply a question of a private intuition. There is no such established fact pertaining to how things should go with Martians: there are only intuitions about science fiction cases which it is very difficult to think about at all. Further, we should remember that it is of course possible for items in the category 'social practice' to come to hold among bearers of different intelligent life forms; through them something in the nature of a Humean justice might come to bind intelligences falling under various natural forms. But such practices would not unite our mutual 'aliens' on first meeting. This, then, is really the case we are considering. And here, I think, the Aristotelian can do no more than plead, as a Humean would in the parallel place, that there are other virtues besides justice, virtues that might protect space aliens even on our first meeting with them; our intuitions about these cases are intuitions about those virtues; they are not intuitions about that elementary justice, claims of which permeate specifically human life.

16. The Received Kantian View has Alarming Metaphysical Commitments

Let us consider finally the received view, which is that the order to which our just agent adverts in the thoughts of true justice induces a manifold of persons that is essentially coextensive with the class of *all agents*, or some slightly narrower class: for example, that of *all rational animals*, or *all Boethian persons*. The just agent, on such a view, looks past the Humean practices into which she and others are sunk; she sees through the particular Aristotelian nature she and others bear; she attaches herself simply to the agency or the rationality of the one *by* whom she proposes thereby to 'do right', or *to* whom she has a horror of doing wrong. It sounds good on paper, it is the currency of academic moral theory, but what are its metaphysical presuppositions?

Let us suppose our heroine, reflecting on the nexus that she registers as binding her to Sylvia, imagines that she is also bound in just the same way not to destroy *any agent*, where the concept 'agent' is taken in the thin and broadly extended sense I explained above, so that it includes Martians and Twin Earthers, but also ExxonMobil and the football team of Action, Arizona. She won't destroy any of them. Can she then view her response to Sylvia as a *response to right*? It seems not. It seems that she cannot reasonably understand *agency* in this exceptionally thin sense to be combined with any tendency, however often its operation is impeded, to register the thoughts she has in imagining these duties. There seems, after all, to be no reason why concept-realizing agency might not sometimes be entirely devoid of dikaiological concepts and incapable of attaining them—or, indeed, corrupted where it does attain them. If a member of this extensive class happens to have otherwise suitable 'correlative' representations, this will just be an accident. It thus seems that a form of deontic thinking that 'protects' *this* entire class will not be a form of dikaiological thinking.

It is the same with the thicker concepts of animal agency, rational animality, Boethian personality and what Kant calls 'humanity'. Given that a suitably robust principle of plenitude operates in the universe in which they are applied, these abstract ideas will determine classes in which *some* have bipolar concepts, some don't. Among those that don't, some indeed will only fail to have them *per accidens*, by youth or idiocy, say; but others, it seems, could only ever *come* to possess such ideas by freak accident or not at all. The virtue that protects this whole class is no doubt very beautiful, but again it seems that it is not justice, the virtue we are analysing.

Let us suppose instead that our heroine attempts to avoid the problem of an over-extensive protected class by definitional fiat, thickening the concept which covers the 'many' of which she sees herself as 'one' by explicit appeal to the idea of bipolar conception. Suppose she imagines that she is bound in 'moral right' not to destroy *any rational animal who deploys concepts of right*. (Or rather, as it would have to be if the supposed manifold is to cover the rights of, for example, the young human beings with whom she is familiar: *any animal that falls under a genus associated with a tendency to deploy concepts of right*.) But of course it is not enough that potential others deploy dikaiological concepts; they must deploy the *same* dikaiological concepts. It is not enough that they are deploying, or tend to deploy, *legal* concepts of right, for example. They must be able to shift, and tend to shift, abstract bipolar deontic vocabulary into the same gear she does.

Perhaps she can do better by attempting to specify the form of bipolar judging in question. But how is she to specify it? It is no use saying that the 'many' of which she sees herself as 'one' is the class of *all rational animals who deploy (or would tend to deploy) not just any conception of bipolarity, but a conception of bipolarity which (say) encompasses all rational animals*. There is no such form of bipolarity, as we have already seen.

It is clear that she cannot specify the form of bipolarity that is to prevail in her imagined manifold by reference to the manifold it induces, since this manifold is the one she is attempting to specify. We are clearly falling into a circle. Can our heroine break out of it by isolating the intended class as that of *all rational animals who grasp or tend to grasp 'this very form of bipolarity'*—namely, the one contained in her thought of Sylvia? Yes, but only because the thought of a 'many' so defined is implicit in every form of dikaiological judgement, legal, ludic, or moral. So this conception of the manifold cannot help to specify the question of its extent. If the true theory of justice is Humean, then our heroine in so thinking will be thinking of the bearers of her 'moral' practice—for these are the ones in whom operates a tendency to grasp 'this very form of practical bipolarity'. If the true theory is Aristotelian, then she will be speaking of all human beings.

The same difficulty would evidently beset the attempt to specify the manifold as the class of *all rational beings who grasp or tend to grasp the 'specifically moral' form of bipolarity*. Here the trouble is with the definite article. On a Humean or Aristotelian theory, the idea of moral bipolarity is akin to the idea of private-legal bipolarity: moral bipolarities might arise independently, and will therefore be different bipolarities, even if they are very similar. To insist that there is just one such form of pairing is to beg the question against them. The class of *all rational beings who grasp a specifically private-legal form of bipolarity* is not a private-legal manifold of persons unless it happens that there is as yet only one system of private law in the universe, as no doubt once there was.

The core question is this. Let our heroine, framing a particular dikaiological judgement, reflectively form the thought of 'this very form of bipolarity' and 'the manifold within which this very form of bipolarity prevails'. And let another agent capable of reflection do something that is qualitatively exactly the same—the person next door or a human on another continent or a twin human or a humanoid in a distant galaxy. What now will make it the case that they are reflectively apprehending the *same* form of bipolarity and through it the same manifold of persons? If we cannot see these thoughts as manifestations of a common practice or a common life form—if we grant that the homogeneity is a mere accident of cosmic history—we seem to have no way of perceiving it as an *identity*; we can only see different forms of practical bipolarity that are as alike, qualitatively, as one pleases. Our heroine and her radically alien science fiction 'other' are in the position of the Lombard and the Schlombard, or the many houses of our heretical Israel.

This conclusion seems to follow if we consider the matter in an even mildly naturalistic way. But perhaps another way of considering things is available. An idealism like Kant's might let us find a suitable common account or ground of our heroine's and the alien's radically separate mental operations—a single intelligible cause hidden below this superficial diversity of crude, empirically given mechanical causes. Thus could the thoughts of our heroine and her alien be opposite poles of the same thought and a true thought. This is indeed how Kant conceives of 'pure practical reason', if I understand him: it is like a Platonic Form which shows itself in the diverse thoughts of many rational beings. Wherever practical reasoning happens in an individual animal, PPR has a foothold, just as it does in me.

On such an account, the idea of an agent not under the 'formula of humanity', is indeed coherent, and thus *logically* possible—and is outlined in the *Religion* discussion of the 'most rational mortal being'.[44] But we were wrong to infer from this abstract conceptual possibility that any such agent is *really* possible—that is, that any could actually appear in nature. Rather, we have synthetic knowledge that this is not a real possibility, founded on our knowledge of the character of the law we find in ourselves. From the judgement that I ought to treat *all reasoning animal agents*—that is, *all Kantian 'humanity'-havers*—thus and so, I will conclude the existence of a law of reason-in-general, a law I will judge present wherever in nature reasoning agency is found, even if consciousness of it has not yet been awakened or developed. The moral law drives me to respect all reasoning agents in practice, but what I properly respect is in a way 'the law of which they give me an example',[45] a moral law which is waiting to operate in them. This I must judge to be *the same law*, not another law with the same content. And so I must think that it is not an accident that otherwise radically alien practical reasoners should all alike develop this way of thinking, and thus thoughts mirroring my own, even though other ways of thinking are perfectly possible conceptually speaking. I must judge that a principle operates in nature which excludes those abstract conceptual

[44] Kant, *Religion within the Boundaries of Mere Reason and Other Works*, ed. A. Wood and G. Di Giovanni (Cambridge: Cambridge University Press, 1998), 50–1 (*Akademie*, 26).

[45] Kant, *Groundwork of the Metaphysics of Morals*, in *Practical Philosophy*, ed. and trans. McGregor, 56 (*Akademie* 401).

possibilities. If I find some reasoners who are not with the programme, then practical faith, governed by the moral law, will lead me to investigate what is impeding the development of this consciousness, and the associated forms of feeling, in their case. And it will drive me to do what it takes to bring this consciousness out. For the aptness, the tendency, to exhibit these thoughts is certainly there in those space aliens, somewhere, if they are thinking practically at all, even in the most elementary 'instrumental' ways; I know this indirectly by reflecting on my own case, from my knowledge that I live under a hyper-extensive formula of humanity.

Thus, on Kant's view, the recognition of another animal agent as reasoning practically is always at the same time recognition of him as a person in relation to oneself. There is no difficulty in specifying the manifold of persons into which our heroine judges herself to be inserted: it is, after all, just the class of all practically reasoning animals in nature, the class of all bearers of 'humanity'. It is just that I have synthetic knowledge 'from within' of a tendency to pairwise judging which prevails across this thinly defined genus, spread as it may be across the cosmos—a tendency which thus constitutes the genus as a manifold of persons. There is present in me a practical law, the operation of which is alas often impeded, which has all the cosmic scope of the laws of interaction of fundamental particles; its operation, we may suppose, is busily being impeded even in distant galaxies.

I have nothing with which to oppose this orthodox Kantian conception of the matter, apart from a mild naturalism. But that is enough, I think we should grant, to make a serious difficulty, and thus to complete the puzzle I have been attempting to articulate: namely, that each of the received accounts of the content of our heroine's distinctive thought— Humean, Aristotelian, and Kantian—is faced with what can readily be felt as a decisive objection. There is in this material a conflict between metaphysical and moral desiderata, and it is difficult to say in which direction we should turn.

The present section poses a more direct objection, I think, to the neo-Kantian view that we can hold to Kant's moral theory, the formula of (Kantian) humanity for example, while rejecting the strange and wonderful metaphysics of reason which would permit us to make sense of it. The mark of such a theory is that, in its lyrical emphasis on the 'autonomy' of each moral agent in respect of the 'moral law' she is under, it compromises the real *identity* of the law to which each agent is thus autonomously related. Neo-Kantian views, if I am right, put morally virtuous agents into the position of the many households at our heretical Sinai, and not into relations of right.

15

The Rightness of Acts and the Goodness of Lives

R. Jay Wallace

A prominent tendency in recent work of Joseph Raz's has been to deny that there is any interesting philosophical problem about the authority of moral considerations to govern our lives. Philosophers who address this problem typically suppose that morality designates a domain of putatively normative considerations that hang together in some non-vacuous way. They then ask whether the considerations within this unified domain really do constitute reasons for action, and how they stack up compared to reasons of other kinds in respect of their normative importance. Thus it is common to contrast moral considerations with considerations of rational self-interest, and to ask whether and why we should conform to the former when they conflict with the latter.

Raz rejects this whole picture. He accepts a thoroughgoing pluralism about the domain of reasons, which denies that there is any context-independent way of classifying normative considerations as moral rather than non-moral.[1] If morality does not constitute a unified normative domain, however, then the general question about the normative force of 'moral' considerations will fail to get a grip—it will be basically unclear what we are even asking about. Raz equally denies that self-interest

[1] Joseph Raz, 'On the Moral Point of View', reprinted in his *Engaging Reason: On the Theory of Value and Action* (Oxford: Oxford University Press, 1999), 247–72; also 'The Amoralist', reprinted in his *Engaging Reason*, 273–302.

represents a significant class of reasons for action.[2] Individual well-being consists in the successful pursuit of valuable ends, but this kind of consideration lacks deliberative significance for the agent to whom it applies. In place of the modern moral philosopher's contrast between morality and self-interest, Raz recommends a 'classical' conception of agency and normative reasons.[3] This holds that reasons are anchored in the value of ends and activities, and that they reflect directly the diversity and plurality that characterize the realm of value. The global question about the normativity of the moral thus gives way to an indefinite succession of first-order deliberative questions that confront individual agents as they make their way through life, questions that can be resolved only by reflection on the nature and significance of the concrete values that are at stake.

There is much to commend in this general approach to the relation between reasons and value. Nevertheless, I am not quite convinced by Raz's arguments that the traditional problem of understanding the normative force of moral considerations can so easily be dismissed or dissolved. To explain my doubts, I will begin by considering some of Raz's own examples, and show how they very naturally suggest a philosophical question about the deliberative significance of ethical[4] requirements. In the sections that follow I shall try to develop a framework to make sense of this question, one that is capable of standing up to the doubts expressed by Raz. While agreeing with Raz that narrow self-interest does not constitute an interesting normative domain, I contend that there is a broader class of 'eudaimonistic' considerations that is significant for practical deliberation. My aim is to explain the challenge that can be posed to morality in terms of this class of reasons, and to make some observations about the resources available within moral philosophy for dealing with the challenge.

1. Goodness for the Agent

Concern about the normative standing of moral considerations is encouraged by cases in which morality demands forms of conduct that do not

---

[2] Joseph Raz, 'The Central Conflict: Morality and Self-Interest', reprinted in his *Engaging Reason*, 303–32. Compare T. M. Scanlon, *What We Owe to Each Other* (Cambridge, Mass.: Harvard University Press, 1998), ch. 3.

[3] See Joseph Raz, 'Agency, Reason, and the Good', in his *Engaging Reason*, 22–45.

[4] I shall use the expressions 'ethical' and 'moral' interchangeably in what follows.

promise any apparent benefit to the agent. We must be faithful to our promises, provide emergency assistance to those in need, refrain from exploiting the vulnerable, etc., even when doing these things is inconvenient for us, or otherwise renders difficult the pursuit of our private aims and goals. Situations of this kind seem to raise a general question about the normative significance of moral requirements, whose grip on us can start to appear puzzling or mysterious.

Raz contends that this appearance is a mere illusion. One of his several arguments for this conclusion begins from reflection on what it is for something to be good *for* a given agent. Thus he suggests that we justify claims to the effect that something is good for a given agent by showing '(a) that the thing is good, and (b) that the agent has the ability and the opportunity to have that good'.[5] This is a schema that can easily be satisfied even in the case of morally required actions that are inconvenient for the agent. An act of helping another person in need, for instance, is clearly good, so when we have the ability and the opportunity to perform such an act, our doing so will be good for us. Granted, it will not be good for us in the same way the act will be good for its direct beneficiary, namely instrumentally; but an act can be good for us without benefiting us in the manner characteristic of instrumental goods.

As Raz himself notes, however, the actions required by morality still seem significantly different from many of the activities that are paradigmatically good for their agents. Take teaching, for instance: we can readily make sense of this as something that can be good not just for the student but also for the teacher, because it is 'a challenging, complex activity which can be fulfilling to those engaging in it'.[6] Such moral actions as keeping a promise or providing emergency assistance, by contrast, hardly seem to resemble the paradigm case of teaching in these respects; they do not seem to be intrinsically good for their agents, just in virtue of being morally good in the ways they are. But this, Raz suggests, would be the wrong lesson to draw from the contrast between teaching and morality. What is at issue here is the contrast not between things that are good for the agent and the requirements of morality, but rather between two different kinds of intrinsic good: namely, the intrinsic good of *activities* and the intrinsic good of *acts*.[7] With activities, such as teaching, what is intrinsically good for the agent lies in the complex, challenging pattern of behaviour over time

[5] Raz, 'On the Moral Point of View', 260.   [6] Ibid. 266.   [7] Ibid. 267–8.

that the activity itself consists in. With morally required acts, by contrast, the value of the behaviour that is required lies principally in the results to be achieved. If I help somebody by giving to charity, for example, the value of what I am doing does not inhere in my writing out a cheque, placing it in an envelope, etc., but rather in the end that is brought about through my donation.

This will address our original worry about the normative standing of moral considerations, of course, only if things that are valuable in the way that acts are can be good *for* the agent who does them. Raz argues that this is in fact the case, using the example of a world-record sprinter to make his point. Running 100 metres in record time is not valuable in virtue of the physical processes and bodily exertions that it involves—which in themselves might well be far from enjoyable for the sprinter—but rather for its result, the setting of a new record. 'Those who achieve it cannot complain that they do not enjoy the activity of racing which led to the result as well. Their reward is in the result.'[8] Similarly for moral acts: the agent who writes out a cheque to a charitable cause is doing something whose reward does not lie in the processes and exertions of writing the cheque, but in the valuable result that those processes achieve. The general schema remains in place that something is good for an agent if it is good and the agent has the ability and opportunity to achieve it. What is distinctive of the things that morality requires of us, at least in a range of central cases, is that they fit into this general schema in the way characteristic of acts rather than activities.

This response, however, does not succeed in removing the worry to which it was addressed. The worry is that what morality requires does not seem to be valuable for the agent in the way our most important endeavours and activities can be. The example of the sprinter is a helpful one, because world-class athletic competition is an enterprise that can clearly contribute to one's own well-being—engaging in this activity well is something that can be better for the person who goes in for it. If the value of the activity lies in the result of setting a record, this is something that seems intelligible as a *reward* for the agent, an *achievement* of the kind that makes their own life better. But the valuable results that moral acts may bring about do not seem to contribute in a similar way to enriching the life of the agents who perform them, as Raz's schematic argument would

---

[8] Raz, 'On the Moral Point of View', 267.

require. At least, it is not obvious how one's own life is made better through one's performing acts whose value lies in results external to the acts themselves, which redound to the benefit of persons other than oneself.

Curiously, Raz seems to concede precisely this point in a separate treatment of the relation between morality and individual well-being.[9] He describes a case involving a young person confronted with a choice between accepting a scholarship to study at university and volunteering to drive a lorry in an emergency operation to bring food to the victims of a severe famine. Raz supposes that the moral reasons in favour of the latter option defeat the considerations that speak in favour of beginning a course of study at the university; they are categorical reasons, whose stringency is grounded in the importance of the lives that are to be saved, in a way that is unaffected by whether or not acting on the reasons would subserve the agent's personal goals. In so far as driving the lorry in the food convoy represents a good that the agent has the ability and the opportunity to realize, choosing that option will be good for the agent. But Raz grants that it will not contribute as greatly to the agent's well-being as would going to university. He explains this by invoking, again, the distinction between acts and activities, noting that the former are typically of shorter duration than the latter, and that assessments of well-being take the 'person's life as a whole as the measure'.[10] The upshot is that the morally required acts involved in driving the lorry, though more valuable than the activity of studying at a university, will make less of a contribution to the agent's well-being, because they ramify less extensively through the agent's life. This seems correct, but it only reinforces the question posed above. Once we are clear that the acts that morality often requires contribute less significantly to our well-being than the alternatives that are open to us, it appears puzzling that they should be categorical in their stringency.

I do not believe this is a decisive objection to the normative significance of moral considerations. My point is rather that there is an intelligible and gripping question about the normativity of moral requirements in this vicinity, and that the question does not seem to be foreclosed by Raz's general animadversions on the concept of something's being good for an agent. Not all of the goods whose realization a given agent has the capacity and the opportunity to achieve are things whose realization is intrinsically

---

[9] Raz, 'Central Conflict', §§ 2–4.   [10] Ibid. 320.

good for the agent, in the way the acts and activities involved in our most important personal relationships and projects typically seem to be. In particular, the goods that are realized by many of the actions that morality requires us to perform do not seem to be important in this way. Perhaps this kind of personal importance is not a general condition of ethical normativity, something without which an agent cannot have reason to perform an action that morality requires. Even if this is correct, however, there is bound to be a question about the capacity of moral reasons to prevail in competition with the acts and activities that are more directly and obviously good for the agent who performs them. This, at any rate, is the idea that I propose to develop in the remainder of the present essay. In doing so, I hope to vindicate, in a limited way, one aspect of the traditional normative project of ethical theory against Raz's attempts at dissolution.

2. Facilitating Goods

First we will need to get a bit clearer about what morality is. As I mentioned above, Raz himself is sceptical about the idea that morality is a unified normative domain, a set of reasons and values that stand apart from other kinds of normative consideration, and that can be characterized in terms that are both substantive and context-independent. Scepticism about this issue is part of what leads Raz to doubt that there is an interesting general question to be joined about the authority of moral reasons and values. For the record, I am less sceptical than Raz that the moral realm exhibits any interesting kind of unity. It seems to me that we can acknowledge the plurality of considerations that go to determining whether acts are right or wrong, while providing an informative account of what these considerations have in common—what makes them determinants of moral right and wrong.[11]

This is an issue to which I shall return below. For the present, however, it seems to me that we can proceed to formulate a question about the normative authority of moral considerations even without having in hand a substantive characterization of the unity of the moral realm. It will suffice if we can identify a group of salient and central moral considerations that both demand sacrifices of us, and appear to be deficient by

[11] See my 'Scanlon's Contractualism', *Ethics* 112 (2002), 429–70, at § 4.

comparison with the activities and projects that are paradigmatically good for the agent who engages in them. Whatever else they may or may not have in common, there seems to be a range of moral requirements that satisfy these two conditions, including (for instance) requirements of fidelity to agreements, fairness, mutual aid, veracity, and non-maleficence.

Now I do not wish to question whether these kinds of moral consideration are genuine reasons for action, or whether they are correctly understood as requirements in some sense or other. There are questions that might be raised at the most fundamental level about the normative standing of these moral considerations, their claim to significance in the deliberations of agents about what they are to do. For purposes of this discussion, however, I would like to put those questions to the side, and focus on an issue that arises even after the normative significance of basic moral requirements has been granted or established.

The issue is raised very clearly by a way of thinking about the values implicated in these central cases of moral requirements that Raz himself has proposed. He suggests that many moral values are what he calls 'facilitating' or 'enabling' values, in that their 'good is in making possible or facilitating the instantiation of other values'.[12] Thus moral requirements such as justice or fidelity or veracity are good, at least in part, in so far as adherence to them facilitates the collective pursuit of other ends that are valuable. Our ability to act effectively to realize complex and valuable goals is clearly enhanced, for example, if we can rely on other people to keep their agreements and fulfil the expectations they lead others to have about what they are going to do, as fidelity requires people to do. Raz notes that enabling or facilitating values can also be valuable in a different way, in so far as acting on them is partly constitutive (for instance) of valuable personal relationships. Let us abstract, however, from situations in which this is the case, to focus on the pure examples of moral requirements whose value lies in their contribution to facilitating the pursuit of other values. Let us also grant that this kind of pure facilitating value provides people with corresponding moral reasons to comply with the requirements in question.

Granting that this is the case, however, does not suffice to remove all basis for questioning the authority of moral principles to govern our lives.

[12] Joseph Raz, *The Practice of Value*, ed. R. Jay Wallace (Oxford: Oxford University Press, 2003), 34.

For morality often requires us to make significant personal sacrifices, compromising or curtailing the pursuit of our individual projects in order to do the right thing. It is typically understood as a kind of highest-level end, laying down fundamental ground rules that are to be complied with as we fashion our more particular plans and decisions.[13] To allow morality to play this role is to structure one's practical reflection in terms of its requirements. Morality leaves room for the pursuit of personal ends, but only within the parameters that are set by moral requirements; it thus functions as a set of constraints on our individual, non-moral activities. If we focus on the central cases in which morality is grounded in facilitating goods, however, there is room to question whether the reasons it provides could possibly be serious enough to constrain our personal attachments and concerns in this way. It does not seem reasonable to grant its requirements this kind of *priority* in shaping our lives.

A worry of this kind seems to me to lie behind some of the more interesting recent critiques of modern morality. Bernard Williams's influential objections to the 'morality system', for instance, turn in part on the idea that no set of purely impartial requirements could hope to prevail in competition with the kinds of 'ground projects' that give our lives meaning and point.[14] A standard response to this suggestion has been to assert that morality itself may be among a person's ground projects, and so at least on a par with the other sorts of commitments over which it is supposed to prevail.[15] But this cannot simply be taken for granted. At least a part of what Williams is trying to question, I believe, is whether impartial morality is the sort of thing to which it would be reasonable to be committed in the way one is committed to one's personal projects and relationships. This question seems especially pressing when we reflect on those central moral requirements that represent facilitating values. The fact that justice and fidelity facilitate or enable the pursuit of valuable ends might

[13] See Joseph Raz, *The Morality of Freedom* (Oxford: Oxford University Press, 1986), 292–93, on the hierarchical structure of human goals.

[14] See Bernard Williams, 'Persons, Character, and Morality' and 'Moral Luck', both reprinted in his *Moral Luck* (Cambridge: Cambridge University Press, 1981), 1–19 and 20–39, respectively. See also Susan Wolf's reflections on the relations between impartial morality and partial attachments, in 'Morality and Partiality', *Philosophical Perspectives* 6 (1992), 243–59.

[15] See e.g. Peter Railton, 'Alienation, Consequentialism, and the Demands of Morality', as reprinted in S. Scheffler (ed.), *Consequentialism and its Critics* (Oxford: Oxford University Press, 1988), 93–133, at 112–13, and Thomas Nagel, *The View from Nowhere* (New York: Oxford University Press, 1986), 198.

well make these things good themselves, and give us some reason to respond to and to care about them. But offhand, it hardly seems very sensible to care about the facilitating goods of morality in anything like the way we care about the ground projects that give texture and substance to our own lives.

This is not, it should be emphasized, merely because the values in question stand in a facilitating relation to other goods.[16] There are cases in which it might well seem sensible to be devoted to a facilitating value in the manner of a ground project or a personal relationship. There are many professional roles, for instance, that primarily involve facilitating the pursuit of other valuable ends or goals—think of the job of an office administrator or a city traffic engineer—and it would not seem unintelligible to us that someone might be committed to performing well in these roles, as a kind of ground project in life. But the facilitating values at issue in morality seem different in this respect. For one thing, they are defined in terms of requirements whose demands on us are episodic rather than continuous; to borrow the distinction from Raz introduced above, we comply with them through a series of apparently disconnected acts, rather than through a pattern of ongoing activity. For another thing, there is a generic quality to the central requirements of morality, in so far as they apply indifferently to all human agents. Acting in conformity with these requirements therefore does not seem to give expression to anything distinctive about the agent's personality or character or outlook on life. This combination of features seems to disqualify impartial morality from acquiring the significance for an agent of personal relationships and ground projects.

If the facilitating values at the heart of morality are not important to us in this way, however, then their capacity to stand up in rational competition with the claims of our projects and relationships may seem insecure. There will be a basis within practical reason for questioning the *priority* that moral requirements are typically taken to possess.

3. Goodness For: Narrow and Broad

The comparison with ground projects returns us to the question of whether the acts that are required by morality can be good for their agent.

---

[16] I owe this point to a very helpful discussion with Niko Kolodny.

For the challenge posed by the work of such critics of impartial morality as Williams is frequently understood in these terms—most notably by Thomas Nagel, who represents Williams as raising a question about the relation between the moral life and the good life.[17] But this way of putting things requires further interpretation. The notion of what is good for an agent is notoriously elastic, but perhaps the most natural way of interpreting it is in prudential terms, as referring to what is in the agent's interests or conducive to the agent's own welfare, where this in turn is understood, in familiar if elusive ways, as a matter of health, material comfort, psychic satisfaction, and so on.[18]

This prudential interpretation seems too narrow, however, to ground an interesting challenge to the deliberative importance of morality. Thus as parents and friends, people involved in our work and committed to various projects and institutions, we are often perfectly willing to put up with sacrifices in our own interests or well-being, narrowly construed; nor does it seem irrational of us to do so.[19] If this attitude is in general not open to rational criticism, there seems no reason to find it objectionable when the ends for which we are willing to make personal sacrifices are moral ones. The narrow or prudential interpretation of the good life, in terms of the agent's own welfare, thus does not look very promising as a basis for challenging the importance of impartial morality. If we reject this interpretation of the question, however, it begins to look as if there is no longer any ground at all for the sceptical challenger to stand on. We might follow Raz in proposing a broader interpretation of 'goodness for', according to which a pursuit is good for an agent just in case it is valuable, and also something that the agent has the ability and opportunity to go in for. But this interpretation is *too* broad for the purposes at hand. Any value, including the merely facilitating values at the heart of morality, is one whose successful pursuit would automatically be good for the agent, and this leaves no basis for a contrast with the kinds of values involved in Williams's ground projects.[20] We seem to lack terms to articulate the intuitive sense

---

[17] See Nagel, *View from Nowhere*, ch. 10.

[18] For further discussion, see Derek Parfit, *Reasons and Persons* (Oxford: Oxford University Press, 1984), Appendix I, and James Griffin, *Well-being: Its Meaning, Measurement, and Moral Importance* (Oxford: Oxford University Press, 1986).

[19] Compare Parfit's arguments against the self-interest theory in *Reasons and Persons*, part II.

[20] As we saw above, Raz at one point qualifies this view, allowing that moral values might contribute less to the agent's well-being than the values whose pursuit occupies a more

that morality might be rationally deficient by comparison with the personal relationships and endeavours around which we structure our lives.

The intuitive concern raised by this contrast is perhaps most naturally expressed in the language of importance. Ground projects in Williams's sense are the sorts of things that are of obvious importance to us; they generate rational claims that are central to our understanding of ourselves, and that we intelligibly and naturally respond to as things that make compelling demands on our attention and concern. The intuitive importance of these kinds of requirements seems to reflect the fact that the values in which they are grounded are things whose pursuit can be made sense of as something that is good for the agent. As we have seen, however, an interpretation of 'goodness for' that is adequate to this intuitive understanding of ground projects seems elusive. The narrow interpretation in terms of prudential self-interest is too narrow to include many of the central cases, whereas Raz's extremely generic interpretation seems too broad to enable us to articulate the central intuition.[21] Is there a third alternative?

I would like to explore the following suggestion: one way in which an activity or pursuit might be good for the agent engaged in it is by making the agent's life *worthwhile* or *meaningful* from the agent's own point of view. Furthermore, being good for the agent in this way is something that has normative significance for the agent's own deliberations. Thus there is a standpoint of practical reflection, reasonably familiar to most of us, which is reached by stepping back from our basic first-order pursuits, and asking whether it is good that we are engaged in these pursuits. In raising this question, we are not asking whether it is good for other people, or humanity as a whole, that we should be engaged in the pursuits we are; nor are we asking whether doing so is good for us in the narrowly prudential sense I have already discussed. We are asking, rather, whether engaging in these pursuits is *worthwhile*, something that makes our own lives choice-worthy as

extensive segment of the agent's life; see, again, 'Central Conflict', § 4. This does not provide a basis for questioning the significance of moral ends, in Raz's view, because 'normally an agent's well-being is not, for him, a reason for action' (ibid. 322). A challenge to the authority of morality requires not merely a demonstration that there are other ends with which morality might conflict, but also that those other ends are themselves deliberatively significant.

[21] Compare Donald H. Regan, 'Why Am I My Brother's Keeper?', this volume, ch. 9, for an expression of deep scepticism about the idea that there is a notion of 'goodness for' that is both coherent and normatively significant.

human lives. We are asking whether our life is made meaningful or worth living as a result of our being engaged in these pursuits.[22] For want of a less misleading expression, we might refer to the point of view from which we pose these questions as the standpoint of eudaimonistic reflection. My suggestion is that our sense of the importance of relationships and ground projects is connected to their salience within eudaimonistic reflection of this kind; they are good for us as individual agents in so far as they can be made sense of as direct contributions to the choice-worthiness of our own lives.

To this it may be objected that any activity that is good in some way, or that we have reason to engage in, will be capable of satisfying this condition. But this does not seem to be correct. A low-level employee's willingness to put in long hours performing inherently uninteresting tasks for the firm may be a response that is grounded in reasons, also one that is valuable in some way or other (e.g., for the firm and its shareholders). But it is far from obvious that it is valuable *for the agent* in the distinctive way I have been trying to characterize: namely, as something that itself contributes directly to making the agent's life meaningful or choice-worthy. Or consider again the facilitating values at the centre of impartial morality. The fact that fidelity or non-maleficence facilitates the collective pursuit of valuable ends makes these moral requirements valuable, and perhaps gives us reason to comply with them as well. But these dimensions of value do not *seem* to render compliance with moral requirements good for the agent in anything like the way our important personal projects and relationships appear to do. This is a thought that Raz himself gives clear expression to in the following passage: 'being a non-murderer, or a non-rapist, or a person who simply gives away everything he has . . . is not something that can give meaning to life'.[23]

A brief survey of some particular kinds of activities that we ordinarily take to be of great personal importance may help to illustrate the notion of 'goodness for' that is at issue here, illuminating both its distinction from

---

[22] Compare Susan Wolf, 'Happiness and Meaning: Two Aspects of the Good Life', in Ellen Frankel Paul, Fred D. Miller, Jr., and Jeffrey Paul (eds.), *Self-Interest* (Cambridge: Cambridge University Press, 1997), 207–25.

[23] Raz, *Practice of Value*, 36. Compare Harry Frankfurt, 'Preface' to *Necessity, Volition, and Love* (Cambridge: Cambridge University Press, 1999), p. x: 'For most people, the relevance of their moral obligations as legitimately binding constraints or as proper determinants of choice and conduct is quite limited. What morality has to say concerning how to live and what to do is important, but its importance is often exaggerated.'

the narrower notion of prudential self-interest and its direct significance for practical deliberation. Consider first the example of personal relationships. People are clearly willing to make fairly great sacrifices for the sake of those they feel attached to as friends, lovers, spouses, and so on. But just as clearly, having relationships of these kinds is among the things that make life interesting and worthwhile. Our lives would be impoverished in all kinds of ways if we did not have the opportunity to experience intimacies of these kinds, and this is itself a powerful reason to nourish and cultivate our personal ties.

A different example involves our professional commitments. There are lots of cases in which people seem quite reasonably willing to make large sacrifices in terms of their own interests and welfare for the sake of professional goals to which they are committed. To take a case of this kind familiar to most of us, there is the scientist or scholar who is willing to put in exceptionally long and grinding hours working on projects that are unlikely to bring fame or financial reward, that render it difficult to develop the range of interests important for a balanced human life, and that introduce their own forms of psychic conflict and distress. Sacrifices of these kinds may without infelicity be said to be good for the agent who makes them, but what renders this conclusion plausible is that the activities in question are direct contributions to the goodness of human lives. Highly structured and complex scientific and artistic pursuits are, after all, characteristically human forms of *achievement*, directed at an appropriate and worthwhile object, and distinguishing oneself in these activities is therefore one way of distinguishing oneself as a human being (compare Raz's example of the sprinter). To the extent that this is the case, engaging well in complex scientific or artistic activities may contribute directly to the goodness of the agent's life, making it choice-worthy and meaningful from the agent's point of view, and this consideration can supply a compelling reason to put up with great sacrifices for the sake of such activities.

There are other kinds of cases, however, in which one has reason to make sacrifices in respect of one's own interests, despite the fact that the activities that impose such sacrifices do not themselves seem to be forms of human accomplishment of this kind. Many people labour virtually to the point of exhaustion in activities that are intrinsically mechanical and unrewarding, such that it is extremely implausible to represent the activities themselves as contributing directly to the choice-worthiness of their lives. Dedication of this sort can nevertheless be good for the agent, if it is a condition for the person's engaging, perhaps at some later point in life, in other meaningful activities. This is a familiar enough pattern: people can have reason to tolerate years of sacrifice and drudgery—law school and the unrelenting grunt work of legal practice, or a long stretch of tedious factory labour—if doing so enables them later to pursue other, more worthwhile endeavours.

In a still different kind of case, a person will toil at an exceptionally tedious and unrewarding occupation not in order to achieve other or later advantages for themselves, but to make possible a better and more choice-worthy life for (say) their offspring. This might of course be a perfectly reasonable thing to do, as a special case of the relationship-based sacrifices already touched on above. But I would maintain that it can remain good for the agent, even when the occupation in question is so consuming that it leaves little time for the person to develop a real relationship with the child whose prospects are to be improved. The condition for its being important in this way, however, is that the agent be able to view the intrinsically tedious activities in a different light: perhaps as a way of participating in something greater than oneself, contributing to a value that will live on when one is gone. Seeing one's activities in this kind of light can enable one to appreciate them as constitutive parts of a life that is worth living. One's own life acquires meaning in so far as it is connected in this radical way to values that lie outside the self, and this supplies a powerful reason to commit oneself to the intrinsically uninteresting acts that fill out the life, which would otherwise be intolerable.[24]

This seems to me recognizable, perhaps as a limiting case, as a way in which a life can be worthwhile from the agent's point of view; but the self-transcending form of value in question is by its nature one that is probably capable of being appreciated only by those who are subject to the transforming effects of personal love or quasi-religious devotion. Outside such personal or religious contexts, most of us would be unable to recognize or endorse the values of self-transcendence in eudaimonistic reflection as sources of meaning. We typically need to see more substantial values embodied in our lives.

---

[24] This is an extreme case of a more general phenomenon to which Harry Frankfurt has called attention, in which the intrinsic value to us of certain activities is a function of their instrumental contribution to an end that we care about; see his 'On the Usefulness of Final Ends', as reprinted in his *Necessity, Volition, and Love*, 82–94.

4. Eudaimonistic Reflection

In the last section I appealed to intuitive convictions about whether the sacrifice of one's own interests could or could not be said to be good for the agent making the sacrifice, and about the relevance of this kind of goodness to practical deliberation. It will now be well to try to be more systematic about these convictions. I have spoken of a standpoint of eudaimonistic reflection, from which we are concerned with the question of the contribution of our activities to the goodness of our own lives. Furthermore, I have suggested that being good for the agent in this way is connected to our sense of the importance of the ends and requirements that stem from our relationships and ground projects. In these terms, the worry that I am trying to articulate about morality is that the facilitating values at its heart do not seem capable of taking on this kind of importance. Compliance with such moral requirements does not appear to be good for the agent in the way that personal values and requirements clearly are—namely, as direct contributions to the goodness or meaning of the agent's own life. To the extent this is the case, and to the extent this dimension of goodness has normative significance, there seems to be a basis *within practical reason* for questioning the deliberative priority of impartial morality, its claim to define a comprehensive framework within which our personal projects and activities are to be pursued.

The appeal to the standpoint of eudaimonistic reflection is an attempt to make out a point of view from which a serious sceptical challenge to the rational authority of morality might be raised. Thus I am in agreement with Raz that the context of amoralist scepticism about morality—defined by the assumption that we are concerned exclusively with our own well-being in the narrow, prudential sense—is not one that defines a serious class of reasons for action; so the suggestion that it might not be prudentially rational to be moral should not be troubling to us. By contrast, the context defined by the standpoint of eudaimonistic reflection is both readily accessible and deliberatively significant; it is important that we are able to justify our most basic projects from this point of view, as things that make our lives worthwhile.

This is not to say that the eudaimonistic point of view is the only one we are capable of occupying for purposes of practical reflection. In addition, there is also (for instance) the point of view of impartial morality itself. As interpreted in the most significant moral theories of the last centuries, such as Kantianism and utilitarianism, impartial morality defines a distinctive way of looking at and thinking about practical questions, one characterized by a kind of abstraction from personal concerns. In certain versions of utilitarianism, and in Nagel's moral theory, for instance, one steps back in moral reflection to a standpoint of impersonality, thinking about practical questions not merely from the first-personal point of view of a particular agent, but as far as possible from the 'point of view of the universe'.[25] In Kant's theory, the moral point of view is defined by a concern with the universalizability of one's maxims or intentions; while some contractualist accounts characterize this perspective in terms of the aim of acting in a way that can be justified to those potentially affected by what we do.[26] Furthermore, all of these theories hold that the characteristically moral point of view is also a comprehensive one, in so far as a moral justification can in principle be demanded for any activity we might be engaged in.

To follow the tradition of modern moral philosophy in this respect is to grant that moral dispositions characteristically enable agents to deliberate about practical problems in a distinctive way. If we go this route, however, then an important question looms about the intelligibility of moral scepticism. Granting that morality defines a characteristic point of view, a challenge to its rational status must apparently be formulated in terms of a standpoint of practical reflection that is distinctively non-moral,[27] and this raises the issue of why the status of moral norms should be answerable to considerations that are external to moral thought itself. (This is a version of Pritchard's question, in his influential paper 'Does Moral Philosophy Rest on a Mistake?'[28]) Furthermore, this is an objection to which Raz too should be sympathetic—despite his scepticism about the unity of anything that might be described as the 'moral point of view'. On the classical account that he favours, there is no interesting context-independent way

---

[25] See Henry Sidgwick, *The Methods of Ethics*, 7th edn. (Indianapolis: Hackett Publishing Co., 1981), and Nagel, *View from Nowhere*, chs. 8–9. (Nagel's view is qualified by the recognition that the impersonal point of view takes in only part of the moral landscape.)

[26] See Scanlon, *What We Owe to Each Other*.

[27] I pass over here the possibility of an 'internal' critique of the status of moral norms, of the sort often attributed (for instance) to Friedrich Nietzsche in the first essay of *On the Genealogy of Morals*, trans. Walter Kaufmann and R. J. Hollingdale (New York: Vintage Books, 1967).

[28] Reprinted in J. O. Urmson and W. D. Ross (eds.), *Moral Obligation and Duty and Interest: Essays and Lectures by H. A. Pritchard* (Oxford: Oxford University Press, 1968), 1–17.

of classifying reasons and values as distinctively moral. But the classical approach remains deeply pluralistic, acknowledging profound differences between the values in which our various reasons for action are grounded. In the spirit of this approach, one might emphasize the categorial discrepancy between the facilitating moral values that have been my main focus to this point and the personal projects and relationships that are significant within eudaimonistic reflection. Even if it should turn out to be misleading to characterize this discrepancy by talking about two distinct, comprehensive points of view, the question arises as to why the normative significance of facilitating values should be answerable to the distinct kinds of value at the bottom of personal projects and relationships.

One way to develop this point is in terms of the notion of importance. I have appealed to the eudaimonistic value of a meaningful or worthwhile life (from the agent's point of view) to elucidate what intuitively seems to be important about the values implicated in personal projects and relationships. But it might be argued that there is more than one kind of importance. An action that is not itself important as a direct contribution to the goodness of the agent's own life might still be important in some other way, say as a contribution to facilitating the general pursuit by humans of valuable ends and activities. If moral values and requirements can be important in the latter way, however, it might be wondered why it should matter if they are not also important in the former. Why should the failure of moral actions to contribute directly to the meaning or choice-worthiness of the agent's own life in any way impugn their claim to determine what the agent is to do? We do not, after all, similarly worry that the claims of our projects and relationships are threatened if they cannot be shown to be important in the distinctive ways characteristic of central moral requirements (i.e., as contributions to facilitating the collective pursuit of valuable ends).

It is far from obvious, however, that these two kinds of importance carry with them equal significance for practical deliberation. The impersonal importance exhibited by facilitating moral values is a function of their relation to the general pursuit of valuable ends by human agents; but things that are valuable and important in this way need not be important *to me*. Personal projects and relationships, by contrast, are things that are paradigmatically important *to* the agents whose projects and relationships they are, in so far as they are good for those agents in the manner I have been trying to trace—that is, as conditions for a meaningful or worthwhile life. It seems manifest that this species of importance *to* the agent is one that has great deliberative significance. Thus we would scarcely know how to interpret someone who conceded that doing X was of great importance to him, but went on to ask why he should care about doing X. The corresponding question posed about the impersonal importance of facilitating moral values, however, seems eminently intelligible. Someone might well grant that fidelity to agreements, for instance, would facilitate the general pursuit of valuable ends by human agents, but wonder why exactly she ought to care about *that*. The intelligibility of this question suggests that the kind of importance exhibited by facilitating moral values does not play the same prominent role within practical reason that importance *to* the agent seems to play.

In saying this I do not mean to deny that we have reason to comply with moral requirements, or to care about the ends that such compliance subserves. But *how much* should we care about doing what is good or important in these ways? If the sceptical challenge I have been trying to articulate goes unanswered, there may be no clear answer to this question at the end of the day. On the one hand, when we reflect on the objective importance of facilitating values for human agents, it seems that moral requirements ought to be given very high deliberative priority, fundamentally structuring the most basic life pursuits of the agents to whom they apply. For it is hardly possible for them to achieve their function if they are not accorded this kind of significance in the lives of individual agents. On the other hand, when we compare moral values with the personal values at the heart of projects and relationships, it appears puzzling that the former should attain the highest deliberative priority. It does not seem to be good for the agent to comply with moral requirements, in the way it clearly can be to comply with the demands that stem from personal values.

We might borrow Sidgwick's image of a dualism of practical reason to express this sceptical aporia.[29] When we attend to the values that define the moral point of view (to the extent there is such a thing), it seems plausible to suppose that moral requirements should have the status of highest-level ends, fundamentally structuring our deliberations and actions. From the standpoint of eudaimonistic reflection, however, it seems doubtful that moral requirements should have this kind of deliberative priority; compli-

---

[29] See Sidgwick, *Methods of Ethics*, 507–9 (e.g.).

ance with them does not appear to be good for the agent, or important to the agent, in the way that is characteristic of the projects and relationships that are of paramount deliberative significance. If this is the problem, however, then the solution would seem to consist in showing that the differing standpoints can be brought into substantive alignment, so that the verdicts arrived at within each are in harmony with one another. To answer the sceptical challenge, it needs to be shown that—contrary to initial appearances—there is a congruence between the standpoint from which the challenge is mounted and the standpoint of morality itself.[30]

To see how this kind of congruence might be brought about, it will be necessary to consider further the standpoint of eudaimonistic reflection from which, on my account, the sceptical challenge is posed. One thing I have already touched on is that this standpoint is not concerned, in the first instance, with the value of particular actions, but rather with our fundamental priorities. Eudaimonistic reflection is reflexive, and focused on our basic projects and comprehensive life goals, the kind of projects and goals that provide the context within which our more particular decisions are posed. It follows from this, perhaps, that the standpoint of eudaimonistic reflection is not one that we actually project ourselves into all that often. Indeed, if things are going well for us—that is, if we are actually engaged in activities that make our lives meaningful from our own point of view—there may be little practical need to stop and reflect about what makes this the case. The reflexive standpoint is nevertheless available to us, and especially in situations in which our projects require sacrifices of us, there will be occasion to make those projects themselves the object of reflection, asking whether it is reasonable to structure our lives in terms of them.

Reflection of this kind involves, as we have seen, fixing our sense of what is important to us.[31] By framing the question of whether we are engaged in pursuits that make our lives worthwhile as we live them, we help to clarify for ourselves what really matters to us, and the degree to which what matters to us is adequately reflected in the most basic priorities

---

[30] For the basic strategy of establishing the congruence between the constitutive standpoints of practical reason, see above all John Rawls, *A Theory of Justice* (Cambridge, Mass.: Harvard University Press, 1971), part 3.

[31] On the general idea of what is important to a person, see Harry Frankfurt, 'The Importance of What We Care About', as reprinted in his *The Importance of What We Care About* (Cambridge: Cambridge University Press, 1988), 80–94.

we have set for ourselves. Thus, not everything that one invests a lot of time and energy in is something that, upon reflection, one really turns out to care about all that much. That one is prepared to invest time and energy in an activity is a necessary condition, perhaps, of the activity's being important, but it is not sufficient; the lesson of a certain kind of mid-life crisis, for example, is that one's actual priorities can be out of alignment with one's sense of what really matters. If this kind of result is to be avoided, the agent herself must be able to endorse her actual patterns of activity reflectively, as an adequate expression of her own sense of what is important in life. We may think of this further, normative condition as a condition of articulation: reflection about our activities must make transparent to us the ways in which our *de facto* priorities contribute to the choice-worthiness of our lives, and the dimensions of value thus articulated must be ones that we can actually succeed in caring about.

Once a conception of what is important is fixed in this way, it establishes a framework for further eudaimonistic reasoning, the task of which can best be characterized in terms of integration. One does not necessarily weigh the various things that matter to one in a balance, with the objective of maximizing the value of something (the goodness or meaningfulness of one's life, say). Rather, one tries to find ways of integrating the various objectives that matter, bringing them together into a single life that makes appropriate room for each. To take the most obvious kind of example, when it comes to degree of importance, many of us would have no trouble concluding that certain intimate personal relationships are more important to us than our professional goals. It in no way follows from this, however, that practical reasoning should be concerned primarily to adjust our priorities in life to reflect precisely this difference in comparative importance of the professional and the personal. The salient desideratum for practical reason is not that the professional is less important than the personal, but that both matter to us greatly (if we are lucky). Given that this is the case, our primary practical objective is to find ways of doing justice to the concrete demands of both spheres within the parameters of a single life. It is only when integrative reasoning of this kind cannot go forward, because circumstances do not allow the demands of the two different spheres to be satisfied together, that considerations of comparative importance may become relevant. And even here, one's decision is apt to have the character of a radical choice or a tragic conflict, rather than of a simple problem of maximization.

That this is the case can be traced to the fact that our most important projects present themselves to us as making claims on us. As friends, lovers, Oakland A's fans, and teachers of philosophy, there are certain things that one simply has to do: provide support for the friend during a difficult phase in her life, follow the play-offs, prepare one's classes, and so on. Each of these projects functions as a highest-level end, defining constraints that structure our more particular deliberations, and partly define who we are.[32] My suggestion is that, once eudaimonistic reflection has determined that these various aspects of one's identity are all of them important, the immediate problem for practical reason is to devise a plan that will enable the various claims to be fulfilled together. Our conception of what is important in this way sets the terms in which practical reasoning about our more particular decisions will go forward.

5. Meaning and Morality

Let us now return to morality and the problem of its congruence with the eudaimonistic point of view. The sceptical challenge that I have been concerned to articulate in this paper begins from the worry that, considered from the perspective of eudaimonistic reflection, compliance with moral norms cannot be endorsed as contributing directly to the goodness of one's own life. The remarks of the previous section suggest that this challenge may be answered if it can be shown that compliance with moral requirements is among the things that matter to us when it comes to determining our basic priorities, defining one of the groups of claims that must be incorporated into the fixed structure of our life plans. If this condition can be satisfied, then one will be able to agree, from the standpoint of eudaimonistic reason, that the meaning and value of one's life will depend in part on the extent to which one succeeds in finding ways of pursuing one's personal goals and projects that are compatible with the requirements of impartial morality. In these terms, the concern articulated earlier in this paper is that impartial morality isn't the sort of end to which we should ascribe this kind of importance.

An adequate response to this challenge would have two parts, one philosophical and one practical. The philosophical aspect of the response

---

[32] Compare the discussion of practical identity and its link with obligation in Christine Korsgaard, *The Sources of Normativity* (Cambridge: Cambridge University Press, 1996), 101–2.

would consist in a re-description of the object of moral motivation, which reveals our moral activities to be the sorts of things that make intelligible contributions to the goodness of our own lives. In the terms of my earlier discussion, this would involve showing how compliance with moral norms can contribute directly to making our lives worthwhile or meaningful, so that we ourselves live better to the extent we achieve such compliance. One might, for instance, seek to establish that compliance with moral principles is a universally necessary condition for a meaningful human life, such that no life can be counted worthwhile which lacks a commitment to moral ends. But this is only the most ambitious version of the kind of argument I have in mind. A more modest version might aim to establish that acting rightly *can* make a direct contribution to the value of the agent's own life; this requires that we articulate the effects of a commitment to moral ends on the life of one who is so committed, so that it becomes transparent to us in what ways such a life is rendered worthwhile by that very commitment. The moral life may not be the only kind of life that can be meaningful from the agent's point of view, but it should at least be on the short list of candidates for such a life.

The second, practical part of the response would consist in bringing it about that the agent whose life is in question actually cares about the relevant dimension of value. After all, not everything that is potentially good for an agent, or that it would be reasonable to attach personal importance to, is something that actually matters to us in fact; so it is possible that we might be left cold by the goods of impartial morality in our own eudaimonistic reflection about our lives. To the extent this is the case, we will face a practical problem about the authority of moral norms to govern our activities, in so far as the eudaimonistic and the moral standpoints will continue to diverge from each other. No moral theory can by itself solve this practical problem—it is in the first instance a social and psychological problem, not a philosophical one. But a philosophical contribution will be satisfying only to the degree that the species of eudaimonistic value it identifies is one that people, as a practical matter, find it comparatively natural to care about.

A brief look at utilitarian and contractualist approaches will serve both to illustrate these observations and to conclude my discussion.[33] On a utilitarian view, the fundamental touchstone for moral rightness lies in

---

[33] For more on these issues, see my 'Scanlon's Contractualism', § 3.

the value of the consequences of that which is to be assessed; actions are morally right, on this account, just in case their consequences are better, on the whole, than those of the alternative actions that are open to the agent at the time of action. Views of this kind deliver an interpretation of moral norms that initially makes it seem puzzling how compliance with such norms could possibly be endorsed from within eudaimonistic reflection. Direct versions of utilitarianism are notoriously demanding, apparently leaving little space in life for the agent to devote to the kind of personal projects that give most of us reason to go on. Indirect versions attempt to address this defect, but with questionable success: either they end up 'ushering themselves from the scene', or they relocate the problem of alienation from one's personal projects by subjecting those projects to a systematic requirement of impartial justification.

I nevertheless believe that utilitarian theories are animated in part by a conception of the goodness of the moral agent's life. They remind us of something that we are perhaps inclined to forget or underemphasize when we think of morality as a set of generic requirements that facilitate human agency: namely, that more is at stake in morality than mere co-ordination of private activities. On the utilitarian approach, morality fundamentally guides us to maximize that which is intrinsically valuable in the world, where this in turn is the sort of aim that could intelligibly become an object of personal devotion. Its teleological structure potentially transforms the moral life into something more than a collection of disconnected episodic acts, imbuing its practical expressions with the coherence and continuity characteristic of ongoing activities that are systematically organized in the way of a project. Seen in this light, moral values begin to seem intelligible, as things whose pursuit could make a direct contribution to the choice-worthiness of the agent's own life.

Here we should recall the example I cited earlier of parents willing to subordinate their own interests radically to the project of improving the lot of their children—to a degree, that is, that precludes their enjoying the normal goods of personal relationship with the children. Thinking about this kind of example, I suggested that it might be recognizable, as a kind of limiting case, as a project that contributes directly to the meaning of the agent's own life, in so far as the agent achieves through the project a kind of self-transcendence, a connection to values that are outside the self, and that will live on when the agent is gone. Utilitarianism seems to me to appeal to a similar ideal of self-transcendence, in so far as moral conduct is seen as an ongoing project of promoting what is ultimately good in the world. Acting rightly may impose immense sacrifices on us in terms of our own interests and welfare, but there is nevertheless something to endorse in it from the standpoint of eudaimonistic reflection: it embodies an attitude of dedication to a higher plane of value.[34]

At this point, however, we need to consider the second, practical aspect of the problem of importance. If congruence in practical reason is really to be attained by a given individual, then not only must it be the case that moral conduct contributes in a recognizable way to the choice-worthiness of the agent's life. It must also be the case that the agent should care about the value in question, taking the incorporation of the value into their life to be a matter of personal importance. In this respect, the utilitarian account of the eudaimonistic significance of morality is deficient. As I mentioned earlier, the value of self-transcendence seems to be something that we tend to care about only if we have a direct and personal interest in the external goods to which our own lives are to be subordinated. Thus it matters to parents that their life should be dedicated to improving the prospects of their children—that it should be choice-worthy as a contribution to this end—because they love their children directly. Similarly, religious love and devotion can make it possible for an agent to take absolute dedication to the divine will to be a matter of supreme importance, in thinking about what it is to live well. In the case of utilitarianism, however, this kind of personal connection to the larger end to which one's life is to be subordinated is seldom present. We are perhaps not indifferent to the greatest good of the greatest number (or however else the impartial values promoted by morality are characterized), but—moral saints apart—most of us don't care enough about those values to make supreme dedication to them important *to us*, as a respect in which our own lives become choice-worthy.

Utilitarianism is often thought of as the paradigmatic secular moral theory. Its account of moral rightness is couched in terms that are utterly congenial to the progressive scientific temperament, and its proponents are notoriously dismissive of the metaphysical and religious baggage that is carried by other moral theories. In light of this, it is a matter of consider-

---

[34] Compare the ideal of transcendence discussed—though not endorsed—in Samuel Scheffler, *Human Morality* (New York: Oxford University Press, 1992), 120–1. A similar ideal is both elaborated and endorsed in Peter Singer, *How Are We to Live? Ethics in an Age of Self-Interest* (Oxford: Oxford University Press, 1997).

able irony that utilitarianism itself should implicitly rely, in its ideal of the goodness of a life, on the idea that the moral personality has an essentially religious structure: the utilitarian agent must be sufficiently attached to a transcendent value outside the self that systematic devotion to that end makes their own life good itself.[35]

In this respect, contractualism seems to me to offer a more attractive response to the problem of the priority of moral requirements. According to contractualism, moral rightness is essentially a matter of justification: what makes an act right is not, say, the value of its consequences, but rather that the act is required by principles that no one concerned to devise a common set of principles could reasonably reject.[36] Acting in accord with principles of this kind can be seen as a way of treating other persons with respect; by striving to comply with moral requirements, we take seriously the status of others as sources of claims, regarding them as people to whom justification is owed. We may put this in Kantian terms by saying that moral conduct represents an appropriate response to the value of persons (as 'ends in themselves').

But the contractualist approach offers at the same time an account of the contribution of moral conduct to the value of the agent's own life. Compliance with moral principles, understood along contractualist lines, not only acknowledges the value of other persons as sources of claims; it also affects directly the agent's own status. By acting in accordance with moral requirements, we enter into a distinctive kind of relationship with other people, one that is based on mutual recognition or acknowledgement, and that involves essentially a form of interpersonal justification. One stands in relationships with other people on this basis to the extent that one can give an acceptable account of oneself to them—that is, an account acceptable to those people themselves. According to contractualism, it is the business of impartial morality to define the terms on which interpersonal justification of this kind is possible. By complying with those terms, then, we ensure that we are able to give an account of ourselves to others—a status that we fall short of when we fail to do what impartial morality requires.

---

[35] Compare Bernard Williams, 'Replies', in J. E. J. Altham and Ross Harrison, eds., *World Mind, and Ethics. Essays on the Ethical Philosophy of Bernard Williams* (Cambridge, England: Cambridge University Press, 1995), 203.

[36] See (again) Scanlon, *What We Owe to Each Other*.

Now it seems to me that attainment of this status is the sort of thing that it is reasonable to care about in contexts of eudaimonistic reflection. It is a respect in which one's own life is transformed by one's compliance with moral principles, and it seems plausible to regard this transformation as a positive dimension of eudaimonistic value, a respect in which one's own life is made more meaningful and worthwhile. If utilitarianism attributes eudaimonistic value to morality by assimilating it to the paradigm of a quasi-religious project, contractualism sees the contribution of morality to the goodness of our lives in the dimension of human relationships. In so far as compliance with moral requirements is constitutive of mutual recognition, such compliance need not be thought of as a series of disconnected episodic performances; instead it is given coherence through the ongoing pursuit of an ideal form of relationship to one's fellows. As a practical matter, it seems that many people care fairly strongly about this dimension of value, taking it to be a matter of considerable importance whether or not they stand to other people in relationships of mutual recognition.[37] This concern is not, perhaps, the immediate motivation to moral conduct in most of us. But it develops very naturally in people who are responsive to moral ends, as a kind of reflexive refinement of our inherent sociability. Granted, mutual recognition lacks the texture and emotional complexity of the personal relationships that we enter into with other people, and that contribute so manifestly to enriching our lives.[38] But it has a personal aspect, in so far as it turns on the possibility of justifying oneself specifically *to* the individuals who might be affected by one's actions. To the extent that morality is connected to this way of relating to other people as individuals, it seems that we both can and should ascribe to it considerable importance within the context of eudaimonistic reflection.

My present aim, however, is not to defend the contractualist answer to the question of the eudaimonistic value of the moral life. I will be content if I have established that there is a question here to be answered, and that philosophical accounts of morality can help us in coming to terms with it. Raz has rightly urged us to reject the simplistic picture of a fundamental opposition between morality and self-interest. Even if we are not egoists, however, we reasonably want to lead meaningful and significant lives, and

---

[37] Compare ibid. 163, on the attitudes of Americans in the 1960s.

[38] Compare the discussion of 'relationship-dependent reasons' in Samuel Scheffler, 'Projects, Relationships, and Reasons', this volume, ch. 11.

it is an ongoing and important problem—both for philosophy and for life—to understand how morality might relate to this aspiration.[39]

[39] I have profited from stimulating discussions of predecessors of this paper at the following institutions: the Free University in Berlin; the Ludwig Maximilian University in Munich; the University of South Carolina; the Central Division Meetings of the American Philosophical Association; the Workshop in Law, Philosophy, and Political Theory at Berkeley; and the US Naval Academy. I am especially grateful to Janet Broughton, Logi Gunnarsson, and Nicholas Sturgeon for thoughtful written feedback on early versions of the paper, and to Niko Kolodny and Samuel Scheffler for very helpful comments on the penultimate draft.

ADLER, JONATHAN, *Belief's Own Ethics* (Cambridge, Mass.: MIT Press, 2002).

ADOLPHS, A., 'Trust in the Brain', *Nature Neuroscience* 5 (2002), 192–3.

AINSWORTH, M. D. S., and BELL, S. M., 'Attachment, Exploration, and Separation: Illustrated by the Behavior of One-Year-Olds in a Strange Situation', *Child Development* 41 (1970), 49–67.

ANDERSON, ELIZABETH, 'What is the Point of Equality?', *Ethics* 109 (1999), 287–337.

ANSCOMBE, G. E. M., *Intention* (Oxford: Blackwell, 1957).

—— 'Modern Moral Philosophy', *Philosophy* 33 (1958), 1–19.

—— 'The Source of the Authority of the State', in *Collected Philosophical Papers*, vol. 1 (Minneapolis: University of Minnesota Press, 1981), 130–55.

AQUINAS, ST THOMAS, *Summa Theologiae*, trans. Fathers of the English Dominican Province (New York: Benziger Brothers, 1948).

ARISTOTLE, *Nicomachean Ethics*, trans. W.D. Ross (Oxford: Oxford University Press, 1917).

ARNESON, RICHARD, 'Equality and Equality of Opportunity for Welfare', *Philosophical Studies* 56 (1989), 77–93.

ARPALY, NOMY, 'On Acting Rationally Against One's Best Judgment', *Ethics* 110 (2000), 488–513.

AXELROD, ROBERT, *The Evolution of Cooperation* (New York: Basic Books, 1984).

BARENDREGT, J. J., BONNEUX, L., and VAN DER MAAS, P. J., 'The Health Care Costs of Smoking', *New England Journal of Medicine* 337 (1997), 1052–57.

BEANEY, MICHAEL (ed.), *The Frege Reader* (Oxford: Blackwell, 1997).

BEARDMAN, STEPHANIE, 'Affective Deliberation: Toward a Humean Account of Practical Reason', (Rutgers University Ph.D. dissertation; Ann Arbor: UMI Dissertation Services, 2000).

BERRIDGE, KENT C., 'Reward Learning: Reinforcement, Incentives, and Expectations', in D. L. Medin (ed.), *The Psychology of Learning and Motivation* 40 (New York: Academic Press, 2000), 223–78.

BLACKBURN, SIMON, 'How Emotional is the Virtuous Person?', in Peter Goldie (ed.), *Understanding Emotions* (Aldershot: Ashgate, 2002), 81–96.

BOGDAN, R. J. (ed.), *Belief: Form, Content and Function* (Oxford: Oxford University Press, 1986).

BOWLBY, JOHN, *A Secure Base: Parent–Child Attachment and Healthy Human Development* (New York: Basic Books, 1988).

BRANDT, RICHARD, *A Theory of the Good and the Right* (Oxford: Oxford University Press, 1979).

BRATMAN, MICHAEL E., 'Autonomy and Hierarchy', *Social Philosophy and Policy* 20 (2003), 156–76.

—— 'A Desire of One's Own', *Journal of Philosophy* 100 (2003), 221–42.

—— *Faces of Intention: Selected Essays on Intention and Agency* (New York: Cambridge University Press, 1999).

—— 'Intention and Means–End Reasoning', *Philosophical Review* 90 (1981), 252–65.

—— *Intention, Plans, and Practical Reason* (Cambridge, Mass.: Harvard University Press, 1987; reissued by CSLI Publications, 1999).

—— 'Reflection, Planning, and Temporally Extended Agency', *Philosophical Review* 109 (2000), 35–61.

—— 'Shapiro on Legal Positivism and Jointly Intentional Activity', *Legal Theory* 8 (2002), 511–17.

—— 'Taking Plans Seriously', *Social Theory and Practice* 9 (1983), 271–87.

—— 'Two Problems about Human Agency', *Proceedings of the Aristotelian Society* 101 (2001), 309–26.

—— 'Valuing and the Will', *Philosophical Perspectives* 14 (2000), 249–65.

BROOME, JOHN, 'Are Intentions Reasons? And How Should We Cope with Incommensurable Values?', in Christopher W. Morris and Arthur Ripstein (eds.), *Practical Rationality and Preference: Essays for David Gauthier* (Cambridge: Cambridge University Press, 2001), 98–120.

—— 'Normative Practical Reasoning', *Proceedings of the Aristotelian Society*, suppl. vol. 75 (2001), 175–93.

—— 'Normative Requirements', *Ratio* 12 (1999), 398–419; repr. in J. Dancy (ed.), *Normativity* (Oxford: Blackwell, 2000), 78–99.

CACIOPPO, J. T., and BERNTSON, G. G., 'Relationship between Attitudes and Evaluative Space: A Critical Review, with Emphasis on the Separability of Positive and Negative Substrates', *Psychological Bulletin* 115 (1994), 401–23.

CASE, MARY ANNE, 'How High the Apple Pie? A Few Troubling Questions about Where, Why, and How the Burden of Care for Children Should be Shifted', *Chicago–Kent Law Review* 76 (2001), 1753–86.

CHALOUPKA, FRANK, WAKEFIELD, MELANIE, and CZART, CHRISTINA, 'Taxing Tobacco: The Impact of Tobacco Taxes on Cigarette Smoking and Other Tobacco Use', in Robert Rabin and Stephen Sugarman (eds.), *Regulating Tobacco* (Oxford: Oxford University Press, 2001), 39–71.

CHANG, RUTH, 'The Possibility of Parity', *Ethics* 112 (2002), 659–88.

COHEN, CARL, and BENJAMIN, MARTIN, 'Alcoholics and Liver Transplantation', *Journal of the American Medical Association* 265 (1991), 1299–1301.

COHEN, G. A., 'On the Currency of Egalitarian Justice', *Ethics* 99 (1989), 906–44.

COLEMAN, JULES L., *The Practice of Principle* (Oxford: Oxford University Press, 2001).

—— and RIPSTEIN, ARTHUR, 'Mischief and Misfortune', *McGill Law Journal* 41 (1995), 91–130.

Commission on Family and Medical Leave, *A Workable Balance: Report to Congress on Family and Medical Leave* (Washington: U.S. Dept. of Labor, 1996).

COPP, DAVID, *Morality, Normativity, and Society* (New York: Oxford University Press, 1995).

—— and SOBEL, DAVID, 'Desires, Motives, and Reasons: Scanlon's Rationalistic Moral Psychology', *Social Theory and Practice* 28 (2002), 243–76.

DANCY, JONATHAN, *Ethics without Principles* (Oxford: Oxford University Press, forthcoming).

—— *Moral Reasons* (Oxford: Blackwell, 1993).

—— *Practical Reality* (Oxford: Oxford University Press, 2000).

—— (ed.), *Normativity* (Oxford: Blackwell, 2000).

DARWALL, STEPHEN, 'Two Kinds of Respect', *Ethics* 88 (1977), 36–49.

—— *Welfare and Rational Care* (Princeton: Princeton University Press, 2002).

DAVIDSON, DONALD, 'Intending', in his *Essays on Actions and Events* (New York: Oxford University Press, 1980), 83–102.

DEL VECCHIO, GIORGIO, *Justice* (Edinburgh: University of Edinburgh Press, 1955).

Department of Labor, 'Balancing the Needs of Families and Employers: The Family and Medical Leave Surveys 2000 Update' (2001), *http://www.dol.gov/asp/fmla.*

DUFF, P. W., *Personality in Roman Private Law* (New York : A. M. Kelley, 1971).

DUNCAN-JONES, AUSTIN, *Butler's Moral Philosophy* (Harmondsworth: Penguin, 1952).

DWORKIN, RONALD, 'Equality of Resources', *Philosophy and Public Affairs* 10 (1981), 283–345.

—— *Sovereign Virtue* (Cambridge, Mass.: Harvard University Press, 2000).

—— 'What is Equality? Part 3: The Place of Liberty', *Iowa Law Review* 73 (1987), 1–54.

DWORKIN, TERRY MOREHEAD, 'It's My Life—Leave Me Alone: Off-the-Job Employee Associational Privacy Rights', *American Business Law Journal* 37 (1997), 47–98.

EISGRUBER, CHRISTOPHER, and SAGER, LAWRENCE, 'Equal Regard', in Stephen Feldman (ed.), *Law and Religion: A Critical Anthology* (New York: New York University Press, 2000), 200–25.

—— —— 'Religious Liberty and the Moral Structure of Constitutional Rights', *Legal Theory* 6 (2000), 253–68.

—— —— 'The Vulnerability of Conscience: The Constitutional Basis for Protecting Religious Conduct', *University of Chicago Law Review* 61 (1994), 1245–1315.

ELSTER, JON, 'Arguing and Bargaining in Two Constituent Assemblies', *University of Pennsylvania Journal of Constitutional Law* 2 (2000), 345–421.

FALK, W. D., 'Ought and Motivation', *Proceedings of the Aristotelian Society* 48 (1948), 111–38.

FICHTE, J. G., *Foundations of Natural Right*, trans. Michael Baur (Cambridge: Cambridge University Press, 2000).

FOOT, PHILIPPA, 'Abortion and the Doctrine of Double Effect' (1968), reprinted in her *Virtues and Vices* (Berkeley: University of California Press, 1978), 19–32.

—— *Natural Goodness* (Oxford: Oxford University Press, 2001).

FRANKE, KATHERINE, 'Theorizing Yes: An Essay on Feminism, Law and Desire', *Columbia Law Review* 101 (2000), 181–203.

FRANKFURT, HARRY, *The Importance of What We Care About* (Cambridge: Cambridge University Press, 1988).

—— *Necessity, Volition, and Love* (Cambridge: Cambridge University Press, 1999).

GIBBARD, ALLAN, *Wise Choices, Apt Feelings* (Cambridge, Mass.: Harvard University Press, 1990).

GILBERT, DANIEL T., 'How Mental Systems Believe', *American Psychologist* 46 (1991), 107–19.

GILBERT, MARGARET, *On Social Facts* (Princeton: Princeton University Press, 1989).

—— 'What Is It for *Us* to Intend?', in her *Sociality and Responsibility* (Lanham, Md.: Rowman & Littlefield, 2000), 14–36.

GOLDMAN, ALVIN, *Knowledge in a Social World* (Oxford: Oxford University Press, 1999).

GREENAWALT, KENT, 'Title VII and Religious Liberty', *Loyola University Chicago Law Journal* 33 (2001), 1–56.

GRIFFIN, JAMES, *Well-being: Its Meaning, Measurement, and Moral Importance* (Oxford: Oxford University Press, 1986).

HABERMAS, JÜRGEN, *A Theory of Communicative Action*, vol. 1 (Cambridge: Polity, 1984).

—— *A Theory of Communicative Action*, vol. 2 (Cambridge: Polity, 1989).

—— *Moral Consciousness and Communicative Action* (Cambridge: Polity, 1990).

HAMPTON, J. E., *The Authority of Reason* (Cambridge: Cambridge University Press, 1998).

HARLOW, H. F., and ZIMMERMAN, R. R., 'Affectional Responses in the Infant Monkey', *Science* 130 (1959), 421–32.

HARMAN, GILBERT, 'Desired Desires', as reprinted in his *Explaining Value and Other Essays in Moral Philosophy* (Oxford: Oxford University Press, 2000), 117–36.

—— 'Practical Reasoning', as reprinted in his *Reasoning, Meaning, and Mind* (Oxford: Oxford University Press, 1999), 46–74.

HART, H. L. A., 'Bentham on Legal Rights', in A. W. B. Simpson (ed.), *Oxford Essays in Jurisprudence: Second Series* (Oxford: Oxford University Press, 1973), 171–201.

HINTON, TIMOTHY, 'Must Egalitarians Choose between Fairness and Respect?', *Philosophy and Public Affairs* 30 (2001), 72–87.

HOHFELD, WESLEY, *Fundamental Legal Conceptions* (New Haven: Yale University Press, 1923).

HOLTON, RICHARD, 'Intention and Weakness of Will', *Journal of Philosophy* 96 (1999), 241–62.

HUME, DAVID, *An Enquiry concerning the Principles of Morals*, ed. P. A. Nidditch, 3rd edn. (Oxford: Oxford University Press, 1975).

—— *A Treatise of Human Nature*, ed. L. A. Selby-Bigge (Oxford: Oxford University Press, 1958; 2nd edn. 1978).

HURKA, THOMAS, 'Parfit on Well-Being and Personal Reasons' (draft MS).

HURSTHOUSE, R., *On Virtue Ethics* (Oxford: Oxford University Press, 1999).

ISSACHAROFF, SAMUEL, and ROSENBLUM, ELYSE, 'Women and the Workplace: Accommodating the Demands of Pregnancy', *Columbia Law Review* 94 (1994), 2154–2220.

JACKSON, JESSICA, 'Colorado's Lifestyle Discrimination Statute: A Vast and Muddled Expansion of Traditional Employment Law', *University of Colorado Law Review* 67 (1996), 143–69.

JAWORSKA, AGNIESZKA, 'Caring, Identification, and Internality', (unpublished MS).

JOLLS, CHRISTINE, 'Accommodation Mandates', *Stanford Law Review* 53 (2000), 223–306.

KAMM, FRANCES, *Morality, Mortality*, vol. 1 (Oxford: Oxford University Press, 1993).

—— 'Rights', in Jules Coleman and Scott Shapiro (eds.), *The Oxford Handbook of Jurisprudence and Philosophy of Law* (Oxford: Oxford University Press, 2002), 476–513.

KANT, IMMANUEL, *Practical Philosophy*, trans. and ed. J. M. Gregor (Cambridge: Cambridge University Press, 1996).

—— *Religion within the Boundaries of Mere Reason and Other Writings*, ed. A. Wood and G. Di Giovanni (Cambridge: Cambridge University Press, 1998).

KORSGAARD, CHRISTINE, *Creating the Kingdom of Ends* (Cambridge: Cambridge University Press, 1996).

—— 'The Normativity of Instrumental Reason', in Garrett Cullity and Berys Gaut (eds.), *Ethics and Practical Reason* (Oxford: Oxford University Press, 1997), 215–54.

—— 'The Reasons We Can Share: An Attack on the Distinction between Agent-Relative and Agent-Neutral Values', *Social Philosophy and Policy* 10 (1993), 24–51.

—— 'Skepticism about Practical Reason', as reprinted in Stephen Darwall, Allan Gibbard, and Peter Railton (eds.), *Moral Discourse and Practice* (New York: Oxford University Press, 1997), 373–87.

—— *The Sources of Normativity* (Cambridge: Cambridge University Press, 1996).

KUTZ, CHRISTOPHER, 'The Judicial Community', *Philosophical Issues* 11 (2001), 442–69.

KYMLICKA, WILLIAM, *Contemporary Political Philosophy: An Introduction* (Oxford: Oxford University Press, 2001).

LEIBNIZ, G. W., *Logical Papers*, ed. G. H. R. Parkinson (Oxford: Oxford University Press, 1966).

LEWIS, DAVID, *Convention* (Cambridge, Mass.: Harvard University Press, 1969).

LOCKE, JOHN, *An Essay concerning Human Understanding*, ed. P. Nidditch (Oxford: Oxford University Press, 1975).

LORMAND, ERIC, 'Framing the Frame Problem', *Synthese* 82 (1990), 353–74.

MCCLENNEN, EDWARD F., *Rationality and Dynamic Choice: Foundational Explorations* (Cambridge: Cambridge University Press, 1990).

MCCONNELL, MICHAEL, 'Free Exercise Revisionism and the *Smith* Decision', *University of Chicago Law Review* 57 (1991), 1109–53.

MCGEER, VICTORIA, 'Is "Self-knowledge" an Empirical Problem? Renegotiating the Space of Philosophical Explanation', *Journal of Philosophy* 93 (1996), 483–515.

—— and PHILIP PETTIT, 'The Self-regulating Mind', *Language and Communication* 22 (2002), 281–99.

MCMAHON, CHRISTOPHER, 'Why There is No Issue between Habermas and Rawls', *Journal of Philosophy* 99 (2002), 111–29.

MELDEN, A. I., *Rights and Persons* (Berkeley: University of California Press, 1977).

MOORE, G. E., *Principia Ethica* (Cambridge: Cambridge University Press, 1962).

NAGEL, THOMAS, *The Possibility of Altruism* (Oxford: Oxford University Press, 1970).

—— *The View from Nowhere* (New York: Oxford University Press, 1986).

—— 'War and Massacre', as reprinted in S. Scheffler (ed.), *Consequentialism and its Critics* (Oxford: Oxford University Press, 1988), 51–73.

NEUBERGER, JAMES, ADAMS, DAVID, MACMASTER, PAUL, MAIDMENT, ANITA, and SPEED, MARK, 'Assessing Priorities for Allocation of Donor Liver Grafts: Survey of Public and Clinicians', *British Medical Journal* 317 (1998), 172–5.

NIETZSCHE, FRIEDRICH, *On the Genealogy of Morals*, trans. Walter Kaufmann and R. J. Hollingdale (New York: Vintage Books, 1967).

NOZICK, ROBERT, *Anarchy, State, and Utopia* (Oxford: Blackwell, 1974).

—— *Philosophical Explanations* (Cambridge, Mass.: Harvard University Press, 1981).

OVERVOLD, MARK, 'Self-Interest and the Concept of Self-Sacrifice', *Canadian Journal of Philosophy* 10 (1980), 105–18.

PARFIT, DEREK, 'Rationality and Reasons', in Dan Egonsson, Jonas Josefsson, Bjørn Petersson, and Toni Ronnow-Rasmussen (eds.), *Exploring Practical Philosophy: From Action to Values* (Aldershot: Ashgate, 2001), 17–39.

—— 'Reasons and Motivation', *Proceedings of the Aristotelian Society*, suppl. vol. 71 (1997), 99–130.

PARFIT, DEREK, *Reasons and Persons* (Oxford: Oxford University Press, 1984).

—— 'Rediscovering Reasons', (draft MS).

PASHUKANIS, EVGENY, *General Theory of Law and Marxism* (London: Pluto Press, 1983).

PETTIT, PHILIP, 'A Consequentialist Perspective on Ethics', in M. Baron, M. Slote, and P. Pettit (eds.), *Three Methods of Ethics: A Debate* (Oxford: Blackwell, 1997), 92–174.

—— *Republicanism: A Theory of Freedom and Government* (Oxford: Oxford University Press, 1997).

—— *A Theory of Freedom: From the Psychology to the Politics of Agency* (Cambridge and New York: Polity and Oxford University Press, 2001).

—— and SMITH, MICHAEL, 'Freedom in Belief and Desire', *Journal of Philosophy* 93 (1996), 429–49.

—— —— 'Global Consequentialism', in Brad Hooker, Elinor Mason, and Dale E. Miller (eds.), *Morality, Rules and Consequences* (Edinburgh: Edinburgh University Press, 2000), 121–33.

—— and T. M. SCANLON, 'Consequentialism and Contractualism', *Theoria* 66 (2000), 228–45.

PETTY, RICHARD E. *et al.*, 'Attitudes and Attitude Change', *Annual Review of Psychology* 48(1997), 609–42.

POJMAN, LOUIS, 'Believing and Willing', *Canadian Journal of Philosophy* 15 (1985), 37–56.

PRITCHARD, H. A., 'Does Moral Philosophy Rest on a Mistake?', as reprinted in J. O. Urmson and W. D. Ross (eds.), *Moral Obligation and Duty and Interest: Essays and Lectures by H. A. Pritchard* (Oxford: Oxford University Press, 1968), 1–17.

QUINN, WARREN, 'Putting Rationality in its Place', as reprinted in his *Morality and Action* (Cambridge: Cambridge University Press, 1993), 228–55.

RAILTON, PETER, 'Alienation, Consequentialism, and the Demands of Morality', as reprinted in S. Scheffler (ed.), *Consequentialism and its Critics* (Oxford: Oxford University Press, 1988), 93–133.

—— 'Normative Force and Normative Freedom: Hume and Kant but not Hume *versus* Kant', *Ratio* 12 (1999), 320–53.

—— 'Truth, Reason, and the Regulation of Belief', *Philosophical Issues* 5 (1994), 71–93.

RAKOWSKI, ERIC, *Equal Justice* (Oxford: Oxford University Press, 1991).

RAWLS, JOHN, 'Social Unity and Primary Goods', in Amartya Sen and Bernard Williams (eds.), *Utilitarianism and Beyond* (Cambridge: Cambridge University Press, 2002), 159–85.

—— *A Theory of Justice* (Cambridge, Mass.: Harvard University Press, 1971; rev. edn. 1999).

—— 'Two Concepts of Rules', in *Collected Papers*, ed. Samuel Freeman (Cambridge, Mass.: Harvard University Press, 2000), 20–46.

RAZ, JOSEPH, *Engaging Reason: On the Theory of Value and Action* (Oxford: Oxford University Press, 1999).

—— *Ethics in the Public Domain* (Oxford: Oxford University Press, 1994).

—— 'Introduction', in Joseph Raz (ed.), *Practical Reasoning* (Oxford: Oxford University Press, 1978), 1–17.

—— *The Morality of Freedom* (Oxford: Oxford University Press, 1986).

—— *Practical Reason and Norms* (London: Hutchinson, 1975; reissued by Princeton University Press, 1990).

—— *The Practice of Value*, ed. R. Jay Wallace (Oxford: Oxford University Press, 2003).

—— 'Promises and Obligations', in P. M. S. Hacker and Joseph Raz (eds.), *Law, Morality, and Society: Essays in Honour of H. L. A. Hart* (Oxford: Oxford University Press, 1977), 210–28.

—— 'Reasons for Action, Decisions, and Norms', as reprinted in Joseph Raz (ed.), *Practical Reasoning* (Oxford: Oxford University Press, 1978), 128–43.

—— *Value, Respect, and Attachment* (Cambridge: Cambridge University Press, 2001).

REGAN, DONALD H., 'How to Be a Moorean', *Ethics* 113 (2003), 651–77.

—— 'The Value of Rational Nature', *Ethics* 112 (2002), 267–91.

ROSS, DAVID, *The Right and the Good*, ed. Philip Stratton-Lake (Oxford: Oxford University Press, 2002).

RUSSELL, BERTRAND, *A Critical Exposition of the Philosophy of Leibniz* (Cambridge: Cambridge University Press, 1900).

SCANLON, T. M., 'Promising', Edward Craig (ed.), *Routledge Encyclopedia of Philosophy*, vol. 7 (London: Routledge, 1998), 740–2.

—— 'Reasons, Responsibility, and Reliance: Replies to Wallace, Dworkin, and Deigh', *Ethics* 112 (2002), 507–28.

—— 'Replies', *Social Theory and Practice* 28 (2002), 337–40.

—— *What We Owe to Each Other* (Cambridge, Mass.: Harvard University Press, 1998).

SCHEFFLER, SAMUEL, 'Agent-Centred Restrictions, Rationality and the Virtues', in S. Scheffler (ed.), *Consequentialism and its Critics* (Oxford: Oxford University Press, 1988), 243–60.

—— *Boundaries and Allegiances* (Oxford: Oxford University Press, 2001).

—— 'Conceptions of Cosmopolitanism', *Utilitas* 11 (1999), 255–76.

—— *Human Morality* (New York: Oxford University Press, 1992).

—— 'Rawls and Utilitarianism', in Samuel Freeman (ed.), *The Cambridge Companion to Rawls* (Cambridge: Cambridge University Press, 2003), 426–59.

—— 'Relationships and Responsibilities', *Philosophy and Public Affairs* 26 (1997), 189–209.

—— 'What is Egalitarianism?', *Philosophy and Public Affairs* 31 (2003), 5–39.

SCHIFFER, STEPHEN, 'A Paradox of Desire', *American Philosophical Quarterly* 13 (1976), 195–203.

SCHNEEWIND, J. B., 'Autonomy, Obligation, and Virtue: An Overview of Kant's Moral Philosophy', in P. Guyer (ed.), *The Cambridge Companion to Kant* (Cambridge: Cambridge University Press, 1992), 309–41.

SCHUELER, GEORGE, *Desire: Its Role in Practical Reason and the Explanation of Action* (Cambridge, Mass.: MIT Press, 1995).

SCHULTZ, W., DAYAN, P., and MONTAGUE, P. R., 'The Neural Basis of Prediction and Reward', *Science* 275 (1997), 1593–9.

SEARLE, J. R., *Speech Acts: An Essay in the Philosophy of Language* (Cambridge: Cambridge University Press, 1969).

SHAPIRO, SCOTT, 'Law, Plans, and Practical Reason', *Legal Theory* 8 (2002), 387–441.

SHERVIN, HOWARD, *et al.*, *Conscious and Unconscious Processes* (New York: Guilford Press, 1996).

SHIFFRIN, SEANA, 'Morality and Agent-Centred Options', *Analysis* 51 (1991), 244–54.

—— 'Paternalism, Unconscionability Doctrine, and Accommodation', *Philosophy and Public Affairs* 29 (2000), 205–50.

—— 'Wrongful Life, Parental Responsibility, and the Significance of Harm', *Legal Theory* 5 (1999), 117–48.

SHOSTAKOVICH, DMITRI, *Testimony*, ed. Solomon Volkov (New York: Harper and Row, 1979).

SIDGWICK, HENRY, *The Methods of Ethics*, 7th edn. (Indianapolis: Hackett Publishing Co., 1981).

SINGER, PETER, *How Are We to Live? Ethics in an Age of Self-Interest* (Oxford: Oxford University Press, 1997).

SMITH, MICHAEL, 'Immodest Consequentialism and Character', *Utilitas* 13 (2001), 173–94.

—— *The Moral Problem* (Oxford: Blackwell, 1994).

—— 'Neutral and Relative Value after Moore', *Ethics* 113 (2003), 576–98.

—— 'Search for the Source', *Philosophical Quarterly* 49 (1999), 384–94.

SOBEL, DAVID, 'Pain for Objectivists' (draft MS).

STAMPE, DENNIS, 'The Authority of Desire', *Philosophical Review* 96 (1987), 335–81.

STOCKER, MICHAEL, 'Desiring the Bad: An Essay in Moral Psychology', *Journal of Philosophy* 76 (1979), 738–53.

—— *Plural and Conflicting Values* (Oxford: Oxford University Press, 1990).

STOCKTON, FRANK R., 'The Lady, or the Tiger?', in Thomas K. Parkes (ed.), *The American Short Story* (New York: Galahad Books, 1994), 202–7.

SUMNER, L. W., *Welfare, Happiness, and Ethics* (Oxford: Oxford University Press, 1996).

THOMPSON, MICHAEL, *Life and Action* (Cambridge, Mass.: Harvard University Press, forthcoming).

—— 'The Representation of Life', in Rosalind Hursthouse, Warren Quinn, and Gavin Lawrence (eds.), *Virtues and Reasons* (Oxford: Oxford University Press, 1995), 247–96.

—— 'Two Forms of Practical Generality', in Arthur Ripstein and Christopher Morris (eds.), *Practical Rationality and Preference* (Cambridge: Cambridge University Press, 2001), 121–52.

THORPE, CRYSTAL, 'A Puzzle about Humean Theories of Practical Reason', (unpublished MS).

TUSHNET, MARK V., 'Questioning the Value of Accommodating Religion', in Stephen M. Feldman (ed.), *Law and Religion: A Critical Anthology* (New York: New York University Press, 2000), 245–57.

ULLMANN-MARGALIT, EDNA, and MORGENBESSER, SIDNEY, 'Picking and Choosing', *Social Research* 44 (1977), 757–85.

VELLEMAN, J. DAVID, 'The Guise of the Good', *Nous,* 26 (1992), 3–26.

—— 'How to Share an Intention', as reprinted in his *The Possibility of Practical Reason* (Oxford: Oxford University Press, 2000), 200–20.

—— *The Possibility of Practical Reason* (Oxford: Oxford University Press, 2000).

WALLACE, R. JAY, 'Normativity, Commitment, and Instrumental Reason', *Philosophers' Imprint* vol. 1, no. 3 (2001); http://www.philosophersimprint.org/001003.

—— *Responsibility and the Moral Sentiments* (Cambridge, Mass.: Harvard University Press, 1996).

—— 'Scanlon's Contractualism', *Ethics* 112 (2002), 429–70.

WATSON, GARY, 'Free Action and Free Will', *Mind* 96 (1987), 145–72.

WEINRIB, ERNEST, *The Idea of Private Law* (Cambridge, Mass.: Harvard University Press, 1996).

WILLIAMS, BERNARD, 'Deciding to Believe', as reprinted in his *Problems of the Self* (Cambridge: Cambridge University Press, 1973), 136–51.

—— *Moral Luck* (Cambridge: Cambridge University Press, 1981).

—— 'Replies', in J. E. J. Altham and Ross Harrison (eds.), *World Mind, and Ethics: Essays on the Ethical Philosophy of Bernard Williams* (Cambridge: Cambridge University Press, 1995), 185–224.

WILLIS, JOSEPH, 'FMLA: A Progress Report', *Brandeis Journal of Family Law* 36 (1998), 95–108.

WINSTON, J. S., *et al.*, 'Automatic and Intentional Brain Responses during the Evaluation of Trustworthiness of Faces', *Nature Neuroscience* 5 (2002), 277–83.

WITTGENSTEIN, LUDWIG, *Philosophical Investigations*, trans. G. E. M. Anscombe (London: Macmillan, 1953).

WOLF, MICHAEL, and SUTHERLAND, DANIEL, *Religion in the Workplace* (Chicago: American Bar Association, 1998).

WOLF, SUSAN, 'Happiness and Meaning: Two Aspects of the Good Life', in Ellen Frankel Paul, Fred D. Miller, Jr., and Jeffrey Paul (eds.), *Self-Interest* (Cambridge: Cambridge University Press, 1997), 207–25.

—— 'Morality and Partiality', *Philosophical Perspectives* 6 (1992), 243–59.

WOLFF, JONATHAN, 'Fairness, Respect, and the Egalitarian Ethos', *Philosophy and Public Affairs* 27 (1998), 97–122.

ZAJONC, R. B., 'Feeling and Thinking: Preferences Need no Inferences', *American Psychologist* 35 (1980), 151–75.

INDEX

The editors are very grateful to Gerardo Vildostegui for assistance in preparation of the index.